JOURNAL FOR THE STUDY OF THE NEW TESTAMENT SUPPLEMENT SERIES
177

Executive Editor
Stanley E. Porter

Editorial Board
David Catchpole, R. Alan Culpepper, Margaret Davies,
James D.G. Dunn, Craig A. Evans, Stephen Fowl, Robert Fowler,
Robert Jewett, Elizabeth Struthers Malbon, Robert W. Wall

Sheffield Academic Press

Paul's Paradigmatic 'I'

Personal Example as Literary Strategy

Brian Dodd

Journal for the Study of the New Testament
Supplement Series 177

To Ingrid, Julia and Kirstie

Copyright © 1999 Sheffield Academic Press

Published by Sheffield Academic Press Ltd
Mansion House
19 Kingfield Road
Sheffield S11 9AS
England

Printed on acid-free paper in Great Britain
by Bookcraft Ltd
Midsomer Norton, Bath

British Library Cataloguing in Publication Data

A catalogue record for this book is available
from the British Library

ISBN 1-85075-914-6

CONTENTS

Acknowledgments 7
Abbreviations 9

Chapter 1
INTRODUCTION 13
   The Imitation of Paul in Recent Study 18
   Identifying the Function and Content of Paul's Use of
      Personal Example 30

Chapter 2
1 CORINTHIANS 1–4: 'THAT YOU MAY LEARN FROM
OUR EXAMPLE' 33
   The Occasion of the Letter 34
   Multiple Models as a Corinthian Problem 37
   A Challenge to Paul's Authority in 1 Corinthians? 40
   1 Corinthians 4.6: An Authorial Intention Statement? 45
   Paul as Exemplum in 1.10–4.13 48
   The Relationship of Chapters 1–4 to the Remainder
      of 1 Corinthians 61

Chapter 3
PAUL, SPIRITUAL PARENT AND PARADIGM IN CHRIST:
1 CORINTHIANS 4.14–15.58 64
   The Significance of the Shift at 4.14 64
   Imitation and Other Uses of Paul's Literary Example in
      1 Corinthians 4.14–15.58 68
   Summary 130

Chapter 4
GALATIANS: PERSONAL EXAMPLE, CONTRASTIVE MODELS 133
   Galatians 1 and 2 136

Galatians 3–6	161
A Summary of Paul's Use of Self-Portrayal in Galatians	168

Chapter 5
PHILIPPIANS: POLEMICAL AND PARADIGMATIC
SELF-PORTRAYAL   171
    The Literary Unity of Philippians   172
    The Opposition: Some Assumptions and Open Questions 174
    The Heart of Paul's Polemic   177
    Paul's Polemical and Paradigmatic 'I' in Philippians 180
    Summary   194

Chapter 6
IMPLICIT USES OF PERSONAL EXAMPLE: PHILEMON AND
1 THESSALONIANS 2.1-12   196
    Personal Example in Philemon   196
    Personal Example in 1 Thessalonians   212
    Summary   220

Chapter 7
A CASE IN POINT: ROMANS 7.7-25   221
    General Observations   221
    The Identity of Paul's 'I' in Romans 7   222
    A Diatribal Origin of Paul's 'I' style?   226
    The Two Functions of 'I' in Romans 7   230
    Summary   234

Chapter 8
CONCLUSION   235

BIBLIOGRAPHY   239
Index of References   262
Index of Authors   277

ACKNOWLEDGMENTS

This study began as an interest in leadership development for church renewal and evangelism, and later focused on social and cultural influences on Paul's style of leadership. The pages herein reflect an installment toward those larger spheres of inquiry. As a result, my desire has only increased to understand and appropriate apostolic models of leadership for the church of the new millennium.

I am grateful to Joel Green who gave early direction to my study, and to Ralph Martin, who wisely steered a previous incarnation of this project to completion in the form of a dissertation at the University of Sheffield. I am grateful, too, for the input of Loveday Alexander and Andrew Lincoln, and the lively cohort of doctoral students and instructors there. Ernest Best and Meg Davies as examiners served to sharpen my thinking, and hopefully their suggestions improved the version that has made it into your hands. It is surely better because of the wise editorial advice of Stephen Fowl, and the carefuly proofreading of Chris Stratton. Vicky Acklam and the high calibre people at Sheffield Academic Press greatly improved this manuscript, but in the end its deficits rest on my shoulders.

I must express my deep gratitude to A Foundation for Theological Education (AFTE) and the Barnsley Circuit of the Methodist Church. Without them, fulfilling my dream to pursue doctoral studies would have been impossible. AFTE's generous John Wesley Fellowship and ongoing support made possible through the vision of Edmund Robb, Jr, were a blessing beyond compare. The Darfield Section of the Barnsley Circuit provided rich fellowship, a warm home and treasured friendship during this part of our journey. We could not have made it through without Bill and Barbara Marsden, dear friends, 'uncle and aunty' to our children and true 'partners in the gospel'.

Although this manuscript has my name on it, I could not have completed this work without the longsuffering good humour and steady encouragement of Ingrid, my wife of 17 years. If ever asked what the secret to my success is, I can honestly answer, 'I married well'. The bonus is two precious daughters, whose energy, antics and indifference to this manuscript helped keep it all in perspective. At the end of the day, I hope this book helps shed light on the understanding of Paul's letters, a precious part of Scripture for me. I believe we have much to learn from how Paul led and lived and ministered—and I am confident that if we listen carefully, we will discover old–new ways of effectively spreading the fragrance of the knowledge of Christ to a world so desperate for his love and grace.

Brian Dodd
Christmas 1998

ABBREVIATIONS

AB	Anchor Bible
ABD	David Noel Freedman (ed.), *The Anchor Bible Dictionary* (New York: Doubleday, 1992)
AnBib	Analecta biblica
ANRW	Hildegard Temporini and Wolfgang Haase (eds.), *Aufstieg und Niedergang der römischen Welt: Geschichte und Kultur Roms im Spiegel der neueren Forschung* (Berlin: W. de Gruyter, 1972–)
ASTI	*Annual of the Swedish Theological Institute*
AUS	American University Studies
AusBR	*Australian Biblical Review*
BAGD	Walter Bauer, William F. Arndt, F. William Gingrich and Frederick W. Danker, *A Greek–English Lexicon of the New Testament and Other Early Christian Literature* (Chicago: University of Chicago Press, 2nd edn, 1958)
BDF	Friedrich Blass, A. Debrunner and Robert W. Funk, *A Greek Grammar of the New Testament and Other Early Christian Literature* (Cambridge: Cambridge University Press, 1961)
BETL	Bibliotheca ephemeridum theologicarum lovaniensium
BHT	Beiträge zur historischen Theologie
Bib	*Biblica*
BJRL	*Bulletin of the John Rylands University Library of Manchester*
BNTC	Black's New Testament Commentaries
BZ	*Biblische Zeitschrift*
BZNW	Beihefte zur *ZNW*
CBC	Cambridge Bible Commentary on the New English Bible
CBQ	*Catholic Biblical Quarterly*
CGTC	Cambridge Greek Testament Commentary
DPL	G. Hawthorne, R.P. Martin and D. Reid (eds.), *Dictionary of Paul and his Letters* (Downers Grove, IL: IVP, 1993)
EBib	Etudes bibliques
EDNT	Horst Balz and Gerhard Schneider (eds.), *Exegetical Dictionary of the New Testament* (3 vols.; Grand Rapids: Eerdmans, 1990–92)
EGGNT	Exegetical Guide to the Greek New Testament
EKKNT	Evangelisch-Katholischer Kommentar zum Neuen Testament
EvQ	*Evangelical Quarterly*

ExpTim	*Expository Times*
FRLANT	Forschungen zur Religion und Literatur des Alten und Neuen Testaments
FzB	Forschung zur Bibel
GNS	Good News Studies
GTA	Göttinger theologische Arbeiten
HNT	Handbuch zum Neuen Testament
HNTC	Harper's NT Commentaries
HTKNT	Herders theologischer Kommentar zum Neuen Testament
HTR	*Harvard Theological Review*
ICC	International Critical Commentary
Int	*Interpretation*
JBL	*Journal of Biblical Literature*
JSNT	*Journal for the Study of the New Testament*
JSNTSup	*Journal for the Study of the New Testament*, Supplement Series
JTS	*Journal of Theological Studies*
KEK	Kritisch-exegetischer Kommentar über das Neue Testament
LEC	Library of Early Christianity
LSJ	H.G. Liddell, Robert Scott and H. Stuart Jones, *Greek–English Lexicon* (Oxford: Clarendon Press, 9th edn, 1968)
LTPM	Louvain Theological and Pastoral Monographs
MNTC	Moffatt NT Commentary
NCB	New Century Bible
NICNT	New International Commentary on the New Testament
NIDNTT	Colin Brown (ed.), *The New International Dictionary of New Testament Theology* (3 vols.; Exeter: Paternoster Press, 1975)
NIGTC	The New International Greek Testament Commentary
NovT	*Novum Testamentum*
NovTSup	*Novum Testamentum*, Supplements
NTD	Das Neue Testament Deutsch
NTS	*New Testament Studies*
RevExp	*Review and Expositor*
SANT	Studien zum Alten und Neuen Testament
SBL	Society of Biblical Literature
SBLDS	SBL Dissertation Series
SBT	Studies in Biblical Theology
SCJ	Studies in Christianity and Judaism
SNT	Studien zum Neuen Testament
SNTSMS	Society for New Testament Studies Monograph Series
SNTU	*Studien zum Neuen Testament und seiner Umwelt*
SR	*Studies in Religion/Sciences religieuses*
ST	*Studia theologica*
TBl	*Theologische Blätter*
TBü	Theologische Bücherei
TDNT	Gerhard Kittel and Gerhard Friedrich (eds.), *Theological Dictionary of the New Testament* (trans. Geoffrey W. Bromiley; 10 vols.; Grand Rapids: Eerdmans, 1964–)

THKNT	Theologischer Handkommentar zum Neuen Testament
TLG	*Thesauras Linguae Graecae*
TLZ	*Theologische Literaturzeitung*
TNTC	Tyndale New Testament Commentaries
TWNT	Gerhard Kittel and Gerhard Friedrich (eds.), *Theologisches Wörterbuch zum Neuen Testament* (11 vols.; Stuttgart, Kohlhammer, 1932–79)
TynBul	*Tyndale Bulletin*
TZ	*Theologische Zeitschrift*
UBSGNT	United Bible Societies' *Greek New Testament*
WBC	Word Biblical Commentary
WMANT	Wissenschaftliche Monographien zum Alten und Neuen Testament
WTJ	*Westminster Theological Journal*
WUNT	Wissenschaftliche Untersuchungen zum Neuen Testament
ZAW	*Zeitschrift für die alttestamentliche Wissenschaft*
ZNW	*Zeitschrift für die neutestamentliche Wissenschaft*
ZTK	*Zeitschrift für Theologie und Kirche*

Chapter 1

INTRODUCTION

The significance of Paul's missionary leadership for the earliest Christians has never been questioned. Whether or not one agrees with his methods, Paul was effective in the missionary propagation of his message about Christ. Undoubtedly Paul's success depended upon the applicability of his message as well as his ability to influence others as an effective leader. Scholars have traditionally given greater emphasis to the content of Paul's message and neglected his practice of leadership for two reasons. First, those who study Paul tend to be drawn from schools of theology with an express interest in studying his ideas, his symbolic universe, and the theologies and symbolic worlds of his churches and the opposition that were a contributing factor in the formation of his letters. This interest is reinforced by the exclusively literary nature of the evidence. To study Paul is to study his letters. A second and more subtle reason that Paul's message has been studied to the neglect of his practice has to do with a spiritualizing tendency in particularly Protestant conceptions of Christian leadership which neglects the human component of leadership, reinforced by a doctrine of depravity that eschews setting fallen persons as exemplary models of the Christian life.[1] Nevertheless, Paul in fact explicitly places himself as a model for his readers through his letters and he implies he did so when he was present with his newly founded churches.

The evidence we have of Paul's practice of leadership is slim, limited to seven undisputed letters, six others which are thought to be more (Colossians, 2 Thessalonians) or less (Ephesians, Pastoral Epistles) Pauline in nature, and the witness of Acts. None of these sources seeks to describe Paul's practice of leadership as such, and so it must be culled from the evidence. One cannot suppose that these brief sources give a full picture of Paul's leadership—his views and practice of

1. E.g. W. Bauder, 'μιμέομαι', *NIDNTT*, I, pp. 490-92.

succession planning, organizational administration, management of personnel and finance, vision casting and goal setting, to name a few issues—given the fact that the primary sources are occasional letters written with particular exigencies in mind. Neither can we know if Paul was always intentional about his style of leadership or even had views on such things just listed. Though the secondary sources are external to Paul, they are no more objective since they evidence their own *Tendenz* and a fairly high view of Paul. The biases of the writings of Paul and his followers hinder investigation of his practice of leadership, an investigation that could not be complete without actual observation in any case.[2]

This study is intended as a contribution to the interest in Paul's leadership style. The sources limit my inquiry to a literary examination, though it is likely that Paul's literary practice reflects something of the leadership style of the historical Paul. Practical concerns place two further limitations. First, this study examines Paul's seven generally accepted letters as primary evidence (Romans 1 and 2 Corinthians, Galatians, Philippians, 1 Thessalonians, Philemon). Secondly, this study is limited to an exploration of how and to what end Paul employs his personal example in the argument of these letters.

The classic literary distinction between showing and telling informs this study. While most studies of Paul have focused on what he 'tells', this study emphasizes what Paul 'shows' in his letters by his self-presentation, self-discussion and self-characterizations. As Wayne Booth puts it, everything an author shows serves also to tell, and 'the line between showing and telling is always to some degree an arbitrary one'.[3] The arbitrary line between showing and telling will not be emphasized here. Rather, this study will focus on the elements of Paul's exhortations that he *shows* through use of his self-portrayal, in the context of what he *tells* his readers in a given letter. It is not claimed that

---

2. The standard treatments are J.H. Schütz, *Paul and the Anatomy of Apostolic Authority* (SNTSMS, 26; Cambridge: Cambridge University Press, 1975); B. Holmberg, *Paul and Power: The Structure of Authority in the Primitive Church as Reflected in the Pauline Epistles* (Philadelphia: Fortress Press, 1980 [1978]). See also the description of Paul's leadership through the lens of recent leadership theory by H. Doohan, *Leadership in Paul* (GNS, 11; Wilmington, DE: Michael Glazier, 1984).

3. W.C. Booth, *The Rhetoric of Fiction* (Chicago: University of Chicago Press, 1983), p. 20.

Paul characterizes himself for only hortatory reasons. Clearly, Paul's self-referrals are sometimes more related to actual or potential criticisms in an apologetic context, as is undoubtedly the case throughout 2 Corinthians.[4] Differently, in Rom. 15.14-32 Paul straightforwardly presents his sense of purpose and missionary agenda as a way of self-introduction in anticipation of his arrival at Rome. No apparent link is made between his introduction of himself and the exhortation of the letter, though even the deliberate interplay of Gentile–Jewish relations evident throughout the letter-essay of Romans plays into his self-portrayal in Romans 15. Even in places in his letters where paraenesis is apparently the central motive for Paul's self-portrayal it is not thought or claimed that this is the only element in these texts, but rather that his personal example depicted for hortatory purposes is one strand woven into the fabric of the argument. In some places Paul's self-presentation is the foremost element of the argument (e.g. 1 Cor. 9; Gal. 1–2; Phil. 3). In other places his self-presentation is a prominent part of complex argumentation that also intertwines authoritative citations of Scripture, social dynamics such as shame and honour, and christological formulations, to name a few (e.g. 1 Cor. 1–4; Gal. 4; Philemon). While in still other parts of his letters there is no explicit reference to his own personal example (e.g. Rom. 2–6; 1 Cor. 11.2-16).

In several places in his undisputed letters Paul explicitly refers to his own personal example as the standard for his churches (1 Thess. 1.5-6; 1 Cor. 4.6, 16; 7.7; 11.1; Gal. 4.12; Phil. 3.17; 4.9). While reference to his personal example is a common feature, the manner in which he refers to his self-exemplification varies. He exhorts his readers to 'become imitators of me' (μιμηταί μου γίνεσθε, 1 Cor. 4.16; 11.1), to 'join together in imitating me…just as you have us as an example' (συμμιμηταί μου γίνεσθε…καθὼς ἔχετε τύπον ἡμᾶς, Phil. 3.17), and to 'become as I am' (γίνεσθε ὡς ἐγώ, Gal. 4.12). In two places Paul refers to his personal example as an object lesson for his readers to learn from (ἵνα ἐν ἡμῖν μάθητε, 1 Cor. 4.6; ἃ…ἐμάθετε, Phil. 4.9), which includes the tradition they have received from him (παρελάβετε), what they have heard (ἠκούσατε), and what they have seen (εἴδετε) 'in

---

4. Contra G. Lyons, *Pauline Autobiography: Toward a New Understanding* (SBLDS, 73; Atlanta: Scholars Press, 1985), p. 226. It is unclear if his generalization that Paul does not make autobiographical remarks to defend himself against charges is meant for Galatians and 1 Thessalonians only or is thought to extend to the entire Pauline corpus (as it seems to read).

me' (ἐν ἐμοί, Phil. 4.9).[5] His example is to become their practice (ταῦτα πράσσετε, Phil. 4.9. ταῦτα unambiguously refers to ἅ at the beginning of the verse). In 1 Thessalonians there is no explicit exhortation to follow Paul's example though the 'recall motif' plays a significant implicit role in the line of thought of the letter, for example 'just as you know what kind of people we were among you on your account' (1.5; see Chapter 6 below, pp. 212-13). The word group is found in 1 Thess. 1.6, 'you became imitators of us and of the Lord' (ὑμεῖς μιμηταὶ ἡμῶν ἐγενήθητε καὶ τοῦ κυρίου), and in 1 Thess. 2.14, 'you became imitators, brethren, of the churches of God in Judaea' (ὑμεῖς γὰρ μιμηταὶ ἐγενήθητε, ἀδελφοί, τῶν ἐκκλησιῶν τοῦ θεοῦ τῶν οὐσῶν ἐν τῇ Ἰουδαίᾳ), but in neither case is there an exhortation to imitation. 'Imitators' is used in 1 Thessalonians as a description of the similarity of the Thessalonians' suffering with the suffering of the apostolic band, the Lord (1.6) and the Judaean churches (2.14).

The emulation of personal example was a common literary and hortatory motif in antiquity, and μιμαυλέω, its derivatives and related ideas have a broad range of usage in Greek literature. There are several excellent surveys that need not be duplicated here, but a brief summary can be given.[6] In its original usage in art, music and drama 'imitation' was used literally as mimicry of another piece of literature or music, and could be employed positively as a means of acquiring competence or negatively as a cheap or fraudulent copy.[7] Ethical emulation of good people, monarchs and deities was a common metaphorical usage of the terminology, and focused on patterning oneself after another rather than slavish mimicry of every detail (e.g. Democritus, *Frag.* 39; Xenophon, *Mem.* 1.2.3). Plato's cosmology made imitation a technical term for the

---

5. An extensive examination of the links between imitation and tradition as pedagogical vehicles is provided by D.M. Williams, 'The Imitation of Christ in Paul with Special Reference to Paul as Teacher' (PhD Dissertation, Columbia University, 1967).

6. H. Kosmala, 'Nachfolge und Nachahmung Gottes: Im griechischen Denken', *ASTI* 2 (1963), pp. 38-85; *idem*, 'Nachfolge und Nachahmung Gottes: Im jüdischen Denken', *ASTI* 3 (1964), pp. 65-110; H.D. Betz, *Nachfolge und Nachahmung Jesu Christi im Neuen Testament* (Tübingen: J.C.B. Mohr [Paul Siebeck], 1967), pp. 48-136; Williams, 'The Imitation of Christ', pp. 31-124; Lyons, *Pauline Autobiography*, pp. 17-73; B. Fiore, *The Function of Personal Example in the Socratic and Pastoral Epistles* (AnBib, 105; Rome: Biblical Institute Press, 1986), pp. 26-163 (based on his 1982 Yale dissertation, unavailable to me).

7. LSJ, *s.v.*

relationship of the phenomenological world to the realm of the ideal (*Tim.* 38a; 48e), a usage followed by Philo (*Op. Mund.* 16, 25). Except for a textual variation in Ps. 30.7, the word group appears in the LXX only in the Apocrypha for 'copy' (μίμημα σκηνῆς ἁγίας, Wis. 9.8) and as an exhortation to emulate a personal example (μιμήσασθέ με, ἀδελφοί, *4 Macc.* 9.23), while Pseudepigrapha urge the imitation of exemplary people (*T. Benj.* 4.1) and God (*T. Ash.* 4.3). However, the LXX commonly employs 'way' (ὁδός) and 'walk' (περιπατέω) in reference to a person's course of life and conduct, terms that Paul uses in connection with the imitation motif,[8] and without the word the Levitical tradition attributes the exhortation to Yahweh with, 'Be holy as I am holy'.[9] Philo, in addition to his Platonic usage of μίμημα, uses μιμέομαι and μιμητής usually for the conscious imitation of a model.[10] In Graeco-Roman letters the paraenetic usage of personal example was commonplace,[11] and Dio Chrysostom (1-2 CE) explicitly uses the language of imitation as a description of effective pedagogy in an often cited passage:

> Then if a follower, he would also be a pupil. For whoever really follows anyone surely knows what that person was like, and by imitating [μιμούμενος] his acts and words he tries as best he can to make himself like him. But that is precisely, it seems, what the pupil does—imitating his teaching and paying heed to him he tries to acquire his art.[12]

What Dio prescribes Epictetus embodies, utilizing paradigmatic 'I' statements as a literary technique, analogous to elements of Paul's usage we will identify below:

> And how is it possible for a man who has nothing, who is naked, without home or hearth, in squalor, without a slave, without a city, to live serenely? Behold, God has sent you the man who will show in practice that it is possible. 'Look at me,' he says, 'I am without home, without a city, without property, without a slave; I sleep on the ground; I have neither wife nor children, no miserable governor's mansion, but only earth, and sky, and one rough cloak. Yet what do I lack? Am I not free

---

8. Judg. 2.17; 1 Sam. 8.3; 1 Kgs 3.14; 9.4; 11.33, 38; cf. 1 Cor. 4.16-17; Phil. 3.17; 2 Thess. 3.6-9.
9. E.g. Lev. 1.45; 11.44; 19.2; 20.26.
10. W. Michaelis, 'μιμέομαι, κτλ.', *TDNT*, IV, pp. 659-74 (664-65).
11. As Fiore has ably demonstrated, *The Function of Personal Example*, pp. 79-163.
12. Dio Chrysostom, *Dis.* 55.4-5.

from pain and fear, am I not free? When has anyone among you seen me failing to get what I desire, or falling into what I would avoid? When have I ever found fault with either God or man? When have I ever blamed anyone? Has anyone among you seen me with a gloomy face? And how do I face those persons before whom you stand in fear and awe? Do I not face them as slaves: Who, when he lays eyes upon me, does not feel that he is seeing his king and his master?'

Lo, these are words that befit a Cynic, this is his character, and his plan of life.[13]

Thus Epictetus exemplifies the character and values of the ideal Cynic with 'I' expressions and, with the final line cited, makes it clear that this practice is paradigmatic for would-be Cynics.

This brief sampling characterizes the variety and commonplace usage of imitation in antiquity, alerting us to the fact that Paul draws upon commonplace Graeco-Roman usage when he exhorts his readers to imitate him. Even so, there has been no consensus on how Paul employs the appeal to imitation of himself, nor are scholars agreed upon what he includes about himself as the object of imitation. I now turn to a brief review of the clashing conceptions of Paul's usage of the imitation motif, and then highlight an emerging synthesis.

The Imitation of Paul in Recent Study[14]

Earlier discussion of this feature of Paul's paraenesis focused on rejecting it as a foundation for ethical idealism, emphasizing the implied assertion of authority in the call to imitation (Michaelis). Later scholars, loosed from such theological concerns, provide a needed corrective that Paul, in fact, was emphasizing his own ethical example based upon his spiritual paternity in Christ (Stanley, de Boer, Schulz, Betz, Gutierrez,

---

13. Epictetus, *Diss.* 3.22.45-50.

14. See Fiore, *The Function of Personal Example*, pp. 164-65, for a thorough bibliography of imitation in Paul through 1986, lacking E. Eidem, 'Imitatio Pauli', in *idem*, *Teologiska Studier Tillägnade Erik Stave* (Uppsala: Almqvist & Wiksell, 1922), pp. 67-85; and Kosmala's two articles cited above in n. 6. Works that treat specific aspects of the imitation of Paul will be treated in the relevant chapters below (e.g. B. Sanders, 'Imitating Paul: 1 Cor. 4.16', *HTR* 74 [1981], pp. 353-63; and M.A. Getty, 'The Imitation of Paul in the Letters to the Thessalonians', in R.F. Collins (ed.), *The Thessalonian Correspondence* [BETL, 87; Leuven: Leuven University Press, 1990], pp. 277-83).

1. Introduction

Fiore, Best). Recently the two emphases of Paul's summons to imitation—the imposition of authority and the pedagogy of personal example—rightly have been held together (Castelli).[15]

Mimesis as Obedience to Paul's Authority
In his 1942 *TWNT* article, Wilhelm Michaelis identifies three uses of μιμέομαι in Paul's letters, and rightly emphasizes that more than one meaning of the phrase in Paul has to be taken into account.[16] The three meanings are (1) simple comparison (1 Thess. 1.6; 2.14), (2) following an example (Phil. 3.17; 2 Thess. 3.7, 9), and (3) obedience to the authority of the apostle (1 Cor. 4.16; 11.1). It is clear that Michaelis believes this third usage is the dominant one in Paul. For example, Michaelis takes 1 Cor. 4.16 to refer to Paul's authority: 'μιμηταί μου γίνεσθε has to mean: [*das muß heißen*] "Be told, take it to heart, keep to it, be obedient"',[17] and 'Certainly 11.1 does not refer to examples to be emulated, let alone to models to whom one is to become similar or equal by imitation, but to authorities whose command and admonition are to be obeyed'.[18] Though he first identifies 1 Thess. 1.6 as a 'simple comparison', he modifies this on the next page with 'the main stress falls on the element of obedience'.[19]

Though Michaelis initially draws attention to the variety of usage, he implies that the element of obedience is almost exclusive in Paul. He clearly has trouble with the imitation of an example, but this is probably best explained as his reaction to the notion of *Vorbild* (ethical example) in ethical idealism rather than a strictly exegetical observation of Paul's usage. When he ventures 'It may be asked how far it is advisable to speak of imitating an example at all', he wrestles theologically rather than exegetically with the implied loss of independence for the one who imitates another, preferring the term 'discipleship' to 'imitation'.[20] Nevertheless, his reductionistic tendency and the absolute manner in which he states his views sets the stage for a continuing

---

15. See E.A. Castelli, *Imitating Paul: A Discourse of Power* (Louisville, KY: Westminster/John Knox Press, 1991).
16. 'μιμέομαι, γκτλ.', *TWNT*, IV, pp. 661-78 (all further citations from 1967 ET in *TDNT*, IV, unless indicated; see n. 10 above).
17. Michaelis, 'μιμέομαι', p. 668.
18. Michaelis, 'μιμέομαι', p. 669.
19. Michaelis, 'μιμέομαι', pp. 672-73.
20. Michaelis, 'μιμέομαι', pp. 671-72 n. 28.

chorus of reactions to his virtual annulment of understanding imitation as a patterning after personal example. Michaelis makes no reference to the relationship of this notion to Paul's self-presentation in his letters.

Imitating Paul as Following his Personal Example
David M. Stanley accepts Michaelis's emphasis on obedience implied by the summons to imitation, but reinserts Paul's ethical example as a mediation of the example of Christ.[21] The suffering motif in 1 Thessalonians and Philippians gives Stanley cause to link the imitation of Paul's *Vorbild* to following the pattern of Christ who attained glory through suffering. For Stanley the imitation of Paul is nothing less than a mediated imitation of Christ the suffering servant.[22] This is confirmed for him by the parallel of τοῦτο φρονῶμεν near Paul's example in Phil. 3.16 with τοῦτο φρονεῖτε introducing Christ's example in Phil. 2.5 (assuming the ethical reading of that text) and by inserting 'imitator' in the second half of 1 Cor. 11.1, 'as I am an imitator of Christ'. Stanley hints at a wider content to Paul's *Vorbild* in 'the specific examples and lessons contained Paul's own version of the Gospel as preached and lived by him'.[23] But, his emphasis remains upon a patternistic relationship between Paul's suffering for the gospel and Christ's redemptive path of suffering.[24] Stanley does not comment upon Paul's epistolary 'self-presentation' in relation to imitation, nor does he demonstrate in any detailed way the relationship of Paul's self-portrait and Christ's portrayal.

In his 1962 dissertation, *The Imitation of Paul: An Exegetical Study*,[25] Willis Peter de Boer develops the views of Stanley while rejecting both Michaelis's emphasis on mimesis as conformity and obedience, and his characterization of 1 Thess. 1.6 and 2.14 as simple comparisons of the Thessalonians' suffering with the sufferings of the apostolic band and the Lord.[26] Against Michaelis's interpretation of imitation as implying

21. D.M. Stanley, '"Become imitators of me": The Pauline Conception of Apostolic Tradition', *Bib* 40 (1959), pp. 859-77 (861).
22. Stanley, '"Become imitators of me"', p. 871.
23. Stanley, '"Become imitators of me"', p. 877.
24. Which he reiterates in his later article, 'Imitation in Paul's Letters: Its Significance for his Relationship to Jesus and his Own Christian Foundations', in P. Richardson and J. Hurd (eds.), *From Jesus to Paul: Studies in Honour of Francis Wright Beare* (Waterloo, ON: Wilfred Laurier University Press, 1984), pp. 127-41.
25. Kampen: J.H. Kok, 1962.
26. Though on this latter point de Boer goes beyond the text to assert that the

primarily obedience to authority, de Boer gathers an impressive array of background materials to demonstrate that imitation (μιμέομαι) and example (τύπος) would be naturally understood as Paul uses them in the sense of following after a personal example.[27] With Stanley, de Boer views the imitation of Paul as a mediated imitation of Christ. For de Boer, however, the imitation of Christ through Paul is not restricted to the way of suffering, but includes the way of humility, self-abnegation and self-sacrifice for the promotion of the gospel and for the salvation of others.[28] Furthermore, the imitation of Paul is a middle step in enabling his followers to imitate Christ directly for themselves. Like Michaelis and Stanley, de Boer somewhat subsumes Paul's usage under broader categories and concerns of theology and ethics.

Unlike Michaelis and Stanley, de Boer briefly explores some suggestions of Paul's pattern for imitation in 1 Corinthians 1–4, particularly the *crux* in 4.6, but then settles for a general interpretation of the object of imitation as a historical allusion to 'the Christian way of life as you saw it in me' without reference to Paul's current literary self-presentation in the letter.[29] The object of imitation in 1 Cor. 11.1 is Paul's self-abnegation (cf. 10.32-33),[30] and de Boer notes that Paul has already presented his personal example in a similar way in 1 Corinthians 9 (comparing 9.22 with 10.33).[31] However, greater emphasis is placed on sorting out the difficulties raised by interpreting καθὼς κἀγὼ Χριστοῦ as 'just as I am *an imitator* of Christ'.[32] Here, too, de Boer changes his literary observation of the object of imitation from Paul's example of self-abnegation to Paul as a mediator of Christ's example. Indeed, he concludes, 'There is little evidence that Paul saw two radically different things in the imitation of himself and the imitation of Christ'.[33] In the

---

Thessalonians actively became imitators in their suffering (*The Imitation of Paul*, pp. 92-126). Michaelis's interpretation is more convincing in these two cases, though perhaps 'resemblance' or 'similarity' are better words than 'simple comparison'.

27. De Boer, *The Imitation of Paul*, pp. 1-50.
28. Making his case from 1 Cor. 11.1; 1 Thess. 1.6; Phil. 2.5-11; 2 Cor. 8.9; Rom. 15.1-3; Acts 20.35; and by taking the Pastoral Epistles as Pauline (1 Tim. 1.16; 2 Tim. 1.13; 3.10).
29. De Boer, *The Imitation of Paul*, pp. 140-54.
30. De Boer, *The Imitation of Paul*, p. 158.
31. De Boer, *The Imitation of Paul*, pp. 155-58.
32. De Boer, *The Imitation of Paul*, pp. 158-69.
33. De Boer, *The Imitation of Paul*, p. 166. This claim is made in various forms

case of Phil. 3.17 de Boer denies any connection between the call to imitation and Paul's literary self-portrait: 'Paul is not here calling their attention directly to himself simply in order to give them a concrete illustration of the things about which he has been speaking.' Rather, Paul's self-discussion has formed a *captatio benevolentiae* to call them to live up to the Christian life they have attained (3.16).[34] In conclusion, de Boer briefly relates in some way the call to imitation in each letter to Paul's literary self-portrait in those letters, only to extract a generalized model for imitation: 'humility, self-denial, self-giving, self-sacrifice for the sake of Christ and the salvation of others'.[35] Though de Boer emphasizes that exemplification is the primary implication of the imitation motif, he ultimately accepts that obedience to authority is also implied.[36]

Pedro Gutierrez develops his understanding of imitation in the context of the teacher–pupil relationship implied by spiritual parenthood. He treats 1 Cor. 4.14-21 under the headings 'The Educational Aspects of Spiritual Paternity' and 'Parental Correction', and views imitation as a derivative of Paul's spiritual engenderment of his converts.[37]

---

by many commentators, a view that makes the grammar of 1 Cor. 11.1 an equation of the examples of Paul and Christ, and leaves unsolved the literary problem that Christ's portrayal in 1 Corinthians has to do with suffering on the cross and the events surrounding the resurrection (cf. 1.17-18, 23-24; 3.11; 7.22; 11.23-26; 15.3-12), surely aspects of Christ's life that Paul regards as inimitable. In 1.30, for example, the soteriological significance of Christ places in doubt an equation of Paul's example with Christ's in 1 Corinthians. What must be avoided are ontologically confused statements like that of J. Roloff, 'Μίμησις Παύλου ist μίμησις Χριστοῦ (1 Kor 11,1)!', in idem, *Apostolat–Verkündigung–Kirche: Ursprung, Inhalt und Funktion des kirchlichen Apostelamtes nach Paulus, Lukas und den Pastoralbriefen* (Gütersloh: Gerd Mohn, 1965), p. 119.

34. De Boer, *The Imitation of Paul*, pp. 176-77.
35. De Boer, *The Imitation of Paul*, p. 207.
36. 'Following his example certainly includes the idea of acting in obedience to apostolic authority' (*The Imitation of Paul*, p. 209). In a study that appeared at the same time, A. Schulz arrives at virtually the same conclusions as de Boer though his interest is in the relationship between following Jesus in the Gospel traditions and the imitation of Christ and *menschliche Vorbilder* in the rest of the New Testament (*Nachfolgen und Nachahmen: Studien über das Verhältnis der neutestamentlichen Jüngerschaft zur urchristlichen Vorbildethik* [SANT, 6; Munich: Kösel, 1962], pp. 308-16).
37. P. Gutierrez, *La paternité spirituelle selon Saint Paul* (Ebib; Paris: J. Gabalda, 1968), pp. 172-97.

1. Introduction

Gutierrez brings to the foreground what all the other scholars in this survey note: 'As an immediate and direct consequence of his position as father of the community, Paul calls upon the Corinthians to imitate him, that is to say, they must become like him. It is a call which Paul makes to all the communities which he has founded.'[38] It is generally accepted that this explains the absence of the call to imitate Paul in Romans. Gutierrez accepts that obedience is implied in imitation, but maintains that 'the accent is put principally upon the paternal instruction which teaches the true way, to which the son must pay attention and obey'.[39] Thus Gutierrez accepts Michaelis's observation that obedience is implied in the motif, but shifts the balance of emphasis toward pedagogy whereas Michaelis has placed the emphasis on authority. This same emphasis on imitation as a part of spiritual paternity is found in the studies of Jürgen Roloff, Hans Dieter Betz, Donald Manly Williams, Bengt Holmberg and Ernest Best.[40]

In his 1982 Yale dissertation, Benjamin Fiore offers a detailed study of the hortatory device of example in Graeco-Roman and New Testament paraenesis.[41] Use of example (εἰκών, παράδειγμα, *exemplum*) and comparison (παραβολή, ὁμοίωσις, *simile*) to increase the authority (*auctoritas*) of a piece's argumentative and hortatory purposes were common in rhetorical discussions.[42] Furthermore, education by example played a significant role in the pedagogical principles of rhetorical education.[43] Fiore demonstrates how these theoretical principles are employed in actual cases from the paraenetic discourses of Isocrates and the kingship literature of Plutarch and Dio Chrysostom,[44] and from examples in official letters and hortatory letters of Seneca[45] and the Socratic letters.[46] Seneca uses personal example not only to emphasize

38. Gutierrez, *La paternité spirituelle*, p. 178.
39. Gutierrez, *La paternité spirituelle*, p. 180; cf. p. 182.
40. Roloff, 'Vaterschaft und μίμεσις', in *Apostolat–Verkündigung–Kirche*, pp. 116-20; Betz, *Nachfolge und Nachahmung Jesu Christi*, p. 144 n. 4; Williams, 'The Imitation of Christ', pp. 31-124; Holmberg, *Paul and Power*, pp. 77-79; E. Best, 'Paul as Model', in *idem, Paul and his Converts* (Edinburgh: T. & T. Clark, 1988), pp. 59-72 (63).
41. Fiore, *The Function of Personal Example*, pp. 26-163.
42. Fiore, *The Function of Personal Example*, pp. 26-33.
43. Fiore, *The Function of Personal Example*, pp. 33-44.
44. Fiore, *The Function of Personal Example*, pp. 45-78.
45. Fiore, *The Function of Personal Example*, pp. 79-100.
46. Fiore, *The Function of Personal Example*, pp. 101-63.

the bond between himself and letter recipients, but explicitly as part of the development of his exhortation and instruction (*Ep.* 6.3-5; 29.4; 52.2, 7; 52.8; 100.12). Fiore cites Hildegard Cancik's conclusion that Seneca's self-testimony serves as an example, and Fiore adds that this effect is created implicitly and explicitly by self-portrayal, an observation salient for our study below.[47] Fiore notes this also is true in the letters of Socrates where 'examples function largely as prototypes, to urge imitation', explicitly and implicitly.[48]

Though the focus of Fiore's study is on the Pastoral Epistles, he casts serious doubt on Michaelis's denial that Paul has exemplification in mind by giving a detailed explication of imitation as following a personal example in common Hellenistic hortatory and pedagogical tracts. Against de Boer, Fiore supports Michaelis's view of simple comparison for 1 Thess. 1.6; 2.14,[49] but he disputes that an assertion of authority is implied in the use of the homologoumena in the parallel materials Michaelis cites, and he insists with Stanley, de Boer, Williams, Gutierrez and Best that the emphasis in imitation is upon its usage as a hortatory and pedagogical technique.[50] To dispute Michaelis's emphasis upon mimesis as obeisance, Fiore briefly examines Paul's use of personal example in 1 Corinthians 1–4, and briefly looks at his other letters to provide a study of Pauline usage salient to his interest in the Pastoral Epistles.[51] He denies that the emphasis is upon an implied assertion of authority, but allows for a complementarity between model and command.[52] Fiore's brief exegetical comments largely agree with the results of this study, and will be commented upon in detail in Chapter 2 below. Fiore's study decisively ends the doubt cast on Paul's summons to imitation as an exhortation to follow the pattern of his personal example, and his cursory exploration of the relationship of Paul's literary self-presentation in 1 Corinthians to the object of imitation is suggestive for the direction of the current study.

---

47. H. Cancik, *Untersuchungen zu Senecas Epistulae morales* (Hildesheim: Georg Olms, 1967), p. 75 nn. 121-24; Fiore, *The Function of Personal Example*, p. 89.

48. Fiore, *The Function of Personal Example*, pp. 137; 143-46.

49. Fiore, *The Function of Personal Example*, p. 165.

50. See Fiore, *The Function of Personal Example*, pp. 165-90, for a detailed critique of Michaelis's views.

51. Fiore, *The Function of Personal Example*, pp. 164-90.

52. Fiore, *The Function of Personal Example*, p. 168.

In her brief article, Adele Reinhartz underlines the commonplace paraenetic usage of models in antiquity and she notes with previous scholars that Paul's exhortation to imitation is based upon his spiritual paternity of the churches to whom he writes, explaining the absence of the phenomenon in Romans. Unlike other scholars she relates Paul's call to imitation to a supposed threat to his authority which she considers 'one of the major themes running through the entire Corinthian correspondence', and indeed Philippians and 1 Thessalonians. She mirror-reads Paul's rhetoric of 1 Cor. 4.3-5 and 1 Corinthians 9 as support for Paul's defensiveness at the time of 1 Corinthians, an approach that will be disputed in Chapter 2 below.[53] Her work, like Fiore's, briefly considers Paul's self-presentation in 1 Corinthians as a 'concrete example of the type of person he wants them to become' (3.1–4.5; 4.8-13; 9.12-15; 9.19-23; 10.32-33).[54] She, like Fiore, points in the direction this study will head, but she overlooks numerous exemplifications in 1 Corinthians and how these numerous instances and their usage give the impression of a literary strategy. She rightly relates the object of imitation in Philippians to Paul's self-presentation in Phil. 3.7-14, but does not consider the parallel Gal. 4.12, nor does she consider Paul's use of exemplification in Galatians, 1 Thessalonians or Philemon.

A Synthesis: The Imitation of Paul as Emulation and Obedience
Much of the discussion to date has been to counteract Michaelis's underplaying of Paul's use of personal example, and his virtual reduction of the summons to imitation as a call to obedience to Paul's authority. Michaelis's bias against imitation as following personal example has now been firmly rejected as a result of critical exegesis.[55] However, the reactionary nature of the discussion has not always made it clear whether or not the issue is where the *emphasis* lies (obedience or personal example), or whether or not imitation as following personal example *excludes* an implication of authority in the motif. Stanley, de Boer, Schulz, Gutierrez and Fiore place the emphasis on personal example, though they do not rule out the implication of obedience (though this element is difficult to discern in their emphasis on personal example). Michaelis allows simple comparison, emulation and implied authority

---

53. A. Reinhartz, 'On the Meaning of the Pauline Exhortation: "*mimētai mou ginesthe*—become imitators of me"', *SR* 16 (1987), pp. 393-403 (397).
54. Reinhartz, 'On the Meaning of the Pauline Exhortation', pp. 396, 398.
55. Best, *Paul and his Converts*, p. 72 n. 14.

as the range of usage of imitation in Paul, though his emphasis is firmly upon obedience to Paul's authority to the virtual exclusion of the others.

The resulting confusion in the debate gives partial impetus to Elizabeth A. Castelli's study. Castelli castigates scholars in general and Fiore in particular for neglecting the power dynamic implied in a mimetic relationship as they have reacted to Michaelis's programmatic formulation of the subject.[56] A close reading of Fiore, for example, makes it difficult to decide whether he is emphasizing personal example following the balance struck in Stanley and de Boer as he claims,[57] or if he is as strong in his bias against an implied obedience as Michaelis is in favour of it. On the one hand, we find a clear statement: 'Whatever obedience he has in mind in these references, imitation lies within his sights as well. *Indeed, the model and the precept work hand in hand in Paul's moral instructions.*'[58] This is the proper balance to keep in mind. On the other hand, Fiore's statement here is in strong tension with his comment two pages later: 'The assumption of an interpretation of the [*sic*] imitation along the lines of accepting or following authority is unfounded and unnecessary'.[59] This last statement leads to some confusion. If Fiore had said 'The assumption of an *exclusive* interpretation of imitation along the lines of accepting authority…', then there would be no difficulty holding his two comments together, and one would think that this is what Fiore meant given the citation above. However, he later says, 'Example has been shown to be a prominent feature in Paul's hortatory method and he aims at imitation rather than obedience of his authoritative prescriptions'.[60] He again places the two interpretations in opposition to one another unnecessarily. One would have thought that emphasis here should be upon example as a 'prominent feature' not excluding an implication of authority, but his interpretations of 1 Cor. 4.14-21 and Phil. 3.17 exclude an implied authority in both the cases.[61] Castelli appears justified in her corrective stance toward Fiore.

---

56. Castelli, *Imitating Paul*, p. 31.
57. Fiore, *The Function of Personal Example*, pp. 165 n. 3, 168.
58. Fiore, *The Function of Personal Example*, p. 184 (emphasis mine).
59. Fiore, *The Function of Personal Example*, p. 186.
60. Fiore, *The Function of Personal Example*, p. 190.
61. Fiore, *The Function of Personal Example*, pp. 182-83, 185.

1. Introduction

Castelli recasts Michaelis's view, maintaining an appropriate awareness of the pedagogical implications of mimesis in antiquity, by approaching the imitation motif from a Foucaldian theoretical framework. From her theoretical perspective she asserts that Paul's exhortation to mimesis may be intended pedagogically, but it functions also as an assertion of power since the asymmetrical model–copy relationship implies a hierarchical power dynamic where the model implicitly possesses authority in the relationship. It is not germane that the readers had a choice to emulate or repudiate Paul's example since a power relationship can and does co-exist with either consent or coercion.[62] Whether or not Paul was conscious of this dynamic and intended this meaning is not a first concern to Castelli since her object of inquiry is the textual effect rather than the textual meaning.[63]

To this theoretical position Castelli adds several cogent *a posteriori* arguments to bolster her *a priori* emphasis on the implication of power in mimesis. First, she rightly emphasizes that the call to unity and mimesis in Philippians (1.27-30; 3.16-21) is an assertion of authority against alternative options available to the Philippians.[64] Secondly, acknowledging the relationship of imitation to the father motif in Paul and in antiquity as Gutierrez has demonstrated, Castelli notes that father imagery evokes not merely feelings of familial warmth and goodwill, but specifically emphasizes the virtually absolute authority that a father possessed over his children. Castelli draws attention to Paul's explicit awareness of this fact in Gal. 4.1-3.[65] She rebukes Fiore for his decontextualization of Epictetus, *Diss.* 3.22.95 to illustrate fatherly concern as 'affectionate urging'.[66] Fiore includes from the Loeb edition,

> When he sees that he has watched over men, and toiled in their behalf; and that he has slept in purity, while his sleep leaves him even purer than he was before; and that every thought which he thinks is that of a friend and servant to the gods, of one who shares in the government of Zeus... why should he not have courage to speak freely to his own brothers, to his children, in a word, to his kinsmen? That is why the man who is in

---

62. Castelli, *Imitating Paul*, pp. 44-45.
63. Castelli, *Imitating Paul*, p. 120.
64. Castelli, *Imitating Paul*, p. 115; NB Phil. 3.2-3, 18-21.
65. Castelli, *Imitating Paul*, p. 101.
66. Only the reference and not the citation is given in Fiore, *The Function of Personal Example*, p. 175, but Castelli reacts to the 1982 dissertation, pp. 325-26 n. 27, where Fiore apparently gives the curtailed citation (I have only had access to Fiore's 1986 published version).

this frame of mind is neither a busybody nor a meddler; for he is not meddling in other people's affairs when he is overseeing the actions of men, but these are his proper concern.

Castelli might have observed that sharing in Zeus's government and overseeing others' actions strongly imply the father's authority, but she accomplishes the same end by continuing the Epictetus citation where Fiore has cut it off:

Otherwise, go call the general a meddler when he oversees and reviews and watches over his troops, and punishes those who are guilty of a breach of discipline.

Castelli's point is well made that when Paul exhorts his followers to imitate him on the basis of his relationship to them as their spiritual father, he places imitation firmly within a cultural context that would understand an implication of authority. The comparison of the father's authority to that of a military general to supervise and discipline his troops in the Epictetus citation underlines this point.[67]

A third argument she develops to support the view that authority is part and parcel of a mimetic relationship is exegetically based upon 1 Cor. 4.14-21.[68] She reads the shift to Paul's singular example in 1 Cor. 4.14-21, Timothy's promised reminder to the Corinthians of Paul's regulative ways that he teaches 'in all the churches' (4.17), and the interwoven father imagery (4.14, 15, 17, 21) as irrefutable evidence that Paul has his regulative authority in mind when he summons the Corinthians to imitate him (4.16; the argument that I advance in Chapter 3 below bolsters Castelli's claim). Furthermore, Paul's proviso when his example is not intended to have this same normative character (cf. 1 Cor. 7.6-7) is explained under Castelli's rubric.

A fourth argument Castelli advances for the implied power dynamic inherent in mimesis is the attachment of the christological modifier to Paul's example in 1 Cor. 11.1.[69] The second half of this verse is usually rendered 'just as I also [imitate] Christ', implying that Paul's example mirrors the example of Christ. However, the reading I prefer is, 'Become imitators of me, just as I also [belong to] Christ'. Support for this is drawn from the technical and perhaps polemical usage of

---

67. Castelli, *Imitating Paul*, pp. 100-101. So also Holmberg, *Paul and Power*, p. 78.
68. Castelli, *Imitating Paul*, pp. 107-10.
69. Castelli, *Imitating Paul*, pp. 112-13.

1. Introduction

Χριστοῦ in the letter as an identifier of one's Christian status (1.1, 12; 3.23; 4.1; 7.22; 15.23; cf. 2 Cor. 10.7; Gal. 3.29; 5.24), suggesting the term is part of Paul's idiolect for 'Christian'.[70] (2 Cor. 10.7 cannot be used to conclude that the notion in 1 Corinthians originated with the opponents, since the nature of the problem by the time of 2 Corinthians 10 has changed dramatically. The expression may reflect the Corinthians' or opponents' side of the dispute, but more likely is Paul's corrective.) However one takes καθὼς κἀγὼ Χριστοῦ in 1 Cor. 11.1b, the implication is that Paul's example is normative because of its relationship to Christ's will.

In summary, Castelli has made an impressive case for understanding Paul's exhortation to imitation as a summons to conform to his normative example. This provides a needed corrective to the tendency of Fiore's work. However, Fiore—and before him de Boer—has made a clear case for understanding mimesis as the pedagogical technique of modelling, a claim which Michaelis has been interpreted to deny. On the face of it Michaelis allows the following of personal example in the case of 2 Thess. 3.7, 9 and Phil. 3.17 alongside an implied assertion of Paul's authority,[71] though in a confusing series of sentences about Phil. 3.17 he appears to repudiate such a balance. On the one hand, Phil. 3.17 'certainly means: Walk as I do, but it also means (and primarily): Recognize my authority, follow what I say, be obedient'. But then Michaelis immediately disowns an understanding of exemplification in Phil. 3.17 with the two sentences which immediately follow: 'Imitation here is not repetition of a model. It is an expression of obedience.'[72]

The scholarly discussion is now ready to move beyond such false dichotomies and acknowledge that the imitation of Paul can and should be understood both as a pedagogical technique and as an implied assertion of authority as a summons to conform to the pattern set by Paul as the regulative model,[73] taking note also of the exceptional usage in 1 Thess. 1.6; 2.14 where the word group is used to compare the Thessalonians' experience with Paul, Christ and the Judaean churches.

---

70. E. Käsemann, 'Die Legitimität des Apostels: Eine Untersuchung zu II Korinther 10–13', *ZNW* 41 (1942), pp. 33-71 (55).
71. Michaelis, 'μιμέομαι', p. 667.
72. Michaelis, 'μιμέομαι', p. 668.
73. A balance maintained by Schütz, *Anatomy of Apostolic Authority*, pp. 226-32; and Holmberg, *Paul and Power*, pp. 77-79; a balance also found, e.g. in Seneca (Cancik, *Untersuchungen zu Senecas Epistulae morales*, p. 89).

*Identifying the Function and Content
of Paul's Use of Personal Example*

The contribution of this study is to venture beyond the aforementioned debate to trace how Paul uses his personal example as an explicit literary strategy in 1 Corinthians, Galatians and Philippians, and as an arguably implicit strategy in 1 Thessalonians and Philemon. (The absence of such a strategy in Romans is explained by the fact that Paul had not established the church in Rome, and the situation of 2 Corinthians may have demanded that Paul not employ such a strategy, perhaps partly due to an unfavourable assessment of his extensive use of this technique in 1 Corinthians; cf. 2 Cor. 4.5.)[74] Whereas previous studies have considered Paul's usage of 'I',[75] or his employment of personal example in particular arguments,[76] this may well be the first study to trace

---

74. Though there are many references to his behaviour when he was in Corinth (2 Cor. 1.12, 17; 2.17; 4.2; 7.2; 10.2, 10; 11.5-7; 12.11-13, 17), Paul's conduct is at issue in 2 Corinthians and cannot be held up as an example when it must be defended (Best, *Paul and his Converts*, p. 66). The few 'I' statements that may be thought to function paradigmatically are clearly related to criticisms or suspicions raised about Paul. For example, Paul's exhibition of the 'meekness and gentleness of Christ' in 2 Cor. 10.1a is clearly linked to some kind of character assassination of Paul in 10.1b. In another place, Paul's boasting in the things that demonstrate his weakness (11.30; 12.5, 9-10) is directly linked to an implied comparison with his opposition rather than an exhortation to emulation by his auditors (e.g. 12.11; 13.3-4).

75. W.G. Kümmel, *Römer 7 und das Bild des Menschen im Neuen Testament* (TBü, 53; Munich: Chr. Kaiser Verlag, 1974 [1929]); W.F. Lofthouse, ' "I" and "We" in the Pauline Letters', *ExpTim* 64 (1952–53), pp. 241-45; M. Carrez, 'Le "nous" en 2 Corinthiens: Contribution à l'étude de l'apostolicité dans 2 Corinthiens', *NTS* 26 (1979–80), pp. 474-86; E. Farahian, *Le 'Je' Paulinien: Etude pour mieux comprende Gal. 2, 19-21* (Analecta Gregoriana, 253; Rome: Editrice Pontificia Universita Gregorina, 1988); G. Theissen, *Psychological Aspects of Pauline Theology* (trans. J. Galvin; Philadelphia: Fortress Press, 1987), pp. 177-201.

76. Notably, 1 Cor. 9: W.L. Willis, 'An Apostolic Apologia? The Form and Function of 1 Corinthians 9', *JSNT* 24 (1985), pp. 33-48; 1 Cor. 13: O. Wischmeyer, *Der höchste Weg: Das 13. Kapitel des 1 Korintherbriefes* (SNT, 13; Gütersloh: Gerd Mohn, 1981); Gal. 1–2: Lyons, *Pauline Autobiography*, pp. 123-76 (and pp. 177-222 on 1 Thess. 2); B.R. Gaventa, 'Galatians 1 and 2: Autobiography as Paradigm', *NovT* 28 (1986), pp. 309-26; Farahian, *Le 'Je' Paulinien*;

Paul's style of argumentation from his personal example in light of its several appearances in his undisputed letters. Indeed, Fiore devotes 19 pages to an exegetical discussion of the non-Pastorals, while Castelli is faulted for allotting a meagre 28 pages to a discussion of the texts.[77] De Boer's study is predominantly exegetical, devoting 104 pages to the task, yet he leaves virtually untouched Paul's self-portrayals in his letters. I attempt to address this lacuna in the current study.

Castelli denies that Paul gives content to his model of imitation and believes this reinforces his power with his followers 'forcing them always to be "policing" themselves, because their model is conspicuously imprecise'.[78] Castelli erroneously extrapolates from Victor Paul Furnish's comments about the absence of the clear *example of the earthly Jesus* in Paul, mistakenly appealing to Furnish as support for her claim about Paul's use of his own example.[79] Later she claims 'one is hard-pressed to produce a univocal, concrete expression of what exactly the Corinthians are being called to imitate'.[80] On the contrary, it will be argued below that Paul's letters give specific content to his personal example, and this literary exemplification is in view when he exhorts his readers to imitate him.

This is not to claim that Paul's example for his readers is to be equated with his literary self-presentation. First, Paul makes numerous self-references in his letters that are inimitable, particularly references about his past (e.g. Phil. 3.4b-6). Secondly, Paul previously had been present with his readers, and presumably he is relying partly on their remembrance of his teaching and behaviour.[81] As we will see below, the recall motif figures significantly in the paraenesis of 1 Thessalonians, and in other references it is clear that Paul's exemplification

---

Phil. 3: W. Schenk, *Die Philipperbriefe des Paulus: Kommentar* (Stuttgart: W. Kohlhammer, 1984), pp. 260-63. Cf. Eph. 5.1-2: E. Judge, 'The Teacher as Moral Exemplar in Paul and in the Inscriptions of Ephesus', in D. Peterson and J. Pryor (eds.), *In the Fullness of Time* (Homebush, Australia: Lancer, 1992), pp. 185-201.

77. So C.J. Roetzel in his review of Castelli in *Critical Review of Books in Religion* 6 (1993), pp. 213-15.

78. Castelli, *Imitating Paul*, p. 32.

79. V.P. Furnish, *Theology and Ethics in Paul* (Nashville: Abingdon Press, 1968), p. 223.

80. Castelli, *Imitating Paul*, p. 109.

81. A common feature of paraenesis, so A.J. Malherbe, 'Hellenistic Moralists and the New Testament', *ANRW*, II.26.1, pp. 267-333 (286-87).

includes the behaviour he modelled when present with his original readers (e.g. 1 Cor. 4.17; Gal. 4.13-15; Phil. 4.9). These historical reference points of his personal example for his first readers count against Castelli's claim that Paul's example is intentionally ambiguous as part of a control technique. Instead Paul's presence apparently left a concrete and specific model that he could refer to and expect them to remember, implying that his epistolary exemplification is only part of the content of his appeal. As I shall argue below, his epistolary exemplification underlines and enhances the forward thrust of the argument that he develops for the exigency of the given letter, and serves to complement the personal example he set when previously present with them.

I shall argue that Paul uses his personal example to ground and illustrate his argumentation in a rhetorically sophisticated manner, that he employs modelling as a technique of effective psychagogy, and that he often structures his argument on the basis of his personal example. In places a crisp statement of his own example serves as a thesis statement of the argument that follows (e.g. Rom. 1.16-17; Gal. 1.10), while at other times it serves to summarize the argument and provide a transition to the next phase (see especially Chapters 3 and 4 below). All the while Paul's self-portrayals in his letters serve not autobiographical nor egoistic purposes but pedagogical and argumentative aims. Paul's exhortation to imitation, then, may recall his personal example when physically present with his churches, but also includes his selective, literary self-portrait, tailor-made for the argumentative and pedagogical situation at hand in a given epistolary situation since he was patently absent when he wrote (Col. 2.5; 4.16; Polycarp, *Phil.* 3.2). An attempt will be made to demonstrate the function and content of Paul's literary example in a study of 1 Corinthians (Chapters 2 and 3), Galatians (Chapter 4) and Philippians (Chapter 5) where Paul explicitly draws attention to his strategy of self-exemplification. An implicit usage of this literary strategy will be suggested for 1 Thessalonians and Philemon (Chapter 6), and then the most disputed 'I' passage in Paul, Rom. 7.7-25, is briefly examined as a case study of Paul's stylistic usage of his personal example (Chapter 7).

Chapter 2

1 CORINTHIANS 1–4: 'THAT YOU MAY LEARN FROM OUR EXAMPLE'

> These things I have applied to myself and to Apollos
> in order that you may learn in us... (1 Cor. 4.6).

The use of personal example as a literary strategy is most prominent in 1 Corinthians among the Pauline corpus, and is crucial to the rhetorical strategy of the letter. In every section of 1 Corinthians, except for 11.2-34, Paul's self-presentation or his paradigmatic 'I' statement is at the heart of his manner of argumentation. This is not to claim that his usage throughout the letter is uniform, when in fact it is quite diverse. In the opening section (1 Cor. 1.1–4.13), Paul's usage of his personal example is quite distinct from his usage in 4.14 to ch. 15. In the first chapters there is no call to imitation nor is Paul's example one that is to be imitated. Instead, Paul and Apollos are presented as exempla for the Corinthians' instruction (4.6). In 1 Cor. 1.1–4.13 Paul's example serves more as a specimen for comparison, whereas in the remainder of the letter he becomes a prototype for imitation.[1] The comparison in 1 Corinthians 1–4 is made in two directions. Implicitly there is a comparison with the boastful, whose self-assurance has contributed to a fractured fellowship. Explicitly, Paul compares—or rather contrasts—himself with Christ to make emphasis on Christ's initiative in the growth, gifting and blessing of the church. A refrain of these chapters is seen, for example, in 1 Cor. 3.5: 'What therefore is Apollos? What therefore is Paul? Servants through whom you believed, and to each one as the Lord gave [faith].' Throughout this opening section Paul depreciates himself for christological emphasis, accents the unity of the missionary workers in their gospel work, and stresses the cruciform nature of life in Christ, laying a foundation for his solution to the church problems that he treats in what follows.

---

1. Fiore, *The Function of Personal Example*, p. 186.

The Occasion of the Letter

The church at Corinth had multiple problems from Paul's point of view, but the interpreter is confronted with the question of the relationship between the apparently disparate issues of party spirit, a misguided emphasis on wisdom and knowledge, intramural lawsuits, sexual immorality, marital relations, idol meat, improprieties in worship, glossolalia, prophecy and disputations about the resurrection from the dead. If one assumes that the canonical letter is a unity,[2] the apparent discontinuity of its parts has invited quite diverse proposals to relate the various parts to a unified theological and/or social understanding of their common source. Ever since F.C. Baur proposed in 1831 that 1.12 describes only two parties—the Paul/Apollos party and the Peter/Christ party—the search for the source of Corinthian problems has tended to look for a single key to unlock the mysterious mixture of theological and ethical problems present in the church.[3] Many suggestions have been offered, including over-realized eschatology (Chrysostom), gnosticism (Schmithals), pneumatic enthusiasm (Ellis), social stratification (Theissen), violation of friendship conventions (Marshall), party politics (Welborn), Cynic-Stoic teaching (Paige), rhetorical sophistication (Pogoloff), factionalism (Mitchell), or problems associated with patronage (Chow, Clarke). Not all of these explanations are exclusive, though Baur's reconstruction of the Peter–Paul divide throughout the earliest churches and Schmithals's 'pan-gnosticism' are not generally accepted.[4]

It is not my purpose here to join this debate, nor to succumb to a reductionist tendency and link all the problems to a single cause. There is, however, a dimension of 1 Corinthians that is best explained in terms of so-called 'realized eschatology' as a contributing factor, though this should not be interpreted to minimize the social sources of

---

2. See H. Merklein, 'Die Einheitlichkeit des ersten Korintherbriefes', *ZNW* 75 (1984), pp. 153-83.

3. For the history of research see W. Schrage, *Der erste Brief an die Korinther (1 Kor 1,1–6,11)* (EKKNT, 7.1; Zürich: Benziger Verlag; Neukirchen–Vluyn: Neukirchener Verlag, 1991), pp. 38-63.

4. Some scholars challenge altogether the endeavour of reconstructing the opponents' theology, e.g. C.B. Cousar, 'The Theological Task of 1 Corinthians: A Conversation with Gordon D. Fee and Victor Paul Furnish', in D. Hay (ed.), *Pauline Theology*. II. *1 and 2 Corinthians* (Minneapolis: Fortress Press, 1993), pp. 90-102.

2. *1 Corinthians 1–4*

some of the Corinthian problems that have been well argued of late.[5] Eschatology as an explanation of the Corinthian matrix of problems was first suggested in the fourth century by John Chrysostom, and its resurgence in this century is credited to H.F. von Soden (1931),[6] accepted in some form by many scholars.[7] This explanation makes sense of some of Paul's comments about some Corinthians' emphasis on the present (4.8; 10.11), is one explanation of the line of thought in ch. 15,[8] relates ch. 15 to the enthusiasm reflected in chs. 12–14 and to the rest of the letter,[9] accounts for references to the angels as Paul picking up a Corinthian theme (4.9; 6.3; 11.10; 13.1), and may partially account for their contempt for the body and ordinary worldly matters.

---

5. E.g. G. Theissen, *The Social Setting of Pauline Christianity: Essays on Corinth* (ed. and trans. J.H. Schütz; Philadelphia: Fortress Press, 1982); W.A. Meeks, *The First Urban Christians: The Social World of the Apostle Paul* (New Haven: Yale University Press, 1983); A.D. Litfin, *St. Paul's Theology of Proclamation: 1 Corinthians 1–4 and Graeco-Roman Rhetoric* (SNTSMS, 79; Cambridge: Cambridge University Press, 1993).

6. H.F. von Soden, 'Sacrament and Ethics in Paul', in W.A. Meeks (ed. and trans.), *The Writings of St. Paul* (New York: W.W. Norton, 1972 [1931]), pp. 257-68; so J.H. Wilson, 'The Corinthians Who Say There Is No Resurrection of the Dead', *ZNW* 59 (1968), pp. 90-107 (95 n. 23).

7. E.g. A.J. Malherbe, 'The Beasts at Ephesus', *JBL* 87 (1968), pp. 71-80 (81); H. Conzelmann, *1 Corinthians* (trans. J. Leitch; Hermeneia; Philadelphia: Fortress Press, 1975 [1969]); C.K. Barrett, *A Commentary on the First Epistle to the Corinthians* (New York: Harper & Row, 1968); A.C. Thiselton, 'Realized Eschatology at Corinth', *NTS* 24 (1977–78), pp. 510-26; G.D. Fee, *The First Epistle to the Corinthians* (NICNT; Grand Rapids: Eerdmans, 1987); Schrage, *Der erste Brief an die Korinther*; V.P. Furnish, 'Theology in 1 Corinthians', in D. Hay (ed.), *Pauline Theology. II. 1 and 2 Corinthians* (Minneapolis: Fortress Press, 1993), pp. 59-89. For a summary of scholarship see A.C. Wire, 'Appendix 12: Resurrection', in *idem, The Corinthian Women Prophets: A Reconstruction through Paul's Rhetoric* (Minneapolis: Fortress Press, 1990), pp. 233-36.

8. See the persuasive response of C. Tuckett, 'The Corinthians Who Say, "There is no resurrection of the dead?" (1 Cor. 15.12)', in R. Bieringer (ed.), *The Corinthian Correspondence* (BETL, 125; Leuven: Peeters, 1996), pp. 247-75, to the objections of G. Sellin, *Der Streit um der Auferstehunge der Toten* (FRLANT, 138; Göttingen: Vandenhoeck & Ruprecht, 1986); and A.J.M. Wedderburn, *Baptism and Resurrection* (WUNT, 44; Tübingen: J.C.B. Mohr [Paul Siebeck], 1987).

9. Though see K. Barth who relates ch. 15 to the problems of the letter without the hypothesis of over-realized eschatology (*The Resurrection of the Dead* [trans. H.J. Stenning; London: Hodder & Stoughton, 1933]).

Inferentially, Paul's multiple references to the future in his eschatological perspective are thereby interpreted as correctives to the Corinthians' overestimation of what has already come their way by the Spirit. This is not to claim that over-realized eschatology is a necessary position demanded by the text, but that it provides an adequate explanation of some elements.[10] If the label 'realized eschatology' begs too many questions it at least draws attention to the strong consciousness among some in Corinth that they possessed spiritual blessings now that somehow precluded self-denial and suffering.[11] As A.C. Thiselton suggests, the question is not so much 'whether the Corinthians believed that their resurrection was past, but whether they placed such weight on the experience of transformation in the past and present that when they thought about resurrection the centre of gravity of their thinking was no longer in the future'.[12]

Apart from their realized eschatological awareness, it is apparent that the Corinthian church was a microcosm of the cultural diversity found in Corinth. The text reveals a number of problems in the church, each of which can be understood to some extent without reference to the other presenting problems.[13] The overriding social problem in the church was disunity, divisions (σχίσματα, 1.10) and quarrels (ἔριδες, 1.11) due to (a) competing claims to a superior church leader (1.12-16; 3.21, 22; 11.16-19), (b) a pretension to wisdom and knowledge divinely mediated by their experience of the Spirit (3.18-19; 8.1-11) which granted them a sense of liberty which issued in (c) ethical and theological disagreements (chs. 5–10; 15), (d) pneumatic enthusiasm[14] and individualism (chs. 12–14), (e) social tension arising from their cultural diversity, boastfulness (5.6), social stratification (7.17-24),[15] and injus-

---

10. Thiselton, 'Realized Eschatology at Corinth'.
11. A.J.M. Wedderburn, 'The Problem of the Denial of the Resurrection in 1 Corinthians 15', *NovT* 23 (1981), pp. 229-41 (234).
12. Thiselton, 'Realized Eschatology at Corinth', p. 524.
13. So W. Baird, '"One Against the Other": Intra-Church Conflict in 1 Corinthians', in R. Fortna and B. Gaventa (eds.), *The Conversation Continues: Studies in Paul and John in Honor of J. Louis Martyn* (Nashville: Abingdon Press, 1990), pp. 116-36 (119).
14. See E.E. Ellis, '"Wisdom" and "Knowledge" in 1 Corinthians', *TynBul* 25 (1974), pp. 82-98, for his argument for a pneumatic/prophetic understanding of 'wisdom' and 'knowledge' in 1 Corinthians.
15. See Theissen, *The Social Setting*, pp. 69-110.

tice and disorder in worship (chs. 11–14). Paul promotes unity throughout the letter,[16] and identifies three or four parties that comprise the church (depending on the significance we attribute to 'of Christ' in 1.12).[17] Throughout, Paul addresses the whole church, and wisely so since 'he attacks the formation of factions as such... and rejects exclusive claims in all four groups as an offence against the missionaries themselves whom he names; he is against the false estimation of leaders by their supporters'.[18] The situation was complicated by difficulties resulting from social stratification, seen most clearly in the celebration of the Lord's Supper (11.17-34).[19] However, the problems cannot be reduced merely to social causes since the problem of idol meat is essentially religious, and the question of the resurrection is essentially theological.[20]

Multiple Models as a Corinthian Problem

Paul characterizes several parties in 1.12 by the names of their leaders, as Graeco-Roman political parties were often labelled.[21] There is no clear indicator of the characteristics of each group, nor is it agreed whether or not all the names reflect actual groups or Paul's fictive creation for the sake of argument. The only group we can be clear in identifying consists of those loyal to Paul. We know some of their names: Chloe and 'her people' (1.11), Crispus and Gaius (1.14), Stephanas and

---

16. M.M. Mitchell, *Paul and the Rhetoric of Reconciliation: An Exegetical Investigation of the Language and Composition of 1 Corinthians* (Louisville, KY: Westminster/John Knox Press, 1992), argues that unification of the church is Paul's single, rhetorical objective throughout 1 Corinthians.

17. Contra J. Munck, 'The Church without Factions: Studies in 1 Corinthians 1–4', in *idem, Paul and the Salvation of Mankind* (trans. F. Clarke; London: SCM Press, 1959), pp. 135-67.

18. F. Lang, *Die Briefe an die Korinther* (NTD, 7; Göttingen: Vandenhoeck & Ruprecht, 1986), p. 36.

19. Theissen, *The Social Setting*, pp. 145-68.

20. So Baird, '"One Against the Other"', p. 131.

21. See L.L. Welborn, 'On the Discord in Corinth: 1 Corinthians 1–4 and Ancient Politics', *JBL* 106 (1987), pp. 85-111. Cf. Theissen, *The Social Setting*, pp. 121-43, who views the distinctions between the groups along the lines of social status rather than the parties named in 1.12, the 'strong' referring to the elite whose business and social relations would be curtailed if they displayed scruples about eating meat sacrificed to idols, an element that surely plays into the Corinthian mix.

Fortunatus (16.15-18). 1.13-16 is framed with them in view, since their boast of Paul would heighten the church rivalries.

The identification of the number and characteristics of the other groups within the church are much more problematic. A second faction may have held up Apollos as their exemplar. They may have displayed a Stoic emphasis on wisdom,[22] and unfavourably compared Paul's speech with Apollos's eloquence.[23] There is no reason to think that Paul and Apollos were themselves having a disagreement but, as S. Pogoloff suggests, they became the source of division without ever intending to. For this reason we may agree with Pogoloff that Apollos's role may be left rather vague.[24] A third faction may have promoted the primacy of Peter, but there is little evidence for this. The Corinthians are familiar with Palestinian Christianity in some fashion, evident in Paul's references to Cephas and the Jerusalem apostles (1.12; 9.5; 15.5-7).[25] If the 'of Cephas' group consisted of converts from Judaism then they like Paul would be angered by the behaviour described in 5.1–8.13 and 10.1–33,[26] and may have brought the practice of glossolalia from Pales-

---

22. As T. Paige argues, 'Stoicism, Ἐλευθερία and Community at Corinth', in M. Wilkins and T. Paige (eds.), *Worship, Theology and Ministry in the Early Church: Essays in Honor of Ralph P. Martin* (JSNTSup, 87; Sheffield: JSOT Press, 1992), pp. 180-93.

23. There is no reason to deny this characterization of Apollos in Acts 18.24-28.

24. S.M. Pogoloff, 'Form and Content in Classical Rhetoric', in *idem, Logos and Sophia: The Rhetorical Situation of 1 Corinthians* (SBLDS, 134; Atlanta: Scholars Press, 1992), pp. 173-96.

25. On this score, is it significant that Paul uses only the Aramaic name for Peter reflecting their name for this Palestinian apostle? 15.5 may be excluded from the argument as part of the creedal material Paul cites, as K. Wegenast has argued, in *Das Verständnis der Tradition bei Paulus und in den Deuteropaulinen* (WMANT, 8; ed. G. Bornkamm and G. von Rad; Neukirchen–Vluyn: Neukirchener Verlag, 1962), pp. 52-70.

26. Some have thought the 'of Cephas' group had been called 'weak' by others because of their Jewish conscience (so T.W. Manson, 'The Corinthian Correspondence [1]', in M. Black [ed.], *Studies in the Gospels and Epistles* [Manchester: Manchester University Press, 1962], pp. 190-209 [200], who interprets 1 Corinthians against 'the apostolic decree'; so also C.K. Barrett, 'Cephas and Corinth', in *idem, Essays on Paul* [London: SPCK, 1982 (1963)], pp. 28-39 [33]). However, 8.10 suggests that the 'weak' were former pagans since it seems unlikely Jews would experience a temptation to join in eating idol meat (Meeks, *The First Urban Christians*, p. 98).

tine.²⁷ Paul may refer to them in 10.32 as he broadens the 'give no offence' rule to include Jews, Greeks and the entire church of God. However, there is general agreement among scholars that Paul is not opposing Judaizers in Corinth.²⁸

The reference to those 'of Christ' has been the cause of much speculation,²⁹ and it is difficult to weigh the evidence. Paul uses the phrase in a positive way in his argument throughout the letter to encourage unity under one head, Christ. Likewise, in 3.21-23 he again lists three of the 'parties' and uses 'of Christ' as the umbrella over all three. This suggests that 'of Christ' may be Paul's corrective of the party spirit in 1.12, though there is nothing in 1.12 that sets it off as such. *1 Clemens* 47 lends support to this reading:

> Truly he wrote to you in the Spirit about himself and Cephas and Apollos, because even then you had split into factions. Yet that splitting into factions brought less sin upon you, for you were partisans of highly reputed apostles and of a man approved by them.³⁰

On the other hand, 'of Christ' has a distinct usage in 2 Cor. 10.7; 11.23 suggesting that Paul may take up his opponents' term there and in 1 Corinthians.³¹ However, the situation has changed dramatically between 1 Corinthians and 2 Corinthians 10–13. Furthermore, there is little in 1 Corinthians to suggest that Paul faced external opponents at the time of

---

27. So Manson, 'The Corinthian Correspondence (1)', pp. 204-205. Barrett finds this attractive but open to question since it is not certain that glossolalia was practised in the Palestinian church ('Cephas and Corinth', p. 34).

28. N.A. Dahl, 'Paul and the Church at Corinth According to 1 Corinthians 1.10–4.21', in W.R. Farmer, C.F.D. Moule and R.D. Niebuhr (eds.), *Christian History and Interpretation: Studies Presented to John Knox* (Cambridge: Cambridge University Press, 1967), pp. 313-35 (315) (all citations from this version unless otherwise noted).

29. E.g. Manson, 'The Corinthian Correspondence (1)', p. 207, suggests that the 'of Christ' party stands at the opposite extreme of the 'of Cephas' party, Greek in their understanding of monotheism, emphasizing 'the sound Greek doctrine of immortality' in place of resurrection, interpreting 'freedom' as 'emancipation from the puritanical rigours of Palestinian barbarian authorities into the wider air of self-realisation'.

30. M. Holmes (ed.), *The Apostolic Fathers* (trans. J.B. Lightfoot and J.R. Harmer; Grand Rapids: Baker Book House, 2nd edn, 1989), p. 55. Holmes dates this 95 or 96 CE (p. 25), but L.L. Welborn dates it between 80 and 140 CE ('Clement, First Epistle of', *ABD*, I, pp. 1055-60 [1060]).

31. Theissen, *The Social Setting*, pp. 46-47.

the first canonical letter. Dahl, reading 1 Corinthians 1–4 as Paul's apology, takes 'of Christ' as a slogan expressing independence from Paul: 'I belong myself to Christ—and am independent of Paul', a meaning he also deciphers in 2 Cor. 10.7.[32] However, before we mirror-read the phrase we must pay attention to Paul's overall usage of it in 1 Corinthians. There are many places where the phrase is unambiguously Paul's and is used in a positive way (1.1; 3.23; 4.1; 6.15; 7.22; 15.23; cf. 2 Cor. 3.3), and two places where 'of Christ' could be taken as Paul's corrective, polemical comment (2.16; 11.1) as 1.12 can be (and this is not ruled out for 2 Cor. 10.7; 11.23). Though grammatically 1.12 does not set off 'I am of Christ' as a corrective, Paul's usage of the phrase elsewhere in the letter suggests that this is his own corrective. Though the Corinthians could not have gathered this from the grammar of 1.12, it would have been immediately apparent if no one had actually claimed to be 'of Christ' against Paul. This immediately raises the question of Paul's status vis-à-vis the Corinthians, and how we should understand the nature of Paul's personal remarks in 1 Corinthians.

A Challenge to Paul's Authority in 1 Corinthians?

There is no direct evidence that Paul also responds to a challenge to his authority in 1 Corinthians, though many interpreters have thought this is the case.[33] Dahl argues that the main evidence for Paul's awareness of opposition is found in 4.18 which uses the indefinite pronoun τίνες to 'refer to some definite persons whose names he does not want to mention'.[34] Dahl's conclusion that the quarrels at Corinth were mainly due to opposition against Paul remarkably ignores the explicit issues in the entire text of 1 Corinthians that were sure to be the basis of quarrelling.[35] Furthermore, 4.18 need not be read as a statement to the opposition, but may be understood as a general exhortation to any who may

32. Dahl, 'Paul and the Church at Corinth', pp. 322-23.

33. E.g. J.C. Hurd, Jr, *The Origin of 1 Corinthians* (London: SPCK, 1965), pp. 111-13; Fee, *The First Epistle to the Corinthians*; Schrage, *Der erste Brief an die Korinther*.

34. Dahl, 'Paul and the Church at Corinth', pp. 318-19. P. Marshall also suggests that Paul uses the rhetorical device of non-naming or periphrasis to shame his opponents ('Invective: Paul and his Enemies in Corinth', in E.W. Conrad and E.G. Newing [eds.], *Perspectives on Language and Text* [Winona Lake, IN: Eisenbrauns, 1987], pp. 359-73 [366-67]).

35. Dahl, 'Paul and the Church at Corinth', p. 329.

have been complacent. As J.B. Chance acknowledges, 'Dahl's reconstruction is the result of a prior assumption; namely, that 1.10–4.21 is an apology'.[36] Dahl himself provides the needed corrective to this and his own earlier position in a footnote attached to his article when it was later reprinted. He acknowledges that characterizing 1 Corinthians 1–4 as an apologetic section may be misleading since, in contrast to Galatians and parts of 2 Corinthians, 1 Corinthians 1–4 is not written in the style of an apologetic letter, and 'to call the section "apologetic" is to downplay the degree to which Paul is critical of his own adherents as well as of his opponents'.[37]

Formal considerations are against reading the letter as an apology. J.B. Chance seeks to support Dahl's earlier position by comparing the 'apologetic letter' of 1 Corinthians 1–6 with Galatians (Chance's paradigm for an apologetic letter).[38] Not all of his points of comparison with Galatians are convincing, nor is it agreed that Galatians is an apologetic letter. Whatever label we accept for 1 Corinthians—'a complex paraenetic and advising letter',[39] 'deliberative'[40] or 'a letter of admonishment'[41]—the letter is not formally an apologetic letter.[42] As J.T. Fitzgerald writes:

36. J.B. Chance, 'Paul's Apology to the Corinthians', *Philosophy of Religion Series* 9 (1982), pp. 145-55 (146). K.A. Plank also draws attention to how one's perspective shapes and organizes the perception of a text's meaning, also supposing that Paul is defensive and adversarial (*Paul and the Irony of Affliction* [Atlanta: Scholars Press, 1987], pp. 62-63).

37. N.A. Dahl, 'Paul and the Church at Corinth According to 1 Corinthians 1.10–4.21', in idem, *Studies in Paul: Theology for the Early Christian Mission* (Minneapolis: Augsburg, 1977), pp. 40-61 (61 n. 50).

38. Chance, 'Paul's Apology to the Corinthians'.

39. S.K. Stowers, *Letter Writing in Greco-Roman Antiquity* (Philadelphia: Westminster Press, 1986), pp. 96-97.

40. E. Schüssler Fiorenza, 'Rhetorical Situation and Historical Reconstruction in 1 Corinthians', *NTS* 33 (1987), pp. 386-403 (393); Mitchell, *Paul and the Rhetoric of Reconciliation*, p. 50.

41. J.T. Fitzgerald, *Cracks in an Earthen Vessel: An Examination of the Catalogues of Hardships in the Corinthian Correspondence* (SBLDS, 99; Atlanta: Scholars Press, 1988), pp. 117-28. The classification of 'epideictic' by W. Wuellner is not generally accepted, though the lines between 'deliberative' and 'epideictic' were not as distinct in practice as in theory ('Greek Rhetoric and Pauline Argumentation', in W. Schoedel and R. Wilken [eds.], *Early Christian Literature and the Classical Intellectual Tradition* [Paris: Beauchesne, 1979], pp. 177-88).

42. Contra W. Schrage, 'Das apostolische Amt des Paulus nach 1 Kor 4,14-17',

> The widespread view that 1.10–4.21 is primarily an apology by Paul is, quite simply, wrong. Paul is concerned here with admonishing the Corinthians, with resolving the problem of their intra-mural strife (1.10-12), not with defending himself. He is as much concerned with those who *overestimate* him and other missionaries as he is with those who would rob any of them of their proper recognition as *God's* collaborators.[43]

In addition to formal considerations there is further, internal evidence against the identification of opponents as a main impulse behind the writing of 1 Corinthians. E.E. Ellis has noted: '(1) This letter is not like other oppositional texts;[44] (2) Paul speaks as a father (4.15); (3) when Paul differs, he does so by concession and qualification (7.6; 8.1-13) or by a reasoned appeal (1 Cor. 1–4; 11.13-16; 14.37; ch. 15); (4) there is no invective; (5) Apollos and Cephas are his co-workers (3.6; 3.22–4.1; 9.5); (6) 'The Corinthians who wish to "examine" or "judge" Paul (4.3-4; 9.3) do not represent an opposition but, as the context in 1 Cor. 2.6-16 shows, only wish to subject Paul to the testing usually given to a fellow pneumatic.'[45]

On the other hand, since some appear to have claimed to be 'of Cephas' or 'of Apollos' it may be supposed that implicit in these claims was a rejection or challenge of Paul's teaching by some of the Corinthians. We need not suppose that the situation was uniform. On the whole, however, Paul must have felt that he stood on firm ground, evident in his assertion of authority in the case of discipline of the incestuous man. This assertion of authority implies that Paul believed their loyalty to his authority as the church's founder was intact. 11.2 gives another hint that the attitude of the congregation seems to have been one of loyalty and respect for Paul: 'I commend you because you remember me in everything and maintain the traditions just as I handed them on to you'.

---

in A. Vanhoye (ed.), *L'Apôtre Paul: Personnalité, style et conception du ministère* (BETL, 73; Leuven: Leuven University Press, 1986), pp. 103-19; M. Bünker, *Briefformular und rhetorische Disposition im 1. Korintherbrief* (GTA, 28; Göttingen: Vandenhoeck & Ruprecht, 1983); J.K. Chow, *Patronage and Power: A Study of Social Networks in Corinth* (JSNTSup, 75; Sheffield: JSOT Press, 1992).

43. Fitzgerald, *Cracks in an Earthen Vessel*, p. 128.
44. Cf. 2 Cor. 10–13; Phil. 1; 3; Gal. 1–2; 5; Rom. 16.17-18; Tit. 1.10-16.
45. Ellis, '"Wisdom" and "Knowledge"', p. 83. To the contrary, Manson, 'The Corinthian Correspondence (1)', p. 191, thinks this period was a critical one for Paul's authority and status which 'were constantly challenged within and without his Churches'.

E. Schüssler Fiorenza disagrees. She reads Paul's rhetoric as 'full of biting irony, and his attempt to shame, belittle, and undermine the Corinthian self-understanding is hardly designed to lessen tensions and to prevent division', and

> while I agree with Dahl [his earlier position] that the rhetoric of 1 Corinthians clearly intends to establish 'the authority of Paul as the founder and father of the entire church at Corinth', I would argue that it does not re-establish, but introduces such unique authority claims. In other words, Paul does not defend his authority as an apostle among other apostles but rather, argues for his authority as the *sole* founder and father of the Corinthian community.[46]

The text of 1 Corinthians raises several problems with her reading: (1) Apollos is given equal status in the missionary work. (2) Paul relies on the status of the other apostles in chs. 9 and 15 to make his case. (3) Paul asserts his authority in ch. 5, and seems to expect his summary judgment to be carried out. Chapter 5 is not the writing of someone whose position is in doubt, whose authority is weak or disputed. Only a respected Paul could deliver the kind of message he does. And if, as some have thought, the situation is referred to in 2 Cor. 2.5-11, it seems that an explosive and divisive situation has been handled without damage to Paul's position. As A.C. Wire says in reference to 4.14-21, 'Paul would not speak so confidently if he did not think that by this point in his argument his readers were ready to accept his authority and take on his ways. This must be given considerable weight.'[47] (4) Schüssler Fiorenza's characterization makes it difficult to understand how Paul could expect the Corinthians to imitate his admonition to humility, patience and kindness when he himself sets such an opposite example in his letter. (5) The purpose of his self-characterization from 4.14 on is different from his self-characterization in 1.10–4.13, and its function in his argument must be contrasted before conclusions are drawn. In the first part of the letter he affirms the unity of the missionary leaders and the oneness of the church. In the second part of the letter he asserts his unique authority as their church founder as he disciplines the infamous man and his stepmother. It makes better sense

---

46. Schüssler Fiorenza, 'Rhetorical Situation', pp. 396-97.
47. Wire, *The Corinthian Women Prophets*, p. 46. This serves as a decisive counter to Reinhartz's view that Paul's exhortation to imitation defensively asserts his authority ('On the Meaning of the Pauline Exhortation', p. 403).

to see Paul's letter as the admonitions of a spiritual father to his children than the belittling utterances that Schüssler Fiorenza suggests.

A methodological consideration must be voiced. Some scholars appeal to 2 Corinthians to support their reconstruction of 1 Corinthians. The appeal to 2 Corinthians must maintain an awareness that it represents a new stage, or stages, in Paul's relationship with the Corinthians. For example, there are no aggressive accusations in 1 Corinthians such as we find in 2 Cor. 11.4, evidently the result of a new situation arising from the arrival of outsiders (11.4, 11-13). P. Marshall, for example, overlooks the circumstantial differences between the two canonical letters, asserting it is correct 'to assume that defamatory accusations underlie 1 Corinthians 9',[48] and he reads them into 1 Corinthians 1–4 as well. Though his study is a valuable contribution to the study of the Corinthian correspondence, he misreads a high level of enmity into 1 Corinthians through the lens of 2 Corinthians.[49] Pogoloff rightly criticizes Marshall's treatment of the first chapters of 1 Corinthians.

> The problem in 1 Cor. 1–4 is not primarily money, or insults, but divisions based on ambitious, boastful, status-seeking attitudes and behavior which led to rivalries and party spirit.[50]

There was no financial criticism of Paul at the time of 1 Corinthians, or if there was, we have no evidence for it since 1 Corinthians 9 serves as an exemplum in Paul's discussion about idol meat (see below, Chapter 3). In fact, Paul considers his position vis-à-vis finances at the time of 1 Corinthians a reason for boasting (1 Cor. 9.15).[51]

1 Corinthians 1–4 will not be read here as an oppositional discourse with covert references to those opposing Paul. Rather I will discuss the function of Paul's self-description in the flow of his argument as it is developed against the prime problem of disunity and the underlying theological, ethical and social tensions which existed among the house churches of Corinth. Paul's argument appears to be assertive rather than defensive, a constructive piece of argumentation and exhortation that

---

48. Marshall, 'Invective', p. 364.
49. P. Marshall, *Enmity in Corinth: Social Conventions in Paul's Relations with the Corinthians* (WUNT, 2.23: Tübingen: J.C.B. Mohr [Paul Siebeck], 1987).
50. Pogoloff, *Logos and Sophia*, p. 234.
51. Chow, *Patronage and Power*, works within the same presuppositional framework as Marshall, supposing that Paul is defensive in 1 Corinthians against patrons in the church because of his refusal to accept their financial support.

seeks to address the issue of disunity that in turn is partly related to heralding one leader in place of another.

1 Corinthians 4.6: An Authorial Intention Statement?

If seeking 'authorial intention' is out of vogue, it is still worth considering 1 Cor. 4.6 as a rare case where the author states the intention of his self-presentation, namely that Paul has referred to himself and Apollos to instruct and exhort those in the congregation who have exalted themselves over others:

> And these things, brethren, I applied to myself and Apollos for your sake, in order that you may learn in us the meaning of 'not beyond what things are written', in order that you may not be puffed up one against another.[52]

Though this brief verse is beset by some enigmas, the gist of it can be ascertained and these difficulties are not insuperable even if there is no decisive way to gain assent to the referent of 'these things' (ταῦτα) nor the meaning of 'not beyond the things that are written'.

It seems that ταῦτα is a general reference to Paul's self-presentation from 1.10. Fitzgerald calls this the 'minority view', the 'majority opinion' taking ταῦτα as a reference to all or part of 3.5–4.5. Fitzgerald supports the view taken here when he writes that 3.5–4.5 is the specific antecedent of ταῦτα, 'but it should not be overlooked that 1.18–3.4 lays the foundation for 3.5–4.5'.[53] Naturally, ταῦτα does not tell us what its precise referent is, but for the sake of this study we shall treat Paul's self-portrayals from 1.10 as part of a composite exemplum that he employs to instruct the Corinthians (μάθητε, 4.6). The line could be drawn at 3.5, but this seems arbitrary when Paul's self-portrayal prior to this fits the pattern also. 'These things' make sense as a reference to Paul's collective self-presentation from 1.10 and his depiction of his interdependency with Apollos in the gospel work.

Paul develops his literary self-portrayal with his paraenetic and pedagogical aims in mind. 1 Corinthians 4.6 is not a reference to the idea of imitation,[54] but to a literary feature of the text, 'transferring as in a

---

52. Ταῦτα δέ, ἀδελφοί, μετεσχημάτισα εἰς ἐμαυτὸν καὶ Ἀπολλῶν δι' ὑμᾶς, ἵνα ἐν ἡμῖν μάθητε τὸ Μὴ ὑπὲρ ἃ γέγραπται, ἵνα μὴ εἷς ὑπὲρ τοῦ ἑνὸς φυσιοῦσθε κατὰ τοῦ ἑτέρου.
53. Fitzgerald, *Cracks in an Earthen Vessel*, p. 120 n. 13.
54. Contra Best, *Paul and his Converts*, p. 64.

figure of speech' (μετεσχημάτισα).⁵⁵ As F.H. Colson has argued, this literary feature applies both to figures of speech such as repetition and antithesis and to figures of thought such as irony.⁵⁶ Paul has applied 'these things' to himself and to Apollos (εἰς ἐμαυτὸν καὶ Ἀπολλῶν), and it is clear that he has argued in these chapters from personal example as a figure of thought to instruct the Corinthians.

'Not beyond the things that are written' (τὸ Μὴ ὑπὲρ ἃ γέγραπται) has the appearance of a saying known to Paul and the Corinthians as its elliptical structure, the negative construction and the introductory marking suggest (τὸ).⁵⁷ Most scholars think this refers either to the Scriptures Paul has cited or to some other saying that is veiled to us.⁵⁸ H. Schlier, relating the phrase to the theme of imitation, suggests that Paul refers to the practice in Hellenistic grammar schools where teachers write letters for children to trace over, thereby teaching them to write correctly.⁵⁹ In this interpretation Paul's preceding self-characterizations form the figurative 'abc's' of community life for the Corinthians to 'trace', emulating Paul in their relations with each other. Fitzgerald cites the characterization of the Corinthians as babes in 3.1-3 as support for taking 4.6 as a reference to their position as schoolchildren.⁶⁰ This reconstruction is imaginative but, as Fiore concedes, 'The exact phrase, unfortunately, has yet to be located in a rhetorical handbook'.⁶¹

In the absence of any textual precursor to support this view full weight must be given to the phrase 'the things that are written' (ἃ γέγραπται), for which there is ample attestation in Paul's usage. 'It is written' (γέγραπται) in each of its other 30 occurrences in Paul refers

55. LSJ, BAGD, *s.v.*
56. F.H. Colson, 'μετεσχημάτισα 1 Cor. 4.6', *JTS* 17 (1916), pp. 379-84.
57. M.D. Hooker, '"Beyond the things which are written": An Examination of 1 Cor. 4.6', *NTS* 10 (1963–64), pp. 127-32 (132). See Fitzgerald, *Cracks in an Earthen Vessel*, p. 123 n. 20, for a recent detailed bibliography on this enigmatic expression.
58. Though some have conjectured this is a scribal gloss (see P. Wallis, 'Ein neuer Auslegungsversuch des Stelle 1 Kor 4,6', *TLZ* 75 [1950], pp. 506-508).
59. H. Schlier, 'ὑπόδειγμα', *TDNT*, II, pp. 32-33.
60. Fitzgerald, *Cracks in an Earthen Vessel*, pp. 123-27.
61. Fiore, *The Function of Personal Example*, pp. 173-74 n. 24. L.L. Welborn, 'A Conciliatory Principle in 1 Cor. 4.6', *NovT* 29 (1987), pp. 320-46 (326), cites putative parallels in Graeco-Roman literature, none that is remotely close to Paul's saying.

to Old Testament citations, and if it does not refer to Scripture in 1 Cor. 4.6 this would be the only exception in Paul's usage.[62] Therefore, L.L. Welborn is simply mistaken when he asserts, 'Proponents of this interpretation must, of course, acknowledge that Paul does not speak of the Scripture in this manner elsewhere in his epistles, but of ἡ γραφή or τὸ γράμμα'.[63] Likewise, Fitzgerald's dismissal of γέγραπται as a reference to Scripture since it is part of Paul's quotation is nonsensical.[64] It is most natural—and the lexical evidence from within Paul's letters is overwhelming—to take the saying as a reference that incorporates the Old Testament citations in 1.19, 31; 3.19, 20.[65]

The verse taken as a whole ties together Paul's self-presentation with the Scriptures he has cited. His self-presentation is, in Paul's own words, a figurative application of these Scriptures to make his case against the futility of human wisdom and arrogance.[66] He appears to say that his personal example has made clear what the Scriptures teach against human arrogance. It is for this reason he makes the regulative statement that derives from his figuratively self-embodied interpretation of Scripture: the Corinthians are not to go 'beyond what is written'.[67] Following the quotation, Paul reiterates the importance of unity, the central point of his extended argument. He exhorts the Corinthians not

62. Rom. 1.17; 2.24; 3.4, 10; 4.17; 8.36; 9.13, 33; 10.15; 11.8, 26; 12.19; 14.11; 15.3, 9, 21; 1 Cor. 1.19, 31; 2.9; 3.19; 9.9; 10.7; 14.21; 15.45; 2 Cor. 8.15; 9.9; Gal. 3.10, 13; 4.22, 27. See C.D. Stanley, *Paul and the Language of Scripture: Citation Technique in the Pauline Epistles and Contemporary Literature* (SNTSMS, 74; Cambridge: Cambridge University Press, 1992).
63. Welborn, 'A Conciliatory Principle in 1 Cor. 4.6', p. 326.
64. Fitzgerald, *Cracks in an Earthen Vessel*, p. 124.
65. E.g. A. Robertson and A. Plummer, *A Critical and Exegetical Commentary on the First Epistle of St Paul to the Corinthians* (ICC; Edinburgh: T. & T. Clark, 1953 [1914]), p. 81; Hooker, ' "Beyond the things which are written" '; E.E. Ellis, *Paul's Use of the Old Testament* (Grand Rapids: Baker Book House, 1981 [1957]), p. 22.
66. Dahl, 'Paul and the Church at Corinth', p. 328, thinks this is a quotation from the Corinthians who are claiming independence, 'We can interpret the Scriptures for ourselves'. Marshall, *Enmity in Corinth*, pp. 194-218, allows this may be an allusion to Scripture, but thinks the emphasis is a counsel of moderation to the '*hybrists*', whose 'excesses' and 'attacks on Paul' are the background to this text. Both presume that Paul is writing apologetically.
67. See Hooker, ' "Beyond the things which are written" ', p. 127-32. There are 16 Old Testament citations in 1 Corinthians (the rest are at 5.13; 6.16; 9.9; 10.7; 10.26; 14.21; 15.27, 32, 45, 54-55).

to exaggerate one's importance over the other in order to remove one of the causes of division in their midst. Whose 'exaggerated importance' does he have in mind? In the immediate context of this verse it means not to exaggerate Paul's importance over Apollos, but as these two are symbolic of the Corinthian divisions it applies to the Corinthians interpersonally. By his intentional statement here we should expect to find Paul's self-presentation in the midst of his argument in 1.10–4.5 to confront one cause of their factionalism.

Paul as Exemplum in 1.10–4.13

Already in 1.4-9 we find a suggestion of the corrective that will follow, an epistolary function of the Pauline thanksgivings.[68] We can hear echoes of the themes which follow in the terminology of the thanksgiving: 'grace' (χάρις, 1.4), 'gift' (χάρισμα, 1.7), 'enriched' (ἐπλουτίσθητε, 1.5), 'word' and 'knowledge' (λόγῳ καὶ πάσῃ γνώσει 1.5), 'awaiting the revelation of Jesus Christ' and 'maturity' (1.7-8), and 'fellowship' (κοινωνία, 1.9-11). If Paul is to provide a corrective of the Corinthian factionalism in what follows, the line that this correction will take is already provided in 1.4-9: it is *in and through Christ* that all gifts and enrichment and speech and knowledge and fellowship come. This christological emphasis—or better, corrective—is accomplished by the repetition of the qualifiers ἐν Χριστῷ and τοῦ Χριστοῦ ten times in the opening nine verses. Notably, Paul's self-presentation in the first several chapters takes the form of self-depreciation to emphasize that the Corinthian experience of the Spirit is 'in Christ' and under his direction rather than 'in Paul' or others (1.13), a view that comes to the fore explicitly in 12.3 but already is implicit given the multiplication of christological qualifiers. Christological emphasis was what was needed and Paul's literary self-depreciation is one vehicle to accomplish that corrective. This gives added reason to suppose that 'I am of Christ' in 1.12 is an indicator of the christological emphasis Paul will make as a corrective to party spirit.

In 1.10 Paul gives another indicator that his central purpose is to confront the Corinthian factionalism. The exhortation begins with παρακαλῶ, a formal marker that Paul uses to indicate the main goal of his

---

68. P.T. O'Brien, *Introductory Thanksgivings in the Letters of Paul* (SNT, 49; Leiden: E.J. Brill, 1977), especially pp. 107-37.

exhortation (Phlm. 8-21 providing the clearest example).[69] Paul's purpose is to emphasize church unity, and to confront the causes of disunity, also treated throughout the letter. It is generally agreed that Paul is addressing the church as a whole in these chapters, and that it is not possible to take any one section to refer to a particular 'party'. Paul's self-characterizations in these chapters may be read in light of this purpose as it is stated in 1.10 and reiterated in 4.6, and we now turn to the task of tracing his self-characterization as it relates to the central thrust of his argument that culminates in 4.6.

1 Corinthians 1.12-17
Paul begins his exhortation on church unity with self-characterization. His self-description here functions to focus attention on Christ, and to remove reason for boasting in a human leader. Paul is self-effacing, contrasting what Christ has done for the Corinthians with what Paul himself cannot do: 'Paul was not crucified on your behalf, and you were not baptized into his name' (v. 13). Because Paul had not baptized many Corinthians, few could claim that they were baptized into his name. It may have been that some Corinthians made this claim, given the mystery cult parallels.[70] Or, it could be the case that Paul creates this rhetorical foil to make his point. The thrust of vv. 14-17 is to draw attention to the crucified Christ as the centre of Paul's proclamation (of which he reminds them in vv. 18-31), and away from human differences and loyalties to different leaders. We may label this use of self-characterization as *self-depreciation for christological emphasis*.

---

69. So C.J. Bjerkelund, *Parakalô: Form, Funktion und Sinn der parakalô-Sätze in den paulinischen Briefen* (Oslo: Universitetsforlaget, 1967), pp. 141-42.

70. U. Wilckens, *Weisheit und Torheit* (Tübingen: J.C.B. Mohr [Paul Siebeck], 1959), pp. 16-17, in this way explains how the Corinthians could be united and yet at the same time champion different teachers. He argues that the Corinthians see themselves as united in Christ, but still attached to their baptizers as their particular bearers of salvation. But, as Koester points out, this explanation makes little sense when one observes not only the lack of attention to baptism after this point, but also that it cannot be a criticism of the 'Christ party', nor of the Pauline group (unless it has only a few members; review in *Gnomon* 33 [1961], pp. 590-95). Furthermore, Wilckens can maintain his view only by having Paul and the Corinthians agree (without understanding that they are agreeing) that the community ought not be divided, that no one is baptized in the name of Paul, and that the whole community belongs to Christ.

Paul may dissociate himself from a Corinthian ideal in 1.17 with his representation of his own gospel commission as 'not in wisdom of word' (οὐκ ἐν σοφίᾳ λόγου). P. Lampe thinks the concentration of σοφίᾳ in chs. 1–3 (16 occurrences; three elsewhere in Paul) 'is best explained by the assumption that Paul picked up on a key word of the Corinthians here: they believed themselves to be "wise" (3.18-20; 4.10; cf. 1.5)'. Lampe thinks they understood this as theological wisdom, and that they praised the theological wisdom of 'their apostle', seen in 3.18-22.[71]

An alternative view of 'wisdom' is that ἐν σοφίᾳ λόγου refers to rhetoric or cultured speech.[72] Pogoloff argues that

> when σοφίᾳ and λόγος are combined in ancient usage, they frequently imply far more than just technical skill at language. Rather they imply a whole world of social status related to speech. For example, one common antonym of σοφός is φαῦλος, which when used 'in point of education or accomplishments', means not just bad or inferior, but '*low* in rank, *common, mean*'.[73]

And it carries implications of social status. 'How one spoke was closely related to issues of social status that included education, power, wealth, birth, social relations, and tensions between urban/rural and Roman/Greek identity.'[74] Pogoloff's argument is based on linguistic parallels, explicit and implicit references linking rhetoric and status in Graeco-Roman culture and 1 Corinthians, and the connection of rhetoric and divisions in the Hellenistic milieu. In an independent study A.D. Litfin also demonstrates the pervasive role the rhetorical tradition played in society, and the general fascination with eloquence and wisdom in Graeco-Roman culture.[75] That this perception held true for Corinth is

---

71. P. Lampe, 'Theological Wisdom and the "Word about the Cross": The Rhetorical Scheme in 1 Corinthians 1–4', *Int* 44 (1990), pp. 117-31 (118).

72. See Pogoloff, 'Form and Content in Classical Rhetoric', in *idem, Logos and Sophia*, pp. 37-69, 108-13, for a detailed argument for this view, and against understanding 'wisdom' as theological (Lampe), gnostic (Wilckens) or Jewish wisdom (J.A. Davis, *Wisdom and Spirit: An Investigation of 1 Cor. 1.18–3.20 against the Background of Jewish Sapiential Traditions in the Greco-Roman Period* [Lanham, MD: University Press of America, 1984]).

73. Pogoloff, *Logos and Sophia*, pp. 108-13; author's italics.

74. Pogoloff, *Logos and Sophia*, p. 127.

75. A.D. Litfin, 'St. Paul's Theology of Proclamation: An Investigation of 1 Cor. 1–4 in Light of Greco-Roman Rhetoric' (DPhil. Thesis, Oxford University, 1983), pp. 22-204 (all citations from dissertation); and see A.D. Clarke, *Secular*

2. *1 Corinthians 1–4*   51

reinforced by the Corinthian discourse of the Sophist Favorinus, who explicitly extols the Corinthians for their devotion to λόγος and σφία. Furthermore there are two Corinthian inscriptions praising *agōnothetai* for their rhetorical capacity.[76] Paul is thus denying the 'dynamic' (i.e. effectiveness) of Graeco-Roman rhetoric in his preaching.[77] Whatever the referent of 'wisdom', Paul dissociates himself from it, and depreciates himself as he emphasizes the power of Christ's cross in his preaching, a christological-soteriological emphasis continued throughout 1.10–4.13.

J.B. Chance has argued similarly that throughout this section Paul de-emphasizes himself.[78] Chance identifies two consistent themes in the sections he identifies as the *narratio* (1.10-31) and the *propositio* (2.1-5): 'Paul, through his continual deemphasis [*sic*] of himself, has, first, removed from his supporters ground for boasting in him and hence removed a barrier to unity and secondly, he has shown himself to be a spokesman for Christ'. As Paul develops his argument throughout 2.6–4.21, 'he will continue to argue along the lines delineated'.[79] 'In 3.5-9 Paul deemphasizes himself as well as Apollos...We can clearly see throughout this passage the note of personal deemphasis.'[80] This may be observed in the self-characterizations that follow.

1 Corinthians 2.1-16
We should read 1 Corinthians 2 from the point of view of Paul's self-presentation, rather than against a presumed backdrop of criticism that Paul was not eloquent like Apollos or a sophist.[81] This reading is

---

and *Christian Leadership in Corinth: A Socio-Historical and Exegetical Study of 1 Corinthians 1–6* (Leiden: E.J. Brill, 1993), pp. 36-39, 101-102.

76. Clarke, *Secular and Christian Leadership*, p. 19 n. 52; pp. 103, 148.
77. Litfin, 'St. Paul's Theology of Proclamation', p. 279.
78. Chance, 'Paul's Apology to the Corinthians', pp. 145-55, even if we reject Chance's main thesis that Paul also defends his weaknesses throughout chs. 1–6.
79. Chance, 'Paul's Apology to the Corinthians', p. 151.
80. Chance, 'Paul's Apology to the Corinthians', p. 152.
81. For a history of research on this text see P. Stuhlmacher, 'The Hermeneutical Significance of 1 Cor. 2.6-16', in G. Hawthorne and O. Betz (eds.), *Tradition and Interpretation in the New Testament: Essays in Honor of E. Earle Ellis for his 60th Birthday* (trans. C. Brown; Tübingen: J.C.B. Mohr [Paul Siebeck], 1987), pp. 328-47. Stuhlmacher understands 1.18–2.16 as the first major argumentative part of Paul's exhortation on party strife (p. 333). Bünker, *Briefformular*, pp. 48-59, argues that Paul consciously uses rhetoric in 1–4, 1.18–2.16 being the *narratio*

impossible to confirm at this point in Paul's relationship with the Corinthians, but his speech has clearly become an object of criticism by the time of 2 Cor. 10.10. Behind 1.17-20 and 2.1-5 may or may not lie attacks against Paul's speaking ability and the plausibility of his message. Alternatively, we cannot rule out the possibility that Paul employs a rhetorical convention, where in the opening 'the speaker is advised to disclaim ability at speaking'.[82] Pogoloff cautions us,

> Despite his weaknesses as a rhetor, the Corinthians still found him persuasive. For this reason, we must be careful not to take his protestations too seriously. Professional rhetors often affected weakness in an ironic method 'by which one urbanely displayed one's own skill by affecting the lack of it'.[83]

Moreover, these assertions are Paul's own, not quotations from the Corinthians.[84]

The emphasis remains on the message of the cross of Christ, and the exhortation against party strife is continued, without directly referring to their divisions in these verses. As Pogoloff notes, 2.1, 4, 13 are rhetorical repetitions, *expolitio*, refining, embellishing and amplifying the theme of 1.17.[85] Lampe identifies 1.18–2.16 as a covert speech that 'is a "Trojan Horse" with which Paul thrusts himself into the middle of the Corinthian party situation. With the Corinthians lulled into security after 1.18–2.16, Paul can attack them openly with the discussion beginning in 3.1.'[86] C.B. Cousar agrees that the '*literary context* and *the continuity of the argument* are all important in understanding 1 Corinthians 2'. Paul treats the problem of divisions as merely symptomatic of the much deeper problem of the Corinthians' fascination with 'the language of worldly wisdom'. Cousar rightly cautions that since we can overhear

between the *exordium* of 1.10-17 and the *probatio* of 3.1-17.

82. G.A. Kennedy, *The Art of Persuasion in Greece* (London: Routledge & Kegan Paul, 1963), p. 11.

83. Pogoloff, *Logos and Sophia*, p. 136, citing E.A. Judge, 'Paul's Boasting in Relation to Contemporary Professional Practice', *AusBR* 16 (1968), pp. 37-50 (37); see H.D. Betz, *Der Apostel Paulus und die sokratische Tradition* (BHT, 45; Tübingen: J.C.B. Mohr [Paul Siebeck], 1972), pp. 14, 88.

84. For a self-conscious reading of the opponents in 2 Corinthians back into 1 Cor. 2.1-5 as an explanation, see T.H. Lim, 'Not in Persuasive Words of Wisdom, but in the Demonstration of the Spirit and Power', *NovT* 29 (1987), pp. 137-49. This methodology has been challenged above.

85. Pogoloff, *Logos and Sophia*, pp. 129-72.

86. Lampe, 'Theological Wisdom', pp. 125, 128-31.

only one side of the conversation, the exact nature of this fascination is obscure.[87]

Paul's self-characterizations here function as much to highlight Christ as to reject false notions of 'wisdom' or a false esteem of polished speech. Scholars have made much of Paul's rejection of rhetoric but have often neglected the christological emphasis here. Pogoloff, for example, writes that 'Paul eschews the Hellenistic role of the ideal public figure'.[88] H.D. Betz, too, overlooks the christological emphasis here when he concludes that 2.1-16 'brings the issues of rhetoric, which have so far remained in the background, into the center'.[89] On the contrary, Paul's self-portrayal, while correcting false-notions of wisdom or the value of speaking ability, functions to bring the message *about Christ* to the centre. This is of a piece with Paul's self-description throughout this section to make a christological-soteriological emphasis.

In 2.1-5 Paul dissociates himself from eloquent wisdom, and perhaps the status attendant to rhetoric,[90] to emphasize the power of God in the proclamation of the crucified Christ. These verses nicely sum up the argument to this point,[91] and re-emphasize Paul's conviction that the basis and foundation for the gospel is divine and not human understanding or persuasiveness. Likewise Paul's example is of one who could not be puffed up because of his own rhetorical ability, whose effectiveness is based upon God and not himself, and whose message is Christ-centred and cross-centred.

In 2.6-16 he sets out to redefine what true wisdom is, and introduces the subject of chs. 12–14.[92] Does the subject shift here since we find a

87. C.B. Cousar, '1 Corinthians 2.1-13', *Int* 44 (1990), pp. 169-73 (169-70). The history of research on 2.6-16 has been dominated by the search for religio-historical parallels. For the history of research, see K.O. Sandnes, *Paul—One of the Prophets? A Contribution to the Apostle's Self-Understanding* (WUNT, 2.43; Tübingen: J.C.B. Mohr [Paul Siebeck], 1991), pp. 77-78.

88. Pogoloff, *Logos and Sophia*, p. 134.

89. H.D. Betz, 'The Problem of Rhetoric and Theology According to the Apostle Paul', in A. Vanhoye (ed.), *L'Apôtre Paul: Personnalité, style et conception du ministère* (BETL, 73; Leuven: Leuven University Press, 1986), pp. 16-48 (36).

90. So Pogoloff, *Logos and Sophia*, p. 131.

91. Chance, 'Paul's Apology to the Corinthians', p. 151, labels it the *propositio*, and Litfin, 'St. Paul's Theology of Proclamation', p. 356, agrees without Chance's parlance.

92. Cf. 2.10/14.30; 2.13/12.1; 2.15/14.37; 2.10, 13/12.4, 7, 8, 9, 11; 2.11, 12,

shift to the plural 'we' between the first-person singulars in 2.1-5 and 3.1-6? If so, to whom does 'we' refer? The options are (1) Paul, used as an epistolary plural;[93] (2) Paul, Apollos and their co-workers, as in 4.1-13; (3) Paul, his co-workers and all the Corinthians;[94] (4) Paul and some of the Corinthians;[95] (5) mature Christians.[96] Whichever answer we give, Paul is included in the 'we'.[97] The word 'God' appears ten times in 2.6-16 leading Lampe to observe, 'Facing the veneration of apostles, Paul calls out "God, God", not "Paul", not "Apollos", not "Cephas"!'[98] Thus, 2.6-16 expands and confirms 1.18–2.5.[99]

2.16 returns to the christological emphasis of the extended argument. In 'but we have the mind of Christ' (ἡμεῖς δὲ νοῦν Χριστοῦ ἔχομεν), Χριστοῦ is a subjective genitive emphasizing that Christ is the source of their knowledge and wisdom, reiterating the thrust of 2.1-5 (cf. Rom. 11.33-34). Along this line W. Willis draws attention to a parallel chris-

---

14/12.3; 2.6, 7; 12.8; 2.6/14.20; as pointed out by T.W. Gillespie, 'Interpreting the Kerygma: Early Christian Prophecy According to 1 Corinthians 2.6-16', in J. Goehring, C. Hedrick, J. Sanders and H. Betz (eds.), *Gospel Origins and Christian Beginnings* (Sonoma, CA: Polebridge Press, 1990), pp. 151-66.

93. Conzelmann, *1 Corinthians*, p. 60 n. 31; B.A. Pearson, *The Pneumatikos-Psychikos Terminology in 1 Corinthians: A Study in the Theology of the Corinthian Opponents of Paul and its Relation to Gnosticism* (SBLDS, 12; Missoula, MT: Scholars Press, 1973), p. 110 n. 95 ('Strictly speaking, Paul is referring in 2.15 primarily to himself. He is the one who has the "mind [= Spirit] of Christ" and is therefore not subject to the criticism of the Corinthians [4.3 and 9.3]'); S. Kim, *The Origin of Paul's Gospel* (Grand Rapids: Eerdmans, 1982), pp. 78-82; Sandnes, *Paul—One of the Prophets?*, pp. 80, 87-88 (who thinks 2.6-16 refers primarily to Paul himself and to his basic revelation on the road to Damascus [following Kim], but has a 'double aspect': Paul has in mind that he is not alone in receiving the 'wisdom of the cross').

94. So Stuhlmacher, 'The Hermeneutical Significance of 1 Cor 2.6-16', p. 334.

95. Ellis, '"Wisdom" and "Knowledge"', p. 83, thinks 'we' here is inclusive of the Corinthian prophets. Welborn, 'On the Discord in Corinth', p. 106, thinks that throughout 2.6–3.3 Paul is speaking to the leaders of the rival factions: 'Like their counterparts in the πόλις, they sought to gain control of the ἐκκλεσία by advancing claims to higher religious knowledge.'

96. Barrett, *First Epistle to the Corinthians*, p. 76.

97. Unless we give credence to the views of M. Widmann, '1 Kor. 2.6-16: Ein Einspruch gegen Paulus', *ZNW* 70 (1979), pp. 44-53, who argues that the entire pericope is a gloss from the Corinthian enthusiasts to correct Paul's attack on wisdom!

98. Lampe, 'Theological Wisdom', p. 127.

99. So Stuhlmacher, 'The Hermeneutical Significance of 1 Cor 2.6-16', p. 334.

tological exhortation to unity in Philippians 2 (τὸ αὐτὸ φρονῆτε, 2.2),[100] a feature found in Rom. 15.5. Likewise in 1 Cor. 2.16 and 12.12-31 Paul makes a christological emphasis to exhort to unity. There are other things going on in 2.1-16, but one element is Paul's submersion of his status under that of Christ and he devalues his own ability by drawing attention to the efficacy derived from Christ's power. This contributes to the composite personal example he offers against being puffed up by one's own ability and status.

1 Corinthians 3
In the next chapter of 1 Corinthians, self-presentation again figures prominently. Paul's portrayal of himself and Apollos in ch. 3 is explicitly set against the party spirit of some Corinthians who claim one leader over the other (3.3-4). In 3.5 the rhetorical questions are meant to depreciate the messengers as mere servants (διάκονοι) through whom the Corinthians came to faith. The agricultural metaphor and the architectural simile in 3.6-10 emphasize the unity of the missionary endeavour and oneness of the church, but more importantly focus on the active part played by God through their work—it is God who gives the growth (3.6) and owns the 'field' and the 'building' and the 'co-workers' (3.9). The plural nouns, διάκονοι and συνεργοί,[101] are applied to both Paul and Apollos and further communicate the sense that they are unified in their efforts (ἕν εἰσιν, 3.8), even though they have different functions as sower and waterer. The characterization of the Corinthians as one field and one building functions toward this same end. There is only one foundation (θεμέλιον) for them as the building of God: Jesus Christ who is the locus of unity throughout this section

100. W.L. Willis, 'The "Mind of Christ" in 1 Corinthians 2.16', *Bib* 70 (1989), pp. 110-22. Sandnes, *Paul—One of the Prophets?*, pp. 107-15, argues per contra that 2.16 is to be interpreted as a thanksgiving for a received revelation, and that an affirmative answer to the rhetorical question in 2.16 refers primarily to Paul himself, attesting to Paul's self-understanding as one who speaks a revealed prophetic mystery.

101. V.P. Furnish, 'Fellow Workers in God's Service', *JBL* 80 (1961), pp. 364-70, is right that this text is about unity of leadership and the church, but he wrongly finds this message in the lone word συνεργοί with a strained reading of the genitive θεοῦ, as the title of his article suggests. There is no lexical or grammatical reason for adding 'service', as he notes, nor is it necessary.

(2.16, 3.1, 11, 23; 4.1-13), throughout the letter,[102] and especially in the architectural simile (3.10-11).

With 'as a wise architect I laid a foundation' (ὡς σοφὸς ἀρχιτέκτων θεμέλιον ἔθηκα, 3.10) Paul emphasizes the enduring and primary nature of his work in establishing the foundation of the church on Christ. This does not exalt Paul in any way since he performs it 'according to the grace of God given to me' (κατὰ τὴν χάριν τοῦ θεοῦ τὴν δοθεῖσάν μοι, 3.10). It should not be thought that Paul characterizes himself as a wise architect as a covert jab at anyone else. Paul cannot be attacking Apollos. He affirms Apollos as his co-servant (v. 5) and as a co-worker of God (v. 9), and in 16.12 Paul urges Apollos to go to Corinth, something he would not do if he felt anxious about him. If the Corinthians took 3.10 to mean Apollos was Paul's opponent, Paul's argument for unity collapses.[103] Rather, Paul's role cannot be separated from that of Apollos, according to the logic of his argument, as the foundation cannot be separated from what is built on top.[104] 'But if another builds upon' (ἄλλος δὲ ἐποικοδομεῖ) is a neutral reference to Apollos, accounting for his contribution to the Corinthian church. It is parallel to the simile in vv. 6-8. Furthermore, the clauses 'let each of you take care how he builds' (ἕκαστος δὲ βλεπέτω πῶς ἐποικοδομεῖ, v. 10) and 'if anyone builds upon the foundation' (εἰ δέ τις ἐποικοδομεῖ ἐπὶ τὸν θεμέλιον, v. 12) directly address the Corinthian auditors, and are not covert references to some adversary.[105] ἕκαστος (1.12; 3.5, 8, 10) and τις (1.15, 16; 3.4, 12) are used in 1 Corinthians 1–3 as

---

102. NB 1.13; 3.21-23; 5.7; 6.15; 7.22; 8.11-12; 9.21; 10.16; 11.1; 12.12-13, 27; chs. 13 and 15.

103. Contra F. Watson, *Paul, Judaism and the Gentiles: A Sociological Approach* (SNTSMS; Cambridge: Cambridge University Press, 1986), pp. 82-83; N.R. Petersen, *Rediscovering Paul: Philemon and the Sociology of Paul's Narrative World* (Philadelphia: Fortress Press, 1985), p. 110; Litfin, 'St. Paul's Theology of Proclamation', pp. 324-30.

104. 3.11-23 seems to be a warning against dividing the 'temple' built on the one foundation of Christ. 3.12 makes the temple metaphor vivid and concrete. See J. Shanor, 'Paul as Master Builder: Construction Terms in First Corinthians', *NTS* 34 (1988), pp. 461-71, who argues that the extended continuity of 3.9b-17 is evident in view of the construction practices of antiquity.

105. Manson, 'The Corinthian Correspondence (1)', p. 194, writes 'the mischief is being done where Paul's work has already been put in—on the foundation'. Manson then reasons from Mt. 16.18 that Peter is the only other foundation that anyone would think of laying.

references to the Corinthians in general, and ἕκαστος takes on a special meaning within the framework of Paul's idea of the body in 12.18. On the basis of its basic meaning referring to individual parts within the whole, ἕκαστος 'was well-suited to express in this special way the idea of the call and the responsibility of each one with a view to the whole, the Church'.[106]

1 Corinthians 3.21–4.13

Paul now draws together his self-portrayal to this point in the letter. At 3.21 Paul continues his self-detraction for christological emphasis. The logic and forward thrust of the text suggests that 4.1-13 is an exposition of 3.21-23, further refining 2.1-5 and 3.5.[107] 4.1-13 is an *expolitio*, a rhetorical amplification intended to redirect the Corinthians' loyalty and sense of belonging to Christ and to diminish their divisive boasting of their favourite human leader.

The thrust of 3.21-23 is straightforward, as it restates the argument from 1.10:[108] 'Let no one boast in human beings [leaders] [v. 21a]... but instead remember that we all belong to Christ and Christ belongs to God [v. 23].' Verse 21b begins the thought that is completed in v. 23, while v. 22 interrupts to explain πάντα ὑμῶν:

> Everything is yours—whether Paul or Apollos or Cephas or the world or life or death, whether things present or things to come—everything is yours, and you are Christ's, and Christ is God's.[109]

There is no reason that the twice repeated πάντα ὑμῶν must be sarcastic, though it has often been read that way. Rather, the emphasis falls on the fact that everything they have is from Christ, they themselves belong to Christ, and therefore they are unified in Christ. The emphasis is on the conclusion, 'You are of Christ/God!', therefore, and not of human leaders.

4.1-13 further develops 3.21-23, emphasizing that the Corinthians' eschatological benefits derive from Christ. Explicit is that Paul and Apollos are mere servants of Christ, the only one on whom the Corinthians' communal life can be founded. 4.1 begins with 'thus' (οὕτως)

---

106. F. Untergassmair, 'ἕκαστος', *EDNT*, I, pp. 403-404.
107. So Pogoloff, *Logos and Sophia*, p. 213.
108. Furnish, 'Theology in 1 Corinthians', p. 84. Similarly, Betz thinks these verses restate the argument from 1.18 ('The Problem of Rhetoric', p. 39).
109. My translation; similarly Betz, 'The Problem of Rhetoric', p. 39.

which refers to the foregoing in a correlative construction,[110] further developing 3.21-23. The christological qualification of Paul's and Apollos's missionary work is emphasized in the next verse, claiming they should be understood 'as servants of Christ and stewards of the mysteries of God' (ὡς ὑπηρέτας Χριστοῦ καὶ οἰκονόμους μυστηρίων θεοῦ, 4.1). These self-descriptions should be read with the emphasis on the genitives 'of Christ' and 'of God' since they further explain 3.23. In this way the contrast is drawn between Paul and Apollos on the one hand and Christ and God on the other. Paul emphasizes his and Apollos's deferential position to Christ as his servants, to God as stewards of his mysteries. This is repetitive parallelism, thus 'servants' and 'stewards' are roughly equivalent, and not contrasted as J.M. Bassler supposes, '*under*lings of Christ and *over*seers for God'.[111] The purpose is not to contrast these two characterizations, but to demonstrate Paul's and Apollos's subservient position to Christ and God. The function of these portrayals is to draw attention to Christ as the one served, and to diminish Paul and Apollos as mere servants.[112]

4.6-13 draws up the line of argument, and makes several points clear: (1) why Paul has referred to himself and Apollos; (2) how his self-depiction is set against those who have exalted themselves over others (4.6); (3) what Paul's corrective is: (a) they wrongly feel in full possession of all blessings but Paul insists that all blessings are received in Christ (4.7b-8; ἐν Χριστῷ, 4.10), and (b) they suppose they have fully realized the blessings of the future, while Paul and Apollos experience suffering, disdain and disrespect demonstrating that for them, at least, the end has not yet come in fullness. The contrast provides an implied critique of the Corinthians' overestimation of eschatological realization.[113] The device of *synkrisis* or *comparatio* was a common

---

110. M. Wolter, 'οὕτω, οὕτως', *EDNT*, II, p. 549.

111. J.M. Bassler, '1 Corinthians 4.1-5', *Int* 44 (1990), pp. 179-83 (181; her italics). Pogoloff, *Logos and Sophia*, pp. 214-17, misses the christological focus of this text, suggesting that Paul's use of these terms implies criticism of the Corinthians who sought higher status.

112. 'Mysteries of God' (μυστηρίων θεοῦ) is reminiscent of 'the mystery of God' (τὸ μυστήριον τοῦ θεοῦ) in 2.1 and the self-depreciation in 2.1-5 for christological emphasis.

113. K.P. Donfried, 'The Kingdom of God in Paul', in W. Willis (ed.), *The Kingdom of God in 20th-Century Interpretation* (Peabody, MA: Hendrickson, 1987), pp. 175-90 (177-78).

2. *1 Corinthians 1–4*

form of admonishment, which probably makes sense of Paul's disclaimer in 4.14.[114]

4.7 continues the central theme of christological emphasis, reiterating 3.22: 'For who divides you? What do you have that you did not receive [from Christ]? And, if you also received it, what ground is there for boasting as not being receivers?' The change to the singular 'you' is familiar in the question and answer of the diatribe style.[115] The implied answer is 'There is no grounds for boasting for everything we have is from Christ!' (cf. Eph. 2.8-10). At once Paul provides both an emphasis on the christological source of what they have received and a corrective on a triumphalist understanding of where they are in the eschatological scheme of things. We should take 4.8 in an ironic sense[116] as a parody of the Corinthians' self-praise and desire for status[117] and, for lack of a better phrase, a critique of their over-realized eschatology, their sense of the 'already' (ἤδη). Though 4.8 trades on Cynic-Stoic language and values that some of the Corinthians may have esteemed,[118] it is a subordinate clause to 4.7,[119] expositing the immeasurable 'riches' that they have received through Christ, a central Pauline theme.[120] Thus, 4.8 explains 4.7 and restates 1.5, which also emphasizes the christological

---

114. Fitzgerald, *Cracks in an Earthen Vessel*, pp. 117-48; M. Ebner, *Leidenlisten und Apostelbrief: Untersuchungen zu Form, Motiv und Funktion der Peristasenkataloge bei Paulus* (FzB, 66; Würzburg: Echter Verlag, 1991), pp. 20-92.

115. S.K. Stowers, *The Diatribe and Paul's Letter to the Romans* (SBLDS, 57; Chico, CA: Scholars Press, 1981). 'Such a change of addressee, from plural to singular, is occasionally noted as rhetorical figure of *apostrophe*' (W. Wuellner, 'Paul as Pastor: The Function of Rhetorical Questions in First Corinthians', in Vanhoye [ed.], *L'Apôtre Paul*, pp. 49-77 [58]).

116. Plank, *Paul and the Irony of Affliction*, pp. 44-48; Fitzgerald, *Cracks in an Earthen Vessel*, p. 137; Fee, *The First Epistle to the Corinthians*, pp. 171-74; Conzelmann, *1 Corinthians*, p. 87; Barrett, *First Epistle to the Corinthians*, pp. 108-109.

117. Pogoloff, *Logos and Sophia*, pp. 222-24.

118. Pogoloff, *Logos and Sophia*, pp. 222-24; Fitzgerald, *Cracks in an Earthen Vessel*, pp. 132-48; Paige, 'Stoicism, Ἐλευθερία and Community at Corinth', pp. 180-93.

119. For a structural analysis of 4.7-13 see Fitzgerald, *Cracks in an Earthen Vessel*, pp. 129-32. Wuellner, 'Paul as Pastor', pp. 61-62, thinks 4.1-7 is a 'presupposition' for 4.8, though he sees 4.8 as ironical.

120. Rom. 2.4; 9.23; 11.12, 33; 2 Cor. 6.10; 8.9; Phil. 4.19. Cf. 1 Cor. 12.13; Eph. 1.7, 18; 2.7; 3.8, 16; Col. 1.27; 2.2.

source of their λόγος and γνῶσις.¹²¹ Overlooking for the moment the irony of this verse, part of the sense is 'Already you are full [through Christ], already you are rich [through Christ], and without either leader [but through Christ] you reign; and it is my wish¹²² that you reigned [with Christ rather than through us], so that we may reign with you [in Christ]'.¹²³ Paul uses language throughout this section that was also used to describe the ideal philosopher, and this may reflect Pauline and/or Corinthian vocabulary and values.¹²⁴ Whatever meaning we ascribe to 'rich', 'wise' and 'knowledge', Paul's argument here emphasizes the *source* of these commodities in Christ.

Fitzgerald makes several cogent observations about 4.9-10. First, 'God has exhibited us apostles last' is the thesis statement for 4.9-13. In 4.9 Paul and Apollos are presented as unworthy leaders of the various factions, since they are ἔσχατοι, 'utterly insignificant'. In the verses that follow 'Paul's hardships, therefore, provide backing for his interpretative claim'.¹²⁵

4.10 emphasizes the superiority of what the Corinthians have received *from Christ*. As in 1.5 and the passage from 3.21, the emphasis is on what they receive διὰ Χριστόν and ἐν Χριστῷ, over what the

---

121. Fee, *The First Epistle to the Corinthians*, pp. 38-39.

122. ὄφελόν may express both an unattainable wish (so BDF §359) and an attainable wish (2 Cor. 11.1; 'ὄφελον', *EDNT*, II, p. 552; *pace* Plank and Fee, *loc. cit.*), and is a term whose meaning is disputed (cf. LSJ, BAGD, *s.v.*).

123. This emphasis is suggested by F. Godet, *Commentary on St Paul's First Epistle to the Corinthians* (trans. A. Cusin; 2 vols.; Edinburgh: T. & T. Clark, 1886–87), I, pp. 222-23.

124. Pogoloff and Fitzgerald have similar views. Pogoloff, *Logos and Sophia*, pp. 115-18, sees the language here as representative of Paul's attack on the Corinthians' ambition for the social status attending wise speech. Fitzgerald, *Cracks in an Earthen Vessel*, pp. 132-48, argues that the Corinthians' 'attitude' was much like the Cynics', taking Paul's language as a mirror to their thinking. However, Fitzgerald demonstrates how Paul's self-depreciating statements are also similar to descriptions of the ideal Cynic. I lose the significance of the language parallels here. Is Paul combating notions like those of the Cynic-Stoics and promoting himself as the ideal Cynic at the same time? We should not over-emphasize the language parallels, as Fitzgerald is aware. See, for example, p. 144 n. 91: 'It is worth noting that the catalogue of what the Lamb is worthy to receive in Rev. 5.12 corresponds in large part to Paul's description of the Corinthians. Kingly power, wealth, wisdom, strength, and glorious honor are all mentioned.' What are we to make of this parallel?

125. Fitzgerald, *Cracks in an Earthen Vessel*, p. 131.

Corinthians could derive from their connection with a mere missionary such as Paul or Apollos. The terms of comparison we find in 4.10 are therefore self-depreciations for christological emphasis, and the christological expansions in 4.10a (διὰ Χριστόν, ἐν Χριστῷ) are implied for the terms of the remaining two antitheses.[126] Paul's self-description focuses on his liabilities, while his characterization of the Corinthians focuses on what they have derived from Christ:

μωροί...φρόνιμοι
ἀσθενεῖς...ἰσχυροί
ἄτιμοι...ἔνδοξοι

These are not simply an explication of the sociological categories in 1.26,[127] but a summarization of the powerful/weak and wise/foolish contrast that underlies the logic of these chapters[128] in which Paul confronts the divisive approach of 'the wise' by using himself as a counter example.[129] Thus, 4.9-13 ties together Paul's self-depreciation for christological emphasis in the preceding chapters.

The Relationship of Chapters 1–4 to the Remainder of 1 Corinthians

1 Corinthians 1–4 are not detached from what follows, and Paul's self-depiction in these opening chapters foreshadows the theme of self-curtailment that is a dominant and recurrent theme from 6.12 through ch. 14. Nevertheless, we must acknowledge that a significant shift occurs at 4.14. Up to 4.13, Paul's self-portrayal provides a contrastive example for the haughty, but from 4.14 Paul, on a literary level, sets a very concrete, ethical example for almost every issue he treats. The relationship of 1 Corinthians 1–4 to the rest of the letter is preparatory for the exhortation that follows, but Paul's usage of his personal example changes significantly. Paul sets the framework of church unity and agreement before treating the divisive issues in chs. 5–15.[130] Chapters

126. Fitzgerald, *Cracks in an Earthen Vessel*, p. 130.
127. Contra D. Sänger, 'Die δυνατοί in 1 Kor. 1.26', *ZNW* (1985), pp. 285-91 (288).
128. Gillespie, 'Interpreting the Kerygma', pp. 152-55.
129. Ebner, *Leidenlisten und Apostelbrief*, p. 394.
130. This is the thesis to which Mitchell devotes her monograph, *Paul and the Rhetoric of Reconciliation*. Dahl, 'Paul and the Church at Corinth', pp. 334-35, thinks that Paul deals with the problem raised by sending a delegation and letter to Paul (the sole cause of quarrels!), so that Paul can proceed to deal with the pastoral

1-4 have a paraenetic function where Paul establishes (1) the importance of unity for the church and church leadership, to exhort the Corinthians to 'be of one mind'; (2) the concept of the church as the temple that should not be destroyed (3.16, 17, 19; cf. 6.19; 9.13); (3) the centrality of the cross to lay a foundation for his teaching on self-denial and voluntary surrender of one's rights; and (4) the destructiveness of boasting and being 'puffed up' (1.29, 31; 3.21; 4.6, 7, 18, 19, cf. 5.2; 8.1; 13.4).

Some have thought that the call to imitation in 4.16 also makes the suffering and hardship referred to in 4.9-13 the object of the Corinthians' conformity to Paul's example.[131] It may be that Paul implies this, but it is not the most apparent application of the list of sufferings as far as these chapters are concerned,[132] nor is it an exhortation that emerges explicitly anywhere else in Paul. Though Paul mentions the sufferings he shares with other Christians (e.g. 2 Cor. 1.6-7; Philippians; 1 Thess. 1.6) and that he conceives of his life in Christ as very much one of suffering like Christ (e.g. 2 Cor. 4.10-11; Phil. 3.10),[133] there is no explicit exhortation anywhere to 'suffer like I suffer', nor is there one in 1 Corinthians 4.[134] Note, for example, the consistent contrast between Paul's experience and that of the Corinthians in 1 Cor. 4.10 (cf. 2 Cor. 4.12). Presumably, this contrast between Paul and the Corinthians is drawn because he is a missionary–apostle (1 Cor. 4.9; cf. Gal. 5.11) and

---

issues. These chapters are preparatory, but for hortatory rather than apologetic purposes.

131. Best, *Paul and his Converts*, pp. 64-65; Fitzgerald, *Cracks in an Earthen Vessel*, p. 122.

132. Schütz, *Anatomy of Apostolic Authority*, p. 203, asserts that the peristasis catalogue functions as an eschatological warning to those whose eschatology is collapsed, and rejects the notion that the exhortation to imitation in 4.16-17 is to call them to suffer. Instead, on the basis of his understanding of the assertion of authority implied in imitation, Schütz thinks the Corinthians are to realize that Paul's existence is exemplary of current Christian existence as their spiritual parent (4.15).

133. Paul's self-presentation throughout 1 Cor. 1–4 cannot be said to 'mirror' the cross, but his status reflects the foolishness of Christ's cross, denigrating himself in social terms. Paul suffers like Christ suffered, but this is not stated in 1 Cor. 4 (contra G.D. Fee, 'Toward a Theology of 1 Corinthians', in D. Hay [ed.], *Pauline Theology. II. 1 and 2 Corinthians* [Minneapolis: Fortress Press, 1993], pp. 37-58 [45]).

134. Sanders, 'Imitating Paul', pp. 358-60.

his sufferings are related to his missionary work and not to his Christian existence per se.

Instead, it has been argued here that 4.6 is the controlling idea for 4.9-13 and what precedes it. By examining Paul's missionary existence the Corinthians, too, can learn 'not to be puffed up' because every blessing that is received is in Christ and through Christ and for Christ and not of or for themselves. Though it is doubtful that 4.9-13 is primarily a call to the Corinthians to a life of suffering like Paul's, in the background is the subject of self-curtailment that will come to the foreground in 6.12, ch. 7, chs. 8–9 and chs. 13–14.

It will be argued in the next chapter that 4.14-21 provides a transition between 1.1–4.13 and the rest of the letter, and serves mainly to introduce what follows rather than as a retrospective summary of what has preceded it. Of course identifying portions of the text as a 'transition' or 'section' is merely an interpretative help since the text in our earliest manuscripts offers no such indicators. By content, 1 Corinthians 1–4 is not detached from what follows. Paul's self-portrayal in these opening chapters prepares the foundation for his consistent call to self-renunciation later in the letter. In these opening chapters Paul has depreciated himself appropriately, drawing attention to Christ as the source and goal of his missionary efforts, a theme that he explicitly carries forward into the second and larger section of the letter, stated explicitly in 1 Cor. 11.1: 'Be imitators of me, just as I belong to Christ'.

Chapter 3

PAUL, SPIRITUAL PARENT AND PARADIGM IN CHRIST:
1 CORINTHIANS 4.14–15.58

> As my beloved children I admonish you...for by means of the gospel I birthed you in Christ Jesus. Therefore I exhort you, become imitators of me (1 Cor. 14-16).

In the previous chapter an attempt has been made to demonstrate how Paul's personal example has been used as a pedagogical and argumentative device to confront factionalism among the Corinthian house churches. 1 Corinthians 4.6-13 summarizes Paul's self-presentation to this point, and provides a transition to the second section of the letter where Paul presents himself as a specific, concrete example of the proper attitude for the Corinthians to maintain and the standard of behaviour they should practise. With 'Be imitators of me' (4.16) Paul introduces this new usage of self-presentation in the letter, and it will be argued below that the content of this exhortation is intended to include the personal example that Paul portrays in virtually every subsequent section of the letter by use of his own paradigmatic 'I', and that his paradigmatic use of 'I' also has an epistolary function of summarizing the argument and providing a transition to the next phase. Highlighting Paul's self-portrayals thus becomes a clear and helpful road map for navigation through the details of the text. This chapter will detail the literary and argumentative signposts that Paul's self-characterizations provide.

The Significance of the Shift at 4.14

1 Corinthians 4.14-17 is a transition that draws up what has preceded it and introduces the remainder of the letter, flows naturally into 4.18, and begins the subject of discipline of the incestuous man. This reading is supported if we take the παρακαλῶ phrase in 4.16, not as an *inclusio*

3. *Paul, Spiritual Parent and Paradigm in Christ* 65

with 1.10,[1] but the setting out of what we find in the following chapters: Paul's self-presentation as a model in Christ for the Corinthians to pattern themselves after. In the previous section, Paul has depreciated himself to make a christological emphasis. In what follows he no longer compares himself with Christ, but reminds them of his privileged, authoritative position as their father in Christ who begot them through the gospel. His tone changes to assert authority in the discipline of the incestuous man, providing a sharp transition from chs. 1–4 to what follows.[2]

Traditionally 1.10–4.21 has been treated as a unit, 4.14-21 forming the conclusion, retrospectively shaping what has come before. However, K.E. Bailey has compiled nine reasons why 4.17 is introductory to the chapters that follow, specifically linked to the assertion of authority and the execution of discipline in ch. 5.[3] Furthermore, 4.14-16 should not be separated from 4.17, primarily since the father imagery there begins Paul's assertion of disciplinary authority through ch. 5. To Bailey's arguments may be added other problems with breaking the text at 4.21 and reading 4.14-21 retrospectively rather than as a transition that introduces what follows:

1. Breaking the text at 4.21 fails to recognize the conspicuous connections of 4.14-21 with 5.1-13 as an assertion of Paul's authority as their spiritual parent in the discipline of the incestuous man.[4]

2. It fails to account for the relationship of the exhortation in 4.16 with the many self-characterizations that follow.

3. It fails to account for the dissimilarity of tone of 4.14-21 with what precedes it, and its congruence with what follows. Fiore notes this phenomenon, but continues to read 4.14-21 in light of the preceding chapters:

---

1. Contra Bjerkelund, *Parakalô*, p. 146; Fitzgerald, *Cracks in an Earthen Vessel*, pp. 117-19, who both think 4.14-17 is merely retrospective.
2. So Mitchell, *Paul and the Rhetoric of Reconciliation*, pp. 221-25.
3. K.E. Bailey, 'The Structure of 1 Corinthians and Paul's Theological Method with Special Reference to 4.17', *NovT* 25 (1983), pp. 152-81 (160-63).
4. E.M. Lassen, 'The Use of the Father Image in Imperial Propaganda and 1 Corinthians 4.14-21', *TynBul* 42 (1991), pp. 127-36, demonstrates the disciplinary authority implied in the father imagery when compared with imperial usage, but links it to Paul's 'covert allusion' to his 'opponents' in the preceding chapters, overlooking the case of discipline in ch. 5. Castelli emphasizes the power dimension of the father imagery, but again there is no mention of ch. 5 (*Imitating Paul*, pp. 98-111).

...while the figurative allusion [4.6] is to the example of Paul and Apollos together, the personal application by Paul to himself intrudes regularly (2.1-5; 3.1-5; 4.3-5) *until it supplants that of the joint laborers in 4.14-21* (and that right after the impassioned description of the common apostolic toils in 4.9-13)... *The intrusion of Paul's example in these first chapters leads to its exclusive application in the rest of the letter*, as the fundamental issue of the community's wisdom and judgment is faced in a variety of settings. *Mimesis* and *metaschematisis* merge, and the virtuous example that Paul urges the community to imitate emerges as his own. Paul's life and teaching become a metaphor for the community's striving, as they seek to become like their founder and father.[5]

It has been argued above that Paul's example in chs. 1–4 does not 'intrude', but rather comprises his strategy of exhortation. It will be argued here that its application in the rest of the letter is explicit, intentional and stated in 4.16, and reiterated in 7.8; 11.1; 12.31. Paul's example does not 'supplant' what goes before, but changes to an assertion of his authoritative pattern in the matters that he treats. In developing the theme of unity in chs. 1–4 Paul emphasizes that he, Apollos and Peter are equal in the service of the gospel and thus loyalty to any one of them should not divide the Corinthian house churches. At 4.14 the emphasis deliberately changes to Paul's exemplary behaviour and thinking related to the specific, concrete issues that follow. The change of usage of his self-portrayal is a literary feature, providing interpretative markers for the reader.

4. Reading 4.14-21 retrospectively fails to account for the introductory function of παρακαλῶ. C.J. Bjerkelund has demonstrated the importance of παρακαλῶ as an introductory formula to the specific contents of Paul's letters. As he observes, 1.10 succinctly introduces 1.10–4.13. Likewise, 4.16 sets the framework through ch. 15, acting consistently with Bjerkelund's identification of the general function of παρακαλῶ. Other scholars appear to be unanimous that 4.16 forms an *inclusio* with 1.10, overlooking that the content of the exhortation has changed from unity to imitation. Furthermore, if we compare 1.10, 4.16 and 11.1 it is clear that 4.16 more likely forms an *inclusio* with 11.1, sharing only the introductory formula, παρακαλῶ...ὑμᾶς, with 1.10:

5. Fiore, *The Function of Personal Example*, p. 174 (emphases added).

3. *Paul, Spiritual Parent and Paradigm in Christ*

1.10   Now *I appeal* [παρακαλῶ] to you, brothers and sisters, by the name of our Lord Jesus Christ, that all of you be in agreement and that there be no divisions among you, but that you be united in the same mind and the same purpose.

4.16   *I appeal* [παρακαλῶ] to you, then, be imitators of me [μιμηταί μου γίνεσθε].

11.1   *Be imitators of me* [μιμηταί μου γίνεσθε], *as I am of Christ.*

An appeal to unity is the theme of 1.10–4.13. It will be argued that an appeal to imitation forms the framework for all of the major arguments that follow. If we divide 4.14–15.58 into topics and set this list next to Paul's self-characterizations throughout these same chapters, we find that Paul's self-presentation is at the heart of each of these texts (except 11.17-34). As M.M. Mitchell says, 'Because the appeal to himself as example is the unifying rhetorical strategy of the letter, enumerating and describing Paul's self-references in 1 Corinthians almost amounts to a summary of the contents of the letter', evidence she adds to support the integrity of canonical 1 Corinthians.[6]

5. Reading 4.14-21 retrospectively fails to account for the change from the 'we/us' in 4.13 to 'I/me' in 4.14. Shifts between I and we are common in Paul's letters, but the significance of the shift here is that Paul refers to his singular example almost exclusively in the chapters that follow.[7]

To summarize, there is ample reason to read 4.14-21 as introductory to what follows, specifically related to the exercise of discipline in ch. 5, and to read 4.16 as a literary introduction to what follows as we have suggested 4.6 can be read retrospectively. Of course, 'section breaks' are an interpretative construct and there is no reason to disavow any connection of 4.14-21 with what precedes it. Rather, the approach below is to explore the connections of 4.14-21 with the subsequent chapters, a neglected topic of study.

---

6.   Mitchell, *Paul and the Rhetoric of Reconciliation*, p. 54; see especially her ch. 4.

7.   See Castelli, *Imitating Paul*, pp. 107-108, who calls this a 'sharp transition from the first-person plural to the first-person singular', and ties it into Paul's assertion of unique authority.

Imitation and Other Uses of Paul's Literary Example in 1 Corinthians 4.14–15.58

1 Corinthians 4.14–5.13

We now turn to an examination of Paul's paradigmatic usage of self-portrayal from 4.14 in light of the above observations. He begins the transition with 'I do not write these things to shame you but to admonish you as my beloved children' (4.14). He asserts that his purpose in writing was to encourage and not to shame. Shame and honour were pivotal issues for the ancient world.[8] The shame-culture in Homeric times was concerned with public esteem and honour rather than the enjoyment of a quiet conscience. 'And the strongest moral force which Homeric man knows is not the fear of god, but respect for public opinion, *aidos*.'[9] As E.R. Dodds demonstrates, the shame-culture of Homeric times gradually became a guilt-culture, but the significance of honour and shame persisted.

The question presents itself, what are 'these things' in 4.14 that the reader might interpret as shaming? Commentators almost universally read ταῦτα here as retrospective, and it most naturally refers to 4.6-13. The irony of Paul's corrective could be construed as shaming, and it may be that the Corinthians' shame might come from Paul as father enjoying inferior status and degrading treatment while his children enjoyed the very best,[10] a source of shame that Aristotle identifies: 'It is also shameful not to have a share in the honourable things which all men, or all who resemble us, or the majority of them have a share in'.[11] Some interpreters understand 'these things' as a reference to previous admonitions (such as 3.1-4),[12] or more generally to Paul's overall argument in 1–4.[13] As Fiore notes, the 'criticized faults' in 4.7-13 'have

---

8. B.J. Malina, *The New Testament World: Insights from Cultural Anthropology* (Atlanta: John Knox Press, 1981), pp. 25-50.

9. E.R. Dodds, *The Greeks and the Irrational* (Berkeley: University of California Press, 1951), pp. 17-18.

10. Litfin, 'St. Paul's Theology of Proclamation', p. 332; Lassen, 'The Use of the Father Image', pp. 135-36.

11. Aristotle, *Rhet.* 2.6.12.

12. Fitzgerald, *Cracks in an Earthen Vessel*, p. 117 n. 1.

13. Fiore, *The Function of Personal Example*, pp. 175-76; Sanders, 'Imitating Paul', pp. 354-55.

been seen to be recurrent in the whole expository section'.[14] These retrospective readings cannot be ruled out, but they should not exclude an application of these verses also to what follows. What needs to be added is that 4.14 is transitional, and therefore is *also* anticipatory of the admonition that follows immediately (the shame attached to the incestuous relationship) and the admonitions throughout the following chapters (lawsuits, disrespect for the 'weak' and the poor, disorderly conduct, etc.). In other words, 4.14 applies equally well to the subsequent chapters as to those which precede it.

Much earlier Aristotle defined shame and offered an exhaustive list of things that would bring shame:

> Let shame be defined as a kind of pain or uneasiness in respect of misdeeds, past, present, or future, which seem to tend to bring dishonour... Such are all those that are due to vice, such as throwing away one's shield or taking to flight, for this is due to cowardice; or withholding a deposit, for this is due to injustice. And illicit relations with any persons, at forbidden places or times, for this is due to licentiousness...[15]

The final sentence gives an indicator that Greek readers like the Corinthians may have found mention of the incestuous relationship in ch. 5 to bring shame upon them. 4.14 does not simply reiterate 4.6, but is tied in with the father imagery that carries into ch. 5.[16] Though we may not rule out a retrospective understanding of 'these things', we must acknowledge the change in argument to an emphasis on authority and pay attention to the argument that follows.

There may be further evidence of the forward-looking intent of 4.14 in the changed usage of γράφειν in 4.14 from 4.6. In 4.6 ἃ γέγραπται refers to the argument built around the Old Testament citations in what precedes it. In 1.19, 31; 2.9 and 3.9 we find the Scriptures introduced with the same perfect passive singular form that we find in 4.6 (γέγραπται). In 4.14, 5.9 and 5.11 (cf. 7.1) various forms of γράφειν are used, all applying to Paul's letter writing, none referring to Scripture per se, and none in the perfect passive form. This may suggest that γράφω ταῦτα in 4.14 looks forward to the things Paul is about to write. If we read 4.6 as a retrospective summary and 4.14 as introductory,

---

14. Fiore, *The Function of Personal Example*, p. 176.
15. Aristotle, *Rhet.* 2.6.2-3.
16. For the connection of Paul's 'spiritual parenthood' with discipline, see Gutierrez, *La paternité spirituelle*, pp. 193-96; Lassen, 'The Use of the Father Image', pp. 127-36.

then the difference may be paraphrased: 'I applied chs. 1–3 to Apollos and myself so that you may learn (4.6)...but now I write what follows about incest to admonish you in a fatherly exertion of authority and discipline (4.14)'.

In 4.15-16 Paul continues his self-presentation as the Corinthians' father in Christ that began in 4.14. The parent metaphor is dominant throughout 4.14-21, and is explicit in 4.14, 15, 17 and 21.[17] Fiore writes:

> He presents himself not as a co-worker among others with God, but as father of the community. And it is this fatherly concern for their well-being that turns the *entropē* to *nouthesia*. Just as in 1 Cor. 11.27ff. Paul considers the divine afflictions as aimed at the community's correction, so here his paternal admonitions look toward community reform.[18]

Paul makes clear in 4.15 that his admonitions are not merely pedagogical, but are an assertion of his authority as spiritual father. When he says 'I begot you', he points to the basis he has 'to call them "his children" and to claim a paternal authority',[19] a point upon which he later trades as he defends himself to these same converts (2 Cor. 3.1-3). As Gutierrez points out, the significance of the modifier ἐν Χριστῷ elsewhere in Paul indicates that in 1 Cor. 4.15 Paul does not think of his spiritual paternity as a purely rhetorical image, but as a reality.[20] When Paul says, 'for you may have many guides in Christ, but not many fathers', he may be taking a side glance at other 'competing' leaders,[21] but we must note that elsewhere Paul recognizes the proper place of Apollos, Chloe, Stephanas, Fortunatus and Achaicus (cf. 16.12-18). Here in 4.15 the contrast is drawn to remind the Corinthians of Paul's primary position among them as their father in Christ. Emphasis shifts to his special authority he asserts in the chapters that follow. In 1.10–4.13, Paul was self-effacing to emphasize their unity in Christ, and his argument focused on Christ as the source of their spiritual benefits. Now, Paul lays claim to his authority as the one who has brought them into Christ.

---

17. Cf. 2 Cor. 12.14; 13.10; Gal. 4.19; Phil. 2.22. See Gutierrez, *La paternité spirituelle*, pp. 119-96.

18. Fiore, *The Function of Personal Example*, p. 175; see also Gutierrez, *La paternité spirituelle*, pp. 188-93.

19. Gutierrez, *La paternité spirituelle*, p. 129.

20. Gutierrez, *La paternité spirituelle*, p. 134.

21. Furnish, 'Fellow Workers in God's Service', p. 370.

3. *Paul, Spiritual Parent and Paradigm in Christ*

If we ignore the fundamental shift in Paul's argument from 4.14, we are left with an understanding of 4.14-21 that undermines the argument against factionalism in chs. 1–4, the very argument it has been thought to conclude. The significance of this exegetical point often has been overlooked, or has been given as support for a partition theory of 1 Corinthians. For example, B. Sanders says that in 4.14-21 Paul 'contributes to the problem of divisiveness which he had been trying to solve'.[22] This is only true, however, if we read 4.14-21 as retrospective to chs. 1–4 rather than anticipatory of the chapters that follow. Instead, if we read 4.14-21 as introductory to what follows we need not suppose that here Paul trips over his own feet, but in a designed way introduces a fairly consistent form of argumentation used in the chapters that follow.

Related to Paul as spiritual parent is the important 'I exhort you therefore, become imitators of me' (παρακαλῶ οὖν ὑμᾶς, μιμηταί μου γίνεσθε, 4.16). Some observations about 4.16 are clear:

1. Paul's call for imitation is a consequence (οὖν) of his fatherhood of the community in Christ.[23] From both a rabbinical and Graeco-Roman perspective, imitation and spiritual parenthood naturally go together. In later rabbinic tradition 'if someone teaches the son of another the Torah, it is as if he had begotten him (*b. Sanh.* 19b). And in 1 Cor. 4.15 Paul replaces the Torah with the gospel as the matrix of generation'.[24] Graeco-Roman usage of the imitation theme is similar:

> It implies the notion of transfer of character or personality from one person to another, e.g., from parents to children, from teacher to pupil, and from God to human beings... Understood in this context, Paul seems to demand imitation by the children of the model given by the father.[25]

2. Paul's example and words together are a part of his instruction of his churches. It is not only Paul's 'word that makes God manifest, but his whole being, his whole life which helps to recognize the effigy and the glory of this announced God, in so far as he himself has been entered and transformed by this word'.[26]

3. It is easy to see how the exhortation in 4.16 introduces the rest of the letter, as Paul's personal example dominates his discussion. Paul as

---

22. 'Imitating Paul', p. 356.
23. Gutierrez, *La paternité spirituelle*, p. 178.
24. Fiore, *The Function of Personal Example*, pp. 178-79.
25. Sanders, 'Imitating Paul', p. 358.
26. Gutierrez, *La paternité spirituelle*, p. 186.

paradigm will recur throughout 1 Corinthians, especially exemplifying the attitude and behaviour of self-curtailment for another's up-building.[27]

4. We should not let a rigid structural understanding of the letter keep us from allowing that the transitionary nature of 4.16 could refer to Paul's immediately preceding self-presentation. Schütz thinks the object of imitation is unclear from the immediate context of 4.16, and so he reasons backwards from 1 Cor. 11.1 that Paul, in 4.16, must be referring to imitating Christ's power in weakness, thus explaining the paradigmatic function of 4.9-13. The call to imitation, in Schütz's view, is to imitate Paul's abstracted theological understanding of the power found in weakness dynamic that Christ also displays in these opening chapters of 1 Corinthians. It is not Paul's specific sufferings that the Corinthians are to imitate, but his normative message that this is how Christ's power is manifested, experienced and appropriated. This reading takes full notice of the eschatological corrective that appears to be going on in the letter (e.g. 2.1-4), a usage of Paul's self-presentation that becomes very pronounced in 2 Corinthians.[28]

5. Paul links his call to imitation in 4.16 with his common teaching 'in all the churches' (4.17b). His teaching in other churches is not the main object of his call to imitation, but serves to emphasize his authority by appealing to the universality of his teaching, a recurrent theme in 1 Corinthians (1.2; 4.17; 11.16).[29]

6. If we take 4.14–5.13 as a unit, the call to imitation in 4.16 is specifically a call to execute discipline on the incestuous man by imitating the judgment that Paul has already made (5.3-5). The image of the disciplinarian's rod (4.21) ties the father motif begun in 4.14 with the exercise of church discipline in ch. 5, a passage to which we now turn.

1 Corinthians 5.1-13 is notoriously difficult for modern readers. The difficulties lie in understanding the rationale for Paul's actions, and in understanding the compatibility of this passage with statements else-

27. So Mitchell, *Paul and the Rhetoric of Reconciliation*, p. 227. Sanders, 'Imitating Paul', pp. 353-63, offers too general an object of imitation, that of 'Paul's communal concern', which indeed Paul taught to all the churches (Phil. 2.4-5; 1 Thess. 5.11-15; Gal. 6.1-5; Rom. 14.1–15.7).

28. Doohan, *Leadership in Paul*, p. 105.

29. See U. Wickert, 'Einheit und Eintracht der Kirche im Präskript des ersten Korintherbriefes', *ZNW* 50 (1959), pp. 73-82.

where in the New Testament about church discipline, judgment and anthropology.[30] These issues are beyond my present purpose but, as a general comment, the references Paul makes to the Corinthians' boasting and arrogance (5.2, 6) imply that the incestuous relationship was not a secret or simply a moral lapse, but related to a theological position that was approved by some of the influential persons in the community.[31] Paul's concern is for the purity of the community, evident already in 3.16-17 where he identifies the church as the metaphorical temple of God, a theme still fresh in the hearers' minds as this letter was read aloud to them.[32] In ch. 5 Paul's concern for the purity of the community is brought forward and applied in this individual case and also broadened to general instruction about church discipline.

The best approach to understanding 1 Cor. 4.14–5.13 is to envision what Paul hoped would take place within the Corinthian community when the letter was read to them,[33] and in this we see Paul's self-presentation serving an exemplary and therefore straightforward function. His concern is for church discipline, and his self-characterization reflects his assertion of authority to chastise an incestuous man. Paul describes himself as the fatherly disciplinarian of his spiritual children (4.14-15), and 4.21 also makes sense as an intimation of disciplinary authority.[34] In 4.18-19 we note a 'bull at a gate approach' to the moral problems that follow,[35] indicating that some of the Corinthians were complacent about the issue of incest.[36] 4.18-19 need not be read as a

---

30. See J.M. Gundry-Volf, *Paul and Perseverance* (WUNT, 2.37; Tübingen: J.C.B. Mohr [Paul Siebeck], 1990), especially pp. 113-20.

31. A.Y. Collins, 'The Function of "Excommunication" in Paul', *HTR* 73 (1980), pp. 251-63 (253).

32. So B.S. Rosner, 'Temple and Holiness in 1 Corinthians 5', *TynBul* 42 (1991), pp. 137-45.

33. G.D. Fee, *God's Empowering Presence: The Holy Spirit in the Letters of Paul* (Peabody, MA: Hendrickson, 1994), pp. 121-27.

34. Cf. C.J. Roetzel, 'The Judgment Form in Paul's Letters', *JBL* 88 (1969), pp. 305-12 (311-12), who locates the exercise of charismatic authority in the context of the Old Testament prophets. 'The apostle Paul, like the prophets, possesses the full authority of the divine judge since as the Lord's messenger he brings God's verdict; however, like the prophets, he does not appear to possess executive power.'

35. Bailey, 'The Structure of 1 Corinthians', p. 163.

36. Clarke, *Secular and Christian Leadership*, pp. 74-88, suggests their difficulty arose because this man may have been a patron of the church, but there is no way to confirm this speculation.

statement against the 'enemies' of Paul, but is better understood as an exhortation to the complacent,[37] anticipating the reading of the letter in their presence.

In 4.21 Paul introduces his epistolary presence with 'Am I to come to you with a stick, or with love in a spirit of gentleness?' Paul's references to himself are directly related to the subject of discipline he is about to broach. The father motif begun in 4.14 is carried forward and developed with reference to a disciplinary rod. The image of the rod may reflect any of three images, either alluding to parental discipline as in the Old Testament,[38] or to the shepherd's rod of Ps. 22.4 (LXX), or to the Roman imperial usage of the father image to assert authority. E.M. Lassen suggests the possibility that the rod refers to one carried by a lector on an assize, or even that carried by Augustus as he is portrayed as a magistrate in a Corinthian statue,[39] and the judicial scenario that follows supports this proposal. Reference to the shepherd's rod causes us to suppose a new metaphor has been introduced, making this less likely (though Paul has been known to mix his metaphors!). We cannot rule out the possibility of a double aspect to this figure, since the political use of father imagery reflected the family institution as Lassen demonstrates. If we cannot decisively choose between one nuance or another, the background only enhances what is clearly in the foreground, namely that Paul prepares to make one of his strongest assertions of authority as founder of the Corinthian church.

After a clear announcement of the dual ethical problem—the πορ-νεία of the man with his stepmother (5.1) and the church's gloating about it (5.2)—Paul's epistolary presence becomes the topic in 5.3-5 where he exemplifies for them the judgment they are to make about the man:

> For though absent in body, I am present in spirit; and as if present I have already pronounced judgment in the name of the Lord Jesus on the man who has done such a thing. When you are assembled, and my spirit is present with the power of our Lord Jesus, you are to hand this man over to Satan for the destruction of the flesh, so that his spirit may be saved in the day of the Lord.

---

37. *Pace* Marshall, *Enmity in Corinth*, p. 346; Dahl, 'Paul and the Church at Corinth', pp. 318-19.
38. Exod. 21.20; Prov. 10.13; 13.24; 2 Sam. 7.14; Isa. 10.24; Lam. 3.1 (cf. 1 Sam. 17.43; though having similar wording as 1 Cor. 4.21, it lacks father imagery).
39. Lassen, 'The Use of the Father Image', p. 136 n. 40.

3. *Paul, Spiritual Parent and Paradigm in Christ*

Paul's 'presence' with them is his spiritual presence conveyed by the power of Christ when the letter is read aloud.[40] Through this epistolary presence Paul's act of judgment is paradigmatic: he exemplifies by his pronouncement expulsion of the man from the church,[41] applying the scriptural allusion in 5.13.[42] Ejection from the community exposes the man to temporal destruction with the hope expressed that he will experience eschatological salvation.[43] Paul models for the Corinthians what they should do with regard to this man, and one cannot help but sense an underlying frustration with the community for moving beyond toleration to supporting openly his behaviour (4.18-19; 5.2, 6).

This interpretation is supported by R.W. Funk's investigation into the epistolary function of the episodes in Paul's letters he has labelled the 'apostolic *parousia*', whether we label these a 'form' or a 'theme'.[44] As Funk demonstrates, Paul's 'presence' may mean his physical attendance or his 'presence' as represented through an emissary or portrayed by a letter.[45] These observations stand even if Mitchell has successfully challenged part of Funk's thesis that the envoy and the letter were less effective substitutes for Paul's personal presence. Instead she plausibly proposes that Paul made strategic use of his envoys and letters precisely

---

40. Fee, *God's Empowering Presence*, pp. 124-25.

41. Gundry-Volf, *Paul and Perseverance*, pp. 117-18; G. Harris, 'The Beginnings of Church Discipline: 1 Corinthians 5', *NTS* 37 (1991), pp. 1-21 (16-19); Meeks, *The First Urban Christians*, p. 130; Collins, 'The Function of "Excommunication" in Paul', p. 259; Fee, *God's Empowering Presence*, p. 126. Other interpreters favour a literal interpretation of the curse of death at the hand of Satan, like the judgment on Ananias and Sapphira in Acts 5.1-11: G.W.H. Lampe, 'Church Discipline and the Interpretation of the Epistles to the Corinthians', in Farmer, Moule and Niebuhr (eds.), *Christian History and Interpretation*, pp. 337-61 (347-48). S.D. MacArthur, '"Spirit" in Pauline Usage: 1 Corinthians 5.5', in E.A. Livingstone (ed.), *Studia Biblica 1978*, III (JSNTSup, 3; Sheffield: JSOT Press, 1978), pp. 249-56; E.E. Ellis, '*Soma* in First Corinthians', *Int* 44 (1990), pp. 137-49 (141).

42. Which may be drawn from Deut. 17.7; 19.19; 22.21, 24; or 24.7; P.S. Zaas, '"Cast the evil man from your midst" (1 Cor. 5.13b)', *JBL* 103 (1984), pp. 259-61.

43. See Gundry-Volf, *Paul and Perseverance*, pp. 114-16; Fee, *God's Empowering Presence*, p. 126.

44. 'Form' is preferred by R.W. Funk, 'The Apostolic *Parousia*: Form and Significance', in Farmer, Moule and Niebuhr (eds.), *Christian History and Interpretation*, pp. 249-68. 'Theme' is preferred by T.Y. Mullins, 'Visit Talk in New Testament Letters', *CBQ* 35 (1973), pp. 350-58.

45. Funk, 'The Apostolic *Parousia*', pp. 258-65.

because he recognized they were *more* effective than his personal presence (cf. 2 Cor. 10.10).[46] Whether standing in their midst literally or 'appearing' to his auditors through representative emissaries or letters, 'Paul must have thought of his presence as the bearer of charismatic, one might even say, eschatological power....Such an understanding of his personal *parousia* accords well with what Paul writes in 1 Cor. 4.18ff.' (NB 4.20).[47] This observation is apropos to 4.14–5.13, where 'my spirit' (5.4) may well refer to Paul's epistolary presence, and perhaps also Timothy's physical presence in the gathered congregation as this letter was read aloud in their worship (cf. 4.17-19; 16.10-11), delivering Paul's summary judgment on the matter, 'perhaps even in a near legal sense'.[48] We find further support for this in an entirely similar approach in 1 Cor. 14.37-38 where Paul links his judgments concerning the exercise of charismata with the text of the letter itself.[49]

The text gives strong support to Funk's observation. In 5.3 Paul contrasts his presence 'by the S/spirit' with bodily presence (ἐγὼ μὲν γάρ, ἀπὼν τῷ σώματι παρὼν δὲ τῷ πνεύματι). It appears that Paul's physical absence was part of the problem, from Paul's point of view in 4.18-19. We are left with an impression of the Corinthian church that while the cat was away the mice did play. The immediate solution is for Paul to come to them vicariously through this letter (carried by Timothy? cf. 4.17-19; 16.10-11). His long-range plan is to arrive bodily (16.3-11).

46. M.M. Mitchell, 'New Testament Envoys in the Context of Greco-Roman Diplomatic and Epistolary Conventions: The Example of Timothy and Titus', *JBL* 111 (1992), pp. 641-62.

47. Funk, 'The Apostolic *Parousia*', p. 265.

48. P. Richardson, '"I say, not the Lord": Personal Opinion, Apostolic Authority and the Development of Early Christian Halakah', *TynBul* 31 (1980), pp. 65-86 (79). Similarly Mitchell, *Paul and the Rhetoric of Reconciliation*, p. 229, says, 'Paul executes an epistolary legal decision'. Meeks, *The First Urban Christians*, p. 128, invents a tension 'between local, charismatic authority and supralocal, unitive governance', based on an inference he draws from how Paul expresses his judgment as a *fait accompli*, and the unmistakable directions Paul gives for the assembly of the congregation when they exercise the discipline and expel the wrongdoer. The two are not in tension with each other, but are to be understood as a unit from the point of view of the public reading of this letter in the gathered assembly. For a different view of the relationship of Paul's authority to the congregation's freedom, see H.F. von Campenhausen, *Ecclesiastical Authority and Spiritual Power in the Church of the First Three Centuries* (trans. J.A. Baker; London: A. & C. Black, 1969 [1953]), pp. 30-54.

49. So G.A. Cole, '1 Cor. 5.4 "...with my spirit"', *ExpTim* 98 (1987), p. 205.

3. *Paul, Spiritual Parent and Paradigm in Christ*

Therefore 'I am coming to you soon' should be understood as inclusive of Paul's epistolary 'arrival' with this letter, perhaps brought and interpreted by Timothy. While we should remain sensitive to the rhetorical aspects of this technique it seems to be more than a mere rhetorical strategy on Paul's part, since his letters demonstrate that he actually relied upon substantial numbers of colleagues in his missionary enterprise.[50]

1 Corinthians 5.12,[51] still on the subject of discipline, suggests a stylistic usage of self-characterization that we will see again below in 6.12; 8.13; 10.28–11.2; 13.1-3; 14.15, 19. This stylistic use is hortatory, and is indicated by the rapid change to a pithy 'I' statement. In this 'hortatory I' Paul says about himself what he intends for the readers to apply to themselves, a point that is emphasized by the appearance of his 'I' statement between two exhortations in the second-person plural (5.11b-12):

> *You* should not[52] even eat with such a one. For what have *I* to do with judging those outside? Is it not those who are inside that *you* are to judge?

The italics highlight Paul's stylistic connection between 'I' and 'you' (see also the discussion under 10.28–11.1 below). The point of this verse is to give a general instruction about discipline. As can be observed Paul's hortative 'I' is really meant from the auditor's point of view (i.e. 'I' = 'you'). Though he presumably presents his self-understanding, the rhetorical question functions as a part of his exhortation of the Corinthians. His idiomatic usage parallels the hortatory plural, but he frames it as an 'I' statement. In this hortative 'I' the auditors are encouraged to appropriate this statement as their own, that is, 'What are we to do with judging those outside?' The point of this verse is to highlight his instruction about discipline, a theme that carries on into ch. 6.[53]

---

50. Contra Mitchell, *Paul and the Rhetoric of Reconciliation*, pp. 224-25. See E.E. Ellis, 'Paul and his Co-workers', *NTS* 17 (1971), pp. 437-52; W.-H. Ollrog, *Paulus und seine Mitarbeiter: Untersuchungen zu Theorie und Praxis der paulinischen Mission* (Neukirchen–Vluyn: Neukirchener Verlag, 1979).

51. On the construction, see BDF §299.

52. Rendering the negated infinitive construction as a prohibitive and making the second-person plural explicit, as the NRSV renders implicitly, 'Do not…'

53. So Barrett, *First Epistle to the Corinthians*, p. 120; Meeks, *The First Urban*

To summarize, Paul's concern in 4.14–5.13 is with the purity and discipline of the community. His self-characterization and pithy personal expressions serve to confront the sour fruit of unbridled libertinism in the church, to assert his authority in the enforcement of discipline, and to portray a model of behaviour and thinking for the Corinthians in order to ensure the community's spiritual and ethical integrity with regard to overt sexual sin. Paul embodies Christ's authority as his emissary, and so he very naturally expresses that authority in personal terms. His example of judgment on the incestuous man is paradigmatic of how the Corinthians are to behave. He employs an 'I' = 'you' technique, a stylistic feature of his paraenesis found also in 1 Cor. 6.12; 8.13; 10.28–11.1; 12.31–13.3; 13.11-12; 14.11, 14, 18.[54] In each of these cases Paul makes 'I' statements which seem intended to express the Corinthian's potential views as they hopefully come to conform to Paul's own. Note also that, except for the examples from ch. 14, all of these 'I' statements occur at summary transitions in the letter's argument.[55] I now turn to an examination of these texts as they demonstrate this stylistic, paradigmatic usage of 'I' in Paul.

1 Corinthians 6.12
Paul's self-characterization in 6.12 functions as part of his larger argument from personal example. Through the device of exemplification he re-emphasizes his teaching on Christian liberty, modelling that freedom does not mean uncontrolled liberty but is compatible with a principled life of self-control and consideration of others. As a rhetorical device, this self-characterization is an effective way of identifying with the Corinthians in their sense of liberty, while modelling self-control and self-denial, a repeated refrain in the chapters that follow.

At key points in his letters Paul often makes 'I' statements that have argumentative significance (e.g. 1 Cor. 5.12; 8.13), and 1 Cor. 6.12 fits this pattern and may be yet another example of Paul's persuasive idiom where he makes an 'I' statement to enhance his exhortation. However, there is a strong scholarly consensus that Paul has cited a Corinthian

Christians, pp. 128-29. J.D.M. Derrett, 'Judgement and 1 Corinthians 6', *NTS* 37 (1991), pp. 22-36, identifies other continuities of chs. 5 and 6.
   54. 1 Cor. 14.6 is a slight variation on this style, cast hypothetically.
   55. Another approach to these 'sudden turns' has been to view them as disruptions in the text, indicators of later redactions. Conzelmann, *1 Corinthians*, p. 137, characterizes these transitions as harsh—surely an exaggeration.

phrase twice, 'All things are lawful...', adding his correction, 'but not all things...', as can be seen in the following table:

'Corinthian Slogan'	Paul's 'Corrective'
1 Corinthians 6.12	
πάντα μοι ἔξεστιν,	ἀλλ' οὐ πάντα συμφέρει.
πάντα μοι ἔξεστιν,	ἀλλ' οὐκ ἐγὼ ἐξουσιασθήσομαι ὑπό τινος.
1 Corinthians 10.23	
πάντα ἔξεστιν,	ἀλλ' οὐ πάντα συμφέρει.
πάντα ἔξεστιν,	ἀλλ' οὐ πάντα οἰκοδομεῖ.

Though there is general agreement Paul cites a Corinthian slogan, R.L. Omanson correctly observes that scholars do not state clearly how they have identified the Corinthians' words.[56]

The influential reading of J. Weiss at the turn of the century appears to have shaped subsequent scholarly opinion on this passage, gaining influence with time. Weiss asserts that the absence of the particle τοῦτο δέ; suggests that this came from the Corinthians' antecedent letter and should be read as Paul's engagement with a Corinthian slogan: 'All things are permissable, you say, but "not all things benefit", I say'.[57] This suggestion is reflected in almost all modern interpretations and recent major translations (NRSV, NIV, RSV, NEB). Before Weiss, F. Godet suggested that Paul himself uttered this 'maxim' repeatedly at Corinth, and Godet simply raised the question 'Did this maxim figure in the letter which the Corinthians had addressed to him?'[58] After Weiss, the suggestion seems gradually to have taken on the force of a fact. A brief survey illustrates the rise of the consensus.

Robertson and Plummer claim these are Paul's own words, though 'they may have been current among the Corinthians as a trite maxim'.[59] J. Moffatt puts the phrase in quotation marks against the background of

---

56. R.L. Omanson, 'Acknowledging Paul's Quotations', *The Bible Translator* 43 (1992), pp. 201-12. See, for example, J. Murphy-O'Connor, 'Corinthian Slogans in 1 Cor. 6.12-20', *CBQ* 40 (1978), pp. 391-96, who assumes 6.12 is of Corinthian origin, and discusses 6.13 and 18.

57. J. Weiss, *Der erste Korintherbrief* (Göttingen: Vandenhoeck & Ruprecht, 1970 [1910]), p. 158.

58. Godet, *First Epistle to the Corinthians*, I, p. 304.

59. Robertson and Plummer, *First Epistle of St Paul to the Corinthians*, p. 121.

Corinth's reputation as the most wanton of cities, a characterization that is now strongly questioned.⁶⁰ C.F.D. Moule simply notes that 'many commentators recognize that v. 12a may represent a "libertine", antinomian slogan', and then uses this reading as an illustration in his discussion on diatribe and implied dialogue.⁶¹ L. Morris thinks 'the way he introduces this makes it seem as though the Corinthians had used the maxim to justify their conduct. Possibly they had derived it from Paul's teaching when he was among them.'⁶² W.G.H. Simon calls this 'possibly a Corinthian catch-phrase'.⁶³ With J. Héring the suggestion begins to take on the force of a fact: 'It goes without saying that *"panta moi exestin"* = "everything is permissible for me", is at each occurrence the rallying cry of the libertines'.⁶⁴ So also for M.E. Thrall: 'The first claim the Corinthians make is "I am free to do anything".'⁶⁵ C.K. Barrett more cautiously reiterates the gathering consensus: 'Paul appears to quote from a Corinthian source'.⁶⁶ F.F. Bruce maintains the RSV rightly places this phrase in quotation marks, a slogan of the 'gnosticising party' in Corinth.⁶⁷ Conzelmann hints that there is a stylistic indication

---

60. J. Moffatt, *The First Epistle of Paul to the Corinthians* (London: Hodder & Stoughton, 1938), p. 67. The historical basis of Corinth's 'reputation' has been challenged and can no longer be asserted with certainty, perhaps reflecting more the effectiveness of Athenian polemic than the historical situation in Corinth. See Conzelmann, *1 Corinthians*, p. 12; J. Murphy-O'Connor, *St. Paul's Corinth: Texts and Archaeology* (Collegeville, MN: Michael Glazier, 1983), pp. 43-46, 56-67, 125-28; D. Engels, *Roman Corinth: An Alternative Model for the Classical City* (Chicago: University of Chicago Press, 1990). Of opposite opinion, see F.F. Bruce, *New Testament History* (Garden City, NY: Doubleday, 1971), p. 314, who thinks Corinth regained its 'former reputation'.

61. C.F.D. Moule, *An Idiom Book of New Testament Greek* (Cambridge: Cambridge University Press, 1959 [1953]), p. 196.

62. L. Morris, *1 Corinthians* (TNTC; Grand Rapids: Eerdmans, 1983 [1958]), p. 99.

63. W.G.H. Simon, *The First Epistle to the Corinthians* (London: SCM Press, 1959), p. 84.

64. J. Héring, *The First Epistle of Saint Paul to the Corinthians* (trans. A. Heathcote and P. Allcock; London: Epworth Press, 1962), p. 45.

65. M.E. Thrall, *1 and 2 Corinthians* (CBC; Cambridge: Cambridge University Press, 1965), pp. 45-46.

66. Barrett, *First Epistle to the Corinthians*, p. 144.

67. F.F. Bruce, *1 and 2 Corinthians* (NCB; Grand Rapids: Eerdmans, 1971), p. 62. On the appropriateness of 'gnosticism', 'gnosis' or 'a kind of gnosis', see R. McL. Wilson, 'Gnosis at Corinth', in M. Hooker and S. Wilson (eds.), *Paul and*

3. Paul, Spiritual Parent and Paradigm in Christ

that Paul cites a source, but does not document what it is: 'the way in which he introduces this statement leads us to the assumption that it was known and used in Corinth; cf. the repetition of it in 10.23'.[68] Presumably he refers to Weiss's observation. In the most recent commentaries and scholarship, Weiss's dialogical reading seems to be established and is represented in recent scholarship by H. Balz, Fee, H.-J. Klauck and Mitchell.[69]

This current consensus is an obstacle to reading 1 Cor. 6.12 as another example of Paul's paradigmatic 'I' in 1 Corinthians, but it is not insurmountable since it stands mostly upon the force of repetition and rests upon some assailable suppositions. Here follows a brief summary and evaluation of the reasons given that Paul cites and responds to a Corinthian slogan in 1 Cor. 6.12. It should be noted that nowhere is the case set forward drawing upon all these points, and this summary may be the strongest existing, explicit argument in favour of the current consensus (a consensus I am seeking here to unground).

1. *The catchphrase is repeated in 10.23.* This is not quite an accurate observation. In 10.23 the personal reference is dropped and the general principle is asserted, 'All things are lawful, but...' That proviso aside, we must challenge the acceptability of an argument which assumes that the repetition of a phrase within a letter confirms that it is a citation from the party to whom the letter is addressed. Alternatively, 10.23 may form an *inclusio* with 6.12, as 11.1 does with 4.16.

2. *The way this phrase is introduced suggests that it came from the Corinthians.* Weiss, followed by Morris and (presumably) Conzelmann, suggests that the absence of the particle τοῦτο δέ is evidence that this is a Corinthian citation.[70] It is difficult to assess this reasoning, but it appears to be an argument from silence. It is true that Paul uses τοῦτο δέ eight times.[71] But, all of Paul's other assertions in his letters lack

---

Paulinism (London: SPCK, 1982), pp. 102-14; E. Yamauchi, 'Pre-Christian Gnosticism, The New Testament and Nag Hammadi in Recent Debate', *Themelios* 10 (1984), pp. 22-27.

68. Conzelmann, *1 Corinthians*, p. 108.

69. H. Balz, 'ἔξεστιν', *EDNT*, II, pp. 5-6; Fee, *The First Epistle to the Corinthians*, p. 215; H.-J. Klauck, *1. Korintherbrief* (Würzburg: Echter Verlag, 1984), p. 47; Mitchell, *Paul and the Rhetoric of Reconciliation*, pp. 33-39.

70. Similarly, D.J. Harrington, *Interpreting the New Testament* (Dublin: Veritas, 1985), p. 58, asserts that 'it is clear to the discerning reader', but he does not say how.

71. Rom. 1.12; 1 Cor. 7.6, 29, 35; 11.17; 15.50; 2 Cor. 9.6; Gal. 3.17.

this introduction, making Weiss's reasoning on this point suspect.⁷² We may be tempted to agree with E.-B. Allo, who identifies this as 'the great weakness of the rich commentary of Weiss', arbitrarily attaching meaning to such an insignificant particular in the text⁷³ or, in this instance, the absence of one. In fact, there are no introductory indicators of a citation here.

In 32 cases in 1 Corinthians, Paul introduces his citations, whether from the Corinthians, other literature or from hypothetical dialogue.⁷⁴ Against these 32 marked citations, there may be only 3 citations in 1 Corinthians that have no introduction, identifiable because they are known to us from the LXX: 2.16 (containing Isa. 40.13); 5.13 (echoing Deut. 17.7; 19.19; 22.21, 24; 24.7); and 15.32 (Isa. 22.13).⁷⁵ However, these may not be intentional citations at all but rather 'echoes' since Paul was thoroughly steeped in the language and imagery of the LXX.⁷⁶

---

72. See Stanley, *Paul and the Language of Scripture*, pp. 33-37, for a sharply defined view of 'citation'.

73. E.-B. Allo, *Saint Paul: Première épître aux Corinthiens* (EBib; Paris: J. Gabalda, 1934), p. 141.

74. 'that each of you says...' (ὅτι ἕκαστος ὑμῶν λέγει; 1.12); 'it is written...' (γέγραπται [for Old Testament citations only]; 1.19, 31; 2.9; 3.19; 9.9; 10.7; 14.21; 15.45, 54-55); 'For when someone says...' (ὅταν γὰρ λέγῃ τις; 3.4; similarly 15.27); 'and again' (καὶ πάλιν; 3.20); 'so that you may learn through us the meaning of the saying...' (ἵνα ἐν ἡμῖν μάθητε τὸ...; 4.6); 'For it is said...' (γάρ, φησίν; 6.16); 'Now concerning the matters about which you wrote...' (Περὶ δὲ ὧν ἐγράψατε; 7.1); 'we know that...' (οἴδαμεν ὅτι; 8.1, 4); 'for...' (γάρ; 10.26; 15.27); 'But if someone says to you...' (ἐὰν δέ τις ὑμῖν εἴπῃ; 10.28); 'and said...' (καὶ εἶπεν; 11.24); 'saying...' (λέγων; 11.25); 'no one...ever says/can say...' (ὅτι οὐδεὶς...λέγει /...δύναται εἰπεῖν; 12.3); 'if the foot/ear/etc. should say...' (12.15, 16, 21); 'declaring that...' (ἀπαγγέλλων ὅτι; 14.25); 'Do not be deceived...' (μὴ πλανᾶσθε; 15.33); 'But someone will ask...' (ἀλλὰ ἐρεῖ τις; 15.35).

75. Stanley, *Paul and the Language of Scripture*, p. 37 n. 13, does not treat these texts since they do not meet his minimum criteria for 'citations'.

76. 1 Cor. 6.12 may fall in this category, echoing Sir. 37.28: 'For not everything is good for everyone, and no one enjoys everything' (οὐ γὰρ πάντα πᾶσιν συμφέρει, καὶ οὐ πᾶσα ψυχὴ ἐν παντὶ εὐδοκεῖ). See the approach of R. Hays, *Echoes of Scripture in the Letters of Paul* (New Haven: Yale University Press, 1989). The possible origin of the phrase in Stoic, Cynic, gnostic or anti-Jewish sources is detailed in the standard commentaries, and see the results of a search of the *TLG* in M.A. Plunkett, 'Sexual Ethics and the Christian Life: A Study of 1 Corinthians 6.12–7.7' (PhD Dissertation, Princeton University, 1988), pp. 167-78. If an exact parallel could be found, it would not foreclose the question: for whom is it a source, Paul or the Corinthians?

3. *Paul, Spiritual Parent and Paradigm in Christ*

Upon close comparison of Paul's allusions with their LXX counterparts, 1 Cor. 2.16 is significantly abbreviated from Isa. 40.13. 1 Corinthians 5.13 seems adapted to the Corinthian context by placing the exhortation in the second-person plural (ἐξαρεῖς becomes ἐξάρατε), unlike all of the Deuteronomy texts to which it may allude. 1 Corinthians 15.32 is the only unmarked citation that is an exact quotation from the LXX. Two other unmarked 'citations' are often attributed to the Corinthians (6.13; 8.8), but they are debatable and in each case the argument may be followed without attributing these lines to the Corinthians.[77] This leaves one unmarked citation in 1 Corinthians (15.32), three at most if we allow 6.13 and 8.8. On balance, then, Paul usually introduces his citations in 1 Corinthians, leaving the burden of proof on those who want to identify parts of his text as quotations which he does not identify as such.[78] The lack of ability to verify or falsify a hypothetical Corinthian slogan has allowed many hypotheses about citations in 1 Corinthians to flourish.[79] M.V. Fox's observation applies: 'If there is no marking at all, we must start with the assumption that there is no quotation, or at least that the quotation is an expression of the speaker's viewpoint and sentiments'.[80] This is the line followed here, with the additional observation that 1 Cor. 6.12 reflects an idiom of Paul's hortatory style in the first-person singular.

3. *The moral problems in the Corinthian church accord well with such a slogan representing their viewpoints*. The strongest point in favour of 1 Cor. 6.12 containing a Corinthian citation is that the expression 'All things are lawful for me' does accord well with the disposition of at least some Corinthian Christians toward sexual promiscuity,

---

77. Contra Murphy-O'Connor, 'Corinthian Slogans', pp. 391-96.

78. It may be worth noting that 6.12 precedes 7.1 ('and now about the matters which you wrote in your letter'), and therefore the cited material. This is negated, however, if M.M. Mitchell is right ('Concerning περὶ δέ in 1 Corinthians', *NovT* 31 [1989], pp. 229-56). She argues that even περὶ δέ is not a clear indicator of a letter citation in ancient epistolary practice, and that chs. 5-6 should not be treated as a separate section from chs. 7-11. Her view is that Paul has shaped the entire letter according to his deliberative rhetorical purpose rather than the lines of their inquiry.

79. For a summary of commentators' views on citations of 'Corinthian sayings' see Omanson, 'Acknowledging Paul's Quotations', and Hurd, *The Origin of 1 Corinthians*, p. 68, who provides a convenient table.

80. M.V. Fox, 'The Identification of Quotations in Biblical Literature', *ZAW* 92 (1980), pp. 416-31 (427).

intramural lawsuits (chs. 5–6; cf. 10.8) and idol meat (chs. 8–10). Moreover, they were boastful about such things (5.2, 6; cf. 10.9, 12). 'All things are lawful for me' could express their theological and moral views in slogan form, a contention that is not disputed here. However, as in 1 Cor. 5.12 and in the passages studied below it will be argued that it is Paul's paraenetic style to make exhortations in the first-person singular that are crafted to confront the hearers' situation. Since he makes 'I' statements in an idiomatic way that the auditors are to appropriate as their own, it is just as plausible that 1 Cor. 6.12 reflects Paul's hortative style to say 'I' when he means 'you'.

4. *Mirror-reading is a legitimate technique to understand Paul's letters.* The commonly adopted reading strategy for 1 Corinthians is dialogical, understanding the letter as direct engagement with Corinthian teaching and arguments by suggesting potential reconstructions of the Corinthian end of the conversation (so-called 'mirror-reading'). It is not my purpose here to take issue with the notion of mirror-reading per se. We must respect that there was another end to Paul's 'conversation' with the Corinthians with which he appears to be well acquainted. And, such a technique can be validated in other parts of 1 Corinthians. For example, if we mirror-read ch. 13, we might suppose that overly enthusiastic attitudes towards tongues and prophecy were present in the Corinthian house churches. By a cursory perusal of chs. 12 and 14 this can be confirmed. Though there is no justification for taking each phrase in the letter as a direct counterpoint to Corinthian teaching and thinking, 1 Cor. 6.12 apparently reflects a 'Corinthian attitude' toward litigation, sexual behaviour and idol meat confirmed from other parts of the letter. All that is argued here is that there is no conclusive reason to take 1 Cor. 6.12 as a Corinthian citation when we have good reasons to read it as an expression Paul's paradigmatic use of 'I' statements to enhance his exhortation in the letter. Here we reject understanding 6.12 as a Corinthian citation without rejecting the legitimate place of mirror-reading as an interpretative technique, even with regard to this particular verse. We may agree with W. Meeks that in 6.12 we find Paul's 'corrective, second-order speech' that takes up specific attitudes known to the readers, without agreeing that Paul takes up specific language of the Corinthians, a possibility that Meeks seems to leave open.[81] Without positing how *they* expressed their views, it is argued below that

---

81. Meeks, *The First Urban Christians*, p. 122.

3. *Paul, Spiritual Parent and Paradigm in Christ* 85

Paul confronts their situation by means of a stylistic 'I' statement that we clearly observe elsewhere in his letters.

This brief review suggests that we need not identify a Corinthian citation in 6.12. We now consider reasons that support Paul as the author of 6.12 in its entirety (and, by implication, 10.23). If we ignore the often-repeated assumption, it is possible to read this verse as Paul's assertion, as do the Revised Authorized Version, J.B. Phillips' Version, W.F. Lofthouse,[82] C. Spicq[83] and E.-B. Allo.[84] Taking 6.12 as entirely Pauline makes sense of two other factors: Paul's persuasive use of 'I' statements, particularly at summary/transitions (see under 5.12 above), and the explicit literary use of exemplification throughout 1 Corinthians. 1 Corinthians 6.12 may be identified as yet another example of this phenomenon. Furthermore, these first-person statements may function like epistolary expressions of self-confidence, thematic statements for their context, a feature demonstrated by S. Olson.[85] This thematic function of Paul's crisp 'I' statements is found, for example, in Rom. 1.16-17; Gal. 1.10; 2.18-21; 1 Cor. 4.6, 16; and is demonstrable also for 1 Cor. 6.12.

If the structural observations made above about the declared strategy of exemplification in 4.16 and 11.1 are valid, then 6.12 has a formal place within the letter's strategy, taken as part of Paul's self-presentation of the free but self-restrained person with concern for the community.[86] Thematic connections of 6.12 with the broader context have previously been demonstrated. As Conzelmann notes, the so-called 'slogan' spans the whole content of chs. 6–10,[87] and Godet makes the case that Christian liberty is the theme through ch. 10.[88] It is not a large step to consider the whole of 6.12 as a Pauline literary invention that ties together his treatment of various issues in these chapters. For example, we see the same theme reverberating, *mutatis mutandis*, in places like 8.9 and 9.19. In 9.19 Paul makes the same emphasis on curtailing

---

82. Lofthouse, '"I" and "We"', p. 242.
83. 'Il s'agit, en réalité, d'une affirmation paulinienne' (C. Spicq, *Théologie morale du Nouveau Testament* [2 vols.; [Ebib; Paris: J. Gabalda, 1965], II, p. 654).
84. Allo, *Saint Paul*, pp. 141-42.
85. S.N. Olson, 'Epistolary Uses of Expressions of Self-Confidence', *JBL* 103 (1984), pp. 585-97.
86. Sanders, 'Imitating Paul', pp. 361-63.
87. Conzelmann, *1 Corinthians*, p. 109.
88. Godet, *First Epistle to the Corinthians*, p. 303.

his own rights for the sake of others as he does in 6.12 (if it is taken as wholly Pauline), as Spicq has noted.[89] If we take 6.12 as wholly Paul's literary device rather than a quotation, this introduces one thread of the argument that extends through ch. 14: Paul models self-limitation of freedom for the sake of other Christians. And 6.12 introduces this thread by Paul placing himself, as it were, in their midst as an example through this literary device. As Lofthouse says, 'In ch. 6, after the vigorous appeal in vv. 1-11 (note v. 3) he puts himself in their midst as an example (v. 12); he passes...from a sharp personal touch...to the interrupted exhortation; now he is distinct from them; now one of them'.[90]

The impression that 1 Cor. 6.12 has a formal function in the letter is reinforced by the repetition of 'all things are lawful' in 10.23, which comes at the beginning of Paul's recapitulation of his argument, and reaches back to 8.1 by topic (idols and idol meat) and to 6.12 by principle (laying down one's rights and freedoms for the sake of others). 10.23 forms an *inclusio* with 6.12 tying together Paul's argument by recapitulating the principle of self-limiting freedom.[91]

Now an alternative reading of 1 Cor. 6.12 is proposed, taking it as idiomatic Pauline persuasion. Here the context of 6.12 is factored in, particularly of the subunit in 6.9-12 which appears to function as both a summary of the argument and as a transition between topics. It is understood that Paul places his assertion in the first-person singular to portray himself as a model of self-restraint out of consideration for the welfare of the church. As outlined above, this appears as a typical example of Paul's persuasive style in 1 Corinthians and is especially prevalent in his summary/transitions.[92]

The immediate context preceding 6.9-12 has a forensic setting in view. In the light of the discussion about lawsuits from 6.1, it seems natural to take 'all things are lawful'[93] with regard to the right to bring

89. Spicq, *Théologie morale*, p. 654.
90. Lofthouse, '"I" and "We"', p. 242.
91. So Wuellner, 'Greek Rhetoric', p. 186, who identifies 6.12–11.1 as a 'ring composition'; Mitchell, *Paul and the Rhetoric of Reconciliation*, pp. 226-27.
92. Cf. 1 Cor. 4.1-13; 5.12; 8.13; 9.24-27; 10.23-11.1; 15.30-32; Gal. 1.10; 2.18-21.
93. According to H. Balz, 'ἔξεστιν, ἐξόν', *EDNT*, II, p. 5, outside the New Testament, ἔξεστιν is used to indicate what is permitted or forbidden according to law or divine will (e.g. Aeschylus, *Prom.* 648; Xenophon, *An.* 7.1.21; Herodotus 1.183). The LXX uses the negative with ἔξεστιν/ἐξόν in the later writings for general prohibitions (2 Esd. 4.14; Est. 4.2; 1 Macc. 14.44) and especially to designate

suit. Initially, 6.12a-b appears as Paul's self-characterization as a person with legal rights, 'All things are legal for me', and then he sharply shapes it with 'but not all things are advantageous'. This appeal to advantage suits the Corinthian situation since, ostensibly, the litigants were resorting to the court system for an advantage over those who had wronged them. This initial impression must be broadened, however, since the *inclusio* in 10.23 suggests application of this general principle over the range of topics enclosed between 6.12 and 10.23. 'All things are lawful' could apply to attitudes about using litigation, but it also is directed toward attitudes about sexual immorality (cf. 5.9-11; 6.9-10, 15-20; ch. 7) and idol meat (cf. 6.13; chs. 8–10).

Most texts and translations place a section break after 6.11 reinforcing the impression that 6.12 is a new start.[94] However if we pay attention to what immediately precedes our verse in 6.9-11, it could be that Paul's self-characterization in 6.12 draws out the ethical boundaries that justification entails. As Lietzmann suggests, 'With a fully effective contrast of the described purity and righteousness with unrighteousness, Paul now brings out the consequence'.[95] That is, by means of a pithy 'I' statement in 6.12 Paul portrays himself as an exemplary embodiment of the effects of the 'washing', 'sanctification' and 'justification' that the Corinthians presumably had experienced in baptism[96] (ἀλλὰ ἀπελούσασθε, ἀλλὰ ἡγιάσθητε, ἀλλὰ ἐδικαιώθητε; 6.11). He reaffirms his teaching on Christian freedom, a notion that the Corinthians had fully appropriated (cf. 8.9: 'your freedom', ἡ ἐξουσία ὑμῶν), but he emphatically shapes it with qualifiers set off by the twice-repeated 'but not' (ἀλλ' οὐ).[97] It is the second half of each statement that Paul wants the Corinthians to hear most of all, to make communal concern the highest priority of their life together. All of 6.12 is an 'I' statement, a literary device through which Paul sets himself in their midst as a model of the characteristics that accompany justification—self-limitation of freedom, self-discipline and a new-found ability to shun sinful behaviour. Taking

what is forbidden by Jewish law (*3 Macc.* 1.11; *4 Macc.* 5.18; cf. Josephus, *Ant.* 20.268).

94. Schrage ends his first volume at 6.11!

95. H. Lietzmann, *An die Korinther*, I–II (HNT, 9; Tübingen: J.C.B. Mohr [Paul Siebeck], 4th edn, 1949), p. 27.

96. Conzelmann, *1 Corinthians*, p. 107.

97. ἀλλ' οὐκ is used in 1 Cor. 9.12 in a similar way, not nullifying what has come before yet emphasizing what follows.

6.12 as following from 6.11 and as a part of Paul's paraenetic strategy of self-presentation in the letter it may be read:

> [Imitate my example:] All things are lawful for me [and for you who have been baptized], but not all things are beneficial. All things are lawful for me [and you], but I will not allow myself to be enslaved by anything [so neither should you].

Of course, further justifications for ethical behaviour are given, and Paul's persuasive use of 'I' is only one aspect of his rhetoric. In the case of sexual immorality, it is not to be permitted because it is not beneficial, it dominates the person involved with it (6.12; cf. Rom. 6.12-23) and it entails joining the 'body of Christ' with immorality (6.15; cf. ch. 12). In the case of idol meat, eating is neither beneficial nor does it edify others. Both sexual immorality and eating idol meat are forbidden because they do not glorify God (6.20; 10.31; further evidence of a ring composition). In none of these do we find Paul arguing for 'Some things are not lawful for me' or 'Not all things are lawful for me'. Rather, he places moral reasoning on a different plane from consideration of Torah restrictions:[98] what is beneficial to the church and therefore Christ himself (6.15; ch. 12), what enslaves, and what does and does not glorify God.

A bold statement of Christian freedom is by no means unlike Paul elsewhere, as most who prefer the Corinthian citation interpretation acknowledge.[99] Paul makes the same kind of bold statement of freedom from the law in Gal. 3.23–5.15. If we take one example, it is clear that Paul can assert radical freedom from the law while at the same time guarding against libertinism:

---

98. So also T.J. Deidun, *New Covenant Morality in Paul* (AnBib, 89; Rome: Biblical Institute Press, 1981), p. 154 n. 13.

99. E.g. Conzelmann, *1 Corinthians*, p. 109; Barrett, *First Epistle to the Corinthians*, p. 145. See further R. Mohrlang, *Matthew and Paul: A Comparison of Ethical Perspectives* (SNTSMS, 48; Cambridge: Cambridge University Press, 1984), pp. 31-32; A. West, 'Sex and Salvation: A Christian Feminist Bible Study on 1 Corinthians 6.12–7.39', in A. Loades (ed.), *Feminist Theology: A Reader* (London: SPCK, 1990), pp. 72-80. M.E. Thrall, 'Christ Crucified or Second Adam? A Christological Debate between Paul and the Corinthians', in B. Lindars and S. Smalley (eds.), *Christ and Spirit in the New Testament* (Cambridge: Cambridge University Press, 1973), pp. 143-56, argues that all of the Corinthian problems may be attributed to a misunderstanding or misapplication of Paul's message.

3. *Paul, Spiritual Parent and Paradigm in Christ* 89

> For you were called to freedom, brothers and sisters; only do not use your freedom as an opportunity for self-indulgence, but through love become slaves to one another (Gal. 5.13).

As we can see, Paul boldly asserts 'freedom' vis-à-vis 'the law' (cf. 5.1), but he is also quick to circumscribe Christian liberty with self-control, in a construction not dissimilar to 1 Cor. 6.12.[100] If we adopt the reading that the entirety of 1 Cor. 6.12 originates with Paul, then he presents himself as the free but communally responsible example to be emulated. He models consideration of what benefits and builds up others, implying that the Corinthians should conform to his pattern, even though they too are 'free' and 'have knowledge' (cf. 8.1-6).

If this interpretation is accepted, Paul's self-characterization in 6.12 has an epistolary function as part of his explicit argumentation from personal example in 1 Corinthians, and operates as an *inclusio* with 10.23. Through this device he re-emphasizes his teaching on Christian liberty by modelling that freedom does not mean uncontrolled liberty, but is compatible with a principled life of self-control in consideration of others. Thus his usage of 'I' here is an effective way of identifying with the Corinthians in their sense of liberty regarding lawsuits, sexual behaviour and idol meat, while modelling self-control and self-denial, a repeated refrain in the chapters that follow. Moreover, Gal. 5.13 is an arguably similar Pauline statement. 1 Corinthians 6.12 and 10.23 in their contexts offer slight variations on the similar argument that spans the topics from chs. 6–10, 'Do not seek your own advantage, but that of the other'.[101]

It has been claimed that 6.12 could be another instance of Paul's hortative 'I' where 'I' = 'you', and is comprehensible without supposing that it is a citation. It has been argued that this nuanced reading is a more accurate and careful way of understanding what is going on in 1 Cor. 6.12 than the dialogical reading which currently holds sway, retrieving this verse from an unnecessary hypothesis and relating it to the larger literary strategy of the letter. If the case here has been persuasive, then using quotation marks to understand 1 Cor. 6.12 and 10.23 will be viewed henceforth as an unnecessary interpretative overlay, and the gain to scholarship will be that quotation marks will disappear in future references to these verses, and an awareness of Paul's 'I' style will be maintained. The macro-strategy of personal example in

---

100. Cf. Gal. 5.14–6.1; Rom. 5–6; 1 Cor. 8.
101. 10.24; cf. 10.28, 33; so Conzelmann, *1 Corinthians*, p. 109.

the letter has suggested such an interpretation. Following the line of interpretation along the trajectory of this strategy now takes us out of the frying pan of 1 Cor. 6.12 and into the fire of 7.1b, another verse which is often interpreted to contain a putative Corinthian citation.

1 Corinthians 7.7-8

Paul's strategic literary usage of personal example throughout 1 Corinthians—if also used in 7.7-8—may provide support for the traditional interpretation that 7.1b is a Pauline rather than Corinthian declaration where he asserts the importance of remaining celibate, a view which he develops in the chapter. Currently, however, the most common approach to 1 Cor. 7.1b is to view it as Paul's citation of a Corinthian ascetic notion that 'it is well not to touch a woman'.[102] The impulse for identifying a Corinthian citation comes from (1) how it is introduced in the first half of the verse, 'Concerning the things which you wrote...' (7.1a), and (2) the somewhat distasteful thought that Paul actually promotes austere sexual abstinence.[103] These two inferences, historical and theological, are combined in the supposition that some Corinthians were ascetics who denied the obligations of the marriage bed, a view first espoused by Origen (though unlike modern scholars he believed Paul endorsed the saying).[104] The presence of ascetic Corinthians has been harmonized with the presence of libertine Corinthians (chs. 5–6; 8–11) by positing two groups current in Corinth—one hedonistic and the other ascetic—or by suggesting a common theological reason that explains their diverse practices, such as the presence of over-realized

---

102. See survey in J. Gundry-Volf, 'Controlling the Bodies: A Theological Profile of the Corinthian Sexual Ascetics (1 Cor. 7)', in R. Bieringer (ed.), *The Corinthian Correspondence* (BETL, 125; Leuven: Peeters, 1996), pp. 519-41.

103. An obvious *Tendenz* in W.E. Phipps, 'Is Paul's Attitude toward Sexual Relations Contained in 1 Cor 7.1?', *NTS* 28 (1982), pp. 125-31; and in Fee, who argues in a circle that 7.1 cannot represent Paul's view because Paul is not an 'ascetic' (*The First Epistle to the Corinthians*, p. 276). The interpretation offered below attempts to demonstrate that if we take into account how 7.1 is qualified throughout the chapter, then 7.1 can be Paul's without thinking he is any more ascetic than 7.8 makes explicit.

104. See Phipps, 'Paul's Attitude'; O.L. Yarbrough, *Not Like the Gentiles: Marriage Rules in the Letters of Paul* (SBLDS, 80; Atlanta: Scholars Press, 1985), pp. 93-122.

3. Paul, Spiritual Parent and Paradigm in Christ

eschatology, which some Corinthians took to license anything at all and others took to imply the end of marriage.[105]

There are at least three issues that remain unaccounted for if 7.1b is thought not to represent Paul's view. First, the introductory phrase in 7.1a is not evidence that Paul cites a Corinthian citation. It is no longer tenable to take περὶ δέ as a reference to specific content of the letter that the Corinthians sent, as M.M. Mitchell has demonstrated. In her study of literary and rhetorical works, literary letters, private and documentary letters and the New Testament, she concludes that περὶ δέ is 'simply a topic marker, a shorthand way of introducing the next subject of discussion', the only requirement of which is that this topic be readily known to both the writer and reader.[106] The extended formula as it appears in 1 Cor. 7.1 (περὶ δὲ ὧν ἐγράψατε) is a known idiom for engaging topics already touched upon in previous correspondence, and the literary evidence makes it inconclusive whether or not περὶ δέ refers to 7.1 or 7.1-24 or all of ch. 7.[107]

Secondly, καλόν is used in two other clauses in 1 Corinthians 7 besides 7.1 that are clearly Pauline:

Περὶ δὲ ὧν ἐγράψατε, **καλὸν ἀνθρώπῳ γυναικὸς μὴ ἅπτεσθαι** (7.1).

Λέγω δὲ τοῖς ἀγάμοις καὶ ταῖς χήραις, **καλὸν αὐτοῖς ἐὰν μείνωσιν ὡς κἀγώ** (7.8).

Νομίζω οὖν τοῦτο καλὸν ὑπάρχειν διὰ τὴν ἐνεστῶσαν ἀνάγκην, ὅτι **καλὸν ἀνθρώπῳ τὸ οὕτως εἶναι** (7.26).

In each case the pattern is καλόν + dative + verb. The dative refers to the subject of the verb that follows. Furthermore, the καλόν + dative + verb pattern is repeated in the next occurrence of καλόν in the letter:[108]

οὐκ ἔγραψα δὲ ταῦτα ἵνα οὕτως γένηται ἐν ἐμοί, **καλὸν γάρ μοι μᾶλλον ἀποθανεῖν** ἤ- τὸ καύχημά μου οὐδεὶς κενώσει (1 Cor. 9.15).

---

105. Hurd, *The Origin of 1 Corinthians*, pp. 276-78; Conzelmann, *1 Corinthians*, p. 115; cf. V.L. Wimbush, *Paul the Worldly Ascetic: Response to the World and Self-Understanding According to 1 Corinthians 7* (Macon, GA: Mercer University Press, 1987).

106. Mitchell, 'Concerning περὶ δέ', p. 234.

107. Mitchell, 'Concerning περὶ δέ', pp. 244-45, 256 n. 118.

108. The only other occurrence of καλόν in the letter is in 5.6 in an entirely different construction (cf. Mt. 18.8, 9; Mk 14.21).

Stylistically, then, the appearance of entirely similar Pauline grammatical constructions in 7.1, 8, 26 and 9.15 strengthens the supposition that 7.1b is Pauline also.[109] Furthermore, this stylistic observation is bolstered by the grammar of 7.1a where 'there is nothing to show that the words which follow are a quotation'.[110]

A third issue that remains unaccounted for in the interpretation of 7.1b as a Corinthian citation is Paul's use of personal example as a unifying argumentative strategy of the letter. If the strategy we have been discussing applies in the case of ch. 7, then the traditional view makes sense of Paul's personal example in 7.7-8 by relating it to his overarching strategy in the letter, while the hypothesis that 7.1b reflects a Corinthian slogan makes us isolate the literary strategy of ch. 7 from the larger pattern of persuasion evident in the letter, marginalizing 7.7-8 as incidental to the chapter. Instead, the weight of Paul's usage of his paradigmatic 'I' throughout 1 Corinthians should lead us to suppose that Paul's references to his personal example in 7.7-8 are also illustrative of a central thrust of his argument, supporting the traditional interpretation of 7.1b as Paul's statement.[111]

It is possible to take ἅπτεσθαι in 7.1 either to refer to sexual intercourse in general or to the marriage bed in particular, both metaphorical extensions of the term and both supported by the subsequent discussion of these related topics in 1 Corinthians 7.[112] For the purpose here, all that is necessary is to demonstrate that it is plausible to take ἅπτεσθαι to refer to marriage. In LXX, though the term is usually used for 'touch' or 'seize', twice it is used euphemistically to refer to sexual intercourse (Gen. 20.6; Prov. 6.29),[113] a minor usage of the term attested in other

---

109. Conzelmann, *1 Corinthians*, p. 115 n. 10.

110. Robertson and Plummer, *First Epistle of St Paul to the Corinthians*, p. 132. More vociferously, C.C. Caragounis argues that the clause in 7.1b cannot (!) be the contents of a quotation referred to in 7.1a ('"Fornication" and "Concession"? Interpreting 1 Cor. 7,1-7', in Bieringer [ed.], *The Corinthian Correspondence*, pp. 543-60). For other difficulties with reading 7.1b as a quotation, see Barrett, *First Epistle to the Corinthians*, p. 154.

111. So also Weiss, *Der erste Korintherbrief*, p. 170; Robertson and Plummer, *First Epistle of St Paul to the Corinthians*, p. 132; Conzelmann, *1 Corinthians*, p. 115; contra Fee, *The First Epistle to the Corinthians*, pp. 275-76.

112. Though as Fee points out, neither view is without its difficulties (*The First Epistle to the Corinthians*, p. 273).

113. G. Schneider, 'ἅπτω', *EDNT*, I, p. 148; Yarbrough, *Not Like the Gentiles*, p. 94.

Greek literature of the period.¹¹⁴ Fee advances a faulty semantic argument when he claims 'There is no evidence of any kind that it can be extended or watered down to mean, "It is good for a man not to marry"'.¹¹⁵ In the first place, the extension of the term that ordinarily means 'touch' to refer to sexual intercourse is a case in point that a term can be extended in usage. It is not unthinkable that this term is being further extended to refer to marriage by referring to the conjugal bed.¹¹⁶ Secondly, terms often are used to refer to a thing signified without the thing signified having even a remote relationship to root meanings of the signifier. Usage and context are all important. In the immediate context of our text there are other instances of terms removed from their ordinary usage to be employed euphemistically, for example, 'have' (7.2), 'to hand over what is owed' (7.3). Thirdly, ἅπτεσθαι has a commonly attested usage to mean 'to fasten oneself to, to cleave to', a usage that is analogous to the euphemistic usage of προσκολληθήσεται for marriage in the LXX and New Testament (Gen. 2.24; Mt. 19.5; Eph. 5.31). As Gundry-Volf notes, ἅπτεσθαι γυναικός is widely used for conjugal relations.¹¹⁷ Therefore, it is plausible that 7.1b may refer to marriage by euphemistically referring to the marriage bed, thus introducing the theme that Paul will bolster by his own example of celibacy (7.8, 32-35).

It is possible, then, that 7.1b is Paul's generalized statement that he qualifies in what follows. If 7.1 is taken as Paul's thesis about marriage, then 7.2-5 (cf. 7.36) are concessions that relax Paul's rigorist ideal (cf. 7.7-8, 27, 32-35, 40). Paul's thesis is a demanding call to celibacy, and so he makes a concession (κατὰ συγγνώμην, οὐ κατ' ἐπιταγήν, 7.6), since he apparently has no teaching 'from the Lord' (7.10), and since he makes space in the church for each one's 'gift from God' (7.7). The language of concession in 7.6 makes sense against 7.2, 5 by asserting that sexuality in marriage is a means of avoiding πορνεία (7.2), which

114. LSJ, *s.v.*; R. Grob, 'Touch', *NIDNTT*, III, p. 859; Fee, *The First Epistle to the Corinthians*, p. 275.
115. Fee, *The First Epistle to the Corinthians*, p. 275.
116. Plunkett, *Sexual Ethics and the Christian Life*, pp. 303-304, supports the interpretation adopted here with a slightly different approach. He takes 7.1 as a Corinthian slogan, but thinks Paul agrees with it only to correct if for pragmatic rather than theological reasons. He takes 7.7 as a clarification of 7.1, suggested by the chiastic structure of 7.1-7: 'Be as I am' = celibate, i.e. 'not touching a woman' (p. 304).
117. Gundry-Volf, 'Controlling the Bodies', p. 4 n. 12.

in turn is a temptation of Satan (7.5). Marriage itself appears to be a part of the concession since 7.7, 29b, 32b-35 present Paul's ideal.

Paul's ideal is not 'ascetic' but eschatological, renouncing sexual pleasure for the sake of having single-minded devotion to God in the light of the impending close of the current age (7.26, 29, 31). If we take 7.1b as Paul's ideal, 7.2-5 makes explicit that this does not apply to the marriage relationship and 7.10-16 makes it clear that the marriage relationship is not to be forsaken to live up to the ideal. Even so, Paul's position is self-confessedly weak on this matter since his view has not been entrusted to him by Christ (7.12). Here he uses θέλω, his least forceful exhortation.[118] If we exclude its usage in the numerous rhetorical constructions that are usually negated (e.g. 'I do not want you to be unknowing'), its usage by itself here is rare in the Pauline corpus (only in 1 Cor. 7.7, 32 and 14.5). His ambivalence is further evident in 7.25a when he concedes that he has no command from the Lord.[119] Nevertheless, his view on celibacy remains the ideal pattern (7.8, 32-35), even if he must acknowledge that not all will attain this ideal. Since some will not it is necessary for him to assure them that 'if you marry you do not sin' (7.28).

In 7.17-24 Paul affirms both celibacy and marriage, as he anticipates in 7.1-6.[120] If 7.1b is Paul's position, then it is clear how 7.2-5 is the concession he mentions in 7.6 (cf. 7.36). Freedom to get married is a relaxation of another principle that Paul develops in the chapter, namely that one should remain in one's current condition, whether single or married, slave or free (7.17-24, 26-27, 40). That marriage is considered to be the concession is further supported by the correctives of 7.9, 28, 36. If 7.1b is taken as Paul's ideal which he excludes from application

---

118. Barrett, *First Epistle to the Corinthians*, p. 158, thinks it is 'almost a command'. However, we should not obscure the clear distinctions Paul makes in ch. 7 between his own thinking and the 'word of the Lord', and therefore 'I wish' or 'I want' is to be preferred, following M. Limbeck, 'θέλω', *EDNT*, II, p. 138.

119. Although Paul distinguishes between his own and the Lord's authority, he still buffers his statement with claims to his own reliability. In 7.25, 40, he strengthens his exhortation by appealing to his pneumatic authority using the *lingua franca* of the Corinthian pneumatics (Hurd, *The Origin of 1 Corinthians*, p. 70). Mitchell suggests that 7.25, 40 are best understood as part of Paul's self-exemplification (Mitchell, *Paul and the Rhetoric of Reconciliation*, p. 56 n. 162), while Olson classifies these as commonplace confidence statements ('Epistolary Uses', p. 593).

120. G.W. Dawes, '"But if you can gain your freedom" (1 Corinthians 7.17-24)', *CBQ* 52 (1990), pp. 681-97.

3. *Paul, Spiritual Parent and Paradigm in Christ*   95

to the marriage bed (7.2-5, 10-16), then it need not be thought that Paul promotes an absolute asceticism as he was later interpreted to say. We need not follow W.E. Phipps when he claims that the interpretation proposed here views this passage 'through the eyes of Tertullian, Jerome, Ambrose, Augustine, and other prominent sexual ascetics who have contaminated the biblical outlook on sexuality'.[121] This is too strong given that 7.7, 8, 27, 32-35, 40 are evidence that Paul himself, by our standards, was sexually austere. (Compared with Graeco-Roman medical texts which regularly deplore the physical harm of intercourse, Paul's example and viewpoint in 1 Cor. 7 is not as 'austere', and is far more positive about the conjugal bed [7.3-5].)[122] Furthermore, it may be held that Paul's proposition in 7.1, if it is indeed his, does not prescribe 'asceticism' but rather as the best option in Paul's eyes (7.6) considering the eschatological situation (7.29). The view that 7.1, if Paul's, expresses a thoroughgoing asceticism as found in church fathers does not give full weight to the fact that this is the only place in Paul's letters where he draws attention to his lack of a command, and it overlooks the allowance he makes for those already married and for those who get married (7.9, 36).

It is possible, then, that Paul again presents his personal example for imitation in 1 Cor. 7.7-8, and that this helps to explain 7.1b, 'I want all people to be as I am' (7.7), and 'it is good for them to remain just as I am' (7.8). The call to imitation is repeated because he sees remaining in one's station as the highest ideal. This view is strengthened if we accept that Paul's self-presentation as a model is the skeletal structure of his argument in 1 Corinthians. In any case, in 7.7-8 Paul presents his personal example as a model for imitation and an attempt has been made to relate this to the argument of the chapter. Identifying a literary strategy employing personal example in 1 Corinthians has led through the quagmire of 6.12 and 7.1. The commonly held hypothesis that these two verses contain Corinthian citations presents a threat to the thesis argued here, but an attempt at an alternative approach to these verses has been suggested. Fortunately the issue of putative citations, as concentrated as it has been in the middle of this chapter, will not deter us again in this study.

---

121. Phipps, 'Paul's Attitude', p. 130.
122. See A. Rousselle, *Porneia: On Desire and the Body in Antiquity* (trans. F. Pheasant; Oxford: Basil Blackwell, 1988).

1 Corinthians 8.13–9.27

To make sense of the broader text of 1 Corinthians 8–10, 1 Corinthians 9 must be read through the lens of Paul's self-portrayals also. First, however, I must confront another obstacle to my thesis, namely that Paul's self-presentation is to be understood against a hypothetical charge sheet against him rather than his own argumentative design in the letter. The reader will not be surprised to find it suggested here that 1 Corinthians 9 fits well within the pattern of usage of personal example in the letter. First, however, the case that Paul defends his authority and apostleship in 1 Corinthians 9 must be dispatched before we can proceed to demonstrate how 1 Corinthians 9 fits into the larger strategy of exemplification in 1 Corinthians.

On first appearance 9.1 seems to be an abrupt shift, detached from what has come before. Conzelmann says, 'Chapter 9 surprisingly introduces a new theme: the apostleship of Paul'.[123] In favour of this view is Paul's claim that this text functions as an ἀπολογία in 9.3, and it has been inferred that his status as apostle was not accepted by 'others' (9.2).[124] In this reading ch. 9 answers the question, if Paul is an apostle why doesn't he allow himself to be supported by the community?[125]

---

123. Conzelmann, *1 Corinthians*, p. 151. See, e.g., C. Dietzfelbinger, *Der Berufung des Paulus als Ursprung seiner Theologie* (WMANT, 58; Neukirchen–Vluyn: Neukirchener Verlag, 1985), pp. 46-48. For a discussion and summary of views on ch. 9 see Willis, 'Apostolic Apologia', pp. 33-48, which range from editorial displacement (so Héring, *The First Epistle*, pp. xiii, 75), to apologetic excursus.

124. If we take εἰ ἄλλοις to include the reality of the supposition 'if, as is in fact the case', Conzelmann, *1 Corinthians*, p. 152.

125. Theissen, *The Social Setting*, pp. 46-47, takes Mk 9.41 as an 'informative parallel' which refers to the 'requirement' for offering hospitality to primitive Christian itinerant charismatics, which Epictetus uses to describe the itinerant Cynic preacher. Similarly, R.F. Hock, *The Social Context of Paul's Ministry: Tentmaking and Apostleship* (Philadelphia: Fortress Press, 1980), pp. 59-63, argues that Paul's refusal to accept support was taken by the Corinthians as a lack of friendship or love. P. Marshall follows Hock and Theissen in *Enmity in Corinth*, pp. 233-51, 282-306. D.L. Dungan, *The Sayings of Jesus in the Churches of Paul: The Use of the Synoptic Tradition in the Regulation of Early Church Life* (Oxford: Basil Blackwell, 1971), p. 6, proposes a compromise position regarding the function of ch. 9. He suggests that even though this chapter functions as part of the argument from 8–10, it also serves the function of self-defence, 'killing two birds with one stone'. This compromise is inviting, but Dungan assumes Paul is defending himself against the charge of why he did not receive support like the Jerusalem apostolate visiting in Corinth, the first stages of the conflict of 2 Cor. 10–13 (pp. 18-19). These

3. *Paul, Spiritual Parent and Paradigm in Christ*

This was apparently the practice of the apostles in Palestine, specifically of 'the brothers of the Lord and Cephas' (9.5). Someone inside or outside the community could have made this unfavourable comparison,[126] and it is presumed that against this challenge Paul addresses his defence.[127]

Three difficulties may be raised against reading ch. 9 as Paul's defence in the face of actual charges:

1. Paul's argument does not demonstrate how he is a legitimate apostle, but how he is *different* from the Palestinian apostles,[128] and how he is different from shepherds, soldiers, farmers and temple servants. Moreover, he makes it clear that his practice ignores the warrants for this right (ἐξουσία, 9.4, 5, 12, 18) granted by the Old Testament (Deut. 25.4)[129] and Jesus (Mt. 10.10).
2. A stronger objection is that Paul presumes his apostleship as a part of his argument. The οὐκ, οὐχὶ and οὐ in the four rhetorical questions of 9.1-2 expect affirmative answers,[130] but Paul does not proceed to defend these claims. If the issue is his apostleship, why does he leave these assertions undefended? It

four studies fall under the same methodological criticism: they read the later developments reflected in 2 Cor. 10–13 as determinative of the situation at the time of 1 Corinthians.

126. Conzelmann, *1 Corinthians*, pp. 152-53.

127. Theissen's explanation is thus: 'The charge could be leveled at him that he has deliberately evaded the requirement of charismatic poverty, and that his work as a craftsman displays a lack of trust in the grace of God, who will also supply the material needs of his missionaries. Seen this way Paul is dependent on his work; he is not free and is no real apostle (9.1), for he has offended against the norm of the primitive Christian ideal of itinerant charismatics set down by Jesus himself. In opposition to all of this Paul is at pains to show that the requirement of charismatic poverty is in reality the missionary's *privilege*. To do that, however, he must reinterpret Jesus' word, which he does with the help of general experience and Old Testament exegesis' (*The Social Setting*, p. 43). Theissen acknowledges this may be seen as 'an artificial intensification of arguments' (p. 43 n. 42), which it is.

128. Who falls within the scope of οἱ λοιποὶ ἀπόστολοι is unclear (see 15.7), but it at least includes Paul and Barnabas (9.6).

129. Paul may interpret this command as Hillel would, but he is not characterizing himself 'als Hillelit', contra J. Jeremias, 'Paulus als Hillelit', in E. Ellis and M. Wilcox (eds.), *Neotestamentica et Semitica: Studies in Honour of Matthew Black* (Edinburgh: T. & T. Clark, 1969), pp. 88-94 (89).

130. P.-G. Müller, 'οὐ', *EDNT*, II, p. 539.

seems that Paul expected the Corinthians to accept the affirmations implied in the rhetorical questions: 'Paul is self-sufficient. Paul is an apostle. He has seen the Lord. We are proof that he is an apostle'. It appears that Paul assumes these for the sake of his argument, seeking to prove something else.

3. Chapter 9 is bracketed by chapters that treat the problem of food sacrificed to idols. If ch. 9 is understandable as part of Paul's extended argument in chs. 8–10, then the surrounding context provides the strongest argument that ch. 9 is not 'an interruption', nor a response to actual charges. This in fact may be demonstrated.

On a thematic level, ch. 9 is related to the material that surrounds it, especially chs. 8–10. Though the topic changes to Paul himself, there is a theme that unifies 6.7–10.33, and the hortatory significance of his change to the first-person singular has already been demonstrated in several places in the preceding chapters. The unifying theme is Paul's ethical principle that, even though the Corinthians have certain rights and freedoms, there are cases when love for others in the church requires that they not claim their rights nor exercise all their freedom. In ch. 7 this principle is applied to two forms of social ἐλευθερία, freedom from slavery and freedom from marriage.[131] The self-exemplification in 7.7, 'I wish that all were as I myself am', abounds in ch. 9, for example the question, 'Do we not have a right to take along a believing wife?' (μὴ οὐκ ἔχομεν ἐξουσίαν ἀδελφὴν γυναῖκα περιάγειν) in 9.5 tacitly may refer to the subject of ch. 7, and tie Paul's example in ch. 9 with his argument there. In any case, in ch. 9 Paul models the self-denial he challenges them to accept as their own standard of behaviour in ch. 7. Chapter 8 again argues that the Corinthians need not act on all their knowledge nor claim all their privileges for the sake of the gospel, a theme that recurs throughout chs. 9 and 10 (9.12b, 15, 18, 22, 23; 10.23, 24, 33), and 9.4 specifically picks up the vocabulary of 8.8-9 and the argument of 8.7-13.[132] On a thematic level we must reject the notion that ch. 9 is an interruption.[133]

---

131. οὐ μᾶλλον ἡμεῖς; ἀλλ' οὐκ ἐχρησάμεθα, κτλ. in 9.12 and εἰς τὸ μὴ καταχρήσασθαι τῇ ἐξουσίᾳ μου in 9.18 are reminiscent of μᾶλλον χρῆσαι in 7.21.

132. See Willis's concise summary of several convincing arguments for the integrity of chs. 8–10 in 'Apostolic Apologia', pp. 39-40.

133. The absence of περὶ δέ at 9.1 is additional support that a new topic is

3. Paul, Spiritual Parent and Paradigm in Christ 99

We may turn to the immediate context of 9.1 to discover the paradigmatic function of Paul's self-presentation here and reject an interpretation of this chapter as a defence of Paul's authority. Most significantly, the 'sudden' change is not in 9.1 but in 8.13 where we find another instance of Paul's hortatory 'I', a stylistic feature of Paul's paraenesis we have already noticed in 5.12 and 6.12. In 8.1-8 the exhortation is framed in the first-person plural. In 8.9-12, the point of the paraenesis is clearly directed at the Corinthians in the second person—in 8.9, 12 as the second-person plural, in 8.10-11 as the second-person singular, characteristic of the diatribal style (v. 8: ἐὰν γάρ τις ἴδη σὲ...; v. 1: ...ἐν τῇ σῇ γνώσει). At 8.13 the shift to the first-person singular is distinct:

> But when *you* thus sin against members of your family, and wound their conscience when it is weak, *you* sin against Christ. Therefore, if food is a cause of their falling, *I* will never eat meat, so that *I* may not cause one of them to fall (8.12-13).

Paul's paradigmatic 'I' statement in 8.13 both summarizes the aim of his argument in ch. 8 and introduces a planned digression built around his personal example to increase the effectiveness of the argument. As J. Jeremias says of 1 Corinthians 9, 'This whole chapter, from the first to the last verse, is nothing else than an explanatory digression to illustrate the point of 8.13: Paul shows the Corinthians his own behaviour, as a Christian who can forego a right due to him'.[134] Paul has been discussing the Corinthian situation in the second-person plural, but changes to a paradigmatic 'I' statement to model the behaviour he expects the Corinthians to emulate (cf. 5.12; 6.12). The self-characterization in 8.13 both summarizes Paul's argument in ch. 8 and introduces his personal example that is elaborated and developed in ch. 9.[135] Chapter 9 is not an interruption in the argument, but is integral to Paul's style, 'a skillful stylistic device',[136] a planned digression to increase the

---

not being introduced, but see the caution on making this inference in Mitchell, 'Concerning περὶ δέ', pp. 229-58.

134. J. Jeremias, 'Chiasmus in den Paulusbriefen', *ZNW* 49 (1958), pp. 145-56 (156).

135. W.L. Willis, *Idol Meat in Corinth: The Pauline Argument in 1 Corinthians 8 and 10* (SBLDS, 68; Chico, CA: Scholars Press, 1985), pp. 108, 122.

136. Willis, 'Apostolic Apologia', p. 39. B.R. Magee, *A Rhetorical Analysis of First Corinthians 8.1–11.1 and Romans 14.1–15.13* (Ann Arbor: University Microfilms, 1989), pp. 71-77, calls 9.1 a 'sharp break', shifting from deliberative to

effectiveness of the argument.[137] This is now the widely recognized scholarly view.[138]

If we take ch. 9 as part of the larger whole, 'Be imitators of me' (anticipated in 4.16 and reiterated in 11.1) summarizes the function of ch. 9 in the line of argumentation in chs. 8–10 as setting a personal example for the Corinthians in their relations with the 'weak'. Paul introduces this principle in 8.9: 'But take care that this right of yours [ἡ ἐξουσία ὑμῶν] does not somehow become a stumbling block to the weak.' In ch. 9 Paul establishes with an accumulation of short assertions (9.5-12a) his own right to 'to eat and to drink' (9.4), which picks up the vocabulary of 8.8-9 and the argument of 8.7-13. As Meeks points out, in all the warrants for Paul's argument none really points out why Paul does not exercise the right he has so carefully defended. 'He is merely presenting himself as example; all the rest is for emphasis.'[139] Paul's argument in ch. 9 turns on his *refusal* to make use of this well-

---

judicial argumentation against an 'implicit challenge to his apostleship'. Yet, he sees Paul's response more like a 'cross-examination' than a defence, as Paul asked between 11 and 14 rhetorical questions in 9.4-15, depending on how the text is punctuated. Yet, he concedes that the rhetorical claims Paul makes are 'Use self-discipline. Do not insist on exercising your rights' (p. 293), inconsistent with a defence about refusing financial support, and entirely consistent with the assertions in 8.9 and 10.23–11.1 (and 6.12, if read as Paul's).

137. Wuellner, 'Greek Rhetoric', pp. 186-87; D.B. Martin, *Slavery as Salvation: The Metaphor of Slavery in Pauline Christianity* (New Haven: Yale University Press, 1990), p. 77; Mitchell, *Paul and the Rhetoric of Reconciliation*, pp. 237-50.

138. So C. Wolff, *Der erste Brief des Paulus an die Korinther* (THKNT, 7.2; Berlin: Evangelische Verlagsanstalt, 1982), pp. 16-35; Willis, 'Apostolic Apologia'; H.P. Nasuti, 'The Woes of the Prophets and the Rights of the Apostle: The Internal Dynamics of 1 Corinthians 9', *CBQ* 50 (1988), pp. 246-64; Stowers, *Letter Writing*, pp. 108, 173; A.J. Malherbe, *Moral Exhortation: A Greco-Roman Sourcebook* (LEC; ed. W. Meeks; Philadelphia: Westminster Press, 1986), pp. 129-30; Martin, *Slavery as Salvation*, pp. 68-80, 140-45; H. Probst, *Paulus und der Brief: Die Rhetorik des antiken Briefes als Form der paulinischen Korintherkorrespondenz (1 Kor. 8–10)* (WUNT, 2.45; Tübingen: J.C.B. Mohr [Paul Siebeck], 1991), pp. 152-99; Meeks, *The First Urban Christians*, p. 99; P.D. Gooch, *Dangerous Food: 1 Corinthians 8–10 in its Context* (SCJ, 5; Waterloo, ON: Wilfred Laurier University Press, 1993), pp. 49-52. Cf. Hurd, *The Origin of 1 Corinthians*, pp. 70-71.

139. W.A. Meeks, *The Moral World of the First Christians* (London: SPCK, 1987), pp. 134-35. Similarly, L.T. Johnson, *The Writings of the New Testament: An Interpretation* (Philadelphia: Fortress Press, 1986), p. 282.

3. *Paul, Spiritual Parent and Paradigm in Christ* 101

established right (9.12b, 15, 18), a refusal that he relates to his missionary aim in 9.19-23 and sums up in the athletic imagery of self-discipline and self-denial in 9.24-27. The message to the Corinthians appears to be an ethical principle that, even though they have certain well-established rights and freedom to eat meat sacrificed to idols, there are cases when love for others in the church requires self-denial, that they should not claim all their rights nor exercise all their freedom. Thus Paul presents himself as 'a personal example for renunciation of freedom'.[140] It should be noted here that if we read 6.12 as entirely Pauline then Paul presents himself there too as an example of the renunciation of freedom. The recapitulation in 10.23–11.1 makes the same emphasis and further supports the exemplary function of ch. 9, restating the argument of chs. 8 and 9 point by point.[141]

With the context in view, this is how ch. 9 reads, developing the paradigmatic self-expression of 8.13:

> Consider these two contradictory facts in my[142] life: I am both self-sufficient[143] and an apostle who has the right to support. You know that I am an apostle because I have seen the Lord and I am the founder of your church. You know apostles have the right to support for several reasons. This is the practice of the other apostles, notably the brothers of the Lord and Cephas [9.1-5]. You count Barnabas and me among them [9.6]. Soldiers, farmers, and shepherds have such a right to gain support [9.7]. The scriptures grant us this right [9.8-10].[144] It is well established that we have a right to support [9.11-12a]. And now this is the example we have set for you: *We have not made use of our right!* [9.12b].[145] Let me add that the temple servants have a right to support from their work

---

140. Wolff, *Der erste Brief*, pp. 16-35; G. Dautzenberg, 'Der Verzicht auf das apostolische Unterhaltsrecht: Eine exegetische Untersuchung zu 1 Kor 9', *Bib* 50 (1969), pp. 212-32.

141. As demonstrated by Hurd, *The Origin of 1 Corinthians*, pp. 128-30.

142. Characteristic of Paul's epistolary style, there is fluidity between 'I' and 'we' (contra Carrez, 'Le "nous" en 2 Corinthiens', pp. 474-86).

143. ἐλεύθερος was an important *topos* for the Cynic-Stoic itinerant philosophers who valued self-sufficiency. Cf. Epictetus, *Diss.* 3.22.48; and Phil. 4.11, 'I have learned in whatever state I am, to be content (αὐτάρκης εἶναι)'. 'The connection here with the philosophical tradition of the αὐτάρκεια of the wise man is unmistakable: Socrates too was considered αὐτάρκης καὶ σεμνός (Diogenes Laertius 2.24)', Theissen, *The Social Setting*, p. 39.

144. See D.I. Brewer, '1 Corinthians 9.9-11: A Literal Interpretation of "Do not muzzle the ox"', *NTS* 38 (1992), pp. 554-65.

145. Rendering the strongly adversative 'ἀλλ' οὐκ as emphatic.

[9.13], and that the Lord himself has commanded that the churches support missionaries [9.14]. We have the strongest possible case for receiving material support from you, *but I have not laid claim to this right!* [9.15-18]. For the sake of the gospel I give up my rights on behalf of any who may be 'weak'[146] [9.19-22]. I exhort you to exercise this same self-control for the sake of the weak and for the sake of the gospel [9.23-27].

If we are to accept this reading, we must explain why Paul casts this paradigmatic exhortation on idol meat in the form of an ἀπολογία. An explanation with two components may be given. The first is stylistic. There are several characteristic diatribal elements from 8.10: (1) the second-person singular is used (8.10-11); (2) there is a sudden turning to address an imaginary interlocutor in 9.1; (3) there are a series of rhetorical questions after turning to the imaginary interlocutor;[147] (4) and, as in Rom. 2.1-3; 9.20; 14.4, Paul specifies the interlocutor with a form of the participle κρίνων (9.3).[148] Reference to 'those who would closely examine me' (τοῖς ἐμὲ ἀνακρίνουσίν) is proleptic, rhetorically anticipating and answering objections before they were raised by the Corinthians.[149] Characteristic of the diatribal style in answering potential objections, Paul refers to his own example and situation, cites authoritative quotations and utilizes single-point analogies.[150] The purpose here is not to demonstrate that ch. 9 is 'diatribe' since there is a looseness and variability of usage of diatribal elements in anticipating and answering objections in argumentation.[151] The function of these diatribal elements in 1 Corinthians 9 is to concretize and sharpen the

---

146. I.e. 'any whom I seek to win for Christ', including both Jews and Greeks, so D.A. Black, 'A Note on "the Weak" in 1 Corinthians 9.22', *Bib* 64 (1983), pp. 240-42; see also his *Paul, Apostle of Weakness: Astheneia and its Cognates in the Pauline Literature* (AUS, 3; New York: Peter Lang, 1984), pp. 84-172.

147. Stowers, *The Diatribe*, pp. 49-77, thinks that rhetorical questions are part of Paul's pastoral technique, having an educational rather than a polemical function. He points out that there are more than 100 rhetorical questions in 1 Corinthians and 20 in ch. 9, the highest concentration of rhetorical questions in the New Testament.

148. Stowers, *The Diatribe*, p. 100.

149. Regarding method, J.L. Sumney rightly says that 'since questions which necessitate a defense can arise without direct opposition, an apology does not require the existence of opponents per se' (*Identifying Paul's Opponents: The Question of Method in 2 Corinthians* [JSNTSup, 40; Sheffield: JSOT Press, 1990], p. 101).

150. Stowers, *The Diatribe*, pp. 131-32.

151. Stowers, *The Diatribe*, p. 129.

3. *Paul, Spiritual Parent and Paradigm in Christ*   103

point of the argumentation, making Paul's self-presentation vivid and engaging.

A second component explaining why ch. 9 is cast as a fictitious defence may lie in the demands of the etiquette surrounding self-discussion and self-praise. Paul implies bold claims about himself in this chapter: 'I am free', 'I am an apostle', 'I have seen Jesus our Lord', 'I am on par with the notable apostles who were with Jesus', and 'I decline a right to financial support that is well established and incontestable'. These implied assertions, concentrated as they are, may have sounded boastful to the Corinthians, drawing upon Paul the odium attached to περιαυτολογία ('self-discussion') in antiquity. Aristotle speaks for Hellenists when he identifies self-praise as dishonourable and shameful as throwing away one's shield, withholding a deposit, illicit relations and making profits on the backs of the weak:

> And to speak at great length about oneself and to make all kinds of professions, and to take credit for what another has done; for this is a sign of boastfulness. Similarly, in regard to each of the other vices of character, the acts resulting from them, their signs, and the things which resemble them, all these are disgraceful, and should make us ashamed.[152]

This stigma attached to self-discussion persisted through the time of Paul's writing, and may further explain why Paul frames ch. 9 in the style of a defence, and may indicate a socially stipulated rhetorical function of other features of his self-presentation in ch. 9.

Plutarch writes of the 'antidotes' to remove the shame of self-praise in his 'On Praising Oneself Inoffensively'.[153] Self-praise is made palatable if the speaker

1. responds to a situation of slander;
2. offers a defence against charges (ἀπολογία);
3. does so because of compulsion (ἀνάγκη);
4. describes triumph over adversity or peril;
5. includes personal shortcomings;
6. credits god or luck for success; or
7. demonstrates that the goal of the self-discussion is the good of others by providing for them a personal example to encourage, admonish or instruct them.

---

152. Aristotle, *Rhet.* 2.6.11-12.
153. Plutarch, *Mor.* 7.539-47.

This last 'antidote' is significant for the interpretation of 1 Corinthians 9 given here, and is worth citing at length:

> It is not enough, however, to praise ourselves without giving offence and arousing envy; there should be some use and advantage in it as well, that we may appear not merely to be intent on praise, but to have some further end in view. Consider first, then, whether a man might praise himself to exhort his hearers and inspire them with emulation and ambition, as Nestor by recounting his own exploits and battles incited Patroclus and roused the nine champions to offer themselves for the single combat. For exhortation that includes action as well as argument and presents the speaker's own example and challenge is endued with life: it arouses and spurs the hearer, and not only awakens his ardour and fixes his purpose, but also affords him hope that the end can be attained and is not impossible.[154]

This latter reason is most reflected in letters. Pseudo-Demetrius (1 BCE to 1 CE) says, 'The letter, like the dialogue, should abound in glimpses of character. It may be said that everybody reveals his own soul in his letters. In every other form of composition it is possible to discern the writer's character, but none so clearly as in the epistolary.'[155]

Plutarch's essay (1–2 CE) reflects a common discussion of rhetoricians, dating back to Demosthenes' 'On the Crown' (330 BCE),[156] and before him to Aristotle. Plutarch discusses rhetoric proper, but this 'queen of the subjects' influenced all subjects in Hellenistic education, including letter-writing. 'Reading was done aloud, so that there was no borderline between the written and spoken word; the result was that the categories of eloquence were imposed on every form of mental activity.'[157] The discussion among rhetoricians is reflected in epistolary theory, though epistolary handbooks were not part of a rhetorical system. Cicero, for example, displays many points of contact with Greek epistolary theory, indicative of how interwoven Greek and Latin rhetoric and epistolary theory were by that time.[158] At least Paul's amanuensis, probably trained in letter-writing and therefore rhetoric, would be

---

154. Plutarch, *Mor.* 7.544D-E.
155. Pseudo-Demetrius, *On Style*.
156. Demosthenes, *De Cor.* 4, 101, 128, 321.
157. H.-I. Marrou, *A History of Education in Antiquity* (trans. G. Lamb; London: Sheed & Ward, 1956), p. 195.
158. A.J. Malherbe, *Ancient Epistolary Theorists* (Atlanta: Scholars Press, 1988), pp. 1-11.

3. *Paul, Spiritual Parent and Paradigm in Christ*

familiar with these customs regarding self-discussion and with other conventions of letter-writing studied in the schools.[159]

Reducing the offence of self-boasting was a social convention undergirded by Hellenistic religious anxiety. It was feared that human success could provoke divine jealousy and punishment. Boasting about such success was sure to offend the heavens and subject one to supernatural danger. This religious anxiety and the rhetorical conventions that sprung from it help explain the importance of the conventions that Plutarch describes.[160]

We find three of Plutarch's antidotes to boasting in 1 Corinthians 9, and this may help explain why Paul frames ch. 9 as a defence. The literary device of defence (2) is used in 9.3,[161] the reason of necessity or compulsion (3) is explicitly mentioned in 9.16, and ch. 9 provides an example for instruction (7) in the issues of chs. 8 and 10. Furthermore, the enigmatic shift at 9.15 is explained. We now turn to this part of ch. 9.

1 Corinthians 9.15b-18 introduces Paul's self-presentation as a slave of Christ that runs through 9.23. By claiming to be compelled in his self-supported work, Paul now mitigates the offence of his self-discussion in 9.1-15. 1 Corinthians 9.15b-18 is not superfluous to the chapter,[162] but serves an important social function necessary since Paul has boasted about himself.[163] He has 'boasted' that he is free, an apostle, a witness to the resurrected Jesus and entitled to support that he does not claim. At the end of 9.15 he makes explicit that he realizes he has

---

159. For the role of the amanuensis in composition of letters, see E.R. Richards, *The Secretary in the Letters of Paul* (Tübingen: J.C.B. Mohr [Paul Siebeck], 1991). For the consistency of Paul's letters with epistolary theory, see J. White, *Light from Ancient Letters* (Philadelphia: Fortress Press, 1986). For the place of rhetoric in education, see H.-I. Marrou, 'Education and Rhetoric', in M.I. Finley (ed.), *The Legacy of Greece: A New Appraisal* (Oxford: Clarendon Press, 1981), pp. 185-201.

160. Dodds, *The Greeks and the Irrational*, pp. 30-31; H.D. Betz, 'De laude ipsius (Moralia 539A-547F)', in *idem* (ed.), *Plutarch's Ethical Writings and Early Christian Literature* (Leiden: E.J. Brill, 1978), pp. 367-93.

161. Betz, 'De laude ipsius', pp. 386-87.

162. Contra E. Käsemann, 'A Pauline Version of the *Amor Fati*', in *idem, New Testament Questions of Today* (trans. W. Montague; London: SCM Press, 1969 [1959]), pp. 217-35.

163. Sandnes, *Paul—One of the Prophets?*, pp. 118, 129-30, notes that these verses define καύχημα, and he draws attention to the tradition of biblical prophets who were obliged to prophesy lest they fall under God's judgment.

boasted, a point already grating against the auditors' sensibilities.[164] Plutarch exhorts those who would discuss themselves 'to remember the distaste and vexation that was felt by all: no other kind of talk is so odious or offensive'.[165] In 9.15 Paul may display an awareness of this Hellenistic etiquette. The offence of boasting is mitigated in 9.16-18a for the reason of ἀνάγκη.[166] This does not make his assertion in these verses any less sincere, but provides a socially necessary alleviation of the negative feelings that his self-discussion would arouse.[167]

Beginning with ἀνάγκη in 9.16 Paul portrays himself as a 'slave of Christ' which he develops in the verses that follow (17-23), a common self-portrayal for him.[168] We may draw a triangle between the three features of Paul's self-portrait as a 'slave of Christ', the parallel of 1 Cor. 9.16 with Jer. 20.9 as an example of someone being entrusted with a commission leading to compulsory speaking, and the common association of ἀνάγκη with slavery and subservience.[169] Slavery to Christ is a significant aspect of Paul's self-understanding (see ch. 4 below under Gal. 1.10), and is one of his key metaphors for salvation (Rom. 8.15-17; Gal. 6–7; cf. Exod. 6.7). He has already introduced slavery as a cipher for the Christian life in the letter (1 Cor. 7.22), a metaphor that was commonplace in Hellenistic moral philosophy (Epictetus, *Diss.* 4.1; 2.123) and Hellenistic Judaism (Philo, *Quod Lib.* 21–25; 156–59). In his slavery to Christ the gospel is the controlling feature, not the communities that Paul serves (9.19; cf. 2 Cor. 4.5; Gal. 1.10; Phlm. 1,

---

164. On the broken syntax in this verse, see R.L. Omanson, 'Some Comments about Style and Meaning: 1 Corinthians 9.15 and 7.10', *The Bible Translator* 34 (1983), pp. 135-39.

165. Plutarch, *Mor.* 7.547D.

166. A word that S. Kreuzer, 'Der Zwang des Boten—Beobachtungen zu Lk 14.23 und 1 Kor 9.16', *ZNW* 76 (1985), pp. 123-28, identifies as 'Fremdkörper' in Paul, and lays out the possible explanations. Against him it must be said that ἀνάγκη appears often in Paul (Rom. 13.5; 1 Cor. 7.26, 37; 9.16; 12.22; 2 Cor. 6.4; 9.5, 7; 12.10; Gal. 2.14; 6.12; Phil. 1.24; 2.25; 1 Thess. 3.7; Phlm. 14).

167. It must be noted that 'boasting' has a different emphasis here than it does in 1 Cor. 1.29, 31; 3.21; 4.7; and 5.6, which reflect the citation of Jer. 9.22-23 in 1.31. See further, C.K. Barrett, 'Boasting (καυχᾶσθαι, κτλ.) in the Pauline Epistles', in Vanhoye (ed.), *L'Apôtre Paul*, pp. 363-68.

168. Martin, *Slavery as Salvation*, pp. 82-83; so also Kreuzer, 'Der Zwang des Boten', p. 127.

169. H. Schreckenberg, *ANANKE, Untersuchungen zur Geschichte des Wortgebrauchs* (Zetemata, 36; Munich: C.H. Beck'sche, 1964), pp. 1-36, 49-54.

9, 13). Paul plays on the theme of the chapter in 9.17-18 to exemplify that he renounced wages because of his slave-like commitment to spreading the gospel.

9.19-23 returns to Paul's use of self-exemplification to persuade the strong to modify their behaviour to avoid offending the 'weak'. In the flow of ch. 9, Paul's example in 9.19-23 again re-emphasizes self-curtailment for the sake of others and on account of the gospel. The target audience is the 'strong' who feel free to eat idol food. As W.L. Willis says, 'The best commentary on both 8.13 and 11.1 is 9.19-23 where Paul stresses his willingness to forego any privileges for the good of others'.[170]

9.19 begins with ἐλεύθερος, picking up the implied affirmative answer to his rhetorical question in 9.1, forming an *inclusio*. ἐλεύθερος in 9.1 refers to Paul's freedom from financial support, which he clarifies in 9.15 and reiterates in 9.18-19.[171] 9.19-23 is part of Paul's exhortation to imitation, similar to 10.31–11.1.[172] Paul asserts, not the 'principle of accommodation',[173] but the personal cost of serving the gospel, a price

---

170. Willis, *Idol Meat in Corinth*, p. 289.

171. Cf. 2 Cor. 11.7. In 1 Thess. 2.5-12 Paul claims he supported himself so that he could avoid the charge that he preached for financial gain, and so that he would not be a financial burden on his churches. It was not part of his preconceived strategy to combat divisions, since this was Paul's practice in Corinth before the divisions (contra H.L. Ellison, 'Paul and the Law—"All Things to All Men"', in W.W. Gasque and R.P. Martin [eds.], *Apostolic History and the Gospel: Biblical and Historical Essays Presented to F.F. Bruce on his 60th Birthday* [Grand Rapids: Eerdmans, 1970], pp. 195-202 [201]). However, 9.19 may indicate that in retrospect Paul saw the value of his practice in combating divisions.

172. Fiore, *The Function of Personal Example*, p. 181.

173. Much of the interest in vv. 19-23 has to do with 'Paul's inconsistency', overlooking the important rhetorical function of these verses and their context. On one side, P. Lapide criticizes Paul for this 'tactical approach to salvation': 'in other words, he was willing to sacrifice valid principles for the sake of propagandistic purposes', P. Lapide and P. Stuhlmacher, *Paul: Rabbi and Apostle* (trans. L. Denef; Minneapolis: Augsburg, 1984), p. 53. On the other side, see P. Richardson, 'Pauline Inconsistency: 1 Corinthians 9.19-23 and Galatians 2.11-14', *NTS* 26 (1979-80), pp. 347-62; D.A. Carson, 'Pauline Inconsistency: Reflections on 1 Corinthians 9.19-23 and Galatians 2.11-14', *Churchman: Journal of Anglican Theology* 110 (1986), pp. 6-45. B. Hall demonstrates the connections of 9.19-23 with chs. 7–10, but overlooks the consistency of these verses with the rest of ch. 9. For example, she sees 9.19-22 as a self-contained chiasm and v. 23 as an unnecessary addition, 'introducing a note not yet sounded' ('All Things to All People: A Study of 1

he wants the Corinthians to pay by foregoing idol meat. As D.B. Martin writes, 'Analysis of these verses reveals that these different exegetical problems are of a piece; they are not to be addressed, as has sometimes been done, as disparate issues. Furthermore, this analysis shows the necessary rhetorical connections between the various motifs of 9.19-23 and 9.1-18...'[174]

For this reason, Marshall cannot be correct that 9.19-23 reflects a charge sheet against Paul. In Marshall's view, 9.19-23 functions as invective against those who charged him as 'the servile flatterer, the one who deliberately adapts his conduct to that of others for his own ends'.[175] On the contrary, in 9.19-23 Paul himself provides the very grounds for such an accusation against him. It is difficult to see how this is a defence on Paul's part. If there were such charges against Paul current in Corinth he foolishly sows here further seeds of his own undoing.[176]

The athletic imagery of 9.24-27 offers another argument for self-denial, and these verses are the climactic summary of Paul's personal example in ch. 9. Paul appeals to a shared value that those resident in the host city of the Isthmian and Nemean games would recognize in the self-renunciation and training of an athlete.[177] He makes a similar appeal in Phil. 3.10-17 which like 1 Cor. 9.24-27 has the elements of exhortation, suffering, athletic imagery of pressing on to the goal, and imitation. In our text, the imagery performs the function of a peroration, to stir the Corinthians to restrict their own personal liberty in following

---

Corinthians 9.19-23', in R. Fortna and B. Gaventa [eds.], *The Conversation Continues: Studies in Paul and John in Honor of J. Louis Martyn* [Nashville: Abingdon Press, 1990], pp. 137-57 [138]). However, 9.23 is the punchline of this paragraph, connecting vv. 19-22 to Paul's overall self-exemplification in ch. 9.

174. Martin, *Slavery as Salvation*, p. 118; see his extended argument on vv. 19-23, pp. 117-35.

175. Marshall, *Enmity in Corinth*, p. 309. Marshall follows H. Chadwick, '"All Things to All Men" (1 Cor. 9.22)', *NTS* 1 (1954–55), pp. 261-75. What is a 'possibility' for Chadwick (p. 263) becomes the controlling principle of reconstruction and exegesis for Marshall.

176. Richardson, 'Pauline Inconsistency', p. 361 n. 41.

177. Wuellner, 'Paul as Pastor', p. 64. V.C. Pfitzner, *Paul and the Agon Motif* (SNT, 16; Leiden: E.J. Brill, 1967), pp. 16-75, demonstrates that the agōn motif and terminology was a common image in both Graeco-Roman and Hellenistic Jewish literature, including in the LXX.

3. *Paul, Spiritual Parent and Paradigm in Christ* 109

Paul's example.¹⁷⁸ The general analogy of self-renunciation of the athlete in training in 9.24 is turned into a direct exhortation (οὕτως τρέχετε ἵνα καταλάβητε), and this exhortation is underlined by Paul's use of his own personal example in 9.26, 'indeed so I run' (ἐγὼ τοίνυν οὕτως τρέχω), consistent with the hortatory function of Paul's self-presentation throughout this chapter. We should resist Conzelmann's notion, 'We are not altogether prepared for the transition to the person of Paul, the return to self-presentation, but it is understandable in the light of the underlying idea of example'.¹⁷⁹ Paul never strays far from self-presentation in ch. 9 for his hortatory purpose. Robertson and Plummer also overlook this point when they write, 'Instead of going on with his exhortation to others, he looks to himself. *He* cannot dispense with painful effort.'¹⁸⁰ On the contrary, the importance of self-chosen discomfort on behalf of others and the gospel *is* Paul's exhortation to the Corinthians. The object of emulation is summed up with the words 'in everything he exercises self-control' (πάντα ἐγκρατεύεται, v. 25),¹⁸¹ the attitude Paul wants the Corinthians to adopt toward idol meat.

Paul does not violate etiquette against self-boasting in 9.24-27. After the self-humbling of 9.15-23 Paul's 'boast' is appropriate since he presents himself as one of the unfortunate slaves who has a right to rise up in the midst of adversity as a boxer (9.26). Plutarch dispenses just such an antidote for the malady of self-praise:

> And so, just as we regard those who strut on a walk and hold up their chin as fatuous and vain, but when in boxing or fighting men rise to their full height and hold the head erect, we applaud; so the man cast down by fortune, when he stands upright in fighting posture
> Like a boxer closing in,
> using self-glorification to pass from a humbled and piteous state to an attitude of triumph and pride, strikes us not as offensive or bold, but as great and indomitable.¹⁸²

In this way Paul concludes the self-exemplification of ch. 9 with a rhetorically effective and non-offensive *peroratio*. His self-characterization and personal example in 9.24-27 serves as a piece and summary of his

178. Pfitzner, *Paul and the Agon Motif*, p. 98.
179. Conzelmann, *1 Corinthians*, p. 162.
180. Robertson and Plummer, *First Epistle of St Paul to the Corinthians*, p. 196.
181. Pfitzner, *Paul and the Agon Motif*, pp. 85-96.
182. Plutarch, 'On Praising Oneself Inoffensively', *Mor.* 7.541B.

overall argument and appeal to self-control and self-denial of idol meat to maintain the unity and health of the church. All the while 'in the background stands the paraenetic motif, μιμηταί μου γίνεσθε, "become imitators of me" (11.1)'.[183] The use of personal example in the letter and the attendant social demands of self-discussion help give a sense of coherency to 1 Corinthians 9, and help us identify the chapter's designed place within the letter as a whole. Although some scholars have made sense of 1 Corinthians 9 by positing antagonistic charges against Paul current in Corinth, the imitation theme and the etiquette of self-discussion make good sense of the parts of this chapter also. My discussion of 1 Corinthians 9 is related to Paul's epistolary usage of paradigmatic self-presentation at the peroration found at the end of this section of the letter, in 10.29–11.2. To Paul's use of self-exemplification in this text I now turn.

1 Corinthians 10.29–11.2

At the end of ch. 10 Paul again uses paradigmatic 'I' statements to concretize and underline his exhortation. He turns to this technique after further developing his case against idol foods by arguing from Scripture (10.1-11, 25-26), tradition (10.16), analogy (10.16-18) and principle (10.31-33).[184] Chapters 8–10 are summarized in the closing section of 10.23–11.2, which is a point-by-point restatement and summary of the argument from 8.1.[185] As such it is a peroration, powerfully summarizing the foregoing and exhorting the Corinthians to action.[186] Key words in this section are sprinkled throughout chs. 8–10. 'Freedom' (ἐλευθερία) is present in 9.1, 19; 10.29; 'judge' (κρίνω) in 10.15,

---

183. Conzelmann, *1 Corinthians*, p. 162; cf. Barrett, *First Epistle to the Corinthians*, p. 218.

184. For a discussion and suggested resolutions of the tensions between chs. 8 and 10, see Willis, *Idol Meat in Corinth*; Probst, *Paulus und der Brief*; and Gooch, *Dangerous Food*.

185. As Hurd has demonstrated, *The Origin of 1 Corinthians*, pp. 128-30. However, he interprets this in light of a 'charge' against Paul that he had been denounced for having eaten meat offered to idols.

186. So Probst, *Paulus und der Brief*, pp. 293-94. D.F. Watson, '1 Corinthians 10.23–11.1 in the Light of Greco-Roman Rhetoric: The Role of Rhetorical Questions', *JBL* 108 (1989), pp. 301-18, offers a finely nuanced identification of rhetorical conventions in this passage. E.g. 10.23–11.1 may be classified as either 'accumulation' or *enumeratio*, that type of *peroratio* in which the points that have been made throughout the 'speech' are gathered together at the conclusion (pp. 311-12).

3. *Paul, Spiritual Parent and Paradigm in Christ*

29; 'conscience' (συνείδησις) in 8.7-12; 10.25, 27, 28, 29; and 'edify' (οἰκοδομεῖ) in 8.1, 10; 10.23. The focus remains on 'the common good' (τὸ σύμφορον) as a limitation of freedom in order that others may be saved (10.33).

Paul concludes this section with two paradigmatic 'I' expressions (10.29b-30 and 10.33–11.2) which are interwoven with the whole of 10.23–11.2. In 10.29-30 we find another sudden shift to the first-person singular where Paul's pithy 'I' statement functions as a hortatory exemplification for his auditors (cf. 5.12; 6.12; 8.13). He shifts back to the second-person plural in 10.31-32 to make his point explicit. He again changes back to the first-person singular in 10.33, forming a readily apparent *inclusio* with 10.23-24 and restating 9.19-23 with its focus upon what is beneficial to and leads to the salvation of those in the community. In 11.1-2, 'I' and 'you (plural)' are woven together, as the italics highlight:

> But if someone says to *you*, 'This has been offered in sacrifice', then do not eat it, out of consideration for the one who informed *you*, and for the sake of conscience—I mean the other's conscience, not *your own*. For why should *my* liberty be subject to the judgement of someone else's conscience? If *I* partake with thankfulness, why should *I* be denounced because of that for which *I* give thanks? So, whether *you* eat or drink, or whatever *you* do, do everything for the glory of God. Give no offence to Jews or to Greeks or to the church of God, just as *I* try to please everyone in everything *I* do, not seeking *my own* advantage, but that of many, so that they may be saved. Be imitators of me, as I am of Christ (1 Cor. 10.28–11.1).

Paul's 'I' appears as a stylistic way of making the exhortation effective where he speaks for the reader as a kind of epistolary ventriloquist, placing the words on their lips that will hopefully express their future commitment. This is a subtle but effective rhetorical technique.

D.F. Watson has provided us with a detailed rhetorical analysis of 10.23–11.1, and has treated the two rhetorical questions of vv. 29b-30. These questions are awkward, 'the major stumbling block to determining the flow of argument in this section'.[187] Watson summarizes three main ways scholars have understood these rhetorical questions, and argues persuasively against all three:[188] (1) Paul portrays, in diatribe

---

187. Watson, '1 Corinthians 10.23–11.1', p. 308.
188. Watson, '1 Corinthians 10.23–11.1', pp. 308-10. Two other possibilities must be excluded on the lack of evidence: (1) these verses are a later scribal gloss,

fashion, the objections he anticipates that the 'strong' will raise to the restrictions he imposes in vv. 28-29b. Against this view, what follows does not provide a response to the questions set forth, the questions are not formed in the second-person singular, and they are not used as indictment.[189] (2) Paul admonishes the 'weak' to consider the position of the strong and not take advantage of it. This is unlikely in light of 8.13; 9.19-23 and 10.24, 'which treat the position of the weak as legitimate concern and do not imply that they were using their position of conscience in an aggressive fashion warranting reprimand'.[190] (3) These questions further elaborate the restrictions of vv. 28-29a, either by defining freedom of conscience as an internal quality, or by providing further reasons for the restrictions of 10.28-29a. Against the former, 'conscience' in antiquity was a judge of action according to set norms, and not the modern notion of an internal quality of subjective freedom.[191] Also, 10.29b-30 does not further explain vv. 28-29a, since this renders Paul's response as feeble, concerned only for the strong to avoid the verbal abuse of the weak.

Watson offers a different explanation based on the observation that the rhetorical questions of 10.29b-30 occur in a section that recapitulates the preceding argument. On the basis of the prescribed function of rhetorical questions in recapitulation in Graeco-Roman rhetoric, there are five rhetorical conventions that may illuminate the rhetorical function of 10.29b-30: (a) *proserotonta*, the use of questions in recapitulation to pit one's strongest points against the weakest points of one's opponents; (b) anticipation, anticipating objections and sweeping them aside; (c) argumentation, where the questions further buffer a premise that may be disputed or introduce an assumption; (d) figures of thought asked, not to gain information, but to emphasize a point; (e) ornament, employing rhetorical questions to add vigour, rapidity and imagination to style. Watson illustrates these in the text, and concludes from the first four that 10.31–11.1 is an indirect response to these questions in 10.29b-30.[192]

---

or (2) are Paul's self-defence against criticism that he ate idol meat while at Corinth, contra Hurd, *The Origin of 1 Corinthians*, pp. 130-31.

189. See Stowers, *The Diatribe*, pp. 85-93, 105-10.

190. Watson, '1 Corinthians 10.23–11.1', p. 310; so also Willis, *Idol Meat in Corinth*, p. 246 n. 117.

191. See von Soden, 'Sacrament and Ethics in Paul', pp. 257-68.

192. Watson, '1 Corinthians 10.23–11.1', pp. 310-18. Watson's method employs

3. Paul, Spiritual Parent and Paradigm in Christ

10.31-32 clearly restates the thesis of chs. 8–10 and answers the questions of 10.29b-30. 10.31 is rhetorically sophisticated, employing euphony (εἴτε οὖν ἐσθίετε εἴτε πίνετε εἴτε τι ποιεῖτε), *epiphora* or *conversio* (the repeated ποιεῖτε at the end of successive phrases), and amplification by accumulation (πάντα in the second part is explained by ἐσθίετε, πίνετε and τι ποιεῖτε in the first part).[193] 10.32 is a refinement of 10.31. Though Paul does not use the term ἀπρόσκοποι in his argument prior to this (and only elsewhere in Phil 1.10), there is nothing new in 'become unoffensive (ἀπρόσκοποι) both to Jews and to Greeks and to the church of God', concisely summarizing an element of his teaching throughout these chapters.

The prominence of exemplification in the letter naturally culminates in the explicit exhortation to emulation in 11.1, forming an *inclusio* with 4.16. Thus 10.31-11.1 forms a fitting conclusion, comprehensively summing up the argument from 8.1 and exhorting the Corinthians to act on the basis of the argumentation and the example of Paul:

> Just as I also in all things do not seek my own benefit but that of the many so that they may be saved. Become imitators of me just as I also belong to Christ (10.33–11.1).

As a summary of chs. 8–10 this may be understood, 'Follow my example, since I belong to Christ. I do not claim all of my rights, nor do I do everything that is lawful for me. My motivation is to keep others from stumbling over my behaviour and to win many to Christ.' Paul has presented himself as a paradigm, alongside his other arguments, and now he calls the Corinthians to follow his concrete example and obey his instructions in these matters, since he belongs to Christ.[194]

In addition to summarizing chs. 8–10, 11.1 is stated generally enough that it exhorts the Corinthians to conform to Paul's example on the various issues presented from 4.16. And, with the anticipatory thanksgiving of 11.2, the appeal to imitation in 11.1 is broadened to imitate all of

---

classical rhetorical method. Employing the 'new rhetoric' Wuellner considers 10.29 a 'self-deliberating question' that involves the 'universal audience' ('Paul as Pastor', p. 69).

193. See Watson, '1 Corinthians 10.23–11.1', p. 307, for other rhetorical elements here.

194. Contra Castelli, *Imitating Paul*, pp. 111-14, who thinks the object of imitation here 'has no specified content, but refers rather to a gesture which would set Christians apart as Christians' (p. 114).

Paul's teaching and example: 'And I praise you because you remember everything of me, just as I handed on to you the traditions you received'.[195]

From the foregoing two things are clear. First, *Paul characterizes himself as part of his hortatory style.* He applies to himself the message he most wants the Corinthians to hear, so that often 'I' is meant as 'you'.[196] This feature takes on a special nuance in 1 Corinthians 13–14. Secondly, it may now be said that *Paul's paradigmatic usage of 'I' statements is a common feature of his perorations*, as we have seen in 4.9-13, 8.13, 9.24-27 and 10.23–11.2.[197]

1 Corinthians 12.31–14.1
In the next major discussion in the letter Paul's literary usage of personal example again plays a key role. The so-called 'hymn to love' in 1 Corinthians 13 has received attention as a literary composition on its own, and many have noticed that 1 Corinthians 13 refers to other salient issues of the Corinthian situation encountered throughout 1 Corinthians, and thus is related to the entire letter as part of Paul's epistolary paraenesis.[198] The topical connections of glossolalia (13.1) and prophecy (13.2) with chs. 12 and 14 are readily apparent,[199] and the thematic connections with the entire letter are not absent. 'Knowledge'

---

195. 11.1-2 may have a transitional function, both summarizing the foregoing and anticipating the subsequent argument though 11.3, by itself, is a characteristic Pauline introduction to a new topic (θέλω δὲ ὑμᾶς εἰδέναι ὅτι). Thus, παρέδωκα ...τὰς παραδόσεις (11.2) may refer forward to the traditions cited in 11.23-25 and 15.3-11. See O. Hofius, 'Herrenmahl und Herrenmahlsparadosis: Erwägungen zu 1 Kor 11.23b-25', *ZTK* 85 (1988), pp. 371-408; Wegenast, *Das Verständnis der Tradition*, pp. 24-33; G.E. Ladd, 'Revelation and Tradition in Paul', in Gasque and Martin (eds.), *Apostolic History and the Gospel*, pp. 223-30; E.E. Ellis, 'Traditions in 1 Corinthians', *NTS* 32 (1986), pp. 481-502.

196. For this reason it matters little which textual variant is chosen for Rom. 8.2 (σε or με), since the resulting implication is the same if the first-person singular is read in this hortatory fashion.

197. So also Watson, '1 Corinthians 10.23–11.1', pp. 307-308.

198. For the history of interpretation see Wischmeyer, *Der höchste Weg*, pp. 11-16; J.T. Sanders, 'First Corinthians 13: Its Interpretation Since the First World War', *Int* 20 (1966), pp. 159-87.

199. On the relationship of ch. 13 with 'die Charismen' of 12–14, see Wischmeyer, *Der höchste Weg*, pp. 27-38.

(13.2) picks up a catchword of the letter (1.5; 4.9; 8.1, 7, 10, 11; 12.8). 'Boasting', though not the only possible textual reading in 13.3,[200] ties into the thread running through 1.29, 31; 3.21; 4.7; 5.6 (cf. 9.15, 16; 15.31). 'Jealousy' (13.4) recalls a source of their division in 3.3. The notion that love does not seek its own (13.5) reiterates Paul's example in 10.33, and the remark that love does not rejoice at wrong (ἀδικία) may be pointed at the attitude represented in chs. 5 and 6.7-8. The importance of love, most fully expressed in ch. 13, recurs throughout the epistle (2.9; 4.14, 17, 21; 8.1, 3; 14.1; cf. 9.20-21; 10.24). Chapter 13 expresses in memorable lyric what 8.1 states in succinct prose: 'We all have knowledge. Knowledge puffs up, but love upbuilds'—in both cases the Corinthians are being admonished to behave in ways consistent with ἀγάπη.[201] Further, we find the term ἀγάπη at the conclusion of the letter (16.14, 24), uncharacteristic in a Pauline conclusion and *sui generis* in the final verse (16.24), further indication of love's importance as a leitmotif of 1 Corinthians. We may conclude with C.R. Holladay, 'Thus, what actually turns out to be a recurrent theme of the epistle as a whole reaches its fullest and richest expression here' in ch. 13.[202]

The verbal and thematic connections between ch. 13 and the rest of the letter are undeniable, and this is strengthened when we consider that the literary strategy of imitation comes to full flower here as well. Paul's repeated paradigmatic usage of 'I' in 1 Corinthians 13 reflects and develops the usage evident throughout the letter. As Jeremias has observed, 1 Corinthians 13 stands between chs. 12 and 14 in an entirely similar way to how 1 Corinthians 9 functions between chs. 8 and 10,[203]

---

200. The other main variant καυθήσωμαι, 'I may be burned', does not have the strong external attestation of 'boasting', and for internal arguments in favour of 'boasting', see J.H. Petzer, 'Contextual Evidence in Favour of καυχήσωμαι in 1 Corinthians 13.3', *NTS* 35 (1989), pp. 229-53. See also J. Smit, 'Two Puzzles: 1 Corinthians 12.31 and 13.3: A Rhetorical Solution', *NTS* 39 (1993), pp. 246-64, who thinks the case in favour of 'that I may boast' 'leaves little room for doubt'.

201. Sanders, 'First Corinthians 13', p. 159.

202. C.R. Holladay, '1 Corinthians 13: Paul as Apostolic Paradigm', in D. Balch, E. Ferguson and W. Meeks (eds.), *Greeks, Romans, and Christians: Essays in Honor of Abraham J. Malherbe* (Minneapolis: Fortress Press, 1990), pp. 80-98 (94-95).

203. Jeremias, 'Chiasmus in den Paulusbriefen', p. 156. See Holladay, '1 Corinthians 13', pp. 83-84, for a detailed comparison of chs. 8–10 with chs. 12–14.

and O. Wischmeyer has noted that 8.13 is 'an exact parallel to this use of the first person singular'.[204] Thus, exhortation to imitation of Paul's literary exemplification is carried forward in 1 Corinthians 13, and therefore the dense usage of the first-person singular we find in this chapter should not surprise us (25 occurrences in 12.31b–13.13, explicit and implied).

With these broader relationships in mind, we may more readily see the connections of 12.31 with ch. 13.[205] The seven rhetorical questions of 12.29-30 relate to the preceding as a hortatory conclusion, but they also introduce the 'hortatory I' that begins in 12.31b. As we have seen above this shift to the first-person singular is typical of Paul's pedagogy and paraenesis. We should no longer consider such a shift as inexplicably abrupt and justifying theories of interpolation, but rather as characteristic, typical and expected as a part of Paul's argumentative style. It is difficult to suppose that ch. 13 is an interpolation, since it is impossibly awkward to jump from 12.31 to 14.1 or 14.2.[206] Wuellner says:

> Logically Paul could have proceeded from 12.31 immediately to 14.1, just as he could have gone from 1.8 directly to 4.1, but only at a loss of what Perelman calls 'presence' or intensified adherence. To paraphrase Paul's own words: logically it would be lawful, but rhetorically it would not be helpful.

How and when ch. 13 was composed remains a mystery but it is clear that chs. 12–14, as we possess them, are interwoven, and ch. 13 has an affective purpose, 'intensifying adherence' to the teaching of chs. 12 and 14.[207] More importantly, if we loose ch. 13 from its context we eliminate a typical example of Paul's paraenetic style that he himself emphasizes in 4.16, 7.8, 11.1, and again in 12.31b (ὁδὸν ὑμῖν δείκνυμι), and demonstrates throughout 1 Corinthians.

---

204. Wischmeyer, *Der höchste Weg*, p. 91.

205. See R.P. Martin, *The Spirit and the Congregation: Studies in 1 Corinthians 12–15* (Grand Rapids: Eerdmans, 1984), pp. 35-37, for a nuanced reading of 12.31b as a further corrective to pneumatic problem.

206. See J. Smit, 'Argument and Genre of 1 Corinthians 12–14', in T. Olbricht and S. Porter (eds.), *Rhetoric and the New Testament: Essays from the 1992 Heidelberg Conference* (JSNTSup, 90; Sheffield: JSOT Press, 1993), pp. 215-34 (211-30), for rhetorical arguments in favour of the integrity of chs. 12–14.

207. Wuellner, 'Greek Rhetoric', p. 188.

3. *Paul, Spiritual Parent and Paradigm in Christ* 117

'And still I will demonstrate to you a superlative way' (12.31b) introduces ch. 13 in a way that leads us to expect Paul's self-presentation as exemplar.[208] 'Way' (ὁδός) can be a technical term for teaching, and δείκνυμι 'is ordinarily used to refer to that which is graphically concrete or, if not, should be'.[209] Smit says,

> Through the choice of this verb Paul indicates that he switches from deliberative argumentation to a demonstrative excursus. As already noticed earlier, Paul does not reason in this passage. He simply places charismata and love against each other and in three steps demonstrates how useless, devoid of virtue and defective the gifts are as contrasted to love.[210]

Holladay further says of δείκνυμι:

> If it is used here in the normal NT sense, its demonstrative rather than pedagogical force is focal and should be rendered *show* in the sense of 'display', 'point out', or 'demonstrate'. That the phrase can be used in paraenetic contexts where a particular ethical life-style is being promulgated, and indeed in a context where the preacher himself provides the paradigm...On this showing, what follows in 1 Corinthians 13 is less a didactic explanation than it is a paradigmatic exhibition.[211]

---

208. καθ' ὑπερβολὴν ordinarily functions adverbially in Paul (Rom. 7.13; 2 Cor. 1.8; 4.17; Gal. 1.13), but here may be attributive to ὁδός, to be understood as 'a superior way'. Holladay suggests the possibility of taking ὑπερβολὴν as a technical rhetorical term ('1 Corinthians 13', p. 88). In this sense 12.31b might read, 'And now I will show you the way by exaggerated metaphor'. The overstated expressions of 13.1-3 such as 'speaking in the tongues of men and angels', 'knowing all mysteries and having all knowledge' and 'having mountain-moving faith' are indeed hyperbolic and lend support to Holladay's proposal.

Sandnes, *Paul—One of the Prophets?*, p. 101, cannot be correct that Paul introduces this chapter in 12.31 as 'a prophetic revelation transcending that of the Corinthian prophets; a higher prophecy, so to say'. To support this claim, Sandnes turns to putative LXX parallels of 1 Cor. 12.31 in 1 Sam. 12.23; Ps. 32(31).8; Isa. 48.17; cf. *Targ. Isa.* 48.16-17; Jdt. 9–10; *4 Ezra* 4.3, but they are not convincing. For example, Ps. 32.8 (LXX 31.8) is apparently the word of God in the oracle, but it is difficult to envision how 1 Cor. 13.1-3 could be an oracle where God is speaking through the words of Paul since God does not speak in tongues nor prophesies without love. 12.31 is not a 'revelatory introduction', but a paraenetic introduction, not unrelated to 'be imitators of me'. Cf. Smit, 'Two Puzzles', pp. 246-64, for the view that 12.31 is ironic.

209. Holladay, '1 Corinthians 13', p. 87.
210. Smit, 'Argument and Genre', p. 230; cf. Mt. 16.24.
211. Holladay, '1 Corinthians 13', pp. 87-88.

Holladay has made an important observation, even if he draws too sharp a distinction between the paraenetic and pedagogical aspects which are not so easily separated. Paul exhorts *and* educates them by this appeal to the apostolic 'I'.[212] From what follows it is clear that Paul intends to continue his exhortation by turning to himself, and I shall treat these paradigmatic expressions in 1 Corinthians 13 in three sections, vv. 1-3, vv. 4-7 and vv. 8-13.

In 1 Cor. 13.1-3 Paul's use of 'I' takes on a hypothetical persona with the conditional ἐάν repeated five times. As Wischmeyer points out, 13.1-2a immediately gives the impression that Paul's 'I' is a caricature of the Corinthian pneumatics whom he seeks to correct.[213] Represented by Paul's hypothetical 'I' are the pneumatics' overemphasis on glossolalia, prophecy,[214] mysteries and knowledge. 13.2b-3 is not as easily related to the rest of the epistle, but 13.2b could reflect the presence of a rigorous enthusiasm. Wischmeyer identifies 13.1-3 as a polemic against the Corinthian enthusiasts, but not completely loosed from Paul's own personal experience, practice and example. She explains the hortatory function of the 'Ich-Stil' 'I style' here as stylistic, but reflecting Paul's personal experience. Thus she says:

---

212. Similarly Smit, 'Argument and Genre', pp. 230-31, who treats ch. 13 as a 'demonstrative excursus': 'Unlike the other genres, in the demonstrative genre not argumentation but presentation holds sway. The speaker does not raise a question for discussion, but purposefully enlarges or reduces a person or cause so as to influence the valuation of the audience in a positive or negative sense.' See further *idem*, 'The Genre of 1 Corinthians 13 in the Light of Classical Rhetoric', *NovT* 33 (1991), pp. 193-216.

213. Wischmeyer, *Der höchste Weg*, pp. 39-75. However, she sees 'know all knowledge' as an assertion inclusive of all Christians due to Paul's affirmations in 1 Cor. 1.5; Rom. 15.14; 2 Cor. 8.7 (p. 69). Differently Mitchell suggests, 'Perhaps the use of himself as a hypothetical negative example is an attempt by Paul to avoid the impression that he is praising himself' (*Paul and the Rhetoric of Reconciliation*, p. 58 n. 177). I see this function of Paul's self-characterization in chs. 9 and 15, but not here since these characterizations are not praiseworthy, and see below on the open question of whether all these qualities could be said to apply to Paul himself.

214. Sandnes, *Paul—One of the Prophets?*, p. 98, uses religio-historical material to demonstrate the correspondence of 13.2-3 and 12–14 'to how prophetic insight in general was defined in antiquity, namely as the capacity, on the basis of revelation, for insight into all the mysteries of God'. On the other hand, D. Hill, *New Testament Prophecy* (London: Marshall, Morgan & Scott, 1979), p. 136, minimizes 13.2 as a source for understanding prophecy since it is hypothetical.

3. *Paul, Spiritual Parent and Paradigm in Christ*

> Clearly, it is a question not of the purely autobiographical 'I', for example, of 1 Cor. 2.1, nor of a merely stylistic figure in the sense of the diatribal general 'one' clothed in a vivid 'I', thereby investing it with a stark moralistic sense. Instead, it is a question of using a generalized 'I' for axiomatic theological assertions which, of course, is not stripped of autobiographical elements, but Paul directly relates his own person and his own experience to accomplish his theological assertions.[215]

The exhortation is framed around Paul's own person, consistent with the explicit hortatory style of the letter. For this reason, Fiore cannot be accurate in his view that Paul refers to himself here in a generalized way in 1 Corinthians 13 ('I' = 'one').[216] This is not nuanced enough to explain Paul's pattern of bringing his exhortation to bear on the Corinthians situation by using 'I' language, nor does it account for how situation-specific ch. 13 is, framed with the Corinthian church as a reference. Wischmeyer and Holladay make observations that help us nuance our understanding of Paul's hortatory style. Wischmeyer identifies the 'I' language as a caricature of the pneumatic enthusiasts and notes the connections to Paul's own life, a view that Holladay develops much further.

Holladay presses the possibility that each of the seven items 13.1-3 are self-referential in a literal sense, functioning as part of Paul's self-presentation. Holladay argues these 'I' statements represent 'the real Paul', both in the protases and apodoses.[217] Holladay surveys Paul's self-characterization elsewhere as it relates to these verses, but has to force the exegesis at several places to make his hypothesis work. For example, Holladay stretches his exegesis of 'faith that moves mountains' (13.2). For his hypothesis to work, Holladay must show that Paul demonstrates such faith. Holladay reads a Synoptic understanding of 'mountain-moving faith' into 1 Corinthians 13, identifying it as the ability to perform miracles of healing and exorcism in particular. But there is no way for us to know that Paul had this understanding of 'faith' as his own, or that he implies such here. Another example of forced exegesis is Holladay's treatment of Paul's pneumatic ability. We know that Paul practised glossolalia (14.6, 18), but nowhere does he explicitly claim prophetic status (13.2). Instead, it seems that he takes pains to express how the authority of his teaching as an apostle super-

---

215. Wischmeyer, *Der höchste Weg*, pp. 90-91.
216. Fiore, *The Function of Personal Example*, p. 183.
217. Holladay, '1 Corinthians 13', pp. 88-94.

sedes the inspired utterances of Corinthian prophets (14.37;[218] implied in 12.28?).[219]

Holladay's position is strained and unnecessary because of his own observation that these verses are hyperbole. He attempts to bring hyperbole and paradigm together with his statement 'The verses are hypothetical, but they are rendered so because of their hyperbolic form, not because they have an imaginary subject'. And, 'the hyperbole recasts the self-portrait so that each item is stretched to the limit of incredibility because it is recast with the assumptions of the Corinthian enthusiasts'.[220] Thus, in the end, Holladay's 'literal' interpretation converges with Wischmeyer's reading.

Paul sets himself up as the hypothetical foil of his own argument. His 'I', cast hypothetically, provides a backdrop against which to highlight and emphasize the centrality of love above all other gifts. His 'I' is a caricature, based on the outline of the problems he confronts. But it also is an exaggeration and therefore we should not overemphasize the literal aspects since they have been distorted by Paul. Nevertheless, the message Paul most wants the Corinthians to hear is framed around his own person. As we have now observed several times in 1 Corinthians, it is Paul's style sometimes to write 'I' when he really means 'This is what *you* should be/do'. We shall encounter this technique again in the study of Gal. 2.15-21 in the next chapter.

We turn now to the second section of the chapter (13.4-7), which on first glance does not contain self-characterizations since ἀγάπη is the

---

218. J.D.G. Dunn, 'The Responsible Congregation (1 Cor. 14.26-40)', in L. De Lorenzi (ed.), *Charisma und Agape (1 Kor 12–14)* (Rome: Abtei von St Paul vor den Mauern, 1983), pp. 201-36, identifies this as one of Paul's strongest assertions of authority.

219. Likewise, 1 Cor. 2.2-16; 7.40; 14.6; and Gal. 1.15-16 do not require that we assign Paul the title 'prophet'. It is clear that he considered his authority as an apostle as supreme. However, see J.D.G. Dunn, *Jesus and the Spirit* (Philadelphia: Westminster Press, 1975), pp. 171, 230, 279-80, who thinks Paul makes distinctions between his assertion of apostolic authority, and his charismatic exercise of the gift of prophecy. Sandnes, *Paul—One of the Prophets?*, pp. 243-44, concludes that Paul's self-understanding is best described as a 'prophet-like apostolate', standing on the shoulders of the prophets yet different in its christological foundation and commission directed outwards, to the nations. He concedes that Paul nowhere claims to be a prophet. Cf. J.M. Myers and E.D. Freed, 'Is Paul Also among the Prophets?', *Int* 20 (1966), pp. 40-53.

220. '1 Corinthians 13', pp. 93-94.

3. *Paul, Spiritual Parent and Paradigm in Christ* 121

subject. However, Holladay raises the possibility that 13.4-7 implies Paul's self-presentation as an apostolic paradigm. Holladay says, 'The personal paradigm is carried over into the characterization but does not dominate it, because the shift now moves toward its implementation', and thus Paul presents his own behaviour positively and therefore as exemplary.[221] Holladay gathers Paul's statements from elsewhere that describe him as valuing patience, devaluing boastfulness, and so forth. Holladay takes this as a confirmation that in 13.4-7 Paul refers to his own example of love. Against this interpretation, it must be noted that Holladay draws most of his examples from 2 Corinthians. Because of Paul's fierce defence of his apostleship in 2 Corinthians, it is more likely to suppose that he defends his loving nature in 2 Corinthians than it is to think that he anticipates and includes his self-presentation in 2 Corinthians implicitly in 1 Cor. 13.4-7.

There are four observations that we may affirm about 13.4-7:

First, there are elements here that are not alien to the rest of the letter, and the function of these verses is hortatory, calling the Corinthians to behave in a loving manner.[222] Second, in the light of vocabulary in ch. 13 that is used of God in the LXX,[223] 1 Cor. 13.4-7 may be understood as having the qualities of an aretalogy.

Third, there are aspects of 'the real Paul' visible here. Fourth, as Wischmeyer has shown, there is an implied christological dimension throughout ch. 13, including vv. 4-7:

a. Charismata are discussed in the context of σῶμα Χριστοῦ theology in both 1 Corinthians 12 and Romans 12, and are clearly in view in 13.1-2;
b. prophecy exercised in love (13.2) has the goal of παράκλησιν καὶ παραμυθίαν (1 Cor. 14.3), which is well-founded christological ethical instruction in the Pauline letters;
c. 13.3 may be a reference to Jesus' and Paul's missionary practice of self-support and self-sacrifice (4.9-13; ch. 9). It is clear

---

221. Holladay, '1 Corinthians 13', p. 94.
222. Cf. Mitchell, *Paul and the Rhetoric of Reconciliation*, pp. 270-79, who argues that these verses show that Paul was combating not 'merely "Corinthian enthusiasm"', but also factionalism, which she believes is the unifying rhetorical situation throughout the letter.
223. See Wischmeyer, *Der höchste Weg*, pp. 92-116.

that Paul understands his lowliness, weakness and suffering in his missionary enterprise 'as the fulfillment of the cross of Christ' (2 Cor. 4.8-11);

d. πίστις (13.2) and πιστεύειν (13.7) have well-established christological significance in Pauline soteriology;

e. 13.4-7 contains an implicit Christology, most evident in the ideas of faith, hope and love, but also in the other predications of love;

f. a cursory reading of passages such as Rom. 5.1-11; 8.35-39; 2 Cor. 5.14 and Phil. 2.1-11 makes evident that Paul portrays the love of God in Christ similarly to the description of personified love in 1 Corinthians 13;

g. the triad 'faith, hope, love' (13.13) contains an implicit Christology when viewed in the light of Paul's other letters.[224]

Another implied christological aspect of ch. 13 may be that ἀγάπη is identified as a central aspect of the ethic of Jesus in all of the Jesus traditions,[225] a point with which Paul seems to be familiar (e.g. Gal. 5.13-15; 6.2).

We need not play the christological and apostolic aspects of 1 Corinthians 13 against one another. If we take 11.1 as a cue we should not draw too sharp a line between 'christological appeal' and 'apostolic paradigm', nor do we need to distinguish the christological elements from the apostolic example. Paul's appeal to imitation does not always explicitly mention its christological implication (e.g. 4.16), but it seems to be implicit (e.g. 4.17) where it is not explicit (11.1). The clear statement of 11.1 may be tacitly embodied in the rhythmic verse of 13.4-7: 'Follow my example of love, just as you and I are in Christ'. In all these we are drawing inferences, and we should not lose sight of the fact that in 13.4-7 love is what is personified and presented as the highest value, rather than an explicit use of Paul's personal example.

In the final section of 1 Corinthians 13 (vv. 8-13), Paul points to the abiding and therefore central place of love. Wischmeyer develops her exposition of these verses along the lines of Pauline eschatological understanding of 'discontinuity' between the present and the future, and may be correct that ch. 13 also functions to provide an eschatological

---

224. Wischmeyer, *Der höchste Weg*, pp. 48-116.

225. E.g. Mt. 5.43-48; 22.24-40; Mk 12.28-34; Lk. 6.27-38; 10.25-37; Jn 13.34-35; 15.9-17. See Mohrlang, *Matthew and Paul*, pp. 94-110.

revision of the Corinthians' theology by marking an eschatological proviso that all is not yet.[226] 13.11-12 functions differently from 13.1-3. In vv. 1-3 Paul frames himself as the hypothetical actor lacking love (ἐάν + subjunctive). The tension he creates between seemingly good things on the one hand and their bankruptcy without love on the other hand renders his exhortation efficient and effective in heightening the reader's focus on the centrality of love. In the next section (13.4-7) love becomes the subject, the personified paradigm of behaviour. In 13.11-12, the first-person singular construction returns, framed as ὅτε + indicative, giving the impression that this 'I' is the 'real Paul'. If this perception is correct, then Paul as model re-emerges, exemplifying the principles of love in vv. 8-10.

In 13.11, Paul dissociates himself from immature behaviour by placing his self-portrayal in the past tense, 'when I was a child...' In so doing, he plays upon the theme he has developed regarding the mature (1.8; 2.6; 10.11; 13.10; cf. 14.20; 15.24) and the strong (1.25, 27; 4.10; 10.22). And, he establishes himself as the fully developed person who has put away the things that attend immaturity. In so doing he sets himself as the model of how the Corinthians are to progress in their spiritual development from immaturity to true maturity.

At 13.12a the first-person singular of 13.11 changes to the first-person plural, and then in v. 12b back to the first-person singular. We have already identified these alternations as evidence of Paul's stylistic use of 'I' for hortatory ends where 'I' is meant to be taken as 'you', though this technique is rhetorically more effective than the simple equation suggests (5.12; 8.13; 10.28–11.1). Paul identifies with the reader where he can, so in 13.12a he addresses the audience in an inclusive 'we', 'For we see now through a murky glass, but then face to face'. As he alternates back to the first-person singular in v. 12b, he models proper humility toward one's partial knowledge in the present eschatological situation. We cannot help but hear echoes of his exhortation in ch. 8 (8.1, 7, 10, 11) reiterated here against the view that knowledge grants unbridled freedom (cf. 1.5; 4.19; 12.8; 13.2; 13.8; 14.6, 7, 9). 'Love'— and therefore the truly mature person—is not puffed up by knowledge since knowledge is only partial and murky at best.

We need not conflate the differences of the hypothetical rhetoric of vv. 1-3, the paradigmatic appeal to personified love in vv. 4-7, and

226. Wischmeyer, *Der höchste Weg*, pp. 128-44. So also Martin, *The Spirit and the Congregation*, pp. 46-56.

Paul's self-presentation as a model for behaviour and maturity in vv. 11-12. These three different yet related appeals are unified around their desired goal: to see the Corinthians value one another in love over temporary things such as knowledge, prophecy or glossolalia. Though Paul's usage of personal example varies from a hypothetical self-presentation to the 'real Paul', his personal example in its various literary forms continues to be used to ground and exemplify the forward thrust of his exhortation. The variety of Paul's usage of personal example is evident also in the next chapter of 1 Corinthians.

1 Corinthians 14: Paul's 'I' Plays Two Roles

1 Corinthians 14 focuses on the importance of love applied to the specific issue of communication that builds up (οἰκοδομή) the church, a refrain throughout this section (14.3-5, 12, 17, 26). In ch. 14 one may find two uses of Paul's 'I' that I have already identified, functioning to highlight and amplify the central theme that speech should be used to edify others. The first usage is that of 'hypothetical negative example',[227] found in 14.6, 11, 14, and already identified in 13.1-3. In 14.6, Paul's 'I' has an air of reality about it since Paul does speak in tongues (14.18), but he makes himself the hypothetical actor of a scene he wants the Corinthians to avoid since glossolalia unaccompanied by intelligible communication does not benefit others.[228] He applies his teaching about love in ch. 13 to the issue of mutual edification, here posed in a rhetorical question, 'what does it profit you...' (14.6). In v. 11, 'I' is the hypothetical casualty of the Corinthian enthusiasm. In v. 14, 'I' again is a conditional negative example, making personal what vv. 6 and 11 frame in interpersonal terms. Unintelligible pneumatic speech leaves 'my mind unfruitful', and therefore is of lesser value than prophecy, teaching, revelation or knowledge (v. 6). Paul's literary use of 'I' in 1 Cor. 14.6, 11 and 14 functions to highlight and amplify his argument that all things should be done in love (ch. 13), and therefore for mutual edification (14.3-5, 12, 17, 26).

A second use of 'I' in 1 Corinthians 14 is its literal function where Paul presents himself as a model for Corinthian behaviour in 14.15, 18-

---

227. Mitchell, *Paul and the Rhetoric of Reconciliation*, pp. 58-59 and 280.
228. Conzelmann, *1 Corinthians*, p. 235, identifies the use of the first person in v. 6 as a rhetorical usage serving, in diatribe style, as an illustration. Wischmeyer, *Der höchste Weg*, pp. 46-47, generalizes this observation to the whole of ch. 14 as 'einer längeren diatribenartigen Ausführung'.

3. *Paul, Spiritual Parent and Paradigm in Christ* 125

19. In 14.15 Paul again uses his 'I' to present his ethical paradigm for communication that builds up the individual and the church: 'What therefore is the point? I will pray with my spirit and I will pray also with my mind; I will sing with my spirit and I will sing also with my mind.' Wuellner identifies this as an example of the self-deliberating use of a rhetorical question expecting a deontic answer. He suggests that the future tenses are best rendered as ethical 'I must...' or 'I should...' rather than simply 'I will...'[229] Regardless of the grammatical consideration, Paul portrays himself as a model of appropriate behaviour for the Corinthian believers. In vv. 18-19, he again models self-curtailment on behalf of others in the community by expressing a willingness to give up his privilege of speaking in tongues for the benefit and upbuilding of others. The self-curtailment theme so dominant in chs. 7–11 is revisited here. As announced in 4.16, reiterated in 7.8, 11.1 and 12.31b, and utilized throughout the letter, Paul presents himself in 14.15, 18-19 as a literal model for appropriate behaviour,[230] while in 14.6, 11, 14 his 'I' functions in a related literary fashion.

1 Corinthians 15.8-11, 30-32
In the last major topic of 1 Corinthians, Paul's paradigmatic use of 'I' follows what we may now call a predictable pattern, even if it is less prominent than in the other parts of the letter. 1 Corinthians 15 turns to the subject of the resurrection, and Paul's personal example plays a reduced role though it is still present. Whatever the precise nature of the Corinthians' eschatology (see above, Chapter 2, pp. 34-36), Paul multiplies arguments against their view, emphasizing that resurrection comes after physical death. As we should expect of the announced literary strategy, Paul's personal example is used twice among the arguments he garners to make his case (15.8-11, 30-32).[231]

---

229. Wuellner, 'Paul as Pastor', p. 60.
230. So also Mitchell, *Paul and the Rhetoric of Reconciliation*, p. 280. L. Hartman leaves these numerous first-person occurrences unmentioned in his otherwise detailed treatment of 14.1-25, '1 Co 14,1-25: Argument and Some Problems', in L. De Lorenzi (ed.), *Charisma und Agape (1 Kor 12–14)* (Rome: Abtei von St Paul vor den Mauern, 1983), pp. 149-69.
231. If we take the first-person plural of 15.14-15 as a self-characterization cast as an epistolary plural, it is another case of the hypothetical negative example we have examined in chs. 13 and 14.

It is often assumed that Paul was in a defensive position vis-à-vis the Corinthians at the time of his composition of 1 Corinthians and therefore the negative self-characterizations in 15.8-11 are taken to reflect a Corinthian 'charge sheet' against Paul, that he was 'illegitimate, the least of the apostles' (ἐκτρώμα, ὁ ἐλάχιστος τῶν ἀποστόλων) and 'not worthy to be called an apostle' (οὐκ...ἱκανὸς καλεῖσθαι ἀπόστολος). On a pragmatic level it is difficult to imagine how Paul could expect to exercise the authority he asserts in 4.17–5.13 or call the Corinthians to imitate himself throughout the letter if his authority was in question.[232] This is exactly the case in 2 Corinthians where there is no such call to imitation and where Paul's position is clearly in question.

Another approach is to read Paul's self-references in 15.8-11 as a corrective of 15.5-7, leading to a substantially different interpretation. U. Wilckens, for example, argues that Paul's uses a tradition embedded in 1 Cor. 15.5-7 in its secondary purpose of demonstrating the centrality of the resurrection for the whole Christian tradition, when originally the purpose of this tradition was to legitimate ecclesiastical leaders. In Wilckens's view, vv. 8-10 are Paul's polemical and apologetic response to this primary function of vv. 5-7, reflecting the long-lasting presence of F.C. Baur's hypothesis of the Peter–Paul divide in the early church.[233] The main problem with this reading, of course, is that there is no way to verify this supposed original use of the tradition, and it requires that we read against the grain of Paul's use of personal example so prominent in the letter.[234]

Paul is not the subject of 1 Corinthians 15. If we suppose that at this point of the relationship Paul was on fairly firm ground with the Corinthians and extend the trajectory of his usage of personal example in the letter through ch. 15, then 15.8-11 may have a rather different place in the argument of ch. 15 as a whole than an apologetic reading of this

---

232. So also S.J. Hafemann, 'Corinthians, Letters to the', *DPL*, pp. 164-79 (174). He notes that Paul's arguments in chs. 8–10 collapse if the Corinthians do not accept his authority.

233. U. Wilckens, 'Der Ursprung der Überlieferung der Erscheinungen des Auferstandenen: Zur traditionsgeschichtlichen Analyse von 1 Kor 15.1-11', in W. Joest and W. Pannenburg (eds.), *Dogma und Denkstrukturen* (Göttingen: Vandenhoeck & Ruprecht, 1963), pp. 56-95 (62-69).

234. For a critique of Wilckens's view, see J. Plevnik, 'Paul's Appeals to his Damascus Experience and 1 Cor. 15.5-7: Are They Legitimations?', *Toronto Journal of Theology* 4 (1988), pp. 101-11.

3. *Paul, Spiritual Parent and Paradigm in Christ* 127

text allows.[235] The thrust of 15.1-11 focuses on the unity and agreement of Paul's message with the other apostles, a move that he may have needed to make in the face of Corinthian revelation referred to in 14.36-37.[236] Against their claim to revelation Paul identifies with other church leaders of high status to bolster the authority of his teaching by stressing the larger recognition of it. These verses focus not on Paul, but on the apostolic agreement concerning the resurrection. It appears to be Paul's approach to adduce as abundant and convincing an array of witnesses as possible,[237] asserting 'I say nothing that the primitive Church did not also say'.[238] Schütz does not agree: 'It is patently absurd to regard Paul's appeal to resurrection witnesses as bolstering the testimony itself'.[239] Schütz thinks this only makes sense if Jesus' resurrection is in dispute. Against Schütz it may be said that the argument makes sense if Jesus' *death* and resurrection is the leverage point of the argument. Jesus' pattern of resurrection after death is then the prime evidence that resurrection is not simply the spiritualized result of baptism, as some Corinthians apparently believed. Also, Paul emphasizes the *unity* of the apostles' witness as a further legitimation of the teaching in 15.12-58.[240] Schütz cannot be correct that 'Paul would scarcely seek to corroborate that on which there is already agreement'.[241] Paul's argumentation in ch. 9 is a case in point against Schütz, and 15.11 contradicts him, 'therefore whether I or they, so we preached and so you believed'. It is plausible then that 1 Corinthians 15 does multiply arguments in order to correct the Corinthians' eschatology.

---

235. Contra G. Klein, *Die zwölf Apostel: Ursprung und Gehalt einer Idee* (FRLANT, 77; Göttingen: Vandenhoeck & Ruprecht, 1961), pp. 38-43.

236. Martin, *The Spirit and the Congregation*, pp. 88-92.

237. W. Schmithals, *The Office of the Apostle in the Early Church* (trans. J. Steely; Nashville: Abingdon Press, 1969), p. 78; R. Bultmann, *Theology of the New Testament* (trans. K. Grobel; 2 vols.; New York: Charles Scribner's Sons, 1951–55), I, p. 295; D.F. Watson, 'Paul's Rhetorical Strategy in 1 Corinthians 15', in Olbricht and Porter (eds.), *Rhetoric and the New Testament*, pp. 231-49 (242).

238. So Barth, *The Resurrection of the Dead*, p. 154.

239. Schütz, *Anatomy of Apostolic Authority*, p. 95.

240. So P.R. Jones, '1 Corinthians 15.8: Paul the Last Apostle', *TynBul* 36 (1985), pp. 3-34 (29-30).

241. Schütz, *Anatomy of Apostolic Authority*, p. 96. His conclusion, pp. 101-102, is that Paul is not defensive or excursive, but presents himself as an 'apostolic paradigm', 'elaborating apostolic activity in terms of his own experience'.

What then is the origin of Paul's negative self-references in 15.8-9? How do they function in the argument? It has been thought that Paul picks up the 'accusations' against him circulating at Corinth, but this would obfuscate his argument. Is there another way to approach these comments that seem like an aside? The hypothesis presented here is simple. When Paul adds his name to the elite group listed in vv. 5-7, he potentially opens himself to the charge of praising himself, a stigma he is careful never to draw upon himself.[242] In the discussion of self-praise in 1 Corinthians 9 above, some of Plutarch's accepted ways of removing the shame of self-boasting were mentioned, but now one more antidote germane to 1 Cor. 15.8-9 is cited at length:

> Again, as those who would spare the susceptibilities of sufferers from sore eyes temper with shade whatever is unduly brilliant, so some do not present their own praise in all its brilliance and undimmed, but throw in certain minor shortcomings, failures, or faults, thus obviating any effect of displeasure or disapproval. Thus Epeius says after his extravagant talk about boxing and his vaunt that a blow from him would rip clean through the skin and smash the bones:
>
> > Nay is it not enough
> > That I am slack in war?
>
> But he indeed is perhaps ridiculous for mitigating his athlete's bragging by a confession of cowardice and unmanliness. There is tact, however, and grace in one who tells of some slip of his own or some mistake... And in general when faults not altogether degrading or ignoble are set down beside the praise they do away with envy. Many also blunt the edge of envy by occasionally inserting into their own praise a confession even of poverty and indigence or *actually of low birth*.[243]

'Least' and 'last' are obviously self-effacing in 15.8-9,[244] as is ἐκτρ-ωμα, which in the LXX is 'the strongest expression for human wretchedness'. In the other Greek literature it can mean both 'stillborn child' and 'monster', sometimes coupled together.[245] Thus, Paul claims 'low birth'

---

242. So Betz, *Der Apostel Paulus*, pp. 75-79.
243. Plutarch, *Mor.* 7.543F-544B; emphasis added.
244. Mitchell, *Paul and the Rhetoric of Reconciliation*, p. 285, observes that Paul's self-renouncing attitude here 'is entirely consonant with Paul's use of himself as the example of humility and conciliatory self-sacrifice throughout the letter'.
245. J. Munck, 'Paulus Tanquam Abortivus (1 Cor. 15.8)', in A. Higgins (ed.), *New Testament Essays: Studies in Memory of T.W. Manson 1893–1958* (Manchester: Manchester University Press, 1959), pp. 180-93; so also Schütz, *Anatomy of Apostolic Authority*, p. 105. G.W.E. Nickelsburg, 'An ἐκτρώμα, Though Appointed

3. *Paul, Spiritual Parent and Paradigm in Christ* 129

(see italicized last line of citation above) amid a passage that could be misconstrued to include his self-boasting. This is supported by the general interpretation in the patristic exegesis that here Paul speaks of himself with humility,[246] bolstering the hypothesis that these words function to reduce the shame of making claim to such a high status as one of those who had seen Jesus. The function of these self-depreciations in vv. 8-10 may be thought to mitigate the potential charge of self-boasting, and the origin of these comments is Paul or perhaps were suggested by his amanuensis (cf. 16.21).[247]

In 15.30-32 Paul again appeals to his own personal example to bolster his argument. If we take 'I fought with beasts in Ephesus' in a literal sense, Paul was contemplating the end of his life in Ephesus and uses himself as a paradigmatic example of the reality of death as a precondition to resurrection.[248] It is also possible to understand these verses in a figurative sense. θηριομαχεῖν comes from the language of the moralists of Paul's day to describe the wise man's struggle against hedonism, and the passage is in the style of the diatribe.[249] It may be that the Corinthians' over-realized eschatology denied the necessity of death and therefore suffering. This is an issue that comes to the foreground in 2 Cor. 6.3-10 and 11.21-33. In our text, Paul may combine a figurative use of death to imply suffering. In either case, he confronts an over-realized eschatology and his appeals to himself are paradigmatic in his argumentation.

In his rhetorical analysis of ch. 15, Watson classifies 15.29-34 as performing the function of a *peroratio*. As he says:

from the Womb: Paul's Apostolic Self-Description in 1 Corinthians 15 and Galatians 1', *HTR* 79 (1986), pp. 198-205, citing the similarities with Gal. 1, considers this a prophet-like reference to Paul's appointment from the womb, in tension with his lack of realization of his potential at the time he saw Christ on the Damascus road.

246. Munck, 'Paulus Tanquam Abortivus', pp. 189-90.

247. In the scholarly discussion of how Paul could have come to know the conventions of rhetoric, almost no attention is paid to the function, freedom and typical education of the amanuensis, and consequently the possibility is overlooked that when composing his letters Paul had at his disposal an assistant trained in rhetoric. See Richards, *The Secretary in the Letters of Paul*.

248. See Martin, *The Spirit and the Congregation*, pp. 121-23.

249. So Malherbe, 'The Beasts at Ephesus', pp. 71-80. Bünker, *Briefformular*, pp. 69-70 considers it a *peroratio*, expressing indignation toward those who resisted his resurrection teaching in Ephesus.

A *peroratio* can be used at the end of a division of a work and throughout a complicated case, as well as at the conclusion of an entire work. Like the peroratio at the conclusion of a work, vv. 29-34 performs the two main functions of recapitulating the main points of the *probatio* and arousing pathos for the case and against the case of the opposition.[250]

In the case of 15.30-32, Watson identifies Paul's peroration as 'recapitulation from interrogation and logical contradictories', a practice Watson illustrates from the rhetorical handbooks.[251] As we have observed above, Paul commonly uses paradigmatic self-portrayal at the conclusion of an argument in several places in 1 Corinthians (4.9-13; 5.12; 7.25, 40; 8.13; 9.23-27; 10.29-11.1), and the use in 15.30-32 is consistent with this pattern.

Summary

It is now time to draw together the observations of this long and detailed chapter. A close reading of Paul's usage of self-presentation in 1 Cor. 4.14–15.58 substantiates the claim 'Paul's references to himself and his apostolic office in 1 Corinthians are evidences of his rhetorical sophistication'.[252] It has been argued that this strategy is explicit, stated (4.16; 7.8; 11.1; 12.31) and worked out in a systematic yet varied way. In the past, many of Paul's self-references in 1 Corinthians have been interpreted against a background of hypothetical charges. Here it has been argued that Paul's self-characterizations, in their various forms in 1 Corinthians, can be understood as well or better as Paul's designed attempt to use exemplification to clarify and strengthen his argumentation and exhortation. We may now gather together several brief conclusions from the the examination of Paul's literary use of personal example in 1 Corinthians.

First, Paul's literary self-portrayal builds on and affirms his previous teaching and practice (4.16-17; cf. 11.2). Secondly, he models behaviour as a pedagogical technique to demonstrate how appropriate behaviour and thinking looks in the life of this apostle in Christ (e.g. 6.12; 8.13–9.27; 15.30-32), or to set a hypothetical negative example to be avoided (13.1-3; ch. 14).

250. Watson, 'Paul's Rhetorical Strategy', p. 246.
251. Watson, 'Paul's Rhetorical Strategy', p. 247.
252. Wuellner, 'Greek Rhetoric', p. 184.

3. *Paul, Spiritual Parent and Paradigm in Christ* 131

Thirdly, the call to imitation is implicitly (ch. 13), and sometimes explicitly (e.g. 4.15-17; 11.1), a christological appeal. Paul depreciates himself to make a christological emphasis in chs. 1–4, and explicitly qualifies his example as one 'in Christ' (11.1). Fourthly, he uses his personal example as an authoritative model of how to enforce discipline with those who have transgressed his teaching (4.17–5.13).

Fifthly, occasionally Paul's self-portrayal verges on 'self-praise' (1 Cor. 9.1-15; 15.5-8a), which a trained rhetor would know required well-defined antidotes to the odious feeling it would arouse in the auditors. It has been suggested that Paul may offer self-description to offset the shame attached to his self-discussion (9.15-18; 15.8-10). (Mitchell thinks that 2 Cor. 3.1; 4.2; 5.12; 6.4; 10.12, 18 show that the Corinthians interpreted Paul's self-presentation in 1 Corinthians as this culturally odious self-recommendation.[253] There are two points to consider against her suggestion. First, 2 Cor. 10.12, 18 make it seem that the issue of self-recommendation arises for the first time in 2 Corinthians in the light of the intruders who have arrived on the scene. Secondly, it is likely that there is at least one other letter between 1 Corinthians and the canonical 2 Corinthians [2 Cor. 7.8], which must be factored in before we draw a straight line of cause and effect from the first to the second canonical letters. Nevertheless, Paul's extensive use of personal example vanishes as a technique in 2 Corinthians, and 2 Cor. 4.5 may be thought to reflect a Corinthian reaction to his earlier usage of personal example so he must disavow 'we do not preach ourselves, but Jesus Christ and him crucified'. All this is inferential.)

Sixthly, he uses 'I' as a tool for rhetorical effectiveness, hypothetically, paradigmatically and with rhetorical questions. Paul's use of personal example yields clarity and provides vividness and concreteness to the line of argumentation. Next, we find Paul's paradigmatic 'I' often in his perorations, summing up an argument and stirring the readers to appropriate behaviour (4.1-13; 5.12; 8.13; 9.24-27; 10.23–11.1; 15.30-32).

Finally, self-references are used as a warrant in argumentation in 1 Corinthians, as common as Old Testament citations or argumentation by analogy.

Nowhere else is Paul's use of personal example so extensively or explicitly used as it is in 1 Corinthians. However, if we take an awareness of Paul's 'I' style so obvious in 1 Corinthians into a reading of his

---

253. Mitchell, *Paul and the Rhetoric of Reconciliation*, p. 303.

other letters, his self-references there may also be found to function implicitly in similar hortatory and argumentative ways. A case for this implicit literary usage of Paul's personal example in Galatians is the subject of the next chapter.

Chapter 4

GALATIANS: PERSONAL EXAMPLE, CONTRASTIVE MODELS

In Galatians Paul's self-portrayal again plays a central argumentative role, presenting himself as Christ's called and enslaved exemplar of radical indifference to the soteriological necessity of circumcision for Gentile converts. Though we do not find the frequent sprinkling of markers of his literary design as we did in 1 Corinthians (4.6, 16; 7.8; 11.1; 12.31), Gal. 4.12 is one such marker that may refer to Paul's earlier self-exemplification in the letter, a clue that should not be underplayed given that Galatians is replete with usages of his paradigmatic 'I' that we discovered in 1 Corinthians (e.g. Gal. 1.10; 2.15-21; 4.12-20; 5.10-11; 6.14). Additionally, Paul employs the device of comparison (*synkrisis, comparatio*) to drive home further his rhetorical agenda by highlighting his own example and denigrating alternative models (2.4-5, 11-21).

Before I highlight Paul's implicit use of personal example in Galatians, I must first lay out my interpretative assumptions that I bring to the exegetical task. Paul's Galatian churches were confronted by pressure to Judaize, that is, to adopt a characteriztically Jewish lifestyle that included calendrical and food law observance and circumcision. It appears that Paul perceived this front was gaining ground (4.10-11) which elicited his letter to the Galatians, a letter in which he presents himself as one sent and possessed by God, bold, confrontational and confident. In this chapter it is argued that Paul's self-portrayal in Galatians is related to his argumentative purpose to repudiate the soteriological necessity for his readers to Judaize. His appeals to Scripture and the Galatians' experience of the Spirit in chs. 3 and 4 are easily understood against this backdrop, but the autobiographical[1] passage in

---

1. 'Autobiographical' rather than 'autobiography', since its explicit purpose is not a narration of the author's past, a distinction maintained in G. Misch, *A History of Autobiography in Antiquity* (trans. E. Dickes; 2 vols.; London: Routledge &

Galatians 1–2 and the other 'I' sections (4.11-20; 5.10-11; 6.14) are not as universally understood against the letter's rhetorical situation.[2] Paul's self-presentation throughout Galatians offers a third major argument against Judaizing, in addition to his appeals to Scripture and the Galatians' experience. It is understood that Paul's self-depiction in Galatians is polemical[3] and paradigmatic[4] rather than his self-defence against charges.[5] As J.L. Martyn puts it, 'In writing this document Paul remains

Kegan Paul, 3rd edn, 1949–50), and made explicit in Lyons, *Pauline Autobiography*, pp. 18-21. The autobiographies studied by Lyons are quite different in style and form from Paul's autobiographical references in Galatians, and so it is questionable what purpose the comparison serves. For a summary of eight forms of autobiographical writing in antiquity, see K. Berger, 'Hellenistische Gattungen im Neuen Testament', *ANRW*, II.25.2, pp. 1031-432 (1271-74).

2. J.C. Beker seems ambivalent on the relation of the first two chapters to the purpose of the letter. He acknowledges the correlation of the authority of the gospel and the apostle (*Paul the Apostle: The Triumph of God in Life and Thought* [Edinburgh: T. & T. Clark, 1980], pp. 46-47), but then betrays this interdependence when he asserts that in 3.1–5.25 'Paul moves from personal to material concerns' (p. 74). C.H. Cosgrove, *The Cross and the Spirit: A Study in the Argument and Theology of Galatians* (Macon, GA: Mercer University Press, 1988), represents the extreme opposite of the view developed in this chapter. He rightly notes that autobiography can serve a variety of purposes and that it is sometimes difficult to differentiate the Antioch horizon from the Galatian horizon (p. 31), but it need not follow that our reading of Galatians should begin at 3.1-14. The blurring of horizons between Galatia and the situations Paul mentions in Jerusalem and Antioch suggests that they are recounted because they are salient to the Galatian setting. Furthermore, Cosgrove overlooks that 1.6-10 clearly addresses the Galatian situation and, if the autobiography is simply an amplification of 1.1-10, it has the Galatian horizon in focus. This is the line of arguementation I shall develop below.

3. Cf. Gal. 1.6-9; 3.1; 4.17; 5.10, 12, 6.12-13. So Schütz, *Anatomy of Apostolic Authority*, pp. 114-58; J.M.G. Barclay, 'Mirror-reading a Polemical Letter: Galatians as a Test Case', *JSNT* 31 (1987), pp. 73-93; J.D. Hester, 'Placing the Blame: The Presence of Epideictic in Galatians 1 and 2', in D. Watson (ed.), *Persuasive Artistry: Studies in New Testament Rhetoric in Honor of George A. Kennedy* (JSNTSup, 50; Sheffield: JSOT Press, 1991), pp. 281-307 (a letter of reproach; a retraction of his earlier views, see n. 5 below); cf. B.C. Lategan, 'Is Paul Defending his Apostleship in Galatians?', *NTS* 34 (1988), pp. 411-30.

4. Cf. 4.12, 19, and the argument for chs. 1–2 below. Lyons, *Pauline Autobiography*, pp. 123-76; Gaventa, 'Galatians 1 and 2', pp. 309-26.

5. E.g. H.D. Betz, 'The Literary Composition and Function of Paul's Letter to the Galatians', *NTS* 21 (1974–75), pp. 353-79; *idem*, 'In Defense of the Spirit: Paul's Letter to the Galatians as a Document of Early Christian Apologetics', in E. Schüssler Fiorenza (ed.), *Aspects of Religious Propaganda in Judaism and Early*

what he was when he first came to Galatia, not fundamentally a rhetorical responder, but rather a situational proclaimer of the gospel, the word that is at its heart *invasive* rather than responsive'.[6] The interconnection of Paul's self-presentation and his defence of the exclusivity of the gospel is generally recognized,[7] further implied by the conjoining of Paul's proclamation *and* his person with Christ.[8] It is maintained

Christianity (Notre Dame: University of Notre Dame Press, 1976), pp. 99-114; *idem, Galatians* (Hermeneia; Philadelphia: Fortress Press, 1979); Berger, 'Hellenistische Gattungen', p. 1272; J.D. Hester, 'The Rhetorical Structure of Galatians 1.11–2.14', *JBL* 103 (1984), pp. 223-33; *idem*, 'The Use and Influence of Rhetoric in Galatians 2.1-14', *TZ* 42 (1986), pp. 386-408 (though he later retracts this view in his 'Placing the Blame'); J.D.G. Dunn, *The Epistle to the Galatians* (BNTC; London: A. & C. Black, 1993). Taking Galatians as an apology is an interpretative decision rather than an exegetical result. For example, Paul does not list explicit accusations in Galatians as he does in 2 Cor. 10–13.

A related topic is the appropriateness of the reconstruction of opponents' views through so-called 'mirror reading', turning a Pauline denial into an assertion of his opponents. Recently the study of Galatians has provided a convenient battleground for this issue. On the one hand is B.H. Brinsmead, *Galatians: Dialogical Response to Opponents* (SBLDS, 65; Chico, CA: Scholars Press, 1982), who believes a reconstruction of the opponents brings coherence to understanding the letter. On the other hand is Lyons, *Pauline Autobiography*, pp. 75-121, who has rightly challenged the reliance upon 'mirror reading' when its results cannot be confirmed apart from the proposed reconstruction. G. Howard, *Paul: Crisis in Galatia. A Study in Early Christian Theology* (SNTSMS, 35; Cambridge: Cambridge University Press, rev. edn, 1990 [1979]), is somewhere between the two, though his counter to Lyons is weak: 'It is virtually impossible to understand Paul's defensive words in Gal. 5.11-12 as mere rhetorical language' (p. xiii). This is his only example, but no 'mirror reading' is necessary to understand these verses because of overt comments in the text. Barclay, 'Mirror-reading a Polemical Letter', pp. 79-83, offers a devastating critique of Brinsmead and sharpens the difficulties that Lyons pinpoints.

6. J.L. Martyn, 'Events in Galatia, Modified Covenantal Nomism versus God's Invasion of the Cosmos in the Singular Gospel: A Response to J.D.G. Dunn and B.R. Gaventa', in J.M. Bassler (ed.), *Pauline Theology* (2 vols.; Minneapolis: Fortress Press, 1991), I, pp. 160-79 (163).

7. Dunn, *Galatians*, p. 51.

8. 2.20; 4.14; 6.17; cf. 1.15-16; 2 Cor. 13.3; Cosgrove, *The Cross and the Spirit*, pp. 119-46. Pace G. Lüdemann, *Paul, Apostle to the Gentiles: Studies in Chronology* (trans. F. Jones; London: SCM Press, 1984), pp. 75-77, who thinks only Paul's gospel was recognized at Jerusalem and not his apostleship, but he has been rightly criticized by B.L. McLean, 'Galatians 2.7-9 and the Recognition of Paul's Apostolic Status at the Jerusalem Conference: A Critique of G. Luedemann's Solution', *NTS* 37 (1991), pp. 67-76.

here that Paul weaves together multiple arguments, including his self-portrayal, to convince the Galatians to reject this 'other gospel' to which they have been exposed.[9]

Galatians 1 and 2

Paul opens the letter with a typical assertion of his authority and apostolic status, but then uncharacteriztically describes how he became an apostle: 'sent neither by human commission nor from human authorities, but through Jesus Christ and God the Father, who raised him from the dead' (NRSV). In these words the reader of Galatians is immediately introduced to one theme that Paul will develop in the opening chapters, namely the origin of his apostleship and its relation to his gospel.[10] In other letter openings Paul describes how his apostleship reflects God's will (as in Gal. 1.4)[11] or God's call.[12] Here the reader is directed to the *inception* of Paul's apostleship, a theme that plays into the larger

9. Galatians is understood as a persuasive letter from Paul to churches he founded. Though Betz has provided helpful stimulus to New Testament studies with his experimental rhetorical analysis in his commentary on the letter, his view that the genre of Galatians is forensic has been criticized from without and countered from within the approach of classical rhetorical criticism. For a survey of critical reviews of Betz, see R.Y.K. Fung, *The Epistle to the Galatians* (NICNT; Grand Rapids: Eerdmans, 1988), pp. 28-32. From 'within' it has been argued that Galatians is either deliberative (so G.A. Kennedy, *New Testament Interpretation through Rhetorical Criticism* [Chapel Hill: University of North Carolina Press, 1984]; R.G. Hall, 'The Rhetorical Outline for Galatians: A Reconsideration', *JBL* 106 [1987], pp. 277-87; J. Smit, 'The Letter of Paul to the Galatians: A Deliberative Speech', *NTS* 35 [1989], pp. 1-26) or epideictic (Hester, 'Placing the Blame', pp. 281-307). R.M. Berchman draws attention to the *cul de sac* that has been reached by attempting to identify a single 'genre' based on the three species of classical rhetoric, and himself identifies all three in Gal. 1.1-5. Berchman emphasizes the unique character of Paul's letters and rightly suggests the proper place of classical rhetoric is to assist in understanding how Paul's argumentative tactics function in a letter ('Galatians [1.1-5]: Paul and Greco-Roman Rhetoric', in J. Neusner and E. Frerichs [eds.], *Judaic and Christian Interpretation of Texts* [London: University Press of America, 1987], pp. 1-15).

10. So Dunn, *Galatians*, pp. 4-5; B.C. Lategan, 'Levels of Reader Instructions in the Text of Galatians', *Semeia* 48 (1989), pp. 171-84; J.S. Vos, 'Die Argumentation des Paulus in Galater 1,1–2,10', in J. Lambrecht (ed.), *The Truth of the Gospel (Galatians 1.1–4.11)* (Rome: Benedictina, 1993), pp. 11-43 (14-17).

11. 1 Cor. 1.1; 2 Cor. 2.1; cf. Eph. 1.1; Col. 1.1; 1 Tim. 1.1; 2 Tim. 2.1.

12. Rom. 1.1.

argument and polemical setting. As K.O. Sandnes correctly observes, Paul utilizes his call story in a way that corresponds to how call narratives function in the Old Testament, that is, to legitimize the authority of the messenger and his message.[13] In this case, it is a legitimization in the face of opposing messengers with a different message. Paul may have known the identity of his opponents given his detailed response to their views, though Gal. 5.10 may suggest otherwise (ὅστις ἐὰν ᾖ).[14] If he did know their identity, then he employs a standard rhetorical practice of non-naming to shame them.[15] His thoughts about their teaching and its results are obvious (cf. 5.14-26), and the initial supposition is that Paul develops his autobiographical comments in Galatians 1–2 to underscore the exclusivity of the gospel he has delivered to the Galatian churches, vis-à-vis the opposing messengers competing for their loyalty.

In 1.6-9 the Galatian setting is addressed omitting the usual thanksgiving period, suggesting the gravity of the situation.[16] We are given some firm indications about the problems Paul perceived and the conditions, at least from his point of view, that shaped the letter and explain why he must reassert the authority of the message he brought to the Galatians. He expresses astonishment[17] that they have 'so quickly'

---

13. Cf. Isa. 6; Jer. 1.8-9; 14.14-15; 23.32; Ezek. 13.6-9; Amos 7.14-16; Sandnes, *Paul—One of the Prophets?*, p. 67; N. Habel, 'The Form and Significance of the Call Narratives', *ZAW* 77 (1965), pp. 297-323. Sandnes's thesis that Paul defends himself against a charge of false prophecy in Galatians is unconvincing. And, Sandnes too confidently presumes the homogeneity or understanding of Paul's audience: 'It is commonly recognized that in Gal. 1.15-16a Paul uses vocabulary which his audience quite certainly associated with a prophetic call' (*Paul—One of the Prophets?*, p. 48).

14. Elsewhere, Paul claims to know even their motives (e.g. 4.17; 6.12-13; cf. 3.1; 5.12), but these seem more for effect than a reflection of his intimate knowledge of their motivations. On 1.7 as a circumlocution for 'the opposition' see Moule, *An Idiom Book*, p. 106 n. 1; and Betz, *Galatians*, p. 49.

15. See Marshall, 'Invective', pp. 359-73; *idem*, *Enmity in Corinth*, pp. 528-38.

16. O'Brien, *Introductory Thanksgivings*, p. 141 n. 1, relates the absence of the thanksgiving to the rhetorical situation: 'Because the Galatians have departed from the gospel of Christ there can be no thanksgiving; instead, a curse is pronounced on anyone who brings another message (v. 8)'.

17. To label this a 'rhetorical' device (Betz, *Galatians*, p. 47) is to draw attention to its persuasive effectiveness, not to suggest that it is an 'artifice' or an inauthentic expression of Paul's feeling (as Dunn takes it, *Galatians*, p. 39; however, cf. his comments on p. 51).

deserted Christ, 'turning to a different "gospel"' (εἰς ἕτερον εὐαγγέλιον). The nature of this 'other gospel' is developed later, but he has in his sights a specific group of troublers (οἱ ταράσσοντες), 'whose desire is to pervert the gospel of Christ' (θέλοντες μεταστρέψαι τὸ εὐαγγέλιον τοῦ Χριστοῦ). In vv. 8-9 the deliberate parallelism[18] and repetition of the curse (ἀνάθεμα ἔστω) castigates his opposition in the strongest possible terms,[19] and urges the readers to remain true to the gospel they had received from Paul (παρ' ὃ εὐηγγελισάμεθα, v. 8; παρ' ὃ παρελάβετε, v. 9). As Dunn says:

> So convinced was Paul that the gospel as he had preached it in Galatia was the gospel from God, the gospel of Christ, that he was prepared to maintain it as the norm by which all other claims to revelation from heaven might be judged.[20]

A Gospel Not from Human Origin

The theme that Paul announces in 1.1-9 is developed in the subsequent autobiographical section to underline the authority of his person, and therefore the supremacy of his message. The widely held view that Paul is out to prove that he is independent of the Jerusalem apostles is not adopted here.[21] Rather it seems that Paul argues from their approval to bolster his claim of the truthfulness of the message he has taught the Galatians, a message he wants them to reaffirm as they reject the need for circumcision and other Jewish practices. In Booth's parlance, Paul 'shows' in the autobiographical section what he 'tells' them in the letter opening about the authority and exclusivity of his message.[22] We may briefly trace this theme that lies so close to the surface in Galatians 1–2.

The antithesis that is set up in 1.1, 'through Christ' versus through human agency, is reiterated in 1.11b-12: Paul was not taught the gospel

---

18. On Paul's use of synonomous parallelism, see J. Weiss, 'Beiträge zur Paulinischen Rhetorik', in *idem*, *Theologische Studien* (Göttingen: Vandenhoeck & Ruprecht, 1897), pp. 165-247 (168-96).

19. Considering the LXX usage of ἀνάθεμα; see H.-W. Kuhn, 'ἀνάθεμα', *EDNT*, I, pp. 80-81. The sarcasm of 5.12 expresses a similar wish.

20. Dunn, *Galatians*, p. 44; so also Schütz, *Anatomy of Apostolic Authority*, pp. 144-45; B.R. Gaventa, 'The Singularity of the Gospel: A Reading of Galatians', in J.M. Bassler (ed.) *Pauline Theology* (2 vols.; Minneapolis: Fortress Press, 1991), I, pp. 147-59.

21. As argued convincingly by Schütz, *Anatomy of Apostolic Authority*, pp. 140-50; and Howard, *Crisis in Galatia*, pp. 20-45.

22. Booth, *The Rhetoric of Fiction*, p. 20.

4. *Galatians*

but received it from God 'through a revelation of Jesus Christ' (δι' ἀποκαλύψεως Ἰησοῦ Χριστοῦ). For this purpose Paul was 'set apart from his birth', reminiscent of prophetic call stories. God commissioned Paul to take the gospel among the Gentiles (1.16; 2.2). Verses 1.16b-17 describe further that he did not receive it from other human apostles but from God. In 1.18-20 he explains a fact the Galatians would surely know: he had been to Jerusalem where he visited[23] Peter and James, but none other. The salient point is that it was *after* three years, mentioned to emphasize the time that lapsed before seeing them and therefore making it unlikely that he received his message from them.[24] The oath of v. 20 gives the evidential nature of his narration of events. If these facts were known to be false, Paul's credibility would have plummeted at this point of the reading. Since no one in Syria or Cilicia recognized him 'by face' but only by former reputation, this demonstrates how he did not consult with those in Antioch previously (1.21-24), and it rounds off the emphasis on the change wrought in him by the 'revelation of Jesus Christ' begun at 1.12.

In 2.1-3 Paul bolsters his evidence to the Galatians that his gospel to the Gentiles was given by God and not by human beings. Additional proof is the approval given to his message by the recognized Jerusalem leaders (οἱ δοκολῦντες, 2.2, 6, 9). Titus is physical evidence of their recognition since he was not forced to be circumcised.[25] In 2.6-10 Paul

---

23. It seems unlikely that Paul would use ἱστορῆσαι in the sense of 'to get information from' in light of 1.1, 11-12, 16-17; 2.2; so Betz, *Galatians*, p. 76. O. Hofius, 'Gal 1.18: ἱστορῆσαι Κηφᾶν', in *idem*, *Paulusstudien* (WUNT, 51; Tübingen: J.C.B. Mohr [Paul Siebeck], 1989), pp. 255-67, argues that 'to get to know' is philologically sound, against G.D. Kilpatrick, 'Galatians 1.18: ΙΣΤΟΡΗΣΑΙ ΚΗΦΑΝ', in A.J.B. Higgins (ed.), *New Testament Essays: Studies in Memory of T.W. Manson* (Manchester: University of Manchester Press, 1959), pp. 144-49. Dunn accepts Hofius's correction, but see his qualifications, 'The Relationship between Paul and Jerusalem According to Galatians 1 and 2', in *idem*, *Jesus, Paul and the Law: Studies in Mark and Galatians* (Louisville, KY: Westminster/John Knox Press, 1990), pp. 108-28 (126-28; cf. 110-13). In the end he concedes the translation should be left 'to get to know'. Cf. N. Walter, 'Paulus und die urchristliche Jesustradition', *NTS* 31 (1985), pp. 498-522 (506-507).

24. Or he received the interpretation of the christophany from them, as in Dunn, 'The Relationship between Paul and Jerusalem', pp. 112-13.

25. E.D.W. Burton, *A Critical and Exegetical Commentary on the Epistle to the Galatians* (ICC; Edinburgh: T. & T. Clark, 1921), pp. 72-75, thinks 2.2c shows apprehension on Paul's part, but the conclusion the Galatians are to draw is to the contrary: Paul's gospel is true and he has not run in vain.

re-emphasizes that they recognized the gospel God entrusted to him (ἰδόντες ὅτι πεπίστευμαι τὸ εὐαγγέλιον, 2.7; γνόντες τὴν χάριν τὴν δοθεῖσάν μοι, 2.9).[26] The repeated reference to the Jerusalem seal of approval of Paul's teaching assumes it would carry additional weight with the Galatians to strengthen Paul's claim to a divine origin of his message.[27] While it is possible to suppose Paul defends himself against charges that his gospel derives from the apostles and not from Christ,[28] the internal logic of the text suggests Paul's amplified argument seeks to demonstrate the truth of his message and, by comparison, to denigrate his opponents' teaching as having a human origin and lacking Jerusalem approval.[29] In this demonstration he both recounts salient

26. Elements of 2.6-10 pose their own difficulties. For example, why the ambivalence toward the Jerusalem apostles in 2.6? Munck, *Paul and the Salvation of Mankind*, p. 99, plausibly suggests that Paul's strategy here is to shake the opponents' position regarding the 'pillars'. This makes sense if the opponents claimed the special status of the Jerusalem apostles against Paul, a point we cannot confirm. Alternatively, Dunn, 'The Relationship between Paul and Jerusalem', pp. 117-22, suggests that Paul's ambivalence reflects a change between 'now' and 'then': the noted apostles recognized his message *then* at Jerusalem, a matter *now* (at the time of Galatians) of indifference to Paul.

Another difficulty is posed by Paul's qualification in 2.10 of his categorical denial in 2.6 (ἐμοὶ γὰρ οἱ δοκοῦντες οὐδὲν προσανέθεντο). The exception in 2.10 weakens Paul's position slightly, as he seems to acknowledge by adding, 'which was actually what I was eager to do' (NRSV). Yet, his admission of a slightly damaging fact may give his overall assertion more credibility, the 'exception that proves the rule'. See Dunn, *Galatians*, pp. 113-14.

27. Lategan, 'Levels of Reader Instructions', p. 177. F.F. Bruce, 'The Conference in Jerusalem: Galatians 2.1-10', in P. O'Brien and D. Peterson (eds.), *God Who Is Rich in Mercy* (Homebush, Australia: Lancer Books, 1986), pp. 195-212, adds that it was also important to Paul for pragmatic reasons and theological reasons. Without Jerusalem's recognition, the opposition to his gospel would have leverage against him. Theologically, Paul believed it was from Jerusalem that the word of the Lord went forth. See Dunn, 'The Relationship between Paul and Jerusalem', pp. 115-16, for the suggestion that Paul follows his own teaching on the importance of community recognition of prophetic utterances (1 Cor. 2.13; 12.10; 14.29; 1 Thess. 5.19-22).

28. Indeed, a dominant exegetical approach to this passage; see Gaventa, 'Galatians 1 and 2', p. 310 n. 2, for an extensive bibliography.

29. Munck, *Paul and the Salvation of Mankind*, p. 94, rightly points out that the narrative about Jerusalem must be evidence of Paul's independence and cannot be counter-evidence that he 'feeds to his opponents'; Paul describes the Jerusalem happenings to show they agree with him *against* the Judaizers in Galatia.

happenings in his life and he asserts that the Jerusalem apostles acknowledge his message, and therefore the origin of it.[30]

Christ's Slave, People Pleasers and Galatians 1.10
It is apparent how 1.1-9 introduces a line of argumentation that Paul develops in Galatians 1–2, but we are still left with a series of unresolved exegetical issues in these first two chapters of Galatians: Why the mention of the intruders in 2.3-4? Why does Paul recount the situation at Antioch with Peter in 2.11-21?[31] Why is 1.10 lodged between 1.1-9 and 1.11 when the transition is greatly improved with it removed? I will propose that these questions are related by a common answer, and the clue to that answer is found in Gal. 1.10.

The usual approach to Gal. 1.10 is to read Paul's denials as an indicator that some charge was made against him by his opponents.[32] Most scholars think Paul responds to a charge that he was a people-pleaser

---

30. G.D. Kilpatrick, 'Peter, Jerusalem and Galatians 1.13–2.14', *NovT* 25 (1983), pp. 318-26, believes the numerous *hapax legomena* in 1.13–2.14 may suggest that Paul uses either his or someone else's notes from the Jerusalem meeting, labelled 'a protocol' of the meeting by Lüdemann, *Paul, Apostle to the Gentiles*, pp. 64-71.

31. Munck, *Paul and the Salvation of Mankind*, p. 102, observes this confrontation is the clearest proof of Paul's independence from Jerusalem and therefore it fits in well with the argument already outlined. Below it will be argued that it does more than this.

32. Other approaches flourish. Some scholars try to make sense of v. 10a by translating πείθω as 'I persuade': A. Feuillet, '"Chercher à persuader Dieu" (Ga 1 10a)', *NovT* 12 (1970), pp. 350-60; Betz, *Galatians*, pp. 54-55; F.F. Bruce, *The Epistle of Paul to the Galatians: A Commentary on the Greek Text* (NIGTC; Exeter: Paternoster Press, 1982), pp. 84-86; and Dunn, *Galatians*, p. 50. Feuillet reads 'seeking to persuade God' as a reference to Peter, vis-à-vis Mt. 16.13-23, where he tries to persuade Jesus to choose another course from the cross. Though this understanding has not been followed here, it is in harmony with the claim made below that Paul anticipates in 1.10 his comparison with Peter in 2.11-14. A redactional explanation is offered by J.C. O'Neill, that ἢ τὸν θεόν is 'far easier to understand as a gloss than as part of the text', but there is no ancient manuscript evidence in his favour, and preference for the more difficult reading weighs against his view (*The Recovery of Paul's Letter to the Galatians* [London: SPCK, 1972], p. 24). On a wholly different line, G. Sass points to 1 Thess. 2.4 as the lens through which to read Gal. 1.10 ('Zur Bedeutung von δοῦλος bei Paulus', *ZNW* 40 [1941], pp. 24-32 [30-31]). The parallel is instructive (as are 1 Cor. 4.3-5; 2 Cor. 1.12; 2.17; 3.4), but should not distort or override the unique rhetorical situation of Galatians.

who had trimmed circumcision from his message for easy acceptance by the Gentiles in Galatia, and evidence can be adduced from Paul himself that he was a self-confessed 'people-pleaser' (1 Cor. 9.19-23; 10.28-33; yet see 2 Cor. 5.11 and cf. Col. 3.22).[33] B.C. Lategan concisely states this hypothetical reconstruction of the opponents' accusations:

> Paul rejects the law—therefore, he attempts to make life easier for his followers—therefore, he wants to be popular—therefore, he is uncertain of himself—therefore, he should not be trusted—therefore, his preaching should be rejected—therefore, the Galatians should accept the message of Paul's opponents and adopt their position.[34]

Alternatively, some scholars suggest that 'people pleasing' refers to Paul's pleasing Jewish colleagues by actually promoting circumcision, and they appeal to Gal. 5.11 as further evidence that this was the current criticism against Paul (cf. Acts 16.3).[35] Gal. 5.11, however, may allude to Paul's practice before the 'revelation from Jesus Christ' ('If I *still* preach circumcision...'), congruent with the now–then distinction he develops in 1.10-24,[36] and may be another self-exemplification, that is, 'my persecution proves that circumcision is not a part of *my* gospel and should not be a part of yours'. The difficulty remains that we have no evidence for either of these reconstructed charges, which are quite

---

33. See R.N. Longenecker, *Galatians* (WBC, 41; Dallas: Word Books, 1990), pp. 18-19. Dunn cites evidence of how the practice of circumcision was an object of derision, suggesting the plausibility of this view (*Galatians*, pp. 49-50).

34. Lategan, 'Levels of Reader Instructions', p. 175.

35. See P. Borgen, 'Paul Preaches Circumcision and Pleases Men', in M.D. Hooker and S.G. Wilson (eds.), *Paul and Paulinism* (London: SPCK, 1982), pp. 37-46. He takes Gal. 6.12-13 as further evidence of this charge against Paul, but these verses are clearly Paul's characterization of his opponents to devastate *their* credibility. Acts 16.3 is evidence only of Paul's missionary principle of accommodation articulated in 1 Cor. 9.19-23, but does not suggest that he preached the necessity of circumcision to others.

36. K.-W. Niebuhr, *Heidenapostel aus Israel: Die jüdische Identität des Paulus nach ihrer Darstellung in seinen Briefen* (WUNT, 62; Tübingen: J.C.B. Mohr [Paul Siebeck], 1992), pp. 10-14, 19-43; Gaventa, 'Galatians 1 and 2', p. 314. To be sure, this rhetoric of antitheses flows from Paul's eschatological frame of reference, as Schütz points out (*Anatomy of Apostolic Authority*, pp. 120-22).

contradictory in what they imply.³⁷ And, as Betz wisely cautions, 'Not every rhetorical denial is an accusation turned around!'³⁸

The impulse for penning Gal. 1.10 is not an accusation against Paul. I will argue here that Gal. 1.10, as the text stands, is integrated into Paul's argumentative design in the letter, and should not be isolated merely 'as an emotional outburst that is to be related in some manner to the curses of vv. 8-9, yet [is] set off as a separate paragraph'.³⁹ The approach followed below is that Galatians is more likely Paul's polemical initiative rather than his defensive response (cf. Gal. 1.6-9; 3.1; 4.17; 5.10, 12, 6.12-13).

To establish a clear understanding of Gal. 1.10 we must interpret the meaning of πείθω, a verb difficult to understand as 'persuade' as it is used in 2 Cor. 5.11, particularly because this leaves a strange combination of 'humans' and 'God' as objects of the verb. However, πείθω is commonly used with the sense 'I conciliate' or 'I seek the approval of'.⁴⁰ If this is correct then the verse should read:

> For now do I seek the approval of humans or of God? Or do I seek to please people? If I were still pleasing people, I would not be Christ's slave.

If we take v. 10b as repeating the first half of v. 10a for effect, as in the case of the parallelism in 1.8-9, this translation is strengthened. Furthermore, this interpretation anticipates v. 10c as Paul's answer to the preceding two rhetorical questions where he moves from self-deliberative questions to an assertion clothed in a conditional construction:⁴¹ 'I am a slave of Christ and not enslaved to human opinion or in need of human approval'.

Galatians 1.10 as Paul's Assertion
Recent classical rhetorical analysis has identified 1.6-11 as an exordium, standing in a carefully planned relationship with the letter as a

37. Similarly, Vos, 'Die Argumentation', pp. 12-14.
38. Betz, *Galatians*, p. 56 n. 115; see n. 5 above.
39. Longenecker, *Galatians*, p. 18.
40. Cf. 2 Macc. 4.45; Mt. 28.14; Acts 12.20; LSJ and BAGD, *s.v.*; Burton, *Epistle to the Galatians*, pp. 30-31; H. Schlier, *Der Brief an die Galater* (KEK, 7; Göttingen: Vandenhoeck & Ruprecht, 1971 [1949]), p. 41; Longenecker, *Galatians*, pp. 18-19.
41. εἰ...ἄν ἤμην is an appropriate conditional construction; Moule, *An Idiom Book*, p. 149.

whole.⁴² Whether or not this rhetorical analysis is accepted, there are four further clues that Gal. 1.10 is integrated into the argument of Galatians rather than merely Paul's defensive response to criticisms. First of all, Gal. 1.10 is formally related to the verses on either side of it. In this case exegesis is hindered by seeking a clear 'section' divider between vv. 9 and 10 or between 10 and 11, succumbing to a pitfall of structural analysis obscuring 'the natural flow of the argument'.⁴³ There are several indicators of the relation of 1.10 to its immediate surroundings. If we take the particle 'for' (γάρ), which occurs four times in 1.10-13, in its general sense as indicating an explanatory construction, v. 13 builds on vv. 11-12, which in turn take up v. 10, which flows from vv. 6-9.⁴⁴ The 'now' (ἄρτι) that begins 1.10 further parallels 'now' in 1.9. In 1.6-9 Paul encourages a Galatian confrontation with outsiders, and 1.10 may be read as bringing forward this emphasis.⁴⁵ 'Now' taken with 'still' (ἔτι) in v. 10 anticipates the subsequent depiction of his former life in 1.12-16 'when he pleased his peers and elders by observing and promoting the Law'.⁴⁶

There is more than an explanatory relationship between these verses, however. The γάρ of v. 10 establishes a logical connection between 1.10 and 1.6-9, as J. Vos has shown. The strong and exclusive claims that Paul makes for his gospel in vv. 6-9 are supported immediately by his character claim in v. 10. Vos presents the syllogism that the reader would intuitively understand from the flow of vv. 6-10:

1a. The gospel is true when it is proclaimed by a true servant of God and Christ.
1b. The gospel is false when it is announced by a flatterer enslaved to humans.
2. The contents and emphasis of vv. 6-9 show that I am not a sycophant and slave of humans, but that I am a servant of God and Christ.

---

42. For a summary of scholarship see Vos, 'Die Argumentation', pp. 17-22.
43. Dunn, *Galatians*, p. 20; cf. Burton, *Epistle to the Galatians*, p. 33.
44. Dunn, *Galatians*, p. 52; contra Betz, *Galatians*, p. 56. We may draw the same conclusion if the textual variant δέ is correct (see S.E. Porter, *Idioms of the Greek New Testament* [Biblical Languages: Greek, 2; Sheffield: JSOT Press, 1992], pp. 207-208), but see Longenecker, *Galatians*, p. 22.
45. Gaventa, 'Galatians 1 and 2', p. 314.
46. Gaventa, 'Galatians 1 and 2', p. 314.

3. It follows that the gospel that I have proclaimed to you is true.[47]

Paul's polemic in vv. 6-9 is founded on his conviction of the truth of the gospel as he has communicated it, which in turn he supports by an assertion about his own character. This sort of character appeal was a stock rhetorical practice where the speaker eschewed flattery.[48] Furthermore, the γάρ of v. 11 also grounds the gospel that Paul reiterates here on his character assertion of v. 10, and adds to that character assertion the divine origin of his message.[49] We may conclude with G. Ebeling: 'What seems to be a mere transition, appearing to turn from the negative curse to the positive revelation of Christ, is intended rather to join them both in an incontestable unity'.[50]

Secondly, Gal. 1.10 seems related to the motif of persecution in Galatians, a theme which E. Baasland has drawn to our attention.[51] As Paul develops the theme of persecution in Galatians he identifies himself as the *former* oppressor (1.13) who has abandoned his violence (1.23). Because he now 'proclaims the gospel of faith' the churches 'give glory to God' because of him (1.24). Already in the opening chapter Paul identifies persecutors with circumcision, and those persecuted with *his* gospel. With this image on the canvas, 4.29 is added: those of the Spirit (τὸν κατὰ πνεῦμα) are shown to be such because they are persecuted by those who are 'born of the flesh' (ὁ κατὰ σάρκα γεννηθεὶς ἐδίωκεν), language which connotes a distinction between those who belong to God and those who do not. Galatians 5.11 makes it clear that Paul believes that *it is the practice of circumcision* which is the 'soft option' that reduces persecution, re-emphasized in the negative characterization of his opponents in 6.12: 'It is those who want to make a good showing in the flesh that try to compel you to be circumcised—only that they may not be persecuted for the cross of Christ'. As Baasland aptly says of 6.12:

---

47. Vos, 'Die Argumentation', pp. 22-24.
48. Betz, *Galatians*, p. 55 nn. 111-13; Vos, 'Die Argumentation', pp. 24-25.
49. Vos, 'Die Argumentation', pp. 25-27.
50. G. Ebeling, *The Truth of the Gospel: An Exposition of Galatians* (trans. D. Green; Philadelphia: Fortress Press, 1985 [1981]), p. 61 (see also pp. 66-67); cf. Betz, *Galatians*, p. 56; Longenecker, *Galatians*, p. 22; Dunn, *Galatians*, pp. 51-52.
51. Gal. 1.13, 23; 4.29; 5.11; 6.12; cf. 3.9. E. Baasland, 'Persecution: A Neglected Feature in the Letter to the Galatians', *ST* 38 (1984), pp. 135-50.

Paul has several things in mind, but the main purpose is to show the clear connection between the teaching of circumcision and renunciation of the cross of Christ for fear of persecutions. If we consider all the διώκω passages together, we cannot fail to notice that the polemical sting becomes more apparent as the letter continues.⁵²

Taken together, Paul's picture of the persecuted and their tormentors paints the former on God's side and the latter as God's opponents. This is further enhanced by Paul's self-depiction as the one who suffers with Christ (2.19-21; 3.13; 5.24-25; 6.14-15, 17). Though Paul's self-portrayal as a co-sufferer with Christ is not unique to Galatians,⁵³ it is significant that the Galatians were under pressure to accept circumcision, pressure that could rightly be characterized as persecution since they were suffering (πάσχειν; 3.4).⁵⁴ This pastoral situation was occasion for the letter and should give us another reason to re-evaluate the relationship of Gal. 1.10 to its context.

A third reason to understand Gal. 1.10 in relation to the argument of the letter rather than against a hypothetical charge is Paul's idiomatic usage of 'I'. In our examination of 1 Corinthians it was demonstrated that Paul uses 'I' statements and self-characterization in a highly stylized way to highlight the thrust of his argument that he develops in what follows. For example, he uses this technique in 1 Cor. 8.13 to introduce the argument of ch. 9, and in 12.31 to introduce ch. 13.⁵⁵ This is a generally recognized feature of Gal. 2.15-21,⁵⁶ and Rom. 1.16-17

---

52. Baasland, 'Persecution', pp. 138-39.

53. Cf. 2 Cor. 4.7-15; 11.23–12.10; Philippians; and see E. Güttgemanns, *Der leidende Apostel und sein Herr: Studien zur paulinischen Christologie* (FRLANT, 90; Göttingen: Vandenhoeck & Ruprecht, 1966).

54. So Baasland, 'Persecution', pp. 139-40. See A.J. Goddard and S.A. Cummins who draw attention to Paul's past persecution among the Galatians and its relation to the current opposition ('Ill or Ill-Treated? Conflict and Persecution as the Context of Paul's Original Ministry in Galatia', *JSNT* 52 [1993], pp. 93-126). For a plausible explanation of the historical circumstances which led to this see R. Jewett, 'The Agitators and the Galatian Congregation', *NTS* 17 (1970–71), pp. 198-212.

55. See Chapter 3 above, and Mitchell, *Paul and the Rhetoric of Reconciliation*, pp. 49-60.

56. As demonstrated by M. Bachmann, *Sünder oder Übertreter: Studien zur Argumentation in Gal. ii. 15ff.* (WUNT, 2.59; Tübingen: J.C.B. Mohr [Paul Siebeck], 1992), pp. 110-51, and Betz, *Galatians*, pp. 114-27 (the '*propositio*'). So also Brinsmead, *Opponents*, p. 201; Bruce, *Galatians*, pp. 136-37; Burton, *Epistle to the Galatians*, pp. 117-18; Longenecker, *Galatians*, pp. 80-81; Dunn, *Galatians*, p. 132.

concisely introduces the following argument in the letter, as is universally recognized. This Pauline style is suggestive for a re-examination of the function of Gal. 1.10 within the argument of the letter. The approach followed below gives Gal. 1.10 a prominent and intentional place in Paul's argument, making sense of a verse commentators usually leave unrelated to Paul's larger contention.[57]

A fourth reason we may take Gal. 1.10 as Paul's argumentative assertion builds upon one purpose of autobiographical writing in antiquity. As G. Misch observes, the highest aim of autobiographical writing was to 'depict an ideal standard of culture or a definite type of character, cast into the form of a self-portrait'.[58] Gal. 1.10 introduces a clear issue of character, and the subsequent autobiographical passage sets Paul's character against others (2.4-5; 11-14). A possible objection that 2.4-5, 11-21 are too far removed from Gal. 1.10 may be dismissed, since we find this same phenomenon of argumentation elsewhere in Paul where he briefly introduces a theme only to develop it later in his letter.[59]

With these features highlighted, it appears that the alternatives of 'people-pleasing' versus 'God-pleasing' in 1.10 are set before the Galatians as rhetorical options with the hope that they will choose 'God-pleasing' and Paul's gospel, and reject 'people-pleasing', circumcision and the teaching of Paul's opponents. On a persuasive level, the effect of 1.10 is that Paul stands as a model for the readers, assured they will reject the option of seeking the approval of humans rather than God.[60] Paul's 'I' statement functions to lead the readers to only one possible conclusion: when they read Paul's 'I am not a people-pleaser', they will

---

57. Gal. 1.10 fits Aristotle's description of a demonstrative enthymeme introduced by 'for' (γάρ; cf. 1 Cor. 5.12; 10.29b; Aristotle, *Rhet.* 2.23). Whether or not the style of Gal. 1.10 derives from a Hellenistic rhetorical influence stemming back to Aristotle, Paul's idiomatic usage of 'I' statements elsewhere gives us enough reason to examine this verse to determine if it introduces a subsequent demonstration. See D.E. Aune, *The New Testament in its Literary Environment* (LEC, 8; Philadelphia: Westminster Press, 1987), pp. 172-74.

58. Misch, *Autobiography in Antiquity*, I, p. 64; so also Lyons, *Pauline Autobiography*, pp. 17-53; Gaventa, 'Galatians 1 and 2', p. 324.

59. E.g. Rom. 9–11 take up the questions of 3.1-7, and Rom. 6 responds to that of 3.8; so A.T. Lincoln, 'From Wrath to Justification: Tradition, Gospel and Audience in the Theology of Romans 1.18–4.25', in *SBL Seminar Papers 1993* (Atlanta: Scholars Press, 1993), pp. 194-226 (210).

60. Similarly, P.E. Koptak, 'Rhetorical Identification in Paul's Autobiographical Narrative: Galatians 1.13–2.14', *JSNT* 40 (1990), pp. 97-115 (109).

want to conclude, 'Neither are we'.⁶¹ When Paul affirms, 'I am Christ's slave', it is his hope that they will adopt this same self-understanding, as is made explicit in 3.29 and 5.24 (cf. 1 Cor. 7.22). Paul's underlying purpose is to claim their total allegiance to the gospel of Christ that he has proclaimed and to make sure they will not Judaize. We now turn to examine the relationship of Gal. 1.10 to the autobiographical section that follows.

The Argumentative Function of Galatians 1.10
The rhetorical questions of v. 10a, b and the conditional construction of v. 10c have the cumulative force of an assertion in which Paul claims that he belongs to and is compelled by Christ and God, and is not controlled by the opinions of human beings. He is not a people-pleaser but a God-pleaser. He is not in bondage to human pressure, but is Christ's slave.

'Christ's slave' (Χριστοῦ δοῦλος) is a familiar self-designation in Paul's letters, as well as a characterization of believers in general (1 Cor. 7.22; cf. Rom. 12.11; 14.4, 18). As a metaphor, he uses it to portray his obedience to his master who compels him (2 Cor. 4.5; cf. 2 Cor. 2.14; 3.6; 1 Cor. 3.5).⁶² Or, to all but the most upper-class readers, it may have been heard as a metaphor of power by affiliation with the most important person in the cosmos, much as a member of the *familia Caesaris* might claim his or her unique social status as Caesar's slave.⁶³ Also significant is the Old Testament usage of 'slave of Yahweh' for prestigious leaders like Moses, Joshua, David and Isaiah (עבד יהוה; LXX δοῦλος κυρίου),⁶⁴ giving the term a connotation of privilege and honour, a sense conveyed when it is found in letter openings (Rom. 1.1; Phil. 1.1; cf. Jas 1.1). Moreover, Paul's usage of 'slave' has a wide

---

61. Reading this verse in light of Paul's idiomatic use of 'I', but other interpretations end up in virtually the same place; e.g. Betz, *Galatians*, p. 55; and Lategan, 'Levels of Reader Instructions', pp. 175-76.

62. Stanley calls this 'the most revealing metaphor' of Paul's relationship with Christ ('Imitation in Paul's Letters', p. 131).

63. See P.R.C. Weaver, *FAMILIA CAESARIS: A Social Study of the Emperor's Freedmen and Slaves* (Cambridge: Cambridge University Press, 1972), p. 2; D.J. Kyrtatas, 'Christianity and the *Familia Caesaris*', in *idem, The Social Structure of the Early Christian Communities* (London: Verso, 1987), pp. 75-86; Martin, *Slavery as Salvation*, pp. 1-49.

64. Deut. 34.5; Josh. 1.1, 13, 15; 8.31, 33; 11.12; 12.6; 13.8; 14.7; 18.7; 22.2, 4, 5; 24.29; Judg. 2.8; 2 Kgs 18.12; Isa. 42.19; Ps. 18.1; 36.1; 2 Chron. 1.3; 24.6.

range of flexibility as he can use its literal sense (1 Cor. 7; Philemon), as a designation of a populist leader 'enslaved' to his constituency (1 Cor. 9.19-23; cf. 2 Cor. 4.5),[65] or to portray the effects of sin (e.g. Rom. 6) or redemption, a use noticeable in Galatians.[66]

With Paul's variable usage of slavery metaphors in mind, there is reason to suspect the use of 'slave' in Jeremiah and Isaiah has partly influenced Paul's usage in Gal. 1.10.[67] As has been often noted, Gal. 1.15-16 has at least three points of contact with Jer. 1.5 and Isa. 49.1: a commission, from the womb of the messenger's mother, to the Gentiles.[68] If we further compare Galatians with Jeremiah we find that slavery as a metaphor is used positively and negatively throughout both.[69] More important for understanding Galatians 1 is the combination in Jeremiah of the sending of the prophets (ἀποστέλλω; cf. ἀπόστολος Gal. 1.1), who are characterized as 'slaves', and are identified with God by a genitive construction (usually μοῦ[70]). These features have striking similarities with Paul's crisp self-designation in Gal. 1.10 within its context in Gal. 1.1-26, and are suggestive that Paul may echo these Old

---

65. Martin, *Slavery as Salvation*, pp. 50-85.

66. 2.4; 3.28; 4.1, 3, 7, 8, 9, 22-23, 24, 25; 5.1, 13; cf. also the redemption language (3.13; 4.5), the frequency of 'free' and 'freedom', and the imprisonment imagery (3.22-23).

67. So Sass, 'Zur Bedeutung', p. 31; T. Holtz, 'Zum Selbstverständnis des Apostels Paulus', *TLZ* 91 (1966), cols. 321-30; F.F. Bruce, 'Further Thoughts on Paul's Autobiography: Galatians 1.11–2.14', in E.E. Ellis and E. Grässer (eds.), *Jesus und Paulus* (Tübingen: J.C.B. Mohr [Paul Siebeck], 1975), pp. 21-29 (23-25); Sandnes, *Paul—One of the Prophets?*, pp. 59-65, 147-48; contra the reductionist approach of J. Bligh, *Galatians: A Discussion of St Paul's Epistle* (London: St Paul Publications, 1970), p. 94.

68. W. Baird gives further parallels ('Visions, Revelation, and Ministry: Reflections on 2 Corinthians 12.1-5 and Galatians 1.11-17', *JBL* 104 [1985], pp. 651-62 [656-57]), following Habel's analysis of the Old Testament call stories ('Call Narratives', pp. 297-323). Yet, in Gal. 1–2 Paul omits 'the objection', 'the reassurance' and 'the sign', three of Habel's six indicators of this *Gattung*.

69. Cf. Gal. 1.10; 2.4-5; 3.23; 3.29–4.9; 4.21–5.1; 5.13; LXX Jer. 2.14, 20; 3.22; 5.19; 8.2; 10.24; 11.10; 13.10; 15.14; 16.11, 13; 22.9; 25.6, 11; 34.6; 41.9, 13; 42.15; 43.31; 44.2, 44.18. On the interchangeability of δοῦλος and παῖς in Jeremiah see the parallelism of Jer. 26.27-28.

70. LXX Jer. 7.25; 25.4; 33.5; 42.15; 51.4. That slaves were property gives support to reading these as genitives of possession. That the prophets were sent in each case supports reading these as subjective genitives, 'the slaves who have come from me'. This same ambiguity exists for 'slave of Christ' in Gal. 1.10.

Testament characterizations of God's messenger. The implication, as in Jeremiah and Isaiah, is that on hearing the words of God's messenger one should not reject them.[71] To reject the words of the messenger is to reject the divine sender. This implication is completely congruent with Paul's purpose to assert the authority of his gospel in Galatians 1–2.

The word order of 'Christ's slave' (Χριστοῦ δοῦλος) is emphatic,[72] unique in Paul,[73] and probably is polemical if we consider the implications of his remarks built around 'slave' and 'free' elsewhere in Galatians.[74] Thus we should understand it as '*Christ* is my master and I am controlled by no one or nothing else'. Paul emphasizes this obligation to Christ against those who are 'enslaved' to a traditional Jewish lifestyle.[75] He portrays himself as compelled by the one who has called and commissioned him, an image that remains in the reader's mind with the elaborate use of slavery metaphors throughout Galatians. This extended treatment of related metaphors gives evidence of 1.10 introducing one of the underlying themes of the letter. Furthermore, the attachment of the genitive 'of Christ' (Χριστοῦ) anticipates its usage later in the letter to designate those who have freedom in Christ in their post-baptismal existence (3.29; 5.24),[76] a sense which Paul explicitly attaches to δοῦλος Χριστοῦ in 1 Cor. 7.22.[77]

Paul's self-characterization as 'Christ's slave' is clearly related to the argument that follows. His 'I' statement is paradigmatic. He is the exemplary 'slave of Christ' whom the Galatians are to emulate and obey. Paul as the model Christian is implicit (cf. 1 Cor. 4.16; 11.1; Phil. 3.17), but is made explicit in 4.12 with his familiar call to imitation, 'Become as I am'. The christological aspect of his example is also explicit, both in 4.14 ('you received me as Christ Jesus') and in 1.10 (he is *Christ's* slave). This much is clear. Yet, if Gal. 1.10 is an interpretative marker, we would expect the contrast of people-pleasing versus

---

71. To cite one of Habel's conclusions about the significance of the Old Testament call narratives ('Call Narratives', p. 317).

72. Moule, *An Idiom Book*, p. 166.

73. Transposed in each other occurrence: Rom. 1.1; 14.18; 1 Cor. 7.22; Phil. 1.1; cf. Eph. 6.5; Col. 4.12.

74. E.g. 2.3-5; 4.7, 26, 30-31; 5.1, 13.

75. Cf. Gal. 4.8 with Jer. 5.19 (11.10; 13.10; 16.11; 22.9).

76. Cf. the use of related phrases of ἐν Χριστῷ in 2.17; 3.26; 5.6 (cf. 5.10); and εἰς Χριστὸν in 2.16; 3.27.

77. We also find 'slave' plus the genitive in Jer. 26.27-28 as a characterization of the personified people who belong to God (δοῦλος μου Ιακωβ; παῖς μου Ιακωβ).

4. *Galatians*

God-pleasing to be exemplified in some way in the autobiographical passage (1.11–2.21). With this expectation we are not disappointed at what we find, and discover that Paul uses the device of comparison with his opponents at Jerusalem (2.4-5) and Peter at Antioch (2.11-14) to accomplish his purpose.

Galatians 2.4-5, 11-21 through the Lens of Galatians 1.10
As Paul describes the scene in Jerusalem some opposition appears in the narration (2.4-5), but the entrance of these 'pseudo-brethren' is neither anticipated nor is it clear why Paul mentions them. Accepting the fairly strong reading of *UBSGNT* (4th edn) text for 2.5, the separation between the Jerusalem and the Galatian horizons is made ambiguous by 'to whom' (οἷς), giving the appearance that even as he writes (πρὸς ὥραν) Paul stands opposed to the same group. If they were the same opponents this would give reason enough for his mention of them, but it is not clear whether Paul believes his opponents in Galatia are the same group he previously confronted, or whether he simply lumps both sets of intruders, in Galatia and in Jerusalem, into a single pejorative category. In Jerusalem they are 'spies', 'pseudo-brethren' smuggled in to enslave (καταδουλεύειν) Paul and Titus. Paul's portrayal of their desire to enslave is not only contrasted with 'our freedom we have in Christ' (2.4), but stands in contradistinction to Paul's self-depiction as enslaved to Christ in 1.10.[78] This self-characterization in 1.10 anticipates his confrontation of his Jerusalem opponents in 2.4-5. The remembrance of them serves as an opportunity for Paul to demonstrate how he is Christ's bondservant, and not a people pleaser. This interpretation makes good sense of the language that follows in 2.5: Paul stands up to them, 'not yielding to their subjection, in order that the truth of the gospel might remain with you'. We would expect, in light of 1.10, that Paul would not subject himself to obey mere humans since he is Christ's slave. His portrayal of his opponents' motivation in the language of bondage is another indicator that he portrays himself as *Christ's* slave as a polemical statement. Paul's model of behaviour is directly applicable to the Galatian situation—Paul wants the Galatians to show the same boldness toward the intruders in Galatia that he modelled in his engagement with the Jerusalem 'false brethren' (NB 1.8-9).

78. So Koptak, 'Rhetorical Identification', p. 104.

In 2.11-14 the theme is further developed. Paul is bold and defiant *even* against Peter.[79] Paul places his boldness in the foreground by portraying his actions *before* he describes the situation which elicited his response (vv. 12-14): 'And when Cephas came to Antioch I resisted him to his face' (2.11). In v. 14, the public manner of his confrontation with Peter is explicit: 'I said to Peter before everyone...' (2.14).[80] Though the historical implications of the Antioch situation have interested scholars, Paul's emphasis in the letter seems to be his own actions towards Peter, and particularly the theological motivation for behaviour (2.15-21).[81] As 'Christ's slave' he does not back down from a confrontation even with the Jerusalem apostle of note, since to do so would nullify Christ's revealed message to him (2.21). In 1.8 Paul adjures the Galatians not to back down from rejecting even an angel from heaven if that messenger brought a contrary gospel to Paul's. In 2.11-14 he models one such confrontation with Peter, whose status he has already acknowledged. F.F. Bruce has observed that Paul's relationship with Peter is not static in Galatians 1–2, but changes from Paul as Peter's guest (1.18) to Paul as his co-apostle (2.1-10) to Paul as Peter's critic (2.11-14).[82] It is contended here that Paul's injunction in 1.8, his self-presentation in 1.10 and his confrontation in 2.11-14, taken together, make sense of these changing characterizations of Peter in Galatians 1–2.

79. For a discussion of other possible reasons that Peter is mentioned, see R.E. Brown, K.P. Donfried and J. Reuman (eds.), *Peter in the New Testament* (Minneapolis: Augsburg; New York: Paulist Press, 1973), pp. 23-32. For the history of interpretation of this passage, see A. Wechsler, *Geschichtsbild und exegetische Studie über den antiochenischen Zwischenfall (Gal 2,11-14)* (BZNW, 62; Berlin: W. de Gruyter, 1991), pp. 1-295.

80. J.M. Everts characterizes this as the *gospel* judging Peter (*Testing a Literary-Critical Hermeneutic: An Exegesis of the Autobiographical Passages in Paul's Epistles* [Ann Arbor, MI: University Microfilms, 1985], pp. 85-89). She is correct in so far as Paul uses 'the truth of the gospel' as his measuring rod in v. 14, but she neutralizes a poignant interpersonal clash for which Paul has an apparently paradigmatic purpose. Not too much should be made of this distinction, however, since he presents his person and the gospel as intertwined.

81. See J.D.G. Dunn, 'The Incident at Antioch (Gal. 2.11-18)', in *idem, Jesus, Paul and the Law: Studies in Mark and Galatians* (Louisville, KY: Westminster/John Knox Press, 1990), pp. 129-82; T. Holtz, 'Der antiochenische Zwischenfall (Galater 2.11-14)', *NTS* 32 (1986), pp. 344-61.

82. Bruce, 'Autobiography', p. 26.

4. *Galatians*

Paul proceeds to explain his reason for his confrontation with Peter, a reason that in its essence was equivalent to the problem in Galatia as Paul saw it: by his example Peter compelled the Gentiles to Judaize (2.14), that is, to adopt a characteristically Jewish way of life.[83] Paul reports that his message to Peter was 'that he stood condemned'. Not coincidentally, this is the same message that he has already communicated about his opposition in Galatia (1.8-9), and it re-emerges in the letter as a threat to the Galatians if they submit to those opposing Paul's gospel (3.10, 13; 5.2-4; cf. 2.21).

But there is another element to Paul's condemnation of Peter in 2.12-13: Peter acted in a transparently fickle manner. Peter is portrayed as the people-pleaser, who was acting properly until outsiders arrived.[84] Paul portrays Peter as fearful of those who promote circumcision (2.12), characterizing Peter as motivated by others' expectations and not by 'the truth of the gospel'. He was a pretender (συνυπεκρίνειν) who led astray even Barnabas by his hypocrisy (ὑπόκρισις; 2.13).[85] It now becomes apparent that 1.10 foreshadows, and 1.11–2.10 builds up to, a deliberate comparison between Peter and Paul: Peter is the people-pleaser; Paul is the slave of Christ who stands against any who oppose the gospel he has proclaimed.[86] Paul and Peter serve as model and

---

83. Dunn, 'Incident', pp. 149-50; H. Boers, 'We Who Are by Inheritance Jews; Not from the Gentile Sinners', *JBL* 111 (1992), pp. 273-81.

84. Against Dunn who maintains that Paul did not 'intend to accuse Peter of being consciously insincere' (*Galatians*, p. 125). Yet see his 'Echoes of Intra-Jewish Polemic in Paul's Letter to the Galatians', *JBL* 112 (1993), pp. 459-77 (460-61), and Howard, *Crisis in Galatia*, pp. 22-27.

85. U. Wilckens points out the almost total negative usage of this word group in Diaspora Judaism(s) ('ὑποκρίνομαι, κτλ.', *TDNT*, VIII, pp. 559-71), a point developed by Dunn ('Intra-Jewish Polemic', p. 461). Gal. 2.12 gives clear indication that Peter did not act consistently with his principles, thus the metaphorical sense of 'pretend' and 'hypocrisy' are most justified here; so also Schütz, *Anatomy of Apostolic Authority*, p. 152.

86. So also Bligh, *Galatians*, p. 93; Bruce, 'Autobiography', pp. 28-29 (who labels this an '*ad hominem* remonstrance'); Vos, 'Die Argumentation', pp. 31-33. Similarly, Lyons identifies 2.11-14 as a rhetorical *synkrisis*, a comparison with another to highlight one's own character (*Pauline Autobiography*, pp. 134-35; cf. Aristotle, *Rhet.* 1.9.38-39). He regards it as a demonstration of how easy it is to set aside the grace of God (p. 163), yet later he may imply an agreement with the interpretation taken here (p. 174).

antitype for the Galatians.⁸⁷ Paul stands as the example of how the Galatians are to resist those promoting circumcision; Peter represents despicable people-pleasers who succumb to the pressure to Judaize.⁸⁸ There has been much speculation on the outcome of this confrontation, but Paul's silence on the consequences of this affray is easily explained in the interpretation adopted here.⁸⁹ Paul is not interested in the Antioch situation as such,⁹⁰ but rather he seeks to model for the Galatians how 'Christ's slave' resists whoever stands against his Christ-revealed gospel.⁹¹ His point is clear: those who want to please God should follow his example by rejecting the addition of Jewish requirements to the gospel Paul has preached, lest they fall under the twofold curse of 1.8-

---

87. On *synkrisis* as a commonplace feature of rhetoric and literature, see C. Forbes, 'Comparison, Self-Praise and Irony: Paul's Boasting and the Conventions of Hellenistic Rhetoric', *NTS* 32 (1986), pp. 1-30; Fiore, *The Function of Personal Example*, pp. 148-61.

88. And, some of the mud sticks to Barnabas, perhaps indicative of Paul's breach with him as Dunn suggests (*Galatians*, p. 89).

89. For the tally of scholars who believe either Paul or Peter 'won' the confrontation, see Holmberg, *Paul and Power*, p. 34 n. 117.

90. See R.G. Hall, who problematizes using Gal. 1 and 2 for historical reconstruction of the events at Jerusalem and Antioch ('Historical Inference and Rhetorical Effect: Another Look at Galatians 1 and 2', in D. Watson [ed.], *Persuasive Artistry: Studies in New Testament Rhetoric in Honor of George A. Kennedy* [JSNTSup, 50; Sheffield: JSOT Press, 1991], pp. 308-20), and Munck, who contends that there was no permanent discord between Paul and the Jerusalem leaders (*Paul and the Salvation of Mankind*, pp. 87-134). His contention is strengthened if Acts 15 came after the incident described in Gal. 2, showing that Peter learned from his confrontation with Paul, as R.P. Martin has pointed out (*New Testament Foundations: Acts–Revelation* [2 vols.; Exeter: Paternoster Press, 1978], II, pp. 151-52). Cf. Bligh, *Galatians*, followed by Dunn ('Incident', pp. 160-62; *idem*, *Galatians*, p. 132), who think the whole letter is in effect Paul's attempt to undo the damage done at Antioch, a confrontation Paul lost. N. Taylor interprets Paul's portrayal of his apostleship in Galatians as 'egocentric and individualistic' (p. 227), resulting from his isolation after the Antioch incident (*Paul, Antioch and Jerusalem: A Study in Relationships and Authority in Earliest Christianity* [JSNTSup, 66; Sheffield: JSOT Press, 1992], pp. 155-70). Yet, this 'psychological' interpretation looks past Paul's persuasive artistry in the text to read in his 'real' mind and motives lying behind the text.

91. Alternatively, Munck observes this confrontation is the clearest proof of Paul's independence from Jerusalem and therefore it fits in well with that part of the argument (*Paul and the Salvation of Mankind*, p. 102). However, it seems that Paul argues *from* his independence from Jerusalem for the God-given nature of his

4. *Galatians*   155

9. The confrontation with Peter carries on through at least v. 17, and it is not clear whether it continues through v. 21. The exemplification of Paul, and particularly the content of his message, is emphasized in 2.15-21 for the Galatians' emulation and obedience so that they, too, may please God and not human beings.

With these features highlighted, it is clear that 'people-pleasing' is not a 'bolt from the blue' in Gal. 1.10, nor is it a defensive remark against a charge that Paul has accommodated the Gentiles, but is rather Paul's polemical phrase that he develops in Galatians as a reference to those who succumb to the pressure to Judaize. Therefore Gal. 1.10 should be treated as another example of Paul's thematic use of the 'paradigmatic I' where it has already been demonstrated that its sudden occurrence heightens awareness of the central thrust of the argument. This usage in Gal. 1.10 lies somewhere between the direct and immediate way that 1 Cor. 8.13 introduces 1 Corinthians 9, and the more general and anticipatory way Rom. 1.16-17 introduces the major theological themes of Romans.

If we read Galatians 1–2 with the sometimes thematic function of Paul's paradigmatic 'I' statements in mind, Gal. 1.10 proves to be an interpretative key that unlocks an element of Gal. 2.4-6, 11-21 that is usually overlooked. The opening of Galatians (1.1-10), then, makes two assertions that Paul develops in the autobiographical section.[92] The first assertion is that his gospel is from God and not from human origin (1.1, 7; 1.11–2.10), as I have discussed above. The second is that Paul does not seek to please human beings but Christ and God (1.10; 2.4-5, 11-21). It is maintained here that this second assertion explains the recounting of Paul's confrontation with Peter at Antioch as a model for how the Galatians are to stand up to the pressure of the heterodox teachers, lest they be 'enslaved' by them. Paul's underlying purpose is to claim their total allegiance to the gospel of Christ that he has proclaimed.

Presumably the confrontation with Peter continues through 2.21, but Paul's argument with Peter from 2.15 continues to be so closely related to his argument with the Galatians that it is difficult to separate the two,

---

gospel rather than *for* his independence, as argued convincingly by Schütz, *Anatomy of Apostolic Authority*, pp. 140-50, and Howard, *Crisis in Galatia*, pp. 20-45.

92. So Longenecker, *Galatians*, pp. 21-22; cf. Jeremias, 'Chiasmus in den Paulusbriefen', pp. 152-53, and Bligh, *Galatians*, who contend there is a chiastic structure for the entire letter. Cf. Longenecker's critique.

though some elements only can be applied to Peter and Paul. For example, 'we' in v. 15 naturally refers to Paul and Peter, who are both 'by nature Jewish', exclusive of a significant portion of Galatian readers. Nevertheless, Paul weaves this confrontation into his epistolary purposes for the Galatians. The whole point of the recounting of his soliloquy is that the Galatians are to 'overhear' his speech to Peter and to apply his teaching to themselves,[93] as can be seen in 3.1 when he brings the message to bear on them ('O foolish Galatians...'), and in 5.2-5 when the same message is repeated. As P.E. Koptak says

> As the Galatians hear Paul tell his story of his past relationships, they are forced to decide whether they will stand with Paul and his understanding of the gospel, or with those who are urging them to be circumcised. What Paul makes clear to them is that they cannot have it both ways.[94]

There are several salient features of Paul's self-presentation to comment on in the four brief verses at the end of Galatians 2. In v. 18 Paul's 'I' occurs as a hypothetical negative example, stylistically not unlike 1 Cor. 13.1-3; 14.6, 11, 14, developing rather than explaining 'certainly not' (μὴ γένοιτο) in Gal. 2.17.[95] On one level, Paul's 'I' statement condemns Peter for building up again what he has previously torn down, and in a sense speaks for Peter as a negative example in Antioch: 'For if I build up again the things which I abolished, I demonstrate I am a transgressor' (2.18).[96] On another level, this condemnation censures his opponents in Galatia, and it serves as a caution to any Galatians who would abandon Paul's gospel.

Whereas v. 18 is a negative formulation, v. 19 comprises positive assertions, picking up the contrast made in v. 16—'we' are justified through 'faith we have in Christ who has acted faithfully'[97] rather than

---

93. W.J. Dalton, 'The Meaning of "We" in Galatians', *AusBR* 38 (1990), pp. 33-44. Contra E.H.-S. Kok, ' "The Truth of the Gospel": A Study of Galatians 2.15-21' (PhD Dissertation, Durham University, 1993), pp. 63, 95, who asserts 2.15-21 is basically Paul's response to *Jewish* Christians. However, he later says, 'Thus with the declaration of 2.21a, Paul (the Jewish Christian) emerges as *the* example for the Gentile believers in Galatia' (p. 282).

94. Koptak, 'Rhetorical Identification', p. 100.

95. So J. Lambrecht, 'The Line of Thought in Gal. 2.14b-21', *NTS* 24 (1977–78), pp. 484-95, who deals with the exegetical difficulties surrounding vv. 17-18; so also Kok, ' "The Truth of the Gospel" ', pp. 170-94.

96. Wechsler, *Geschichtsbild*, p. 385.

97. Gal. 2.16 is perhaps the best support for the multiple conclusions of M.D.

'out of works of the law'.[98] In v. 19, Paul 'died to the law' in order that he 'might live to God'. Verses 19b-20a develop v. 19a into a christological and cross-centred statement, suggested by the parallelism:[99]

> I, through the law, *died to the law* in order that *I will live to God* (v. 19a).
>
> I have been *crucified with Christ*, it is no longer I who live but *Christ lives in me* (vv. 19b-20a).

'I am crucified with Christ' (Χριστῷ συνεσταύρωμαι) is participationist language in which Paul sets his current life 'in Christ' against his former life under Torah. He explains that his transference from one mode of living to the other took place eschatologically in Christ's death on the cross. The eschatological understanding of this phrase need not

---

Hooker, 'ΠΙΣΤΙΣ ΧΡΙΣΤΟΥ', *NTS* 35 (1989), pp. 321-42, particularly that Paul includes both Christ's faithfulness (διά / ἐκ πίστεως Ἰησοῦ Χριστοῦ) and human faith (ἡμεῖς εἰς Χριστὸν Ἰησοῦν ἐπιστεύσαμεν) in the mix, and that human faith flows out of participation with Christ, an element strongly present in 2.19-20 (so also Longenecker, *Galatians*, pp. 92-94). Furthermore she makes the case that we need not settle for an either-or interpretation in Paul's varied usage of πίστις Χριστοῦ. For example, Rom. 4.24–5.1 is not about Christ's faithfulness, but Gal. 3.22 clearly is. R.B. Hays, *The Faith of Jesus Christ: An Investigation of the Narrative Substructure of Galatians 3.1–4.11* (SBLDS, 56; Chico, CA: Scholars Press, 1983), is a strong proponent for a 'faith of Christ' only approach, as in his 'Jesus' Faith and Ours: A Rereading of Galatians 3', in M. Lau Branson and C. Padilla (eds.), *Conflict and Context: Hermeneutics in the Americas* (Grand Rapids: Eerdmans, 1986), pp. 257-80. However Dunn, *Galatians*, pp. 138-39, offers further compelling reasons why we need not settle for 'faith of Christ' only. See my 'Romans 1.17—A *Crux Interpretum* for the Πίστις Χριστοῦ Debate?', *JBL* 114 (1995), pp. 470-73.

98. The current discussion on the meaning and background of this phrase between Sanders, Dunn and Räisänen are beyond the scope of this essay. See E.P. Sanders, *Paul and Palestinian Judaism: A Comparison of Patterns of Religion* (Minneapolis: Fortress Press, 1977); *idem*, *Paul, the Law, and the Jewish People* (Philadelphia: Fortress Press, 1983); *idem*, 'Jewish Association with Gentiles and Galatians 2.11-14', in Fortna and Gaventa (eds.), *The Conversation Continues*, pp. 170-88; H. Räisänen, *Paul and the Law* (Tübingen: J.C.B. Mohr [Paul Siebeck], 1983); *idem*, 'Galatians 2.16 and Paul's Break with Judaism', *NTS* 31 (1985), pp. 543-53; J.D.G. Dunn, *Jesus, Paul and the Law: Studies in Mark and Galatians* (Louisville, KY: Westminster/John Knox Press (collection of his earlier articles); *idem*, *The Partings of the Ways between Christianity and Judsaism* (London: SCM Press, 1991); *idem*, 'Intra-Jewish Polemic'.

99. So also Kok, ' "The Truth of the Gospel"', pp. 241-43.

be set against its baptismal overtones (cf. Gal. 3.26-29; Rom. 6.3-6).[100] Even though baptism is not mentioned here,[101] Rom. 6.3-6 makes it clear that Paul believes baptism includes recognition of eschatological participation in Christ's death. In this case the perfect tense need not imply that he is 'still immersed' as Dunn supposes,[102] but simply that the past action has abiding consequences, namely, because of Paul's identification with Christ's death in baptism Torah remains nullified with regard to soteriology.[103] Yet, Dunn rightly points out that this phrase ties into Paul's rich 'together with' vocabulary (cf. Rom. 6.4-6; 2 Cor. 4.10; Phil. 3.10), and he takes us in the right direction with his suggestive 'I have been nailed to the cross with Christ, and am still hanging there with him'.[104] 2 Corinthians 4.10 and Phil. 3.10 are particularly instructive here, and taken with Gal. 6.17, demonstrate that Paul understands Christ to be manifest in his own present, literal sufferings, and that these troubles have a revelatory function in communicating the crucified Christ to others. The christophany of the Crucified *to* Paul (1.12, 16) has become a christophany to others *through* Paul's hardships and message. Therefore, although Kok is probably correct that Gal. 2.20a is to be understood 'in the sense that Paul is dethroned; he is no longer in power or jurisdiction over his own life',[105] this metaphorical rendering risks obscuring the way in which Paul connects his current traumas with the sufferings of Christ, explicit in the texts just cited and implicit in Gal. 2.19-20.

Galatians 2.20b explains further the christocentric life mentioned in 2.19-20a, how it is lived 'in the flesh' yet 'by the faithfulness of the son of God, the one who loved me and gave himself on my behalf'. Equally correct grammatically is 'by faith in the son of God', and yet the emphasis in this particular text is on Christ's actions rather than Paul's faith (Paul 'no longer lives'!). Christ shows his faithfulness as 'the one who loved me and gave himself for me' (v. 20). The specific choice of

100. Schlier, *Der Brief an die Galater*, pp. 99-100, is a strong proponent of a baptismal reading of these verses.

101. C.K. Barrett, *Freedom and Obligation: A Study of the Epistle to the Galatians* (London: SPCK, 1985), p. 20; for others who object to this as a baptismal reference see Kok, '"The Truth of the Gospel"', pp. 255-56.

102. Dunn, *Galatians*, p. 144 n. 1.

103. E. Schweizer, 'Dying and Rising with Christ', *NTS* 14 (1967–68), pp. 1-14 (3).

104. Dunn, *Galatians*, p. 144.

105. Kok, '"The Truth of the Gospel"', p. 66.

language deliberately echoes the opening verses of the letter (1.1, 4), giving the impression of a carefully crafted construction and suggests that vv. 19-21 may not have been part of the original speech to Peter. Verse 21 completes the section, setting this Christ-centred life totally against an acceptance of 'righteousness through the law'. Or, more accurately, 'righteousness through the law' is presented as a setting aside of God's grace.

At the end this rich soliloquy in 2.18-21, Paul's forceful presence is felt as he restates his case in personal terms, recounted for the benefit of the Galatian auditors. The first-person singular pronoun is emphatic, occurring seven times in these four verses, not counting the seven additional times 'I' is implied by the verb form. Though we have no way of confirming the relationship of these words to the actual confrontation between Peter and Paul, this speech now has a triple epistolary function, in addition to crisply stating key aspects of Paul's theology.[106] First, Paul completes his self-presentation as a model of how to be Christ's slave in confronting a 'people-pleaser', a subtext from 1.10. He stands his ground against Peter and 'those of circumcision' (2.12) in Antioch and rebukes them. This rhetorical comparison ends with Paul's example fixed firmly in the reader's mind, a feature that is heightened by Peter's unannounced exit from the narrative of events. Paul's 'performance' at the end of the scene is robust and confident.

Secondly, Paul's statement in 2.18-21 is an inclusive 'I' statement, modelling for the Galatians the theology they are to espouse.[107] Paul directs these comments to the Galatian audience, so that *they* will not 'build up again the things' that have been 'torn down' (v. 18). As Longenecker says of v. 18, the use of the first-person singular 'is rhetorical feature that allows Paul to make his point in more diplomatic fashion— i.e., by applying to himself a charge really directed against others'.[108] Ebeling observes of vv. 19-21:

106. On the theological significance of this passage, see Dunn, *Galatians*, pp. 147-49; and Kok, '"The Truth of the Gospel"', esp. pp. 27-46, for a survey of scholarly views on 2.15-21.

107. Bachmann, *Sünder oder Übertreter*, pp. 41-45; Betz, *Galatians*, pp. 121-23; W.G. Kümmel, '"Individualgeschichte" und "Weltgeschichte" in Galater 2, 15-21', in B. Lindars and S. Smalley (eds.), *Christ and Spirit in the New Testament* (Cambridge: Cambridge University Press, 1973), pp. 157-73; Lyons, *Pauline Autobiography*, p. 164; Hester, 'Placing the Blame', pp. 304-306.

108. Longenecker, *Galatians*, p. 90; BDF §281; similarly Ebeling, *The Truth of the Gospel*, pp. 119-20; Kok, '"The Truth of the Gospel"', p. 273. Longenecker

But despite the explicitly confessional note, these statements in the first person singular are not limited to Paul. They exemplify the situation of every Christian. The Galatians are thus invited for their own good to identify with this 'I' in the contrast to the other 'I' of v. 18, which referred at least indirectly to the Judaizers with whom the Galatians are on the point of identifying themselves, with disastrous consequences.[109]

Congruent with the style we identified in 1 Corinthians, Gal. 2.19-20 should be read as 'you', as made explicit in 5.2-5, 24 (cf. Rom. 6.6), and even has a polemical dimension (cf. 6.13-15). When he says 'I', he models for the Galatians the bold and exclusive faith in Christ *they* are to hold and profess. Thus in Galatians 2 Paul's 'I' is intended to re-emphasize his gospel, to influence the Galatians to reject the necessity of circumcision, and to demonstrate for the Galatians how they are to act toward those who think differently.[110]

Thirdly, the speech in 2.15-21 is programmatic for the letter setting out what will be argued in the chapters that follow, as is widely recognized.[111] In this connection, 2.18-21 as an 'I' statement serves as a summary/transition at the conclusion of a section, and if our observations of 1 Corinthians apply here, this is another case of Paul's stylized

---

thinks the 'I' changes to a gnomic 'I' in vv. 19-20, and then back to a literal 'I' in v. 21, responding to a charge (pp. 91-95). If we apply Longenecker's comment on v. 18 to v. 21, it is more likely a part of Paul's exemplification rather than engagement with a charge against him. As Dunn notes, *Galatians*, p. 148, 'grace' is probably Paul's word and not a Jewish-Christian criticism of him. Betz, *Galatians*, pp. 126-27, takes 2.21 as a charge, but acknowledges that it should be found in the *peroratio*. Instead, in 6.12-13 what is found is an accusation against his opponents, making it more likely that 2.21 is Paul's *synkrisis* rather than his engagement with a criticism against him.

109. Ebeling, *The Truth of the Gospel*, p. 120. As demonstrated above, this usage of 'I' is typical for Paul rather than 'peculiar'; *pace* Betz, *Galatians*, p. 121.

110. If Paul incorporates pre-pauline material here familiar to the Galatians then the authority of his exemplification is enhanced as in his appeals to the 'universality' of his teaching (e.g. Gal. 1.2; cf. 1 Cor. 14.33). On the other hand, such an inclusion might weaken his claim that he was 'not taught it by humans'. For a discussion, see G. Berényi, 'Gal. 2.20: A Pre-Pauline or a Pauline Text?', in Vanhoye (ed.), *L'Apôtre Paul*, pp. 340-44, who rightly notes that the paradoxes, antitheses and references to himself in Gal. 2.15-21 are typical of Paul's style.

111. As demonstrated by Bachmann, *Sünder oder Übertreter*, pp. 110-51, and Betz, *Galatians*, pp. 114-27 (the *'propositio'*). So also Brinsmead, *Dialogical Opponents*, p. 201; Bruce, *Galatians*, pp. 136-37; Burton, *Epistle to the Galatians*, pp. 117-18; Longenecker, *Galatians*, pp. 80-81; Dunn, *Galatians*, p. 132.

way of highlighting the thrust of his letter. As Longenecker says, 'this passage in reality is not only the hinge between what has gone before and what follows but actually [is] the central affirmation of the letter'.[112] As such, Paul's self-presentation comes at the centre of the argument and is critical for its development.

Galatians 3–6

The remaining self-characterizations in Galations enhance our understanding of what we have already touched upon. It remains to comment on these incidental occurrences, and then to summarize Paul's use of personal example in Galatians. In chs. 3–4, he further elaborates the point that nothing can be added to his gospel and that the Old Testament teaching about circumcision is no longer valid having served its purpose. He argues by appealing to the Galatians' experience of the Spirit that they received by faith (3.2-5; 4.8-10), to the compilation of Scripture citations and explanations clustered around the example of Abraham (3.6-14), to a word-play on the singularity of Abraham's 'seed' (3.15–4.7),[113] to further self-exemplification and personal appeal (4.12-20), and to an allegory on the sons of Hagar and Sarah (4.21-31). All of these contribute to Paul's paraenetic and polemical point, outlined in 2.18-21 and recapitulated in 5.1-2:

> For freedom Christ has set us free. Stand firm, therefore, and do not submit again to a yoke of slavery. Listen! I, Paul, am telling you that if you let yourselves be circumcised, Christ will be of no benefit to you.

By his comments elsewhere it does not appear that he was against circumcision as such (cf. Galatians 5.6; 6.15), but he opposed those who made it an additional soteriological requirement for his Gentile converts.

An Explicit Call to Imitate Paul (Galatians 4.11-20)

Paul's personal appeal and self-depiction in Gal. 4.11-20 supports the reading adopted for his self-presentation in Galatians 1–2. In 4.11, his personal feelings re-emerge as he pauses amid his scriptural argumentation to address the Galatian situation and to express his pastoral concern as a veiled threat. He expresses fear that his gospel labour has been

---

112. Longenecker, *Galatians*, p. 83.
113. Following Longenecker, *Galatians*, pp. 135-36, and Dunn, *Galatians*, p. 151, that this is not a digression but integral to the argument.

pointless, but the polemical implication is clear. If he has laboured in vain with the Galatians, then they have no eschatological hope.

In 4.12 we read a familiar Pauline appeal for imitation, though the word itself (μίμησις) is lacking.[114] It seems natural to take this appeal to include the self-presentation that has already occurred in the letter, since it has already been argued that the earlier self-portrayal is intentionally paradigmatic.[115] But, there are further clues that lend support to this contention. Surrounding 4.12-20, there is explicit use of the slavery metaphor introduced in 1.10. In 4.8-11 there is an implied contrast between 'slavery to those who are not gods' with slavery to Christ, though the latter half of the comparison is inferred.[116] Likewise, slavery imagery is developed in what follows 4.21. As we have already noted, 5.1-2 applies the slavery imagery explicitly to the Galatians, as it applies implicitly throughout the letter.[117] Moreover, within 4.12-20 we

114. So de Boer, *The Imitation of Paul*, pp. 188-96; contra Michaelis, 'μιμέομαι', p. 672 n. 29; Vos, 'Die Argumentation', p. 35. However, chs. 1–2, taken as a model of behaviour, are problematic since Paul hardly asks the Galatians to mirror his call (1.13-24) or to re-enact his confrontations with the 'pseudo-brethren' (2.4-5) and Peter (2.11-14). These chapters can only stand as a model in a general sense, that is, that the Galatians are to stand firm boldly against Paul's opponents in Galatia as he has exemplified in Jerusalem and Antioch. It must be added that Paul's style of a paradigmatic use of 'I' renders irrelevant the objection of Sandnes that the direct appeal to imitation does not appear before Gal. 4.12 (*Paul—One of the Prophets?*, pp. 49-50). Lyons, however, overstates the case when he claims this call to imitation 'would be scarcely intelligible apart from the autobiographical narrative in Galatians 1 and 2 which precedes it' (*Pauline Autobiography*, p. 165). He overlooks that the Galatians had personal knowledge of Paul from his visits, and Paul could be referring to his example set when present with them (cf. 4.13). See Goddard and Cummins who give 4.13-14 full weight and emphasize Paul's *past* dealings with the Galatians and arrive at a similar interpretation, but they overlook Paul's *present* exemplification in chs. 1–2 ('Ill or Ill-Treated?', pp. 93-126).

115. De Boer, *The Imitation of Paul*, p. 191; contra Sandnes, *Paul—One of the Prophets?*, pp. 49-50.

116. The στοιχεῖα of 4.9, as in 4.3, need not be understood more precisely than 'elements or principles' which vie for control of the Galatians, since in both cases Paul affiliates them with enslavement (see the excursus in Burton, *Epistle to the Galatians*, pp. 510-18). In 4.9-10 Jewish calendrical observance is characterized as an example of elements that enslave (Bruce, *Galatians*, pp. 202-204; Dunn, *Galatians*, pp. 227-29). In place of this 'bondage' Paul wants the Galatians instead to be 'steered by the Spirit' (5.25, also employing στοιχ-). See also Goddard and Cummins, 'Ill or Ill-Treated?', pp. 117-18.

117. Cf. 5.13; 6.2-5 for further traces of this imagery.

find traces of Paul's self-presentation as a slave of Christ. In v. 13 Paul hints that there was an element of compulsion in his proclamation of the gospel to the Galatians. In vv. 14-15, he refers to his sufferings which he explicitly mentioned as part of his earlier exemplification (2.19-20). The appeal to imitation in 4.12, then, is naturally to be taken to include his earlier epistolary exemplification.

Our understanding of the content of Paul's example to be imitated must be slightly nuanced, however. As Gaventa rightly notes, the Galatians 'could never duplicate the βίος Paul characterizes in Gal. 1.11–2.14, especially because the fulcrum of that βίος is God's action (1.15) —not Paul's'.[118] Her understanding is that Paul calls the Galatians to imitate his single-minded response to the gospel that was revealed to him, and to allow Christ to live in oneself (cf. 2.20) to the exclusion of the law or of any other tradition or category (cf. 3.27-28). In agreement with this, we may add that Paul's example of how to resist 'people-pleasers' is, for him, a part of his single-minded response to the gospel.

The call to imitation in 4.12-14 carries explicit christological implications since, rather than rejecting Paul because of his physical condition (ἐν τῇ σαρκί μου), they received him 'as a messenger of God, as Christ Jesus' (ὡς Χριστὸν Ἰησοῦν, 4.14). He believes he models not his own will but the will of God in Christ, and it is this christological life pattern that Paul exhorts the Galatians to imitate (cf. 2.19b-20).[119] This christological dimension, as in 1 and 2 Corinthians, paradoxically embodies the weakness of a cruciform life (2.19b-20; 4.13).[120] As Paul draws attention to the christological dimension of his message and life, his words take on an unsurpassed claim to authority because he speaks 'as Christ Jesus'.[121] This implicit assertion of authority bolsters the exclusive claims he has already made for his teaching in the letter.

The enigmatic 'as I also you' poses difficulties. The elliptical construction most likely should be read 'Become as I am [εἰμί], for I also have become [ἐγενόμην] as you were/are', inserting either ἦτε or ἐστέ.[122] This phrase is made more difficult if we read the 'as I also you'

118. Gaventa, 'Galatians 1 and 2', p. 322.
119. See further R.B. Hays, 'Christology and Ethics in Galatians: The Law of Christ', *CBQ* 49 (1987), pp. 268-90 (280-87).
120. See Goddard and Cummins, 'Ill or Ill-Treated?', pp. 93-126.
121. Cf. 2 Cor. 5.20.
122. Schlier, *Der Brief an die Galater*, p. 208; Burton, *Galatians*, pp. 236-37; de Boer, *The Imitation of Paul*, p. 191.

as an equation, that is, the Galatians' imitation of Paul is a mirror of his imitation of them. But as de Boer has pointed out, this second phrase is a statement of fact, whereas the call to imitation is an imperative.[123] With an ironic reversal of roles Paul probably speaks of how he became free of Torah like the Gentile Galatians had been before their conversion, and now calls them to pattern themselves after his radical indifference to the Mosaic law.[124] With the threat of their Judaizing Paul becomes the example of their former liberty: 'become like me (i.e., free from the Torah) as I have become like you'.[125] This nicely recapitulates the earlier self-presentation in 2.18-21 and, as Schlier notes, is Paul's stated missionary strategy among the Gentiles in 1 Cor. 9.21.[126]

Paul's Spiritual 'Maternity' (4.19-20)
Galatians 4.19 carries forward the theme of the imitation of Paul. As in 1 Cor. 4.14-16, the summons to imitation is related to spiritual parenthood (Gal. 4.19). Paul's parenthood of the Galatians is at once a further implication of his authoritative status with them,[127] but also is derivative of God's parenthood as all believers are God's children (Rom. 8.16-17; Phil. 2.15; cf. Gal. 4.27-31). Furthermore, there is an element of this personal language (τέκνα μου) that fits the rhetorical situation. The Galatians are Paul's *own* children and do not properly belong to the interlopers. In 4.20, he models his parental concern by acknowledging the harshness of his tone (cf. 1 Cor. 4.14), yet he nevertheless returns to the fray in the next verse.

Gaventa has raised the possibility of a unique understanding of Paul's self-presentation in her article, 'The Maternity of Paul: An Exegetical Study of Galatians 4.19'.[128] She notes that the verb ὠδίνειν customarily

123. De Boer, *The Imitation of Paul*, p. 193. As Castelli says, 'Paul remains the privileged model for the community he addresses' (*Imitating Paul*, p. 116). Differently, Betz, *Galatians*, pp. 221-23, takes this as *topos* from popular philosophy that 'true friendship' is only possible among equals.

124. Doohan, *Leadership in Paul*, p. 33.

125. De Boer, *The Imitation of Paul*, p. 191; Hays, 'Christology and Ethics in Galatians', pp. 281-82; similarly, Hooker, 'ΠΙΣΤΙΣ ΧΡΙΣΤΟΥ', pp. 332-33; Gaventa, 'Galatians 1 and 2', p. 321.

126. Schlier, *Der Brief an die Galater*, pp. 208-209.

127. See Holmberg, *Paul and Power*, pp. 78-79.

128. B.R. Gaventa, 'The Maternity of Paul: An Exegetical Study of Galatians 4.19', in Fortna and Gaventa (eds.), *The Conversation Continues*, pp. 189-201. She makes it clear that her agenda is to reclaim Paul from a solely 'paternal' portrayal

refers to the physical pain accompanying childbirth. Because begetting (fathering) is different from birthing (mothering), Gaventa is against equating 4.19 with Paul's familiar representation of his relationship with his converts as a father with his spiritual children (cf. 1 Cor. 4.14-15; 2 Cor. 12.14; 1 Thess. 2.11; cf. Phlm. 10). For that reason she understands 'gentle as a nurse' (1 Thess. 2.7) as a closer parallel, and thinks Paul's self-presentation should be understood through other Pauline parallels that employ childbirth imagery (Rom. 8.22-23; 1 Cor. 3.1-4; 1 Cor. 15.8). She argues that, in addition to maternal self-presentation, Paul associates his apostolic vocation with the anguish anticipated in the apocalyptic era (cf. 1 Thess. 5; Rom. 8). He 'reflects the anguish of the whole created order as it awaits the fulfillment of God's action in Jesus Christ'.[129]

Though her approach is stimulating, she presses it too far to suggest that Paul claims 'to be doing something that is manifestly impossible—giving birth (again!)'.[130] In J. Barr's parlance, this is an 'illegitimate identity transfer', requiring the word to bring its literal implications in another place to a particular metaphorical usage in this text.[131] This is surprising since Gaventa notes the variability of usage of ὠδίνειν for metaphors of any great pain,[132] and that the LXX reserves the verb and its related noun almost entirely for metaphors, usually for a situation dealing with the people collectively (e.g. Mic. 4.10; Isa. 13.6, 8; Jer. 6.24).[133] Moreover, Paul does not develop the image in the direction of birthing, but of *Christ's* formation in the Galatians (μορφόω; cf. Rom. 12.2; 2 Cor. 3.18; Phil. 3.10), and so suggestion of a birthing connotation breaks down. Furthermore, the attention Gaventa draws to the apocalyptic groaning of creation is hardly applicable in this text. Paul's anguish concerns the threat that his converts in Galatia will abandon his

of his apostleship (pp. 198-99). Her characterization that scholars relegate the language of maternity to the footnotes is not borne out in the work of Holmberg, *Paul and Power*, pp. 73, 78, nor Gutierrez, *La paternité spirituelle*, pp. 213-23, which she cites. Gutierrez characterizes Paul's concern as 'la sollicitude maternelle'. Cf. Castelli, *Imitating Paul*, p. 116, who reads Paul's self-presentation in Gal. 4.19 as both hierarchical and paternal.

129. Gaventa, 'The Maternity of Paul', p. 194.
130. Gaventa, 'The Maternity of Paul', p. 189.
131. J. Barr, *The Semantics of Biblical Language* (London: Oxford University Press, 1961), p. 218.
132. LSJ, *s.v.*
133. Gaventa, 'The Maternity of Paul', p. 192.

gospel, a theme that precisely fits his exhortation in the total letter (1.6; 3.1; 4.11, 16; 5.7; 6.16-17).[134] His expression of anguish communicates how seriously he considers this new 'gospel' a threat, and how strong his desire is that they return to his gospel.

Paul's concern for the Galatians to reject Judaizing is nothing less than a concern for them to remain faithful to Christ. If they have accepted 'another gospel' (1.7) they have lost their christocentricity, implied since Paul has agony over them 'again' (πάλιν, 4.19). He suggests that there is now an unfulfilled aspect to their formation in Christ (μέχρις οὗ). Especially related is Gal. 2.19-20. As the crucified Christ lives in Paul (ἐν ἐμοὶ Χριστός, 2.20), his desire is that they will be indwelt by this same crucified Christ (Χριστὸς ἐν ὑμῖν, 4.19). As Gaventa rightly says, 'For Christ to be formed in the Galatians is not simply for them to develop spiritually or morally or christologically. The formation of Christ among the Galatians is simultaneously their crucifixion with Christ.'[135] Paul's pastoral concern for them remains an interest in their relation to Christ. An unfavourable reading of Paul places his motives in the realm of personal defensiveness for his own reputation or ego. Instead, his representation of his concern remains christocentric throughout.

The Basis of the Galatians' Persuasion (5.10-11)
Galatians 5 is punctuated with Paul's paradigmatic 'I' as well. The theme of 1.10 is picked up in 5.8: '[Your] persuasion does not come from the one who calls you'. The opponents' persuasiveness has already been alluded to (cf. Gal. 1.7; 3.1a; 5.8, 10), and now is characterized as the little leaven that corrupts the whole lump of dough (5.9). His rhetorical purpose throughout Galatians has been to drive a wedge between these outsiders and 'his children' in Galatia, and he repeats his appeal for them to conform to his thinking (5.10). The NRSV translation 'I am confident about you in the Lord' obscures the way in which Paul speaks for them, literally rendered, 'I am persuaded for you [εἰς ὑμᾶς] in the Lord that you will not think otherwise'. Paul steps in as their surrogate, persuaded on the proper grounds that they agree with him (οὐδὲν ἄλλο φρονήσετε; cf. 2 Cor. 13.11; Phil. 2.2, 5; 3.15, 19; 4.2).

Galatians 5.10 amounts to a reference to Paul's whole purpose in writing to the congregation: that they may accept his teaching and

134. Gutierrez, *La paternité spirituelle*, p. 213.
135. Gaventa, 'The Maternity of Paul', p. 195.

reject that of his opponents. As Olson has pointed out, the 'confidence expression' is a stylistic feature of Hellenistic letter writing in antiquity. It cannot be characterized as formulaic since the verbal variation is great in the papyri and New Testament (cf. Rom. 15.14; 2 Cor. 7.4, 16; 9.1-2; Gal. 5.10; 2 Thess. 3.4; Phlm. 21), but the usage shows *functional* parallels.[136] In each case, Olson notes, the expression is linked to the purpose of the letter.

As in the case of 1.10, 5.11 seems to be another comparative statement with his opponents. Though the syntax is awkward,[137] Paul's meaning is straightforward enough: he no longer preaches circumcision as he once did, but is now the recipient of persecution by those who do (cf. 1.13, 23). Paul's argument makes sense in light of the content of the letter. He would not be opposed by the Galatian intruders if he had been preaching circumcision. Yet, there is a further negative characterization of his opponents implied here. They have abolished the scandal of the cross, and have chosen the easy path rather than the way of the crucified Christ. That they are portrayed with disdain in v. 11 seems assured as Paul expresses his contempt for them in the next verse: 'I wish that the ones who trouble you would castrate themselves'.

The Conclusion of the Matter (Galatians 6.14, 17)
In 6.11-18 Paul sums up the thrust of the letter as we would expect in an autographic postscript, adding confirmation to the interpretation of Galatians already offered.[138] Paul's usage of his personal example here echoes his earlier self-portrayals in Galatians.

Galatians 6.14 on its own appears as a confessional statement, recapitulating 2.19-20:

> May I never boast of anything except the cross of our Lord Jesus Christ,
> by which the world has been crucified to me, and I to the world.

But, the mention of boasting (καυχᾶσθαι) is offered as a direct comparison with those mentioned in the previous verse who promote circumcision in order to 'boast in your flesh' (v. 13). And, Paul centres his confidence on the cross, which these interlopers have set aside to avoid persecution (v. 12). Paul's confession serves as a *synkrisis* with the

---

136. Olson, 'Epistolary Uses', pp. 585-97.
137. See T. Baarda, 'ΤΙ ΕΤΙ ΔΙΩΚΟΜΑΙ in Gal. 5.11: Apodosis or Parenthesis?', *NovT* 34 (1992), pp. 250-56.
138. Betz, *Galatians*, pp. 312-13; Lyons, *Pauline Autobiography*, p. 168.

intruders in Galatia, but more than that, it functions as a paradigmatic confession for the Galatians. His hope is that they will avow with him a belief in christocentric and cross-centred theology that eliminates the necessity for circumcision. Paul wants them to reaffirm that in Christ they are a 'new creation' (v. 15; cf. 5.2-6; 2 Cor. 5.16-17).

He goes on to promise a conditional blessing for those who submit to his rule (6.16), followed up by an implied threat to those who oppose him (6.17). He identifies himself again with the crucified Christ, enhancing the impression already given that he is their exemplar in Christ (2.19-20; 5.24; 6.14)[139] whom they received as Christ himself (4.14). The 'marks of Jesus in my body' (6.17) re-emphasizes again Paul's self-description as a representative of the crucified Christ (cf. 1.1, 12, 16; 2.19-20; 4.14; 5.24; 6.14).[140] It is likely that 'the marks of Jesus' refers to the physical scars he has acquired from 'suffering with Christ' on his missionary campaigns,[141] which he bears as tattoos marking him as 'Christ's slave' (1.10).[142] Paul closes his letter as he began, identifying himself and his message with the crucified Christ.[143] The warning is explicit: to oppose Paul is to oppose Christ.

A Summary of Paul's Use of Self-Portrayal in Galatians

The general thrust of Paul's self-depictions in Galatians is that if the Galatians want to please God, then there is no way they can reject the

---

139. Betz, *Galatians*, p. 325.
140. Betz, *Galatians*, pp. 323-25.
141. Cf. 2 Cor. 4.10; 1.5; 4.16; 13.3-4.; Phil. 3.10. So Burton, *Galatians*, p. 360.
142. Burton, *Galatians*, p. 361; Schlier, *Der Brief an die Galater*, p. 285; Bruce, *Galatians*, pp. 275-76; Longenecker, *Galatians*, p. 300; cf. Dunn, *Galatians*, pp. 346-47; and see LSJ, *s.v.*, on στίγματα as slave brands. Cf. Betz, *Galatians*, p. 324 n. 26, for the suggestion that these refer to religious tattoos widely used in the ancient world.
143. Two other plausible nuances have been suggested. First, the mention of these marks may have a polemical intent as 'the spiritual counterpart of circumcision' in view of the context (Bligh, *Galatians*, p. 496). Secondly, could Paul be referring to visible trouble with his eyes, taking 6.17 with 4.15, 6.11 and the story in Acts 9.8-19? If so, he closes the letter leaving a vivid picture in their minds: he has physical signs that he encountered Christ on the Damascus road. This nuance would further emphasize his contention of the divine origin of his calling and message. See E. Hirsch, 'Zwei Fragen zu Gal 6', *ZNW* 29 (1930), pp. 196-97, and the reply by O. Holtzmann, 'Zu E. Hirsch, Zwei Fragen zu Gal 6', *ZNW* 30 (1931), pp. 82-83.

message of the apostle who pleases God. If they want to be accursed of God and be seen as 'people pleasers', a choice not realistically open to them, then they should choose the teaching of Paul's opponents. His rhetoric leaves no options open for them but to return their loyalty to him and his teaching. Paul's use of personal example in Galatians is not marked by the same explicit indicators of a deliberate literary strategy as it was in 1 Corinthians, Gal. 4.12 notwithstanding. Implicitly, however, his use of self-exemplification and self-portrayal serves the following:

1. To drive a wedge between the Galatians and the Judaizers by convincing them to side with Paul against his opponents.
2. To identify the divine nature and origin of Paul's message, the Jerusalem approval of it, and therefore its truth and exclusivity for the Galatians. This assertion is strengthened by his close identification of himself with Christ as Christ's slave.
3. To denigrate, by comparison, the teaching of the Judaizers as deriving from a merely human source and lacking the Jerusalem seal of approval. No reference needs to be made to hypothetical charges against Paul to interpret Gal. 1.10. It may have been that Paul was charged with being a people-pleaser, but there is no evidence for this, and the text has been made sense of without resorting to this hypothetical reconstruction. Furthermore, it has been argued that Paul introduces people-pleasing as a part of his persuasive tactics with the Galatians, and part of his characterization of Peter serves as an exemplum along this line of his argument.
4. To exemplify defiance against Judaizing which Paul sees as 'people pleasing', providing a paradigmatic expression of the views the Galatians are to espouse (Gal. 1.10; 2.15-21; 6.14). Galatians 1.10 introduces Paul's personal example for the Galatians to imitate as they reject the teachers who seek to alter his teaching dramatically.
5. To highlight the thrust of Paul's argument as in Rom. 1.16-17; 1 Cor. 8.13; 12.31. Thus, Gal. 1.10 provides the reader with an interpretative clue for exegesis by anticipating thematically part of the argument that follows.
6. To offer a third major argument against Judaizing—an argument from Paul's apostolic example—in addition to the argu-

ments from experience (3.1-6) and scriptural examples (chs. 3–4).

Implicitly, then, Paul's use of himself as an exemplum in his argument in Galatians serves a refined literary and argumentative function. Though the explicit discourse markers for such a usage are not prevalent as they were in 1 Corinthians, the employment of the same sort of technique and style of argumentation is unmistakable. Nevertheless, there is a new situation encountered and Paul's letter to his converts in that new situation is shaped to the needs of their situation. Thus, while the use of self-portrayal in Galatians is similar to that in 1 Corinthians, it is not claimed that it is exactly the same nor could it be given the differing demands of the rhetorical situation. In the next chapter it will be argued that this same technique is adapted again to the new demands of the Philippian church, and again there are explicit literary indicators of this style (Phil. 3.17; 4.9).

Chapter 5

PHILIPPIANS: POLEMICAL AND PARADIGMATIC SELF-PORTRAYAL

After a survey of the literary usage of self-depiction, paradigmatic 'I' statements, and personal example in 1 Corinthians and Galatians, it is very apparent that Paul's references to himself are by no means informed by a uniform strategy. Sometimes Paul literally portrays himself or his past to underline his calling and authority, while at other times his 'I' takes on a rhetorical flair and rather is meant as 'you'. In places Paul's self-references engage the pastoral situation faced, while in other places his self-characterizations may have more to do with generally held social requirements surrounding self-discussion. He often uses paradigmatic 'I' expressions as punchlines, summarizing and providing a transition to the next phase of his letters, and at other times his self-exemplification and personal example is the heart of his argument. He also sets against his own exemplary model the contrastive, negative examples of others, employing the commonly practised technique of *synkrisis*. For these reasons it is misleading to conceive of Paul's self-presentations in his letters as 'autobiography', since this suggests that the purpose of his self-presentation is merely to express himself and the details of his life. Rather, his self-characterizations are highly selective, serving as antidotes for the particular rhetorical situation by seeking both to undermine his opposition and to provide a clear model for his readers.

One of Paul's most personal letters, Philippians, employs 'I', 'me' and 'my' more than 50 times,[1] and adds to the complex collage of Paul's usage of personal example. In light of our foregoing study of Paul's stylistic usage of self-presentation, we should reject R.T. Fortna's interpretation of Philippians as Paul's most 'egocentric' letter.[2]

    1.   G.F. Hawthorne, *Philippians* (WBC, 43; Waco, TX: Word Books, 1983), p. 3.
    2.   R.T. Fortna, 'Philippians: Paul's Most Egocentric Letter', in Fortna and

Fortna seems unaware of the common paraenetic practice of Hellenistic moralists in their use of imitation in paraenesis, and thus he misinterprets the function of Paul's self-references labelling them 'self-absorbed' and 'grandiose'. This interpretation is anachronistic, overlooks Paul's nuanced usage outlined above, and it fails to give full weight to the Graeco-Roman principle that a good letter should substitute for one's personal presence, a feature which Paul accomplishes quite nicely in Philippians. Furthermore, it is evident that the Philippians were very interested in, even financially committed to, the subject of the letter, having sent Epaphroditus to care for Paul and deliver their material support (implied by λειτουργία: 2.25, 30; cf. 2.17).[3] An awareness of Paul's 'I' style, already highlighted in 1 Corinthians and Galatians, should give us reason to explore the rhetorical, hortatory and polemical purposes of Paul's self-references in Philippians. It will be argued here that Paul indeed discusses himself with persuasive intentions for a paraenetic purpose. First, however, some general issues that confront the interpreter of Philippians must be faced.

The Literary Unity of Philippians

Philippians is treated below as a literary unit and partition theories are not heeded, a stance that requires a brief justification. The integrity of Philippians has been a matter of considerable debate for internal, formal reasons—the dramatic shift of tone at the beginning of ch. 3 and suspected seams at 4.10 and 4.21.[4] However, in a recent formal analysis and comparison of Philippians with Hellenistic letters L.C. Alexander demonstrates that 'the *formalia* of Hellenistic letters give us no warrant

---

Gaventa (eds.), *The Conversation Continues*, pp. 220-34.

3. C.O. Buchanan, 'Epaphroditus' Sickness and the Letter to the Philippians', *EvQ* 36 (1964), pp. 157-66 (158-59).

4. F.W. Beare, *A Commentary on the Epistle to the Philippians* (BNTC; London: A. & C. Black, 1959), pp. 1-5; B.D. Rahtjen, 'The Three Letters of Paul to the Philippians', *NTS* (1960), pp. 167-73; J. Gnilka, *Der Philipperbrief* (HTK; Freiburg: Herder, 1968), pp. 5-11; J.-F. Collange, *The Epistle of Saint Paul to the Philippians* (trans. A. Heathcote; London: Epworth Press, 1979), pp. 3-8; Schenk, *Die Philipperbriefe*, pp. 331-35. See D.E. Garland, 'The Composition and Unity of Philippians: Some Neglected Literary Factors', *NovT* 27 (1985), pp. 141-73 (see p. 155 n. 50, for a chart summarizing the various proposals for separate letters contained in Philippians).

for the dismembering of Philippians'.[5] Moreover, several scholars have demonstrated a literary and rhetorical unity between the putative parts of the letter, in addition to identifying rare words that occur in two presumably separate letters.[6] These lexical parallels—especially *hapax legomena*—and thematic parallels in the various proposed fragments provide the strongest argument for the unity of the letter.[7] R. Jewett, for example, traces the introductory themes of the thanksgiving (1.3-11) through the letter,[8] while other scholars have shown that the concepts and vocabulary of the Christ hymn (2.6-11) are integrated into the argument of the whole.[9] Furthermore, the presence of suffering is woven throughout Philippians as a leitmotif.[10] These internal indicators

---

5. L.C. Alexander, 'Hellenistic Letter-Forms and the Structure of Philippians', *JSNT* 37 (1989), pp. 87-101 (98).

6. W.J. Dalton, 'The Integrity of Philippians', *Bib* 60 (1979), pp. 97-102; Garland, 'The Composition and Unity of Philippians'; D.F. Watson, 'A Rhetorical Analysis of Philippians and its Implications for the Unity Question', *NovT* 30 (1988), pp. 57-88; L.G. Bloomquist, *The Function of Suffering in Philippians* (JSNTSup, 78; Sheffield: JSOT Press, 1993), pp. 101-103, 119-38.

7. So Collange, *Philippians*, p. 5, though he favours a partition theory.

8. R. Jewett, 'The Epistolary Thanksgiving and the Integrity of Philippians', *NovT* 12 (1970), pp. 40-53.

9. T.E. Pollard, 'The Integrity of Philippians', *NTS* 13 (1966–67), pp. 57-66; M.D. Hooker, 'Philippians 2.6-11', in E. Grässer and E. Ellis (eds.), *Jesus und Paulus* (Göttingen: Vandenhoeck & Ruprecht, 1975), pp. 151-64 (152-53); R.A. Culpepper, 'Co-Workers in Suffering: Philippians 2.19-30', *RevExp* 72 (1980), pp. 349-58 (350-51); S.E. Fowl, *The Story of Christ in the Ethics of Paul: An Analysis of the Function of the Hymnic Material in the Pauline Corpus* (JSNTSup, 36; Sheffield: JSOT Press, 1990), pp. 77-101; P.S. Minear, 'Singing and Suffering in Philippi', in Fortna and Gaventa (eds.), *The Conversation Continues*, pp. 202-19; and Bloomquist, *Function of Suffering*, p. 165, for a convenient chart summarizing the lexical data.

10. Bloomquist, *Function of Suffering*. See also L.M. White, 'Morality between Two Worlds: A Paradigm of Friendship in Philippians', in Balch, Ferguson and Meeks (eds.), *Greeks, Romans, and Christians*, pp. 201-15 (206 n. 22), who asserts that 'the consistency with which the semantic complex of "friendship" (and its related fields) appears through the various sections of the letter is one of the chief arguments in favor of its literary integrity', an argument that is given considerable force by S.K. Stowers, 'Friends and Enemies in the Politics of Heaven', in J.M. Bassler (ed.), *Pauline Theology* (2 vols.; Minneapolis: Fortress Press, 1991), I, pp. 105-21.

are weighed in favour of treating Philippians as a literary unity in the argument that follows.[11]

The Opposition: Some Assumptions and Open Questions

Although there is no consensus on the nature of the opposition Paul confronts in Philippians,[12] most scholars generally agree that opponents are a main reason for the letter's composition drawing their clues from 3.1-2 and 18-19.[13] 'Opponents' and 'opposition' are used here as collective nouns without implying whether or not they offered a unified or multiple front, an issue that is energetically debated by others.[14] Though there is a lack of general consensus on the composition of the opposition, certain assertions are widely agreed and are understood for discussion of Philippians below.

1. Paul had a pipeline to Philippi where he could be updated on the situation there. At least two messengers came to Paul from the Philippians, Epaphroditus and someone informing Paul that the Philippians were disturbed by Epaphroditus's illness (1.25-30; 2.26-28). He had the means to be informed about any new teaching introduced into the community.

2. Paul develops his self-portrayal against opponents who had arrived in Philippi or were on the horizon. This impression is firmly in the

---

11. So E. Lohmeyer, *Die Briefe an die Philipper, an die Kolosser und an Philemon* (Göttingen: Vandenhoeck & Ruprecht, 1964 [1930]), pp. 4-8; J.L. Houlden, *Paul's Letters from Prison: Philippians, Colossians, Philemon, and Ephesians* (Philadelphia: Westminster Press, 1970), pp. 40-41; R.P. Martin, *Philippians* (NCB; Grand Rapids: Eerdmans, 1980 [1976]), pp. 10-22; Hawthorne, *Philippians*, pp. xxix-xxxii; P.T. O'Brien, *The Epistle to the Philippians: A Commentary on the Greek Text* (NIGTC; Grand Rapids: Eerdmans, 1991), pp. 10-18.

12. J.J. Gunther, *St. Paul's Opponents and their Background: A Study of Apocalyptic and Jewish Sectarian Teachings* (NovTSup, 35; Leiden: E.J. Brill, 1973), p. 2, lists 18 different assessments of the opponents in Philippians.

13. Two recent exceptions are White, 'Morality between Two Worlds', and Stowers, 'Friends and Enemies'.

14. Unified opposition: e.g. W. Schmithals, 'The False Teachers of the Epistle to the Philippians', in *idem*, *Paul and the Gnostics* (trans. J. Seeley; Nashville: Abingdon Press, 1972), pp. 65-122; H. Koester, 'The Purpose of the Polemic of a Pauline Fragment (Philippians 3)', *NTS* 8 (1961–62), pp. 317-32; C. Mearns, 'The Identity of Paul's Opponents at Philippi', *NTS* 33 (1987), pp. 194-204. Multiple threat: e.g. R. Jewett, 'Conflicting Movements in the Early Church as Reflected in Philippians', *NovT* 12 (1970), pp. 362-90; Martin, *Philippians*, pp. 22-34.

reader's mind since Paul places his autobiographical remarks within a polemical frame, introducing and concluding this section with a side glance toward this theological threat to the community (3.1-2, 18-19).

3. The opposition envisaged in the letter exert pressure to be circumcised and obey Torah. They 'mutilate the flesh' (3.2), a caustic description of circumcision in which they 'boast' (3.3). Against them Paul asserts '*we* are the circumcision' who truly worship God (3.3). Paul's Jewish self-presentation in 3.4-6 is apparently contrasted with their emphasis on circumcision and the importance of 'righteousness from the law', a point made explicit when Paul repudiates his past in 3.7-9.

4. The opposition were triumphalists with a radically realized eschatology who considered suffering to be inconsistent with faithfulness to God (see argument below).

5. There was dissension in Philippi (2.2, 5; 3.15; 4.2; cf. 3.19; 4.10), and this dissension is somehow related to the problem of suffering in the letter.

There are several further issues on which there is no general agreement, but on which I state my view for the reconstruction that follows.

1. It cannot be determined whether or not the Judaizers were Jewish or Gentile. 'Dogs' (3.2) is a common Jewish pejorative for Gentiles, but it also is an attested epithet for one's enemies (Ps. 22.16, 20; Isa. 56.10-11; *1 En.* 89.41-50), or it may be an ironic use of a slur on Gentiles turned back on them.[15] Likewise, Paul's renunciation of his Jewish past may be against Jewish opponents,[16] but it could just as likely be Paul's *Jewish*-Christian one-upmanship over Gentiles who promote circumcision, 'the disdain of a real Jew for the Jewish fantasies of Gentile propagandists'.[17] The Philippians would know which, but we may never know for sure.

2. It is most likely that the opponents presented themselves as Christians. There is no explicit indicator of this as is the case for some of Paul's opponents where he was imprisoned (1.15-18), but it is unlikely Paul would need to warn the Philippians so sharply if these

---

15. See Martin, *Philippians*, p. 125.
16. Beare, *Philippians*, p. 101; A.F.J. Klijn, 'Paul's Opponents in Philippians 3', *NovT* 7 (1964), pp. 278-84; Hawthorne, *Philippians*, pp. xliv-xlvii; Niebuhr, *Heidenapostel aus Israel*, pp. 88-92.
17. K. Grayston, 'The Opponents in Philippians 3', *ExpTim* 97 (1986), pp. 170-72 (171); Gnilka, *Philipperbrief*, pp. 186-87.

opponents did not have access to the Christian community (3.1-2).[18] A supplementary argument is that their Christian identity is further indicated if there is anything to the parallel between the 'deceitful workers' (ἐργάται δόλιοι) of 2 Cor. 11.13, who clearly claim to be Christians, and the 'evil workers' (κακοί ἐργάται) of Phil. 3.2. That Paul 'weeps' for these antagonists (3.18) does not contribute to their identification since he may be displaying a passion either for wayward fellow missionaries[19] or for his fellow unconverted Jews (cf. Rom. 9.2).

3. Philippians 3.19 is ambiguous and cannot be used to clarify the portrait of the opponents. The phrase at issue is 'whose God is their belly, whose glory is their shame'. For some interpreters, this is simply a further indication of the Jewish nature of the opposition, referring to their scruples about keeping food laws, as commentators in the ancient church took this phrase.[20] A recent refinement of this interpretation is provided by C. Mearns, who argues that κοιλία and αἰσχύνη are being used, as in the well-attested LXX usage, as euphemisms for the male organ, and as such are further sarcastic references to circumcision, parallel to the sarcasm of κατατομή in 3.2.[21] For other interpreters 'belly' and 'shame' are indicators that a libertine opposition is present, either in their willingness to eat idol meat (cf. 1 Cor. 6.13; 8.1–11.1)[22] or of immorality in a more general sense of gluttony and sexual freedom.[23] ('Dogs' in 3.2 cannot be appealed to as a libertine epithet because it is just as likely an ironical turn of phrase against Jewish opponents.)[24] The

---

18. So E.P. Sanders, 'Paul on the Law, his Opponents, and the Jewish People in Philippians 3 and 2 Corinthians 11', in P. Richardson and D. Granskou (eds.), *Anti-Judaism in Early Christianity*. I. *Paul and the Gospels* (Waterloo, ON: Wilfred Laurier University Press, 1986), pp. 75-90 (83-84); Schmithals, 'False Teachers'; J.B. Tyson, 'Paul's Opponents at Philippi', *Perspectives in Religious Studies* 3 (1976), pp. 82-95; O'Brien, *Philippians*, pp. 26-35; Koester, 'The Purpose'; Jewett, 'Conflicting Movements', pp. 383-84; Martin, *Philippians*.

19. Collange, *Philippians*, pp. 136-37; Martin, *Philippians*, p. 143.

20. Koester, 'The Purpose', pp. 326-27; Gunther, *St. Paul's Opponents*, p. 98; W.S. Kurz, 'Kenotic Imitation of Paul and of Christ in Philippians 2 and 3', in F. Segovia (ed.), *Discipleship in the New Testament* (Philadelphia: Fortress Press, 1985), pp. 103-26 (116).

21. Mearns, 'Paul's Opponents at Philippi', pp. 198-200.

22. Schmithals, 'False Teachers', p. 109.

23. Jewett, 'Conflicting Movements', pp. 379-80; Martin, *Philippians*, pp. 145-46.

24. Contra Schmithals, 'False Teachers', pp. 84-85.

objection that there is no indicator that a new set of opposition in 3.18-19 is plausibly mitigated by Jewett who suggests that 3.12-16 bridges two groups, where 'perfection' refers backwards to Judaizers and forwards to triumphalist libertines. If there were libertine tendencies present, however, Paul does not develop his self-presentation in the letter against them as such.

The evidence of 3.19, then, is ambiguous enough to allow two quite differing and plausible interpretations. Furthermore, it may be that 3.19 is a generic polemical warning as is the case in Rom. 16.17-18 where Paul uses 'serve their own belly' in contrast with 'serving our Lord Christ'. Philippians 3.19 may reflect a Pauline style of criticism of his opponents, that they are enemies of Christ and enslaved to earthly things.[25] If this is the sense, then 'their end is destruction; their god is the belly; their glory is in their shame' is a rhetorical flourish, summarized in the final phrase of 3.19, 'their minds are focused on earthly things'.[26] This expression in turn may paraphrase what he has already implied about them, that their 'confidence is in the flesh' (3.3, 4). Taken together, the appellations of 3.18-19 negatively characterize the opposition as earthly minded enemies of Christ's cross, while Paul and the Philippians are heavenly minded servants of Christ. D. Patte interprets these verses with similar results, arguing that 3.17-18 exhibits the 'dialogic level' of the text, while 3.19-21 functions on the 'warranting level'. On the dialogic level Paul wants the Philippians to follow his teaching (3.17), which he warrants by claiming that he and his imitators will be saved (3.20-21). His opponents should not be followed (3.18) because their path leads to destruction (3.19).[27]

The Heart of Paul's Polemic

There are two problems that Paul confronts in the letter for which a credible reconstruction has to account: the prominence of suffering[28] and the repeated emphasis on the 'not yet' of eschatology. Suffering presents itself as a major issue from the beginning of the letter, where

25. So Sanders, 'Paul on the Law', pp. 80-82.
26. Similarly Gunther, *St. Paul's Opponents,* pp. 98-99.
27. D. Patte, *Paul's Faith and the Power of the Gospel: A Structural Introduction to the Pauline Letters* (Philadelphia: Fortress Press, 1983), p. 171.
28. 1.7, 12-18, 21-26, 29-30; 2.8, 17, 25-30; 3.10, 18; 4.11-14; and see Bloomquist, *Function of Suffering,* for a full demonstration of suffering as a leitmotif in Philippians.

the tone of 1.12 suggests that Paul seeks to justify his imprisonment, perhaps against a doubt raised by the interlopers. Paul characterizes the opponents as 'enemies of the cross' (3.18; cf. 2.8[29]), and everyone in the letter (except Timothy[30]) suffers for the gospel—Paul, the Philippians, Christ, Epaphroditus. Taken together, these strongly suggest that Paul argues against the notion that suffering is incongruent with the life experience of those who are truly faithful to God.

From where did their objection to suffering arise? Bloomquist surveys the history of interpretation,[31] but he leaves untreated the *prima facie* explanation that the Judaizing tendency of the opposition could account for Paul's 'defence' of suffering in the letter. The Old Testament would provide many resources for them to interpret Paul's and Christ's afflictions as signs that they were cursed by God (e.g. Gen. 3; Ps. 32). In this, they would not simply be enemies of Christ, but explicitly 'enemies of the cross' (3.18). That is, they opposed the notion that Paul could call the cross a part of the purpose of God when Deut. 21.23 labels it 'cursed' (cf. Gal. 3.13). Opposition from Judaism or Judaizers could account for much of Paul's description and treatment of suffering as a 'defence', though it must be noted that the Old Testament offers other solutions to the problem of suffering, as in Habakkuk, Job and Isaiah 52–53.[32]

There is another strand of evidence that is not yet explained, however, namely the strong emphasis in the letter on the future nature of fulfilment, the 'not yet' of eschatology.[33] The strongest evidence that

29. If Lohmeyer's suggestion could be verified that θανάτου δὲ σταυροῦ is Paul's 'interpretierende Gloße' to a hymn known to them that originally celebrated the victory of Christ in a triumphalist manner (*Die Briefe an die Philipper*, p. 96); a contention supported by J.A. Fitzmyer's retroversion to a hypothetical Jewish Christian original ('The Aramaic Background of Phil. 2.6-11', *CBQ* 50 [1988], pp. 470-83). R.P. Martin, *Carmen Christi: Philippians 2.5-11 in Recent Interpretation and in the Setting of Early Christian Worship* (Grand Rapids: Eerdmans, rev. edn, 1983 [1967]), p. xvii, fully exploits Lohmeyer's observation, but it is contested by, among others, Hooker, 'Philippians 2.6-11', pp. 157-59.
30. Contra Bloomquist, *Function of Suffering*, pp. 174-75.
31. See Bloomquist, *Function of Suffering*, pp. 18-70.
32. Bloomquist imaginatively interprets 1.12 as a question of whether the gospel's preaching, Paul's suffering and their financial support were 'in vain'. Bloomquist argues that the opponents rejected the notion of providence, but his argument based on putative parallels with 2 Peter is not convincing (*Function of Suffering*, pp. 123-24, 132-33).
33. 1.6, 10-11; 2.8-11; 3.10-21; 4.19-20; cf. 1.19-21; 2.16, 19, 23-24; 4.5. So

this is an issue for the opposition is that in the midst of dealing with the opponents Paul develops the currently unfulfilled nature of the Christian life (3.10-21).[34] What is most significant is that suffering and death are connected both to Paul's identity in Christ and to his future expectancy (3.10-11).[35] Thus, Koester rightly identifies the contrast between Paul's earthly minded opponents with his heavenly minded example in 3.17-21 as 'the contrast between a realized eschatology and an apocalyptic expectation. The two so strictly exclude each other that Paul in 3.20 can introduce his expectation of the heavenly, that is, future, realization as the reason for his derogatory judgment of his opponents'.[36] It is entirely inferential, but the suggestion presents itself that Paul and the Philippians were confronting triumphalist proponents of a too-strongly realized eschatology for whom suffering was incompatible with their 'presentation of the believer's life in terms of triumphalism and present glory. At all costs suffering and persecution must be avoided',[37] and so Paul characterizes them as 'enemies of the

---

Schmithals, 'False Teachers'; Koester, 'The Purpose'; Martin, *Philippians*; A.T. Lincoln, *Paradise Now and Not Yet: Studies in the Role of the Heavenly Dimension in Paul's Thought with Special Reference to his Eschatology* (Cambridge: Cambridge University Press, 1981), pp. 92-95; Mearns, 'Paul's Opponents at Philippi', pp. 196-97; J.T. Fitzgerald, 'Philippians, Epistle to the', *ABD*, V, pp. 318-26 (323).

34. Bloomquist, *Function of Suffering*, p. 181, offers a different explanation of the data, asserting that Paul's 'Epicurean "opponents" reject suffering and cling to all they have—that is, fleshly existence—for there is no after-life', but later he revises his position claiming it is not necessary to assume they rejected suffering, but rather that they rejected that suffering has meaning (pp. 196-97).

35. J.S. Pobee, *Persecution and Martyrdom in the Theology of Paul* (JSNTSup, 6; Sheffield: JSOT Press, 1985), p. 91, views 'conformed to his death' (3.10) through the lens of Rom. 8.29, and the 'key is sonship'. But, the theological description of the revelatory function of suffering in 2 Cor. 4.10-11 may be as significant. As pointed out by B.M. Ahern, Rom. 8.17; 2 Cor. 1.6-7 and 2 Cor. 4.11 (cf. 1 Thess. 1.6; 2.14-15) point to the fact that Christian suffering is rooted in union with Christ ('The Fellowship of his Sufferings [Phil. 3.10]: A Study of St. Paul's Doctrine on Christian Suffering', *CBQ* 22 [1960], pp. 1-32), which C.M. Proudfoot labels a *participatio Christi* ('Imitation or Realistic Participation? A Study of Paul's Concept of "Suffering with Christ"', *Int* 17 [1963], pp. 140-60).

36. Koester, 'The Purpose', p. 330.

37. Martin, *Philippians*, p. 34 (see also pp. 70-73); so also Jewett; Koester; Tyson, Schmithals, Lincoln. Cf. Collange, *Philippians*, p. 14, who points to parallels with the opponents in 2 Corinthians, but rightly cautions against a complete identification of the opponents in 2 Corinthians with those in Philippians.

cross' (3.18). That is, by shunning suffering they oppose the work of Christ. Paul's response to this sort of opposition would account both for the prominence of suffering in the letter and for the emphasis on the unrealized nature of eschatology, and it would account for the combination of these two topics in several places in the letter (1.6-7, 10-12; 2.8-11; 3.10-21; 4.11-20).

In summary, clear identification of Paul's opponents lying behind Philippians is not possible, nor can we decide if they were a united front or separate groups. Yet even with these ambiguities certain characteristics of their portrait are apparent and make up the background of the interpretation followed below. Paul perceived these opponents as a theological threat to the Christian community in Philippi, suggesting they were most likely Christian missionaries who had entrée to the community. At least some were Judaizers who emphasized obedience to Torah requirements. At least some were proponents of a triumphalist message who espoused a radically realized eschatology which was incompatible with suffering, effectively displacing the centrality of the cross. They appear to emphasize the power of the Christian or of the Christian leader, and cast aspersions on a form of Christianity that entails suffering, death or any sign of human weakness and degradation.[38] If there were two fronts, it may be that both Judaizers and those for whom the end had come were united in their sense of perfection or completeness, though they defined τέλειος differently (3.12-16)—Judaizers in the sense of rigoristic expectation of Torah compliance and radically realized eschatologists for whom all had already been obtained. Both would have strong theological objections to including suffering as a part of the Christian life and especially among the credentials of a Christian apostle, hence explaining elements of ch. 3.

Paul's Polemical and Paradigmatic 'I' in Philippians

Against these general emphases of Torah observance, triumphalism and a strongly realized eschatology, Paul presents himself both as a paradigm for the Philippians and as part of his polemic against those whose teaching he wants them to reject. The framing comments of 3.1-2 and 18-19 and the line of argumentation cast Paul's self-depiction in a

---

38. E.g. Collange, *Philippians*; Martin, *Philippians*; Alexander, 'Hellenistic Letter-Forms'; Mearns, 'Paul's Opponents at Philippi'.

polemical mode.³⁹ The stark warning of 3.2 with its triple 'beware'⁴⁰ creates this expectation for the reader (even for scholars who take ch. 3 as a fragment), which is already introduced at 3.1b, 'To write the same things to you is not troublesome to me, and for you it is a safeguard' (NRSV).⁴¹ The flow of 3.3-5 suggests that the comparison is meant to be against these intruders. '*They* are the mutilators, confident in the flesh... *we* are the [true] "circumcision", confident in Christ Jesus' (3.3-4). The change to the first-person singular comes at 3.4, and Paul lists his Jewish credentials (3.5-6) only to renounce what appears to be his opponents' values, a point made explicit in 3.7-11.⁴² Paul's polemical point turns on the contrast of life 'in Christ' (ἐν Χριστῷ)⁴³ with life 'in flesh' (ἐν σαρκί; 3.3, 4; cf. 3.19), which is identified with life 'in Torah' (ἐν νόμῳ; 3.6, 9).⁴⁴ The polemical setting is reiterated at the close of the chapter with another stark characterization of the outsiders (3.18-19), even if we cannot be certain if these are the same opponents as those in 3.2. As 3.17 calls the Philippians to imitate Paul, Phil. 3.18, in effect, presents those who compete for his readers' loyalty as unworthy of imitation.⁴⁵ Thus, Paul's self-characterization in this chapter is clearly set against a polemical target, but this does not fully explain the occurrence of his self-portrayals we find here.

Paul's self-references in Philippians 3, though shaped by the polemical setting, also maintain a paraenetic function. That is, Paul presents himself in Philippians as a model for his readers, which he makes explicit in 3.15-17 in four ways. First, he calls the 'mature' to 'think this way' or 'have this mind' (v. 15; cf. 2.5). It is most natural to take τοῦτο in 3.15 to refer to the example of self-renunciation of confidence in the

---

39. Something stronger than 'contrastive' is required, though Stowers plausibly identifies these comparisons as the well-known rhetorical strategy of contrastive models (*synkrisis*; Stowers, 'Friends and Enemies', pp. 115-17). In his view, the 'dogs' are not impinging upon the community, but are known and therefore are an effective negative example in the argumentation.

40. See O'Brien, *Philippians*, pp. 352-54, for a treatment of Kilpatrick's proposal that this should have the softer sense of 'consider' or 'take due note of'.

41. In favour of taking 3.1b with what follows, see V.P. Furnish, 'The Place and Purpose of Philippians 3', *NTS* 10 (1963–64), pp. 80-88; Stowers, 'Friends and Enemies', pp. 115-16.

42. Gnilka, *Philipperbrief*, pp. 187-91; Martin, *Philippians*, pp. 126-29.

43. 3.3, 9, 14; and 1.1, 13, 23, 26; 2.1, 5; 4.7, 19, 21 (cf. 3.7, 8, 10, 12, 18, 20).

44. Bloomquist, *Function of Suffering*, pp. 130-31.

45. Patte, *Paul's Faith*, p. 170.

flesh, christocentricity and eschatological reserve that he has portrayed for them in 3.3-14, to which we shall return below. Secondly, in 3.17, the familiar Pauline call to imitation is present, if in a slightly nuanced form, employing here the unique compound 'co-imitators' with a familiar call to imitation (see below). Thirdly, he calls them to 'look at' or 'mark' (σκοπεῖτε) his model embodied in faithful followers of his own example. Fourthly, at the end of 3.17, he calls himself and others a 'type' (τύπος) that the Philippians have as a model for how they are to think and behave (περιπατέω). As Kurz points out, 'Both περιπατέω and τύπος are technical terms in first century exhortation, often applied to imitation of people as examples (e.g. 2 Thess. 3.9; 1 Tim. 4.12; Tit. 2.7)'.[46] It is noteworthy that this theme is repeated in 4.9: 'the things which you learned and received and heard and saw in me, these things practise'.[47] Thus in Philippians we find a characteristic marker of Paul's usage of pastoral imitation, and this urges us to reflect on his earlier self-references in Philippians to discover if he uses the same literary technique here that he employs in 1 Corinthians and Galatians. Before we can address the question of the content of Paul's literary example in Philippians, we must acknowledge three factors that hinder full identification of Paul's model for imitation.

1. Paul makes numerous self-references in the letter, but some of these are inimitable. This is the case of the description of 3.4b-6 since most of the Philippians would not be able to be confident of their circumcision, able to trace their Israelite lineage to the tribe of Benjamin, have training as a Pharisee, nor boast of their past as a persecutor of the church. Thus the too-generalized statement made by B.M. Ahern needs to be moderated, 'Paul understood well that his "I" is the "I" of every Christian and that the new life which he received through conversion is the same reality which every Christian possesses through baptism'.[48] While this may be true of 3.3, 10, it is clearly not the case for 3.4b-6.

2. A second factor which limits our ability to identify the model Paul calls the Philippians to pattern themselves after is that Paul was previously present with them and presumably he relies partly on their remembrance of his teaching and behaviour, a common feature of

46. Kurz, 'Kenotic Imitation', p. 114; cf. E.K. Lee, 'Words Denoting "Pattern" in the New Testament', *NTS* 8 (1961–62), pp. 166-73.

47. And see Schenk, *Die Philipperbriefe*, pp. 259-74, for implied semantic indicators of Paul's 'paradigmatische Ich' in Phil. 3.

48. Ahern, 'The Fellowship of his Sufferings', p. 29.

paraenesis.⁴⁹ Whereas 3.17 seems to point to living examples, 4.9 gives a strong impression that it refers to the example of Paul in the past with its four aorist verbs (ἐμάθετε, παρελάβετε, ἠκούσατε, εἴδετε). This distinction between his historical example and epistolary exemplification should not be pressed too far, however. These verbs could be taken as epistolary aorists just as well as simple past aorists. Furthermore, the nature of a good letter was that it was to attempt to substitute for one's personal presence, and the distance between one's historical personage and literary persona were to be minimized. This is not to make a historicist argument in favour of the reliability of Paul's self-presentation in his letters, but rather an argument in favour of wedding his epistolary example with his past example as the content of the model he calls his readers to emulate. Nevertheless, the content of 'the things which you learned...' (ἅ) and 'these things' (ταῦτα) may include Paul's past example for which we have no literary evidence.

3. A third factor limiting our identification of the model Paul sets for his auditors is his inclusion of the example of other appropriate models (3.17b). Although it is clear that Paul's model is meant to be primary (3.17a; 4.9), he sees his pattern as reproducible in others who can also model proper doctrine and practice (3.17b, τοὺς οὕτω περιπατοῦντας). Therefore he relies on the example of his co-worker Timothy who accompanied the letter and most likely elaborated on it, and 1.1 and 2.19-22 give us reason to take seriously Timothy's place among the plural 'us' of 3.17b, 'just as you have a type in us'.⁵⁰

'Be Imitators of Me'
In spite of these hindrances to a full identification of the modelled behaviour and beliefs that Paul lifts up for the Philippians, there are perhaps as many as six components of Paul's literary self-presentation as an exemplar in Philippians that can be included in the personal example he sets for their imitation and instruction:

1. *Self-renunciation of confidence 'in the flesh'*. In 3.4 the turn to the first-person singular, 'even though I have [reason] for confidence in the flesh', echoes what must be Paul's implied characterization of his opponents in the previous verse, who were 'confident in the flesh' (3.3). In 3.4-6 Paul portrays his inimitable past to set up his example for the

49. Malherbe, 'Hellenistic Moralists', pp. 286-87.
50. De Boer, *The Imitation of Paul*, pp. 182-83; contra Hawthorne, *Philippians*, pp. 160-61.

Philippians in 3.7: he renounces his Jewish past as confidence ἐν σαρκί in the strongest possible terms, 'considering it loss' (3.7) and 'filth' (3.8). In 3.9-10 the readers are clearly in view with this crisp expression of Paul's gospel in the form of his paradigmatic 'I'. Most likely, this is a pre-emptive paradigm for the Philippians, akin to 2 Corinthians and unlike Galatians, since apparently they had not yet succumbed to Judaizing pressure to be circumcised.[51]

2. *Affirmation of confidence 'in Christ'.* In one sense, Paul's self-renunciation of his confidence in the flesh acts as a foil for what seems to be his more important point, his expression of confidence in Christ (καυχώμενοι ἐν Χριστῷ, 3.3), which Hawthorne identifies as the dominant theme of 3.4-11, 'the superlative significance of Christ',[52] which is anticipated in 1.21 when Paul announces, 'For me to live is Christ and to die is gain'. In 3.3, 'the true circumcision' are those who worship by the Spirit of God, and boast in Christ. It is because of Christ (διὰ τὸν Χριστὸν, 3.7) that Paul's Jewish credentials are regarded as a loss. But he expands this to claim that he regards 'all things' forfeit contrasted with knowing Christ (3.8). He desires to 'gain Christ' (3.8b), that is, to be found 'in him' by faith, not thinking that righteousness before God comes from the law (3.9). The christocentric focus of Paul's example is reiterated again in 3.10 with the fourfold him/his as the centre of Paul's passion: 'that I may know him and the power of his resurrection and the fellowship of his sufferings, becoming like him in his death...' (and cf. 3.14). The example Paul provides for the Philippians affirms the soteriological necessity of Christ and renounces the soteriological place of Torah requirements. Paul models confidence in Christ, a confidence in which he is hopeful the Philippians will continue.

3. *Eschatological reserve.* As mentioned above, beginning with 3.11 Paul presents himself as one who accepts the eschatological 'not yet' of life in Christ (cf. 3.20-21),[53] a theme that is present throughout the letter.[54] In 3.11 emphasis on the 'not yet' of the general resurrection is reaffirmed as Paul expresses uncertainty as to whether or not he will be

---

51. This is to agree with what Garland affirms, but to deny what he rejects, namely that Paul does not have opponents in view ('The Composition and Unity of Philippians', p. 173).

52. Hawthorne, *Philippians*, p. 149.

53. Koester, 'The Purpose', pp. 323-24.

54. 1.6, 10-11; 2.8-11; 3.10-21; 4.19-20; cf. 1.19-21; 2.16, 19, 23-24; 4.5.

alive at the parousia.[55] This point is developed in 3.12-14 in the *locus classicus* of Pauline eschatological tension of 'now–not yet'.[56] Paul's eschatological reserve may be developed against a background that contains both an emphasis on Judaizing perfectionism[57] and an over-realized eschatology.[58] If Paul must wait to receive the full blessings of the kingdom, then so too must the Philippians. This is gathered up in the future expectancy of 3.20-21, which has the added element of living now as people regulated by the heavenly commonwealth.[59] If models in the letter must suffer—Christ, Paul, Epaphroditus—then Philippians presents multiple examples to illustrate that life in Christ this side of the eschaton embraces rather than excludes the afflictions for the sake of the gospel that come to those who are faithful to the crucified Christ.

4. *Eschatological encouragement*. Paul's paradigmatic 'I' in 3.11-14 also has a paraenetic function, providing an example of one who continues to pursue 'the goal for the prize of the heavenly call of God in Christ Jesus' (3.14), a confidence he earlier had expressed (1.24-26) to supply further motivational stimulus for the Philippians to press on amid their struggles.[60] He creates a tangible sense of longing and eagerness by his compilation of words and phrases. He ardently pursues (3.12, διώκω) that which he has yet to obtain, and this incompleteness itself creates a sense of desire for more (3.12: Οὐχ ὅτι ἤδη ἔλαβον ἢ ἤδη τετελείωμαι; 3.13: οὐ λογίζομαι κατειληφέναι). This is intended paradigmatically for all his auditors, and the understatement of 3.15 tacitly may address their lack of hunger for heaven by referring to them as τέλειοι (cf. τετελείωμαι, 3.12). By contrast, future satisfaction lies ahead of Paul as a goal which he pursues (3.13: τοῖς δὲ ἔμπροσθεν ἐπεκτεινόμενος), which draws him as an incentive (3.14: κατὰ σκοπὸν διώκω). It is for this purpose that Christ 'took hold' of him, and by implication the Philippians (3.12: ἐφ' ᾧ καὶ κατελήμφθην ὑπὸ Χριστοῦ). Paul has already set the example of what he has left behind in order to

---

55. A. Perriman, 'The Pattern of Christ's Sufferings: Colossians 1.24 and Philippians 3.10-11', *TynBul* 42 (1991), pp. 62-79 (70-71).
56. Collange, *Philippians*, pp. 132-35; Martin, *Philippians*, pp. 135-38.
57. Pfitzner, *Paul and the Agon Motif*, pp. 139-53; Gunther, *St. Paul's Opponents*, p. 61; Hawthorne, *Philippians*, pp. 149-58; Schenk, *Die Philipperbriefe*, pp. 291-304; Watson, 'Rhetorical Analysis', p. 75.
58. Jewett; R.P. Martin; and O'Brien, *Philippians*, pp. 418, 423.
59. Lincoln, *Paradise Now and Not Yet*, pp. 97-99.
60. Hawthorne, *Philippians*, pp. 149-58.

gain Christ (3.4-9), and his exemplary 'I' here reminds his auditors to leave the past behind (3.13: τὰ μὲν ὀπίσω ἐπιλανθανόμενος), and to seek the eschatological reward found 'in Christ' (3.14: εἰς τὸ βραβεῖον τῆς ἄνω κλήσεως τοῦ θεοῦ ἐν Χριστῷ Ἰησοῦ). Thus these verses enhance the already noted eschatological corrective, and provide encouragement to the Philippians to press on amidst opposition.

5. *Obedience to Paul*. The call to imitation is paraenetic and pedagogical, but always with an element of obedience implied. It is irrelevant that Paul does not explicitly use the language of command. Who he is vis-à-vis the community determines how his rhetoric will be heard.[61] Paul does not conceive of his example as one option among many, but rather as the regulative type. Thus in 3.17-18, Paul's example and those who 'walk' according to his way are contrasted with the 'many' who 'walk' as 'enemies of the cross'. There are other indications in the letter that Paul expects his model to be regulative. In 2.12 the theme is explicit, 'Therefore, my beloved, just as you have always obeyed [me], not only in my presence, but much more now in my absence...' In 3.15 conformity to Paul's way is implied, and those who dissent will be enlightened by God (3.16). In 4.1-2, Paul's expectation of obedience may be implied. Thus, while Paul's 'I' is paradigmatic for the Philippians, there remains an implied assertion of authority to ensure their conformity to Paul's modelled way of thinking and living.

6. *Contentment from trusting prayer*. Paul calls the Philippians to a grateful attitude in prayer as the path to God's peace amid their afflictions (4.6-7). In 4.9 this same 'peace of God' comes as a result of following Paul's example. It may be that Paul includes in the scope of his own example (4.9) his model of prayer when he was with them (cf. Phil. 1.3-11; Acts 16.13, 16, 25).[62] Furthermore, it may be that Paul models this godly contentment (4.11-13) and the inner peace from God of which he speaks in 4.7, 9. Though αὐτάρκης (4.11) is a significant term in Stoic thought, 4.13 makes it clear that Paul has in mind the provision of God rather than self-sufficiency.[63] Philippians 4.11-13 is not a 'confessional' statement, but is self-exemplification.[64] Out of his

---

61. Malherbe, 'Hellenistic Moralists', pp. 285-86, and see above under 1 Cor. 4.16. Contra de Boer, *The Imitation of Paul*, pp. 184-87; Fiore, *The Function of Personal Example*, p. 185.

62. Cf. O'Brien, *Philippians*, pp. 491, 494.

63. Martin, *Philippians*, pp. 162-63.

64. Contra O'Brien, *Philippians*, p. 522.

own contentment he expects the same for the Philippians, expressed with the encouraging 'My God will supply all of your needs… (4.19).[65] He expresses confidence the Philippians will receive the same treatment from the One who has met all of Paul's needs, the God who hears their requests (4.11-13).

'As I Am "of Christ"'
Many interpreters have pointed out the parallel depictions of Christ and Paul in Philippians, and from this it has been suggested that Paul conceives of his example as a reflection of Christ's example.[66] This interpretation has sometimes gained support by an appeal to 1 Cor. 11.1, interpreted as 'Be imitators of me as I [imitate] Christ'.[67] This appeal should be discounted, however. As suggested above ('Introduction', p. 28), 'Be imitators of me as I am "of Christ"' should probably be read as 'Be imitators of me since I belong to Christ' in light of the significance Χριστοῦ acquires in 1 Corinthians as shorthand for belonging to Christ in a single, undivided church.[68] The sense is that since Paul is 'in Christ' he is a model of the quintessential Christian. The call to imitation in 1 Cor. 4.16 contributes to this impression since it is based upon Paul's spiritual paternity 'in Christ' (4.15). In the same way, the call to imitation of Paul in Phil. 3.17 is based upon Paul's standing in Christ (cf. 1.1, 8, 13, 20-21; 3.7-10, 12). Some have suggested that the compound 'co-imitators' (συμμιμηταί) should be taken as 'be co-imitators with me [of Christ]',[69] but 'with me' strains against the normal use of the genitive, 'of Christ' must be supplied, and 1 Cor. 11.1 is not support for this reconstruction as has been thought. A more plausible

---

65. Differently, see G.W. Peterman, '"Thankless Thanks": The Epistolary Social Convention in Philippians 4.10-20', *TynBul* 42 (1991), pp. 261-70 (270), who reads this as a formalized expression of thanks communicated by a declaration of indebtedness. Here Peterman thinks God discharges Paul's debt to the Philippians as a variation on a conventional way of expressing gratitude.

66. E.g. Hooker, 'Philippians 2.6-11', pp. 155-57; Kurz, 'Kenotic Imitation', pp. 106-108; Minear, 'Singing and Suffering in Philippi', pp. 202-19; Bloomquist, *Function of Suffering*, pp. 135, 168.

67. E.g. C. Wolff, 'Niedrigkeit und Verzicht in Wort und Weg Jesu und in der apostolischen Existenz des Paulus', *NTS* 34 (1988), pp. 183-96; Stowers, 'Friends and Enemies', p. 120.

68. 1 Cor. 1.12; 2.16; 3.23; 6.15; 7.22; 12.27; 15.23.

69. W.F. McMichael, '"Be ye followers together of Me": Συμμιμηταί μου γίνεσθε—Phil. 3.17', *ExpTim* 5 (1893–94), p. 287.

translation is 'join together in imitating me', which looks to one of the letter's themes for an explanation, reinforcing Paul's emphasis on corporate unity of the community in Philippi.[70] Paul's example comes as a result of his existence 'in Christ', and the Philippians are able to emulate him because they too are 'in Christ' (e.g. 2.1, 5).

The material correspondence between Christ and Paul in Philippians, therefore, must be carefully considered before it is concluded that Paul consciously presents himself as an imitator of Christ. The parallels between Christ and Paul, expressed in terms of elements found in the Christ hymn of 2.6-11, may be more a matter of verbal echoes than actual or formal patterning on Paul's part. For example, the first material correspondence between Christ and Paul is that they both renounce a privileged position (2.7-8; 3.4-8), but it is too much to say that Paul, like Christ, exhibits self-abasing, downward movement. There is nothing in Paul's self-depiction in 3.4-8 that is self-abasing or suggests that his movement to Christ was a downward one; on the contrary, Paul has moved to a superlative condition (3.8). Though there is a general correspondence between the self-renunciations of Christ and Paul, they differ significantly in what they renounced and why they renounced it since they start from entirely different vantage points. Jesus gave up the image or glory of God (2.6)[71] and Paul forsook 'a righteousness of my own, based on the law' (3.9)—there is no apparent parallel or equation of these former positions.[72] There is another correspondence between how they reckoned their former position (ἡγοῦμαι, 2.6 and 3.7-8), but here too the parallel breaks down. Christ did not 'count' his former position 'as something to be exploited' (2.6, NRSV),[73] but Paul 'counted' his former status as 'loss' and 'rubbish' to gain Christ. Another correspondence is that Christ humbled himself (ἐταπείνωσεν, 2.8) and Paul 'knows what it is like to be humbled' (ταπεινοῦσθαι, 4.12; cf. 2.3; 3.21), but again the parallel breaks down since

70. De Boer, *The Imitation of Paul*, pp. 177-79; Hawthorne, *Philippians*, pp. 159-60; contra T.C. Geoffrion, *The Rhetorical Purpose and Political and Military Character of Philippians* (Lewiston, NY: Edwin Mellen Press, 1993), p. 131, which he himself contradicts on p. 146.

71. See Martin, *Carmen Christi*, pp. xix-xxi.

72. Contra Minear, 'Singing and Suffering in Philippi', pp. 205-206.

73. See N.T. Wright, 'ἁρπαγμος and the Meaning of Philippians 2.5-11', *JTS* NS 37 (1986), pp. 321-52 (343), for a convenient comparison of ten (!) different approaches to the crux of 2.6.

Christ's humbling was part of his act of self-renunciation, while Paul's 'humbling' is not related to his self-renunciation of his Jewish past but depicts human life in eschatological anticipation (3.21), and in 4.12 is only partially expressive of missionary conditions (which also include times of abundance). These verbal echoes of humility do not create an impression that Paul is like Christ, but on the contrary that Christ took on the lowly conditions of human existence in his incarnation (2.8) that Paul hopes will be transformed in the consummation (3.21). A further implied comparison between Christ and Paul as self-abasing in their obedience is the use of 'slave' for Paul in 1.1 (cf. 2.22) compared with Christ who 'took the form of a slave' in 2.7. This is perhaps the strongest material parallel between Paul and Christ in Philippians, but even so Paul remains subordinate to Christ as slave (1.1) to his now exalted Lord (2.11). In the light of these texts, Paul's appeal to the Philippians in 2.3 (τῇ ταπεινοφροσύνῃ ἀλλήλους ἡγούμενοι ὑπερέχοντας ἑαυτῶν) completes a triangle of correspondence between Paul, the Philippians and Christ, but this is not an equation of Paul's and Christ's examples.[74] Christ's motivation provides the mindset that the Philippians are to emulate in their community relations,[75] and they are able to have 'Christ's mind' because they are 'in Christ' (2.1-5).[76] If Paul's character echoes humility this also reflects that he is 'in Christ', but there is nothing like an equation of Paul's example with Christ's story. Furthermore, Paul's humility is not an explicit part of his self-exemplification in Philippians, though his self-depiction echoes several terms from Christ's story.

Secondly, both Christ and Paul suffer, carrying obedience to the extent of death. For Christ, this description entails the suffering and death of the cross (2.8), as Paul's slavery to Christ entails suffering for Christ.[77] Though Christ has died and Paul's death is discussed in worried anticipation (1.23; 2.17), Paul's current sufferings are identified as a partnership with Christ's own (3.10). The pattern is repeated as the Philippians experience suffering like Paul and Christ (1.29-30; 4.14; cf.

---

74. Contra White, 'Morality between Two Worlds', p. 214.
75. Following P.T. O'Brien, 'The Gospel and Godly Models in Philippians', in M.J. Wilkins and T. Paige (eds.), *Worship, Theology and Ministry in the Early Church: Essays in Honor of Ralph P. Martin* (JSNTSup, 87; Sheffield: JSOT Press, 1992), pp. 273-84.
76. A balance struck by Hooker, 'Philippians 2.6-11', p. 156.
77. 1.12-13, 20, 29-30; 3.10; 4.13-14.

1 Thess. 1.6; 2.14), a pattern embodied by Epaphroditus as well (2.25-30).

In the case of Epaphroditus, we must reject O'Brien's claim that Paul consciously presents him, too, 'as a godly example of the way the Philippians should imitate Christ'.[78] This is initially supported since both Epaphroditus and Christ have brushes with death, described by a phrase that is used twice in Philippians 2 and nowhere else in Paul or the New Testament (μέχρι θανάτου, 2.8, 30). After careful consideration, however, this initial impression must be set aside. While it is striking that this unique combination of terms is used for both Christ and Epaphroditus, we commit a lexical *faux pas* if we isolate these lexemes from the sentences that shape them in quite different ways. In the case of Christ, he does not simply have a brush with death, but demonstrates his obedience to God by dying on a cross (2.8, γενόμενος ὑπήκοος μέχρι θανάτου, θανάτου δὲ σταυροῦ). Epaphroditus is indeed sick to the point of death, but he does not experience death as Christ did, indeed he does not experience death at all. In the case of 2.8, μέχρι θανάτου expresses the reality of Christ's death, 'to the actual extent of dying' while the phrase in 2.30 is used in a wholly different sense as the verb suggests, 'he came near to the point of death without actually experiencing it' (μέχρι θανάτου ἤγγισεν; cf. 2.27: γὰρ ἠσθένησεν παραπλήσιον θανάτῳ). Furthermore, as in 1 Thess. 1.5-6; 2.14-16, the correspondence of their sufferings is a description of what is in fact already the case rather than an ethical exhortation to suffer like Christ and Paul or Epaphroditus, more of a comparison than a conscious following of an example.[79]

While O'Brien is correct that Paul (1.12-14; 2.17; 3.15, 17; 4.9), Timothy (2.19-24) and Epaphroditus (2.25-30) are godly examples for the Philippians of how to live worthily of the gospel in its service (1.27-29),[80] and that Christ's portrayal in 2.6-8 provides an ethical archetype of humility and obedience to God, there is a significant difference between their life-patterns that is undervalued in his analysis. Namely, although Paul, his co-workers and the Philippians are to live worthily of the gospel and even suffer for it, the depiction of Christ in Phil. 2.6-11 *is* the very gospel of which the Philippians are to live

78. O'Brien, 'Godly Models in Philippians', p. 278; cf. Geoffrion, *The Rhetorical Purpose*, pp. 128-52, 191-201.
79. As Michaelis says of 1 Thess. 1.6 ('μιμέομαι', p. 667).
80. So also Geoffrion, *The Rhetorical Purpose*, pp. 140-46.

worthily. Furthermore, the depiction of Paul, Christ and Epaphroditus as sufferers has a unified purpose as an eschatological corrective, locating the unity of Paul's portrayal of them all, not in Christ's example, but in the corrective that was needed in Philippi.

Thirdly, another implied correspondence may be found in the portrayal of Christ's exaltation by God (2.9-11) in parallel with Paul's expected exaltation out of his own suffering and death (1.20-23; 3.10-11, 14, 21).[81] As God is the agent in Christ's exaltation (2.9-11), so he is the deliverer of the Philippians (1.28) and of Paul together with the Philippians (3.20-21, though the agent here is identified as 'the Lord Jesus Christ'). The portrayal of Christ's humility now—vindication later creates a positive expectation of the future for Paul and the Philippians which is intended to bring them eschatological comfort in light of 3.20-21. Nevertheless, the exaltation of Christ is accomplished by God in 2.9-11 and cannot be viewed as an ethical *Vorbild* for the Philippians to pattern themselves after.

What are we to make of this 'grammar of correlations'[82] between Paul, Christ and the Philippians? We have shown that Paul's self-presentation in Philippians is related to his depiction of Christ only on the level of verbal echoes and a comparison of the experience of suffering. Now we need to make three points in relation to the use of the Christ story vis-à-vis Paul's employment of his own personal example in Philippians:

1. Most elements of the Christ story in 2.6-11 are arguably inimitable. It is apparent that Paul does not nor cannot pattern his autobiographical remarks after his portrayal of Christ in Philippians. Although a very specific element of Christ's story, namely humbling himself in obedience (2.8), functions as an ethical example for the Philippians in their situation (2.3, 12),[83] the story of 2.6-11 as a whole

---

81. M.D. Hooker, 'Interchange in Christ', *JTS* NS 22 (1971), pp. 349-61 (356-57); Bloomquist, *Function of Suffering*, pp. 112-14.

82. To use a phrase from Minear, 'Singing and Suffering in Philippi'.

83. Betz, *Nachfolge und Nachahmung Jesu Christi*, p. 167; A.J.M. Wedderburn, 'Paul and the Story of Jesus', in *idem* (ed.), *Paul and Jesus: Collected Essays* (JSNTSup, 37; Sheffield: JSOT Press, 1989), pp. 161-89 (185-86). In a discussion of Phil. 2.5-11 with Rom. 15.1-6, the later Käsemann allows for a usage of example that combines *Urbild* and *Vorbild*, not in the idealist sense but as an adapted conventional paradigmatic usage found in Graeco-Roman literature (Käsemann, *An die Römer* [HNT, 8a; Tübingen: J.C.B. Mohr (Paul Siebeck), 1973], p. 369; cf. his earlier 'Kritische Analyse von Phil. 2.5-11', *ZTK* 47 [1950], pp. 313-60).

only partially applies to them.[84] Neither Paul nor the Philippians could make the choice Christ made to become human from their heavenly dwelling or to be exalted as the heavenly Lord after an ignoble death, a key point for the so-called 'soteriological interpretation' of the hymn.[85] L.W. Hurtado's suggestion that 2.9-11 underlines Christ's authoritative example does not account for the fact that these verses themselves must be excluded from that example.[86] While it is true that 'There is a similarity-in-difference between the traditions about Christ formulated in 2.6-11 and the situation of the Philippian church that allows Paul to use the tradition to speak to the present',[87] the differences between Christ's story and Paul's example strain the comparison and are best understood as correlative.

2. There is no explicit equation of Paul's ethical example with Christ's in Philippians, even though there are implicit material correlations between Christ, Paul and the Philippians. Paul's self-renunciation of his Jewish past has similarities with Christ's renunciation of his privileged position if we leave the comparison on that level of generality, but when we compare the elements of their self-renunciation this comparison is transformed to a strong contrast. Furthermore, it appears that Paul's appeal to the Philippians is *not* to give up their privileged position in Christ by receiving circumcision rather than to encourage them to renounce something they already have. Likewise, the pattern of Christ's exaltation provides the pattern for Paul's hope, but the exaltation is accomplished by God, and is not something that the Philippians can choose to imitate. While it is true that there are several striking similarities between Paul's composite self-portrayal in his letters and

---

84. Fowl, *The Story of Christ in the Ethics of Paul*, pp. 92-101, describes this as an analogous use of an 'exemplar' which acknowledges the similarities and differences.

85. Martin, *Carmen Christi*, pp. xii-xix, 287-89.

86. L.W. Hurtado, 'Jesus as Lordly Example in Philippians 2.5-11', in Richardson and Hurd (eds.), *From Jesus to Paul*, pp. 113-26 (124-26).

87. Fowl, *The Story of Christ in the Ethics of Paul*, p. 101. See Martin's recent qualification of his earlier position, which reiterates the significance of the theory of a two-stage development of the hymn: although the hymn is now put to ethical use in its setting in Philippians, Christ's inimitable qualities in 2.9-11 (the hymn's 'center') are still best explained by positing a pristine form of the hymn which celebrated the cosmic authority of the exalted Lord ('Hymns, Hymn Fragments, Songs, Spiritual Songs', *DPL*, pp. 419-23 [422]); an observation made independently by Wedderburn, 'Paul and the Story of Jesus', pp. 185-86.

the incarnate Christ depicted in the Gospels (C. Wolff points out four: deprivation, renunciation of marriage, humble service, suffering persecution),[88] we do not find in Philippians a reflected image of Christ's example in Paul's self-depiction. This is not to argue in favour of discontinuity between Jesus and Paul,[89] but rather to argue against an explicit equation of Christ's and Paul's examples in Paul's exhortation to imitation in Philippians.

3. To approach the question vis-à-vis Paul's example, the content of Paul's personal example in Philippians gives further reason to deny a literary parallelism with Christ's model in Philippians. The main lines of Paul's paradigmatic self-presentation in Philippians outlined above are:

(a) self-renunciation of confidence 'in the flesh';
(b) confidence 'in Christ';
(c) proper eschatological reserve;
(d) encouragement to press on;
(e) the regulative teacher to be obeyed; and
(f) one who has contentment from trusting prayer.

This is the telling point: *Christ is not portrayed as an example of any of these in Philippians, and thus the example of Paul cannot be conceived of as a mirror image of Christ's model in the letter.* To say that 'Christ is personified in Paul',[90] beyond lacking textual warrant, collapses distinctions that Paul apparently is at pains to maintain, nor can it account for these difficulties: Are all parts of Christ's example personified in Paul? Some parts? Which parts? Why only some parts of Christ's pattern if Paul is Christ's personification? These questions still have force against Bloomquist's more moderate statement that Paul is 'the fulfilment of the Christ-type'.[91] This interpretative conclusion is too imprecise to address the questions asked. Are there correlations between Christ and Paul? Yes, verbal and material. Is this an intentional self-

---

88. Wolff, 'Niedrigkeit und Verzicht'.
89. On the history of the question of continuity between Jesus and Paul, see V.P. Furnish, 'The Jesus–Paul Debate: From Baur to Bultmann', *BJRL* 47 (1964–65), pp. 342-81, and the other essays that bring the discussion up to date in A.J.M Wedderburn (ed.), *Paul and Jesus: Collected Essays* (JSNTSup, 37; Sheffield: JSOT Press, 1989).
90. Bloomquist, *Function of Suffering*, p. 135.
91. Bloomquist, *Function of Suffering*, p. 168.

identification of Paul with Christ? No, it collapses the obvious differences that Paul himself portrays. We may acknowledge the correspondences without collapsing the clear differences between Christ, Paul and the Philippians.

Instead, it may be better to conclude that Paul's paradigmatic 'I' exemplifies the soteriological significance of life 'in Christ'. The differences between Christ's lordly example and its correlations with Paul and the Philippians cause us to reject the notion that Paul presents himself as an imitator of Christ in Philippians. Against Bloomquist, the text does not justify an assertion that Paul intentionally demonstrates how he 'fulfills' or 'mirrors' the 'Christ-type', and that he included the hymn specifically to cast himself in this light.[92] 'Fulfilment' and 'mirroring' are misleading ways of identifying the correlations between Christ and Paul when the essence of Paul's paradigmatic self-presentation reflects little of Christ's pattern in the hymn, nor can Paul mirror Christ's now lordly estate (2.9-11). The relationship between Christ and all others is firstly soteriological (2.1, 5), though his example of self-abnegation remains exemplary for the Philippians' way of thinking with regard to one another. The correlations between Paul and Christ make Paul's example that much more credible for those 'in Christ' (2.5) because by his teaching and behaviour he models what is possible for those who are also in Christ. Paul's self-portrayal in Philippians may echo verbally Christ's *sui generis* pattern, but it is probably better to describe the relationship of Paul's example to Christ's as one of 'analogy' or 'correspondence',[93] where Christ is the 'archetype' (*Urbild*) for Paul and the Philippians while Paul is their 'type' (3.17; *Vorbild*) because he and they are 'in Christ'.

Summary

Paul's use of self-characterization in Philippians combines persuasive artistry, polemics and paraenesis. In Philippians 3, it has been maintained, Paul presents his renunciation of Jewish credentials against those who were flouting theirs, probably promoting circumcision. The rhetoric of his paradigmatic 'I' is shaped by his polemical purpose against these 'dogs' who are 'evil workers'. Thus, Paul's Jewish self-

---

92. Contra Bloomquist, *Function of Suffering*, pp. 195-97.
93. K. Barth's preferred parlance, so J.B. Webster, 'The Imitation of Christ', *TynBul* 37 (1986), pp. 95-120 (115).

5. *Philippians*

presentation is with the express purpose of exemplifying his renunciation of these qualities because of Christ. He models soteriological confidence in Christ, and a proper eschatological reserve against those for whom the kingdom was already fully realized. When he presents himself as a model, he knows that another option exists for his readers, thus his use of self-characterization in Philippians is at once paradigmatic and polemical. We found this same pattern in Galatians 1–2 where he attacks those who would add any Jewish requirements to the gospel while at the same time modelling for his readers how to stand firm against the pressure these Judaizers brought to bear on them. In Philippians, Paul's self-presentation is explicitly exemplary, as is made clear in 3.15-17 and 4.9, and flows from his life 'in Christ', a life that at points is analogous to, but not equated with, Christ's unique story. With Philippians we complete an examination of Paul's explicit, textually announced use of personal example as a literary strategy, but now we turn to two other letters where the strategy may be used implicitly.

Chapter 6

IMPLICIT USES OF PERSONAL EXAMPLE: PHILEMON
AND 1 THESSALONIANS 2.1-12

In 1 Corinthians, Galatians and Philippians there is a convergence of two factors that strongly indicate Paul's designed usage of personal example as a literary strategy: literary markers exhorting the auditors to imitation (1 Cor. 4.6, 16; 7.8; 11.1; 12.31; Gal. 4.12; Phil. 3.17; 4.9) and a corresponding self-portrayal that serves to model behaviour and attitudes appropriate to those who are 'in Christ'. We turn now to two other Pauline letters where we arguably find the latter without the former. In Philemon and 1 Thessalonians there is no explicit literary exhortation to imitation, but there are passages in each letter where Paul implicitly utilizes his personal example as a literary strategy similar to usages we have identified in 1 Corinthians, Galatians and Philippians. In this chapter this suggestion will be developed and, if correct, demonstrates that this strategy and leadership style spanned Paul's career as a letter writer from his earliest (1 Thessalonians) to his latest letters (Philemon). I begin with Philemon since Paul's implicit exemplification is worked out here in a thoroughgoing way, and end with 1 Thessalonians, Paul's earliest letter, where the pattern of exemplification is present, but only in seedling form.

Personal Example in Philemon

Paul's hortatory use of personal example is worked out with substantial rhetorical sophistication in Philemon. There is no explicit literary marker to indicate that this is what is going on, but Paul's self-references in this short letter have demonstrable hortatory relevance and rhetorical effect.

6. *Implicit Uses of Personal Example*

The Story behind the Letter of Philemon

The letter of Philemon, like other letters, implies a story that must be inferred from the text and reconstructed within the possibilities that the social context permits. The implied story behind Philemon begins with Philemon incurring a debt to Paul (19) and ends with Paul's anticipated arrival at Philemon's house (22). Between these two ends, Philemon's slave Onesimus comes to Paul, and Paul writes a letter to favourably influence Philemon's reception of his slave.[1]

The traditional explanation for why Onesimus came to Paul is that he was a runaway,[2] but the recent modification of this view by P. Lampe, B.M. Rapske, S.S. Bartchy and A.G. Patzia is more likely: Onesimus sought a respected third party (an *amicus domini*) to become his advocate before his aggrieved owner, a common case in Roman legal evidence and thus referred to in v. 15a.[3] The latter option is preferred because the traditional view suffers from crucial flaws in its various presentations—the legal obligation of the authorities to return a slave or the proceeds from his sale to his master (if he were a prisoner); the difficulty of imagining why Onesimus would seek the company of a friend of his master (if he were seeking to disappear); or why Onesimus as a runaway was permitted by the authorities to visit Paul who was under their guard[4] (a location not recognizable as a place of asylum[5]), and why Paul could feel free to send him back to Philemon (12). The elements of Philemon make better sense if Onesimus's goal was not to run away

---

1. Petersen, *Rediscovering Paul*, pp. 43-88. For the outline of the full 'story', see *Rediscovering Paul*, pp. 69-71.

2. Defended recently by J.G. Nordling, '*Onesimus Fugitivus*: A Defense of the Runaway Slave Hypothesis in Philemon', *JSNT* 41 (1991), pp. 97-119, who does not consider Lampe's view.

3. P. Lampe, 'Keine "Sklavenflucht" des Onesimus', *ZNW* 76 (1985), pp. 135-37; followed by B.M. Rapske, 'The Prisoner Paul in the Eyes of Onesimus', *NTS* 37 (1991), pp. 187-203; S.S. Bartchy, 'Philemon, Epistle to', *ABD*, V, pp. 305-10 (307); and A.G. Patzia, 'Philemon, Letter to', *DPL*, pp. 703-707 (705).

4. C.F.D. Moule, *The Epistles to the Colossians and to Philemon* (CGTC; Cambridge: Cambridge University Press, 1962), notes that this theory must suppose that Paul's imprisonment 'was of a lax sort' suggested by Acts 24.23; 28.16, 30, but even in these cases Paul remained under the supervision of a centurion or soldier who presumably would be compelled to uphold the law. For the legal obligations, see Nordling, '*Onesimus Fugitivus*', pp. 114-17, who overlooks the difficulties these obligations raise for the runaway theory.

5. S.C. Winter, 'Paul's Letter to Philemon', *NTS* 33 (1987), pp. 1-15 (2). Some but not all temples had the right of asylum (Moule, *The Epistles*, p. 37).

successfully but rather to return to his owner's household under improved conditions, a strategy that would not make him a *fugitivus*.⁶ He sought Paul to adjudicate a grievance he had with his master Philemon, precisely because he knew Philemon respected Paul. The whole case may revolve around Onesimus's wrongdoing (τι ἠδίκησέν σε; v. 18).⁷ While he was with Paul Onesimus converted to Christ (10-11, 15-16), and the combination of Onesimus's new Christian status and Paul's previous relationship with Philemon forms the basis of Paul's appeal to Philemon.⁸

The Force of Paul's Appeal
Paul begins his appeal in v. 8 only to qualify continually his petition until it is finally stated in v. 17: Paul asks Philemon to receive⁹ Onesimus back with favourable regard (cf. 10-12, 17),¹⁰ acting in a way that

6. Bartchy, 'Philemon', p. 307.
7. Verse 18 is a notorious crux. Cf. C.J. Martin ('The Rhetorical Function of Commercial Language in Paul's Letter to Philemon [Verse 18]', in Watson [ed.], *Persuasive Artistry*, pp. 321-37 [330-35]), who argues that the conditional form and its place in the peroration show that v. 18 is 'merely for the sake of argument' (p. 334) to 'appeal to pity'. If Onesimus has not wronged Philemon in some way, why would the letter of Philemon be necessary? We may accept that this is 'for the sake of argument' while rejecting that it is 'merely' for that purpose—an appeal to the pocketbook would carry as much force as an appeal to pity. Furthermore, what is the point of Paul's reminder of v. 19b if in fact there were no outstanding obligation owed to Philemon?
8. We should reject the other recent hypothesis that Philemon sent Onesimus to Paul (suggested in Houlden, *Paul's Letters from Prison*, p. 226; developed by Winter, 'Philemon'; and followed by W. Schenk, 'Der Brief des Paulus an Philemon in der neueren Forschung [1945–1987]', *ANRW*, II.25.4, pp. 3439-95). Verse 13 cannot be taken as support for this view since the ἵνα clause suggests Philemon's vicarious 'ministry' (διακονῇ) through Onesimus would come as a *result* of Paul's retention of the slave rather than Philemon's *previous* design, as Paul elaborates in v. 14.
9. 12: ἀνέπεμψά; 15: αὐτὸν ἀπέχῃς; 17: προσλαβοῦ αὐτὸν ὡς ἐμέ. A.H. Snyman's study suggests the 'discourse inferences' of vv. 8-11, 17-20, mark the reception of Onesimus as the overall theme ('A Semantic Discourse Analysis of the Letter to Philemon', in P.J. Hartin and J. Peter [eds.], *Text and Interpretation: New Approaches in the Criticism of the New Testament* [Leiden: E.J. Brill, 1991], pp. 83-99 [98-99]).
10. If Onesimus were, in fact, a runaway he could be whipped, imprisoned and even crucified according to Oxyrynchus papyrus 1643 (cited in R.P. Martin,

is congruent with love (5, 7; cf. 1, 9, 16).[11] The specifics of this directive are not detailed, rather 'the accent is on Philemon's spirit of love and not on any specific actions'.[12] Equally unspecified are 'what is proper' (8: τό ἀνῆκον; cf. Eph. 5.4; Col. 3.18),[13] 'what is good' (14: τό ἀγαθόν) and what things will fill Paul with joy and refresh him 'in Christ' (20). Presumably, Philemon would recognize what his obligations were. If Onesimus's wrongdoing was the impetus for his seeking out Paul as his advocate then Paul's appeal, without mentioning it, is that Philemon will put aside his somewhat justified anger and be reconciled to his slave.[14] Paul does not overlook the financial loss that Philemon has incurred by the absence of his slave Onesimus (and perhaps by his wrongdoing),[15] but in good rhetorical fashion deflects a potential objection by promising to make recompense to Philemon (18-19),[16] which the law would have required of him if he had harboured Onesimus as a runaway.[17]

As all commentators acknowledge, Paul does not explicitly go beyond this to ask for Onesimus to be manumitted, though this may be

---

Ephesians, Colossians, and Philemon [Interpretation; Atlanta: John Knox Press, 1991], p. 136). If this were the case Paul's appeal is for clemency.

11. E. Lohse, *Colossians and Philemon* (Hermeneia; trans. W. Poehlmann and R. Karris; Philadelphia: Fortress Press, 1971 [1968]), p. 187.

12. Patzia, 'Philemon', p. 703.

13. P.T. O'Brien, *Colossians, Philemon* (WBC, 44; Waco, TX: Word Books, 1982), p. 288. Neither Zeno's *Concerning That Which is Fitting* (Περὶ τοῦ καθήκοντος) nor Hellenistic Judaism (e.g. 1 Macc. 10.42; Josephus, *Ant.* 13.66) tell us what is that 'proper' thing to do in Philemon's case; see E. Schweizer, *The Letter to the Colossians: A Commentary* (trans. A. Chester; Minneapolis: Augsburg, 1982), pp. 221-22. J. Bauer, 'ἀνήκω', *EDNT*, I, p. 98, does not add any clarity although he gives us the sense of the appeal, 'to command you *to do what is required* (of a Christian)' (author's italics).

14. N.T. Wright also argues that this is the main aim of the letter (*The Epistles of Paul to the Colossians and to Philemon* [TNTC; Leicester: Inter-Varsity Press, 1986], pp. 166-68).

15. See R.P. Martin, *Colossians and Philemon* (NCB; London: Marshall, Morgan & Scott, 1973), p. 167.

16. F.F. Church, 'Rhetorical Structure and Design in Paul's Letter to Philemon', *HTR* 71 (1978), pp. 17-33 (29); Martin, 'The Rhetorical Function', pp. 329-30; Bartchy, 'Philemon', p. 307.

17. Oxyrynchus papyrus 1422 'contains a notice that persons who gave shelter to escaped slaves were to be held accountable in law and could be prosecuted by the slaves' master' (Martin, *Colossians and Philemon*, p. 167).

implied in vv. 13-14, 21. Though Paul makes it clear that Onesimus is precious (10, 12) and valuable to him (11, 13) we can only suppose that Philemon would have felt obliged, because of Paul's suggestion in vv. 13-14, to send Onesimus back to Paul to work as Philemon's slave in Paul's service, or to make him a freedman so that he could work alongside Paul.[18] If this is the implicit message, it stands in tension with the implied permanence of Onesimus's return in vv. 15-16. White summarizes what can be only a tentatively held conclusion, 'The request may then, in fact, be two pronged—Philemon is both asked to accept Onesimus back without retribution and, if right minded, to return him to Paul —though it is never fully concretized'.[19]

Paul's appeal is as compelling as it is vague. His persuasive artistry in Philemon is not limited to his use of rhetorical techniques[20] and his implied authority in the letter (see below). There is a third component to the force of the letter's appeal, implied by references to Philemon's community. Though Paul directly addresses Philemon over 30 times in this short letter giving the impression that this is a personal appeal,[21] this petition is not private since it is bracketed by references to his co-workers and the church in his house at the beginning and end of the letter (2-3, 22-25; cf. textual variant for v. 6). Furthermore, the 'grace [and peace]' formulae (3, 25) anticipate a liturgical setting for the letter's first hearing.[22] This is more than an epistolary convention of maintaining personal contact,[23] since it places Philemon's honour on the line as his reaction to the letter would be scrutinized by his community.[24] As Bartchy says, 'His house-church was watching, and Paul hoped to

---

18. E.g. Lohmeyer, *Die Briefe an die Philipper*, p. 191.

19. J.L. White, 'The Structural Analysis of Philemon: A Point of Departure in the Formal Analysis of the Pauline Letter', in *SBL Seminar Papers 1971* (Atlanta: Scholars Press, 1971), pp. 1-47 (36-37).

20. Church, 'Rhetorical Structure and Design'.

21. Moule, *The Epistles to the Colossians and to Philemon*, p. 17; contra J. Knox, *Philemon among the Letters of Paul* (London: Collins, 1960).

22. Martin, *Ephesians, Colossians, and Philemon*, pp. 142, 145.

23. White, 'The Structural Analysis of Philemon', p. 27.

24. Derrett's novel suggestion that Philemon 'was directed in reality to pagan scrutineers of his church, and also to equally curious synagogue-leaders' goes against the grain of the text (J.D.M. Derrett, 'The Functions of the Epistle to Philemon', *ZNW* 79 [1988], pp. 63-91 [65]).

be there soon to see for himself'.[25] This communal aspect in Paul's thought is not distinct from his understanding of life 'in Christ' (8, 23) or 'in the Lord' (16, 20).[26] Paul's appeal to Philemon is in the context of this shared life, as v. 6 arguably makes explicit: as Philemon acts among the community so he acts toward Christ (τοῦ ἐν ἡμῖν εἰς Χριστόν). As M.L. Soards puts it, in Philemon 'God as Father and Jesus Christ as Lord relate to humans—vertically—in such a manner that humans who are related to God and Christ now [are to] relate to one another—horizontally—in terms of their identities formed in relation to God and Christ'.[27] Furthermore, we might expect that since Paul teaches that the 'body is one' (1 Cor. 12), actions toward Onesimus 'in Christ' are actions toward Paul (17: Εἰ οὖν με ἔχεις κοινωνόν, προσλαβοῦ αὐτὸν ὡς ἐμέ). Paul addresses Philemon as a member of the community, a condition he owes to Paul's own ministry (19).[28] By identifying the community to which Philemon is accountable, Paul increases the likelihood that Philemon will 'obey' (21) without resorting to a direct command, a component that deserves further comment.

Against the backdrop of Philemon's watching community, Paul develops a distinction between commanding and appealing, a feature that is not peculiar to Philemon.[29] He exploits his right 'in Christ' to command (8) only in order to contrast it with his loving appeal (9-10) while crediting Philemon with the sense freely to do what is good and right

---

25. Bartchy, 'Philemon', p. 309 (cf. p. 307); Petersen, *Rediscovering Paul*, pp. 99-100 (see pp. 89-199, for a full treatment of the complex and conflicting social obligations implied by the various roles depicted in the letter).

26. T. Preiss, *Life in Christ* (SBT, 13; trans. H. Knight; Chicago: Allenson, 1954), pp. 32-42; E. Best, *One Body in Christ: A Study in the Relationship of the Church to Christ in the Epistles of the Apostle Paul* (London: SPCK, 1955), pp. 1-33; F. Neugebauer, 'Das Paulinische "in Christo"', *NTS* 4 (1957–58), pp. 124-38 (131-34); cf. A.J.M. Wedderburn, 'Some Observations on Paul's Use of the Phrases "in Christ" and "with Christ"', *JSNT* 25 (1985), pp. 83-97.

27. M.L. Soards, 'Some Neglected Theological Dimensions of Paul's Letter to Philemon', *Perspectives in Religious Studies* 17 (1990), pp. 209-19 (214).

28. Whether directly or indirectly through one of Paul's co-workers since v. 5 employs language that Paul usually reserves for those he has not known in person ('having heard'); see Martin, *Colossians and Philemon*, p. 160.

29. E.g. 1 Cor. 7; 2 Cor. 8. See Bjerkelund, *Parakalô*, pp. 13-19, 24-28, 188-90; Holmberg, *Paul and Power*, pp. 83-86, 183-88; Petersen, *Rediscovering Paul*, pp. 131-51.

(14). Petersen has demonstrated the chiastic rhetorical sequence with the following table:[30]

A	B	B[1]	A[1]
command (8)	appeal (9–10)	consent (14)	obey (21)

It may be the case that Paul's open abandonment of a strong line of argument is itself a rhetorical technique (ἀντίφρασις).[31] However, because the request Paul makes of Philemon is 'so oblique, so faltering', and because this is an uncommon feature of the appeal in common Greek letters,[32] some further explanation for Paul's hesitation must be sought. J. Knox explains Paul's ambivalence in light of the weighty request, since Knox (followed by Winter) believes Paul explicitly appeals for Onesimus to be returned to assist Paul in his missionary work.[33] However, the appeal (παρακαλῶ...περί) is most naturally rendered 'I appeal on behalf of',[34] and Knox's view is somewhat undermined by vv. 15-16.

J.M.G. Barclay explains Paul's ambivalent appeal as an indication of his uncertainty of what should be done in the circumstance, that is, Paul did not know what to recommend. Barclay suggests (1) that Paul was aware of the social difficulties of suggesting that a slave be freed, and (2) that he pondered the irreconcilable nature of being truly 'brothers' and remaining master and slave,[35] a tension that Petersen calls 'inherent'.[36] Against the first part of Barclay's argument, neither Greek nor Roman slavery was usually a permanent state, and owners could release bondservants for various reasons.[37] Many slaves may have had reason to expect emancipation by their thirtieth birthday and so Philemon's

---

30. Petersen, *Rediscovering Paul*, p. 132.

31. Church, 'Rhetorical Structure and Design', pp. 24-25.

32. White, 'The Structural Analysis of Philemon', pp. 35-36. Cf. the clarity of request in Pliny's letter to Sabinianus (*Ep.* 9.21).

33. Knox, *Philemon*, p. 20.

34. So Bjerkelund, *Parakalô*, pp. 120-22; Nordling, '*Onesimus Fugitivus*', pp. 110-12; Derrett, 'Functions of the Epistle to Philemon', p. 64; contra Winter, 'Paul's Letter to Philemon', p. 6.

35. J.M.G. Barclay, 'Paul, Philemon and the Dilemma of Christian Slave-Ownership', *NTS* 37 (1991), pp. 161-86.

36. Petersen, *Rediscovering Paul*, pp. 76-78.

37. S.S. Bartchy, *First-Century Slavery and the Interpretation of 1 Corinthians 7.21* (SBLDS, 11; Atlanta: Scholars Press, 1973), pp. 88-91.

consideration may have been *when* and not *if* he would release Onesimus, as Bartchy suggests.[38] Against the second part of Barclay's argument, the incomprehensibility to us of how Philemon could remain both a master and a 'brother' would not necessarily have produced the same conflict of conscience for Philemon or Paul (though this may be the noblest implication of Gal. 3.27-28). Patron–client relationships were a part of the fabric of society, paradoxically embracing the unstable combination of mutual solidarity and inequality of power—the very tension that is incomprehensible to us.[39] The commonplace acceptance of patron–client relationships renders anachronistic Petersen's comment, 'It is logically and socially impossible to relate to one and the same person as both one's inferior and as one's equal'[40]—for us, but it may not have seemed that way to Philemon, nor to Paul (NB 1 Cor. 7.21-22), nor to the author(s) of Eph. 6.5-9 and Col. 4.1 who were far closer to, if not in an identical position as, Paul.[41]

Paul as Paradigm in Philemon
How then do we understand the ambivalence of Paul's request, since he repeatedly appeals to Philemon's volition so he may freely choose the right thing (8-9, 14, 17, 20), all the while allowing the undercurrent of his authority to flow freely (21-22)? The answer may lie in his implied paradigmatic strategy in the letter. That is, Paul's ambivalence itself may exemplify the attitude he wants Philemon to adopt in his reshaped relationship with his slave: as Paul refuses to assert the authority that he clearly possesses, Philemon is coached in the responsibilities of his newly reformed relationship with Onesimus. Paul wants to gain Philemon's consent so that he will 'freely' (κατὰ ἑκούσιον) do what is good, not 'by compulsion' (κατὰ ἀνάγκην; v. 14). By this example the seed is sown for a new phase of the master's relationship with his slave. Paul does not compel Philemon to act, thus patterning for him a new style of interaction with his slave-become-brother, Onesimus.

38. Bartchy, 'Philemon', p. 308.
39. J.H. Elliott, 'Patronage and Clientism in Early Christian Society', *Forum* 31.4 (1987), pp. 39-48.
40. Petersen, *Rediscovering Paul*, p. 289.
41. Cf. J.H. Elliott, 'Philemon and House Churches', *The Bible Today* 22 (1984), pp. 145-50; Bartchy, 'Philemon', p. 308-309. Contra Barclay, 'Christian Slave-Ownership'; D. Daube, 'Onesimus', *HTR* 79 (1986), pp. 40-43.

What is implied by Paul's paradigmatic self-presentation for Philemon's reformed view of his slave is reinforced by the explicit appeal of v. 17, 'Receive [Onesimus] as me'. Formerly Onesimus was merely a slave who was perhaps not all that useful (11), but now he has become a 'beloved brother' (16) in the spiritual family in Christ, and thus Onesimus gains status with Philemon based on his intimate affiliation with Paul as one of his spiritual protégés.[42] Philemon's mutual brotherhood with Paul and Onesimus defines how his slave is to be received: as Paul himself.

In the next verse (18) Paul further models, consciously or unconsciously, how to be gracious and generous. Though Onesimus's absence and perhaps wrongdoing caused Philemon a financial loss, Philemon may well have been able to cover this amount from his holdings of Onesimus's personal funds.[43] By offering to pay this amount Paul sets the tone for Philemon's future dealings with Onesimus. Church and Bartchy note this exemplification, though they link it to Paul's self-deprivation of Onesimus's service by urging Onesimus to return home.[44] It is difficult to imagine how Philemon could appreciate their point since, after all, Onesimus was *his* slave and not Paul's with whom to be generous. However, generosity is exemplified with the financial commitment of vv. 18-19, suggesting the liberality Philemon could show to Onesimus.

Paul also portrays himself as an example of love (9; ἀγάπη), a model which he affirms that Philemon has already followed (5, 7). Philemon and Onesimus are identified as equally beloved (1, 16; ἀγαπητός). Paul's self-exemplification of compassion for Onesimus (12; τὰ ἐμὰ σπλάγχνα) and his affirmation of Philemon's mercy toward other Christians (7) is masterfully brought together in the identification of this same compassion as the appropriate behaviour toward Onesimus 'in Christ' (22). In the repetition of the words 'love' and 'compassion' there can be no doubt that Paul's love for Onesimus as a beloved brother (16) is paradigmatic parenesis for Philemon's future relationship with him.[45]

42. Cf. 1 Cor. 4.14-21; 2 Cor. 6.13; 12.14-15; Gal. 4.19; Phil. 2.22; 1 Thess. 2.7, 11. See Gutierrez, *La paternité spirituelle*.

43. Bartchy, 'Philemon', p. 309; *idem*, 'Slavery (Greco-Roman)', *ABD*, VI, pp. 65-73 (70).

44. Church, 'Rhetorical Structure and Design', p. 27; Bartchy, 'Philemon', p. 307.

45. Church, 'Rhetorical Structure and Design', pp. 22-24, 27.

6. *Implicit Uses of Personal Example*

M.A. Getty further suggests that the mention of Timothy may also function paradigmatically in the letter:

> Paul wishes to give to Philemon an example of his own 'team ministry' with Timothy whom he joins to himself not as apostles possessing authority, but as servants. Paul is thus portrayed as one who lives and acts out [of] a communal context just as he exhorts Philemon to do.[46]

At first this observation does not seem specific to Philemon since Paul often makes references to his co-workers in his letters. However, there is a strong partnership theme in the letter that gives support to Getty's observation. As N.T. Wright argues, Philemon is an outworking of the nature of 'mutual participation' or 'interchange' 'in Christ' expressed in the idea of κοινωνία (6, 17).[47] Implicitly, then, it is likely that Paul presents his relationship with Timothy, and we may add the eight others mentioned in the letter (including Philemon; vv. 1-2, 23-24), in order to emphasize the community relationships to which Onesimus has gained entry by his conversion (see 'Paul as Partner', pp. 210-11).

Thus, Paul paradigmatically presents himself in Philemon as one who renounces his authority and is full of generosity, love and compassion in regard for other members of the community of believers, in order that Philemon will emulate (21b) his example in his relationship with Onesimus.[48] We now turn to an examination of Paul's explicit self-depictions as prisoner, πρεσβύτης and partner to examine briefly their relationship to Paul's implicit argumentation from personal example in the letter.

Paul as Prisoner
From the first descriptor used of himself in Philemon, we are introduced to Paul's current status as a prisoner in chains. The sender in common Greek letters qualified himself, at the fullest, by name, patronymic, vocation, and place of residence. J.L. White suggests that 'prisoner of

---

46. M.A. Getty, 'The Theology of Philemon', in *SBL Seminar Papers 26* (Atlanta: Scholars Press, 1987), pp. 503-508 (504).

47. Wright, *Colossians and Philemon*, pp. 175-78; idem, *The Climax of the Covenant: Christ and the Law in Pauline Theology* (Edinburgh: T. & T. Clark, 1991), pp. 49-55.

48. Does Paul's expressed desire for freedom (22b) give Philemon food for thought about Onesimus's future?

Christ Jesus' stands as a vocational description,[49] which the christological qualifier (1, 9: δέσμιος Χριστοῦ Ἰησοῦ), and v. 13 support, but it also tells us that the place of writing was Paul's current residence in prison. The christological qualifier is the only constant among his letter introductions besides his name (lacking only in 1 Thessalonians among the entire 13-letter corpus). F. Staudinger quite rightly calls this a genitive 'of source, quality, and possession' which 'expresses the apostle's inner relationship to Christ together with its missionary effect'.[50] Paul's self-characterization elsewhere as 'Christ's slave' and his depiction of Epaphras's imprisonment 'in Christ' (23: ὁ συναιχμάλωτός μου ἐν Χριστῷ Ἰησοῦ) lend credence to a metaphorical implication here, 'Christ Jesus took Paul as a prisoner',[51] in addition to a literal reference to his incarceration.

In total, the self-depiction as a prisoner is reiterated six times in this brief letter (1, 9, 10, 13, 22, 23). He is in chains (10, ἐν τοῖς δεσμοῖς), but they are for the gospel (13, τοῦ εὐαγγελίου), reminiscent of Phil. 1.7, 16. In Philemon 22, Paul draws attention to his imprisonment again by mentioning his anticipated release which, reminiscent of Philippians 1, will be granted due to the prayers of the letter's recipients. In Philemon 23 Paul's imprisonment is consciously or unconsciously reiterated when he characterizes Epaphras as a 'fellow prisoner in Christ Jesus'. The repeated emphasis on the image of Paul as a prisoner makes it likely that Paul emphasizes his current condition as a rhetorical *captatio benevolentiae*, using it as one of the several means of persuasion that he adopts in this short appeal (cf. Eph. 4.1). Moreover, in his refusal to 'compel' Philemon (14) he employs a term (ἀνάγκη) that was frequently associated with chains, yokes and slavery.[52] This common semantic association accomplishes a three-way identification between himself, Philemon and Onesimus. As Paul is obligated to Christ (in chains 'to' Christ), Philemon is indebted to Paul (19) and Onesimus to Philemon. There may be an implied identification of Paul as an indentured prisoner to Christ with Onesimus as an indentured slave to Philemon, so that Philemon will feel the full force of Paul's appeal to receive Onesimus as himself (v. 17).

49. White, 'The Structural Analysis of Philemon', pp. 28-29.
50. F. Staudinger, 'δεσμος, κτλ.', *EDNT*, I, pp. 290.
51. Soards, 'Some Neglected Theological Dimensions', p. 213.
52. Schreckenberg, *ANANKE*, pp. 1-36.

Paul as Presbutēs

Paul interrupts the beginning of his appeal to characterize himself: 'but rather through love I appeal to you—since I am Paul an old man/ambassador [πρεσβύτης] but now also a prisoner of Christ Jesus—I appeal to you...' (v. 9). πρεσβύτης] has the support of the entire manuscript tradition.[53] The suggestion of R. Bentley that the manuscript should be emended to πρεσβ[ε]υτής has been partially adopted and popularized by Lightfoot and subsequent scholars, and gains support from the contrast drawn in v. 9, the authority asserted in the letter, and Paul's self-characterization elsewhere as an ambassador, especially in 2 Cor. 5.20 (cf. Eph. 6.20). It will be argued here, however, that the text should read πρεσβύτης and that the most common translation for this Greek word, 'old man' or 'elder', is the best translation here and can be supported in spite of these objections.

J.N. Birdsall has compiled compelling reasons to reject Bentley's textual emendation. Beyond the fact that conjectural emendation for Philemon 9 has no manuscript support, the most significant reasons Birdsall gives are (1) that textual errors or changes from /ευ/ to /υ/ are extremely rare in all periods; (2) by both the earlier pitch-accent system and the later stress-accent system the words are clearly distinct; (3) all subsequent manuscripts saw no problem with reading πρεσβύτης which confirms that the established text is not so problematic that it demands conjectural emendation; (4) Paul could accurately be called νεανίας in Acts 7.58 and πρεσβύτης in Philemon 9 if account is made both for the several calculations of these ages that were current then, and for the multiple Pauline chronologies that are promulgated now.[54] If Birdsall has decisively established the text as πρεσβύτης, he has not dealt with the argument that this term was used occasionally for 'ambassador', for which πρεσβευτής was the usual term.[55] So the problem remains with us as a translation problem, though it is clearly not a textual one.

---

53. B.M. Metzger, *A Textual Commentary on the Greek New Testament* (New York: United Bible Societies, 1975 [1971]), p. 657.

54. J.N. Birdsall, 'ΠΡΕΣΒΥΤΗΣ in Philemon 9: A Study in Conjectural Emendation', *NTS* 39 (1993), pp. 625-30.

55. E.g. cf. 1 Macc. 13.21 and 14.21, 22 (א); 2 Macc. 11.34; 2 Chron. 32.31 (B); Ignatius, *Smyr.* 11 (examples given by Lohmeyer, *Die Briefe an die Philipper*, p. 185 n. 2); so also Lohse, *Colossians and Philemon*, p. 199; Moule, *The Epistles*, p. 144; O'Brien, *Colossians, Philemon*, p. 290.

Bentley's conjecture also would have changed Παῦλος to πάλαι, reading 'as a former ambassador but now a prisoner' (ὡς πάλαι πρεσβευτής, νῦν δὲ καὶ δέσμιος), which attempts to draw out the significance of the νυνί δέ comparison here analogous to its then–now force in v. 11. However, νυνί δέ in v. 9 may merely indicate that Paul's imprisonment has just begun.[56] Whatever we make of νυνί δέ, both translations of πρεσβύτης can be taken as honourable self-characterizations, if we understand by 'old man' the implied honour and respect he is due because of his seniority. Indeed, the honourable senior status of a πρεσβύτης may be why this term came to be a designate for an emissary.[57] Either way the sense is, 'I deserve the respect as an elder/ambassador in my current imprisonment for Christ Jesus'.[58] Combined with πρεσβύτης, 'prisoner of Christ' further stresses Paul's honourable status, since he is metaphorically imprisoned to and for Christ.[59]

Paul's assertion of authority in the letter is taken as another reason to prefer the more obscure translation for πρεσβύτης, equivalent to his self-characterization as God's 'ambassador' in 2 Cor. 5.20 (πρεσβεύομεν; cf. Eph. 6.20)[60] and congruent with his self-portrayal elsewhere as Christ's apostle. To be sure, Paul makes several side-glances to his authority in Philemon. Even though he ostensibly disavows using such authority (8, 14), the mention of the authority he is *not* using serves to remind Phlmn that he has it in reserve. Likewise, he interrupts the beginning of his request by reminding Philemon who he is (9b) and, whichever way we take πρεσβύτης, we have to recognize that this self-characterization is intended to strengthen the force of the appeal. By form, Paul's request is an appeal, but by innuendo it takes on the force of a command.[61] Paul's understanding of his authority comes com-

56. Martin, *Colossians and Philemon*, p. 163.
57. E.g. *Test. Epict.* 4.28, 6.29 (LSJ, *s.v.*).
58. Thus answering Petersen's objections that the contrast is meaningless if πρεσβύτης is taken as 'an old man of Christ' (*Rediscovering Paul*, pp. 126-27).
59. F.F. Bruce, *The Epistles to the Colossians, Philemon, and to the Ephesians* (Grand Rapids: Eerdmans, 1984), p. 205.
60. E.g. O'Brien, *Colossians, Philemon*, p. 290; Petersen, *Rediscovering Paul*, pp. 126-28. O'Brien contradicts himself with his statements about v. 1, claiming that the absence of 'apostle' is to be explained because Paul 'has no intention of appealing to his apostolic authority' (p. 272). This same denial is made by Patzia, 'Philemon', p. 704.
61. Petersen, *Rediscovering Paul*, p. 65. Similarly, R.P. Martin takes δέσμος in

pletely out of the shadows in v. 21, expressing confidence in Philemon's 'obedience' (ὑπακοή).⁶² Philemon's obedience, in the rhetoric of the letter, is predicated upon his honour to act properly (8, 14) but, in the social chemistry implied behind the letter, his obedience is influenced by the status and authority of the one who makes the appeal.⁶³ Paul exerts the influence of his authority without actually asserting his authority—and the difference between the two is negligible.⁶⁴ The impact of Paul's authority underlying his request is openly indicated by the 'head-on insinuation' that he will come to see for himself what Philemon has made of this 'appeal' (22).⁶⁵ Despite its thin veil Paul's authority is implicit throughout the letter.

Nevertheless, there is no reason why Paul must call himself an 'ambassador' for Philemon and his church to grant him an authoritative status; it is a *non sequitur* that Paul must identify himself as an 'apostle' to assert his authority as one. Furthermore, we must resist the temptation to read Paul's self-characterization elsewhere into the text here.⁶⁶ Coherency in Paul's letters does not require that contingent *hapax legomena* should be expunged or reinterpreted to obtain uniformity of Paul's self-presentation, particularly in this case where the textual evidence is unwavering until the suggestion of Bentley.⁶⁷ While 'ambassador' remains a possible translation, 'old man' is the most common translation of this term.⁶⁸ The nuance of this depictor, lodged where it is amid the appeal of vv. 9-10, emphasizes the senior status of the one making the appeal to strengthen the force of his entreaty. Paul's self-identification as an elder strengthens the function of his imprisonment

---

the sense of, 'respect my fetters by obeying my teaching' (*Colossians and Philemon*, pp. 141, 163; cf. Eph. 4.1).

62. 'Compliance' may 'seem more in keeping with the delicate tact of the letter' (M.J. Harris, *Colossians and Philemon* [EGGNT; Grand Rapids: Eerdmans, 1991], p. 278), but its softer tone does not alter the implied authority that is being asserted.

63. Holmberg, *Paul and Power*, p. 86; Petersen, *Rediscovering Paul*, p. 106.

64. Petersen, *Rediscovering Paul*, p. 190 n. 128.

65. Martin, *Ephesians, Colossians, and Philemon*, p. 145; contra Bruce, *Colossians, Philemon, Ephesians*, p. 220.

66. As in the case in Soards's over-interpretation: 'Thus one may conclude [from Phlm. 9] that *God...made Paul an ambassador of Christ Jesus*' ('Some Neglected Theological Dimensions', p. 21; author's italics).

67. Contra Petersen, *Rediscovering Paul*, p. 126, who explicitly asserts that coherence with Paul's other letters should be decisive in this case.

68. Lohse, *Colossians and Philemon*, p. 199.

as a *captatio benevolentiae*, drawing the portrait of a high-status missionary enduring the afflictions resulting from his service to Christ.[69] In any case, he is a prisoner 'for Christ Jesus' (9c), and it is this christological qualifier that is, in his eyes, his highest claim to status and authority.

Paul as Partner

In v. 17 Paul seeks to establish Philemon's treatment of Onesimus on the basis of Philemon's sense of partnership (κοινωνός) with Paul. This imagery is probably not referring to a Roman partnership contract (κοινωνός = *societas*),[70] but rather to their mutual participation 'in the Lord/Christ' (20), linking in with Paul's rich use of κοινωνία (cf. v. 6). Their 'partnership' (κοινωνός) comes from their 'mutual participation' (κοινωνία) in Christ. G. Panikulam rightly emphasizes that the primary stress of κοινωνία is on the christocentric life, and is never merely individual.[71] The 'fellowship of faith' (6)[72] and their partnership 'in Christ' (17, 20) form the basis of Paul's appeal for Onesimus. Their partnership is not simply a sense of mutual belonging but is a shared commitment to a common missionary effort, and so O'Brien and Petersen are probably correct that a Pauline synonym of κοινωνός in v. 17 is the esteemed designation of 'co-worker',[73] explicitly applied to Philemon in v. 1 (cf. 2 Cor. 8.23).

Paul implicitly characterizes himself and further develops the communal ethos that was anticipated in the thanksgiving (6) by how he characterizes every other person in the letter. As Philemon is a 'co-worker' (1, συνεργός), so are Mark, Aristarchus, Demas and Luke (24). Apphia, probably Philemon's wife, is identified as 'the sister' (ἡ

---

69. Bruce agrees that this is the sense if 'old man' is accepted as the translation (*Colossians, Philemon, Ephesians*, p. 212).

70. Winter, 'Philemon', pp. 11-12. Cf. J.P. Sampley, *Pauline Partnership in Christ: Christian Community and Commitment in Light of Roman Law* (Philadelphia: Fortress Press, 1980), pp. 79-81.

71. G. Panikulam, *KOINONIA in the New Testament: A Dynamic Expression of Christian Life* (AnBib, 85; Rome: Biblical Institute Press, 1979), pp. 1-5.

72. On the interpretative difficulties of v. 6, see H. Riesenfeld, 'Faith and Love Promoting Hope: An Interpretation of Philemon v. 6', in M. Hooker and S. Wilson (eds.), *Paul and Paulinism: Essays in Honour of C.K. Barrett* (London: SPCK, 1982), pp. 251-57.

73. O'Brien, *Colossians, Philemon*, p. 299; Petersen, *Rediscovering Paul*, p. 105.

ἀδελφή) and thus is located within the same spiritual family as are the 'brothers', Timothy (1) and Philemon (2, 7, 20). Paul's characterization of these three is explicitly applied to Onesimus who has become one of their number as their 'most dear brother' (ἀδελφός ἀγαπητός; v. 16). With similar missionary connotation to 'co-worker', Archippus is a 'co-soldier' (2, συστρατιώτης). This comparatively rare word in general literature and Paul (only elsewhere in Phil. 2.25 and there linked with 'co-worker'), carries the sense of '"comrade", to designate a helper in time of need, an ally, a befriender'.[74] Epaphras is a 'co-prisoner' (23, συναιχμάλωτός), presumably imprisoned near Philemon rather than with Paul. Onesimus has become one of them as their 'brother', thus becoming a partner of their shared service to Christ. Not only is he Paul's disciple (10) and 'very heart' (11), but vicariously he carries on Philemon's ministry (12). Thus, the partnership that is portrayed in egalitarian relief is leveraged to full effect for Onesimus's benefit. When Paul asks Philemon to receive Onesimus 'as you would receive me', he means that Philemon should give Onesimus full acceptance as one of those who shares in the work of the family of Christ (Rom. 15.7).[75] Furthermore, there may also be an implied admonishment, as Petersen suggests, 'If you do not receive Onesimus as you would receive me, you will prove to me that you are neither my partner nor a brother'.[76] The cumulative dynamics of the letter suggest that the fellowship that Philemon extends to all the other saints will also be extended to Onesimus who is now counted as one of their number.[77] By characterizing others as his co-labourers Paul creates an implied portrait of himself as a partner, worker, soldier and brother.

Summary
In Philemon, Paul exhibits self-restraint of his authority by explicitly refusing to command as he appeals to Philemon to forgo freely his grievance with Onesimus. This display of Paul's self-limitation of authority is combined with an example of love and generosity to demonstrate paradigmatically the manner in which Philemon is to treat his slave-who-has-become-a-brother. Though Philemon has the legal right to be harsh with Onesimus, Paul asks him to grant Onesimus the

74. Knox, *Philemon*, pp. 58-59.
75. Martin, *Ephesians, Colossians, and Philemon*, p. 144.
76. Petersen, *Rediscovering Paul*, p. 105.
77. See Panikulam, *KOINONIA*, pp. 86-90.

same loving and generous treatment that he would extend to this elder missionary. This is because Onesimus has become a member of the Christian family as a beloved brother, and has become a sharer in the missionary partnership. The community stands witness to Philemon's honour in carrying out the request of Paul, the elder who is in chains because of his gospel service. Paul's status as an elder and as Christ's metaphorical prisoner affirms Paul's authority in the community in the strongest terms, and his repeated emphasis on his imprisonment creates an emotional receptivity to his appeal as a *captatio benevolentiae*. Whether or not Philemon would have or should have taken the letter as a suggestion that he manumit Onesimus cannot be ascertained, but it may be implied by v. 21: 'I am confident of your obedience to the things I write, knowing that you will do more than the things I have asked.'

Thus, by the time of Philemon Paul's rhetorical use of self-portrayal has bloomed into a full and intricate flower, and the paradigmatic aspects are difficult to extract from their intrinsic relationship with the other aspects of his nuanced epistolary persuasion. Philemon is the apex of a literary style that is already evident in Paul's earliest letter, 1 Thessalonians. It is to this earliest use of personal example as a rhetorical strategy that we now turn.

Personal Example in 1 Thessalonians

The Recall Motif in 1 Thessalonians

At first glance, it appears that 1 Thessalonians actually fits the dual pattern of 1 Corinthians, Galatians and Philippians, with the exact word group for imitation appearing in 1.5-6 and 2.14-16 bracketing autobiographical statements that could be partially construed as ethically exemplary. Upon closer examination, however, the coincidence of the word group in 1 Thessalonians is undermined by its totally different usage: here the 'imitation' is a description of what is in fact the case rather than an exhortation to become like Paul.[78] Ἐγενήθητε, used in 1.6 and 2.14, is an indicative verb, whereas the exhortations in 1 Cor. 4.16; 11.1; Gal. 4.12; Phil. 3.17 are imperatives. The Thessalonians, like Paul, his colleagues (2.2; 3.3-5), and the Judaean churches (2.14) experienced tribulation as a result of receiving the gospel. 'What makes the Thessalonians "imitators" of others is not that they follow their example

---

78. Michaelis, 'μιμέομαι', p. 670; Castelli, *Imitating Paul*, p. 192.

(although they also do this) but that the same things *happened* to them'.[79] The use of μιμηταί in 1 Thessalonians is therefore used as a simple comparison.

There is, however, a surrogate literary feature for emulation in 1 Thessalonians, found in the predominant use of the 'recall motif'[80] where Paul repeatedly appeals to the Thessalonians' recollection of his past presence with them. Paul's past personal example is in the foreground already at 1.5, 'just as you know what kind of persons we were when we were with you for your sake' (καθὼς οἴδατε οἷοι ἐγενήθημεν [ἐν] ὑμῖν δι' ὑμᾶς). Appeal to their reminiscence becomes a dominant feature in the letter with continually repeated phrases like 'For remember brothers' (μνημονεύετε γάρ, ἀδελφοί, 1.3, 2.9); 'you yourselves know...', or 'as you know...' (αὐτοὶ γὰρ οἴδατε, 2.1; 3.3; 5.2; καθὼς οἴδατε, 1.5; 2.2, 5; 3.4; καθάπερ οἴδατε, 2.11; οἴδατε γάρ, 4.2). This feature is even more striking when compared with Paul's correspondence with the church in Rome that had no prior experience of him. These phrases are not found in Romans except where Paul appeals to 'what any human being or any Christian would know and hold'.[81] By contrast, in 1 Thessalonians

> he makes explicit references to what he himself had said earlier. He appeals to what the faithful had already heard from him, to what they had witnessed, but also to their own Christian experience. In no other letter does the apostle make so many allusions to what the community has already learned from him. This is a characteristic feature of this epistle, and concerns the circumstances of his mission in Thessalonica, a mission that had been interrupted by a persecution. His earlier instruction of the Thessalonians is still very fresh in his mind.[82]

---

79. Patte, *Paul's Faith*, p. 132; so also C.A. Wanamaker, *The Epistles to the Thessalonians: A Commentary on the Greek Text* (NIGTC; Grand Rapids: Eerdmans, 1990), p. 112.

80. This apt phrase is derived from R.F. Collins, '"The Gospel of Our Lord Jesus" (2 Thess. 1.8): A Symbolic Shift of Paradigm', in *idem* (ed.), *The Thessalonian Correspondence* (BETL, 87; Leuven: Leuven University Press, 1990), pp. 426-40 (430).

81. J. Plevnik, 'Pauline Presuppositions', in Collins (ed.), *The Thessalonian Correspondence*, pp. 50-61 (53).

82. Plevnik, 'Pauline Presuppositions', pp. 53-54.

To add to this impression, 1 Thess. 2.8, characteristic of Paul's approach, combines the centrality of both the message and its messenger.[83] As J. Gillman says, 'The gospel of God is manifested in the life of the apostle; he is the visible incarnation of the divine message of salvation. In that sense the life and character of the apostle is the key to the credibility of the message in the eyes of the community.'[84] And, as Malherbe puts it, 'In short, Paul's method of shaping a community was to gather converts around himself and by his own behavior to demonstrate what he taught. In doing this, he followed a widely practiced method of his day particularly by moral philosophers.'[85]

This utilization of reminiscence draws attention to the past nature of Paul's example which he exemplified when he was present with them, but in each case this past example is related to the present epistolary topic. So although there is no explicit literary marker of personal example in 1 Thessalonians as we found in 1 Corinthians, Galatians and Philippians, there are indicators that leadership by personal example was practised by Paul during this earlier part of his missionary career, even if he had yet to develop fully the literary style. In his use of personal example in 1 Thessalonians, as in so many other epistolary features of this 'experiment in Christian writing',[86] we find *in nuce* what will later become a hallmark of Paul's developed use of personal example.[87] Before we examine 1 Thess. 2.1-12 for elements that reflect Paul's later, more fully developed paradigmatic and polemical uses of his self-presentation, we must first acknowledge the conflicting historical reconstructions about this pericope which have diverted attention from Paul's employment of his personal example here.

---

83. 1 Thess. 4.1 may refer to Paul's personal example also. Though παρελάβετε may be a technical term for the reception of tradition, περιπατεῖν and περιπατεῖτε may suggest that Paul has in mind his past exemplification.

84. J. Gillman, 'Paul's ΕΙΣΟΔΟΣ: The Proclaimed and the Proclaimer (1 Thess 2:8)', in Collins (ed.), *The Thessalonian Correspondence*, pp. 62-70 (69).

85. A.J. Malherbe, *Paul and the Thessalonians: The Philosophic Tradition of Pastoral Care* (Philadelphia: Fortress Press, 1987), p. 52.

86. H. Koester, '1 Thessalonians—Experiment in Christian Writing', in F. Forrester Church and T. George (eds.), *Continuity and Discontinuity in Church History* (Studies in the History of Christian Thought, 19; Leiden: E.J. Brill, 1979), pp. 33-44.

87. So Getty, 'The Imitation of Paul', pp. 277-83 (278, 282). Getty also interprets Paul's example in 1 Thessalonians to be model of self-support, but she does not justify this interpretation from 1 Thessalonians (pp. 279-80).

6. *Implicit Uses of Personal Example* 215

1 Thessalonians 2.1-12: Apology or Stoic Clichés?
Throughout this study we have encountered quite diverse views on the background of Paul's denials about himself, and this schism in Pauline scholarship also impinges upon examination of 1 Thess. 2.1-12. On the one side, in line with a long and well-established scholarly method, the form of the apology evident in 1 Thess. 2.1-12 is thought to contain defensive remarks that relate to intrigues not specified in the text. The text could be thought to imply that Paul had run away from Thessalonica like a coward; while he was in Thessalonica he deceived his hearers and flattered them in order that he might gain some financial return and personal prestige from them; and his motives and character as a preacher would not stand up to examination. Whether thought to be charges against or suspicions about Paul, this approach is well represented in recent scholarship.[88]

On the other side, this approach vis-à-vis 1 Thess. 2.1-12 has been strongly contested by E. Best, A.J. Malherbe, G. Lyons and C.A. Wanamaker. Against the general trend, Best compiles several arguments

---

88. J.E. Frame, *A Critical and Exegetical Commentary on the Epistles of St. Paul to the Thessalonians* (ICC; Edinburgh: T. & T. Clark, 1912), p. 90; W. Marxsen, *Introduction to the New Testament* (trans. G. Buswell; Oxford: Basil Blackwell, 1968 [1964]), p. 35; W. Schmithals, *Gnosticism in Corinth* (trans. J. Seeley; Nashville: Abingdon Press, 1971), pp. 140-45; F.F. Bruce, *1 and 2 Thessalonians* (WBC, 45; Waco, TX: Word Books, 1982), pp. 23-28; I.H. Marshall, *1 and 2 Thessalonians* (NCB; London: Marshall, Morgan & Scott, 1983), p. 61; T. Holtz, *Der erste Brief an die Thessalonicher* (EKKNT, 13; Neukirchen–Vluyn: Neukirchener Verlag, 1986), pp. 92-95; R. Jewett, *The Thessalonian Correspondence: Pauline Rhetoric and Millenarian Piety* (Philadelphia: Fortress Press, 1986), pp. 102-104. Marxsen's view alters between his third edition of his New Testamant introduction and his commentary on 1 Thessalonians. Earlier, he interpreted 1 Thess. 2.1-12 as a personal apology for the apostle, not with respect to enemies at Thessalonica, but with reference to the troubles which Paul had met at Philippi. By the time of his commentary he interprets this passage as an 'Apologie seines Evangeliums' (*Der erste Brief an die Thessalonicher* [Zürich: Theologischer Verlag, 1979], p. 43). For an excellent summary of the scholarly issues facing the interpreter of 1 Thessalonians, see R.F. Collins, 'Recent Scholarship on the First Letter to the Thessalonians', in *idem*, *Studies on the First Letter to the Thessalonians* (BETL, 66; Leuven: Leuven University Press, 1984), pp. 3-75; E. Richard, 'Contemporary Research on 1 (& 2) Thessalonians', *Biblical Theological Bulletin* 20 (1990), pp. 107-15.

against the identification of opponents lying behind 1 Thessalonians:[89] (1) there is no reference to Judaizer controversies; (2) nor is there mention of a clear, distinct group; (3) nor an emphasis on the need for unity (overlooking 5.13); (4) there is a mild tone in Paul's writing; (5) reconstructions such as Schmithals's or Jewett's 'assume there are opponents to be described and then they set out to discover them in every nook and cranny of the letter'.[90] He concludes, 'The enemy, if there really is one, is vague, and the defence can be nothing other than vague; there is no passion as there is in so many of Paul's other letters because there is no group against which Paul can be passionate'.[91]

Malherbe and Lyons, followed by Wanamaker, dispute that the negative self-references in 1 Thess. 2.1-12 are indications of criticisms when they, in the stock practice of the day, reflect a pattern of self-definition where popular philosophers compared themselves with others with negative formulations. Malherbe draws attention to the common use of several phrases from Cynic-Stoic rhetoric,[92] and makes a stylistic comparison of 1 Thess. 2.1-12 with Dio Chrysostom's 'To the Alexandrians' (*Diss.* 32.11-12). In Malherbe's view, Paul's use of antitheses, like Dio's, does not indicate that negative statements are being made against Paul, but rather that Paul depicts himself in a manner evident in Dio also.[93] Lyons argues for a monolithic usage of autobiographical remarks toward paraenetic ends, which he thinks excludes an apologetic function.[94] Lyons, for example, sharply delineates what for him are acceptable approaches to autobiographical texts:

> Antithetical constructions require a literary and rhetorical rather than a historical explanation. They were far too common in the normal synagogue preaching of Hellenistic Judaism and the moral discourses of itinerant Cynic and Stoic philosophers in clearly non-polemical settings

---

89. E. Best, *The First and Second Epistles to the Thessalonians* (BNTC; London: A. & C. Black, 1972), pp. 16-22.
90. Best, *First and Second Epistles*, pp. 21-22.
91. Best, *First and Second Epistles*, p. 22.
92. A.J. Malherbe, '"Gentle as a nurse": The Cynic Background to 1 Thessalonians 2', *NovT* 12 (1970), pp. 203-17.
93. Malherbe, *Paul and the Thessalonians*, pp. 3-4. See, however, B.R. Gaventa's criticisms of this comparison in her 'Apostles as Babes and Nurses in 1 Thessalonians 2.7', in J. Carroll, C. Cosgrove and E. Johnson (eds.), *Faith and History: Essays in Honor of Paul W. Meyer* (Atlanta: Scholars Press, 1990), pp. 193-207.
94. Lyons, *Pauline Autobiography*, pp. 95-112, 183-84.

to assume, as the consensus of New Testament scholarship has done, that Paul's antithetical constructions uniformly respond to opposing charges.[95]

As we have seen, though, literary and historical explanations are not mutually exclusive. One senses here a reductionistic tendency, urging sharp limits on the exegete's ability to reconstruct the historical setting based on the *Gattung* of this pericope, and there is an implied critique against historical reconstruction in general. This tendency is reflected in the recent commentary by Wanamaker who draws this very inference as he commends the results of the studies of Malherbe and Lyons.[96]

Are we really forced to choose between one option or the other? The demand for a unilateral usage or approach to autobiographical remarks in Paul is undermined in the current study. Instead, we have seen that Paul combines quite diverse elements, and displays a range of usage of his self-portrayal. In the case of Philippians 3, for example, disparate elements of polemical and paradigmatic self-presentation are interwoven. There is no reason to reduce 1 Thess. 2.1-12 to either an apology or exemplification, since elements of both may be present. In what follows, a suggestion is made that there is an element of Paul's self-portrayal here that is at once paradigmatic and polemical, modelling industry and chastising the indolent.

1 Thessalonians 2.1-12: Polemical and Paradigmatic Self-Portrayal
An element of Paul's self-representation in 1 Thess. 2.1-12 is polemical against the ἄτακτοι (5.14), paradigmatic for those who would conform to Paul's pattern. The textual evidence is thin but can be pieced together. The most natural reading of 2.7, 'able to be a burden as Christ's apostles' (δυνάμενοι ἐν βάρει εἶναι ὡς Χριστοῦ ἀπόστολοι), is likely since 2.4-5 focuses the auditor's attention on the apostle's financial dealings. In 2.9 the appearance of the lexeme again (ἐπιβαρῆσαί) confirms this translation of ἐν βάρει in 2.7, as 2.9 explicitly ties the pericope in with the well-known Pauline practice of self-support (1 Cor. 9; 2 Cor. 11.7-11; 12.14-18; cf. 2 Thess. 3.6-11).[97] Paul's missionary style

---

95. Lyons, *Pauline Autobiography*, p. 184.
96. Wanamaker, *The Epistles to the Thessalonians*, p. 57. So also B. Johanson who, following Malherbe, identifies the 'anticipitative apologetic function' of 1 Thess. 2.1-12 (*To All the Brethren: A Text-Linguistic and Rhetorical Approach to 1 Thessalonians* [Stockholm: Almqvist & Wiksell, 1987], pp. 164-65).
97. Bruce, *1 and 2 Thessalonians*, pp. 30-31; A.J. Malherbe, 'Exhortation in

is characterized by paying his own way with the work of his own hands, eschewing his right to financial support as an apostle. Another hint of the relation of 1 Thess. 2.1-12 to the imitation motif is the characteristic attending reference to spiritual paternity in 2.11 (cf. 1 Cor. 4.14-16; Gal. 4.19), where an imperative note is added.[98] There are several indicators, then, that Paul's example of hard work with his own hands in 1 Thess. 2.1-12 contains a polemical and paradigmatic aspect for the auditors, a reading that finds confirmation in the co-texts in 4.10b-12; 5.14; and 2 Thess. 3.6-13.

Paul's example in 2.9 is linked with the specific, concrete exhortation in 4.10b-12 to labour with one's own hands:

> We exhort you...to make it your aim to live a quiet life and to tend to your own business and to work with your [own] hands, just as we directed you, so that you may walk in a way that is respectable to those outside the church and be dependent on no one.

Paul exhorts the Thessalonians, in effect, to imitate the literal example he set in their presence, and the literary example in 2.1-12 which reminds them of his past practice.[99] They are to work with their own hands (4.11, πράσσειν τὰ ἴδια καὶ ἐργάζεσθαι ταῖς [ἰδίαις] χερσὶν ὑμῶν), as Paul 'toiled and laboured night and day' (2.9, τὸν κόπον ἡμῶν καὶ τὸν μόχθον· νυκτὸς καὶ ἡμέρας ἐργαζόμενοι). They are not to have financial need of anyone (4.12, μηδενὸς χρείαν ἔχητε), as Paul has kept them free of his financial obligations (2.9, πρὸς τὸ μὴ ἐπιβαρῆσαί τινα ὑμῶν ἐκηρύξαμεν εἰς ὑμᾶς τὸ εὐαγγέλιον τοῦ θεοῦ), a hallmark of his missionary strategy.[100] Thus, the hortatory remarks of 4.10b-12 dovetail with elements of Paul's exemplification in 2.1-12 lending further credence to the hypothesis that he uses personal example in a characteristic manner.[101]

---

1 Thessalonians', *NovT* 25 (1983), pp. 238-56 (242-43); Holtz, *Der erste Brief*, p. 78; Marshall, *1 and 2 Thessalonians*, p. 68. 'Weighty', that is, 'having authority' is possible in 2.7 but made less likely by the repetition of the lexeme in 2.9 (contra Marxsen, *Der erste Brief*, pp. 42-43). Getty suggests, if this translation is followed, that 'Paul exemplifies the appropriate attitude toward authority, not as a means of power and domination' (Getty, 'The Imitation of Paul', p. 281).

98. Schütz, *Anatomy of Apostolic Authority*, p. 228.

99. Lyons, *Pauline Autobiography*, p. 200.

100. R.F. Hock, 'The Workshop as a Social Setting for Paul's Missionary Preaching', *CBQ* 41 (1979), pp. 438-50.

101. Cf. also 2.3 with 4.7; 2.5 with 4.6. Williams rightly points out that the

6. Implicit Uses of Personal Example

Another confirmation in 1 Thessalonians for this reading is found in 5.14 where the offenders are called ἄτακτοι, 'undisciplined' or 'idle'. There are two semantic reasons to settle on this translation of ἄτακτοι rather than Jewett's preference for 'disobedient' or 'insubordinate' (following Spicq's 'refractaires').[102] First, while 'insubordinate' is a lexical possibility,[103] the line of argument already outlined has suggested a context in which indolence is an issue, and the forward thrust of the text is a significant semantic factor in determining the nuances of a lexeme in a given context. (Indeed, Jewett has employed this lexical principle by contending that Paul's defensiveness about his authority in 1 Thessalonians tips the scale in favour of identifying the ἄτακτοι as insubordinate to his direction.) Secondly, the lexeme ἀτακτ- is used only four times in the entire New Testament corpus, only in 1 Thess. 5.14 and 2 Thess. 3.6, 7, 11. In 2 Thess. 3.6, 7 the term is clearly endowed with the sense of not earning one's keep, reiterated in 3.11. 2 Thessalonians 3.10, 12 confirm this sense of the term with a stark, *quid pro quo* ethic, 'if they won't work, neither let them eat!'

The explicit use of the imitation of Paul vis-à-vis self-support in 2 Thess. 3.6-13, regardless of its dating and authorship, is a very early indication that Paul implicitly presents his personal example in 1 Thess. 2.1-12 against the pastoral situation indicated in 1 Thess. 4.10b-12; 5.14.[104] Not only is the typical Pauline word group for imitation employed in 2 Thess. 3.7, 9 (μιμεῖσθαι ἡμᾶς [2]; τύπος), but the very pattern exemplified and reiterated in 1 Thess. 2.9 is mentioned in 2 Thess. 3.8b as an indisputable echo of that earlier text:

μνημονεύετε γάρ, ἀδελφοί, τὸν **κόπον ἡμῶν καὶ τὸν μόχθον· νυκτὸς καὶ ἡμέρας ἐργαζόμενοι πρὸς τὸ μὴ ἐπιβαρῆσαί τινα** ὑμῶν ἐκηρύξαμεν εἰς ὑμᾶς τὸ εὐαγγέλιον τοῦ θεοῦ (1 Thess. 2.9).

οὐδὲ δωρεὰν ἄρτον ἐφάγομεν παρά τινος, ἀλλ' ἐν **κόπῳ καὶ μόχθῳ νυκτὸς καὶ ἡμέρας ἐργαζόμενοι πρὸς τὸ μὴ ἐπιβαρῆσαί τινα** ὑμῶν (2 Thess. 3.8b).

---

demand to interpret 2.1-12 against purely apologetic motives leads commentators to overlook these obvious correlations ('The Imitation of Christ in Paul', p. 162).

102. Jewett, *The Thessalonian Correspondence*, pp. 104-105.
103. H. Hübner, 'ἄτακτος', *EDNT*, I, pp. 176-77.
104. Williams, 'The Imitation of Christ in Paul', pp. 287-93.

If H. Grotius's view is followed that 2 Thessalonians is considered both Pauline and earlier than 1 Thessalonians,[105] then the pastoral issue would already be highlighted for the readers at their reception of the presumably later letter of 1 Thessalonians. If 2 Thessalonians is Pauline but later than 1 Thessalonians, then it may be thought that the earlier problem is still an issue that Paul must confront again with this later letter.[106] If 2 Thessalonians was written by a follower of Paul or someone seeking to forge a Pauline letter,[107] then we have in 2 Thess. 3.6-13 the earliest expression of the *Wirkungsgeschichte* of 1 Thessalonians, confirming that the reading adopted here is actually how the text was received by an early Paulinist.[108]

Summary

In summary, as Paul's earliest letter 1 Thessalonians embodies in incipient form the literary use of personal example that Paul develops for persuasive impact in 1 Corinthians, Galatians and Philippians, and that comes to full flower in Philemon. If the exegetical argumentation and literary insights in this and the previous chapters have adequately established Paul's stylistic use of 'I' in the rhetorical construction of his letters, then we are ready to apply these insights to the most disputed 'I' passage in Paul, Rom. 7.7-25.

---

105. A view defended most recently in Wanamaker, *The Epistle to the Thessalonians*, pp. 37-45.

106. See Jewett, *The Thessalonian Correspondence*, pp. 26-30, for a recent defence of the traditional view of authorship and dating of 1 and 2 Thessalonians.

107. E.g. W. Trilling, *Der zweite Brief an die Thessalonicher* (EKKNT; Zürich: Benziger Verlag; Neukirchen–Vluyn: Neukirchener Verlag, 1980), pp. 22-32.

108. It is beyond the scope of our enquiry to relate idleness to an eschatological position of some Thessalonians, but the connection is not hard to make, i.e. a lack of confidence in the parousia (1 Thessalonians) or an over-realized eschatology (2 Thessalonians) could have been culpable of destroying the work ethic of the community (e.g. Marxsen, *Der erste Brief*, p. 71; Williams, 'The Imitation of Christ in Paul', p. 288).

Chapter 7

A CASE IN POINT: ROMANS 7.7-25

Paul does not explicitly exhort the reader in Romans to imitate him, explained by his auditors' lack of-personal knowledge of him, but his use of 'I' in a stylized way in Rom. 7.7-25 does reflect elements of his usage we have already discussed in 1 Corinthians, Galatians, Philippians, Philemon and 1 Thessalonians. This highly disputed passage in Romans serves as a good case study for what has been identified in this study as Paul's literary 'I' style. Now we are ready to apply some of the above conclusions to the interpretation of this text. I shall examine this passage in four sections: (1) general observations, (2) a consideration of the possible identity of the 'I', (3) a brief consideration of the origin of this literary 'I' style, and (4) an exploration of the two ways in which Paul uses this dramatized 'I' statement as part of his persuasive programme in Romans.

General Observations

Romans 7.7-25 is found within the larger unit of chs. 5–8 that deal with a series of objections raised against the doctrine of righteousness through faith, further developing the thesis of 1.16-17 from 1.18–4.25.[1] The transition to address those who know the law in 7.1 is obvious and significant, as Minear notes.[2] It is to this delimited group of readers that Paul now turns his attention, but all the auditors have something to

---

1. R. Jewett, 'Following the Argument of Romans', in K.P. Donfried (ed.), *The Romans Debate: Revised and Expanded Edition* (Edinburgh: T. & T. Clark, 1991), pp. 265-77 (271).
2. P.S. Minear, *The Obedience of Faith: The Purposes of Paul in the Epistle to the Romans* (London: SCM Press, 1971), p. 64, though his overall theory of five audiences addressed in the letter is strained.

learn from the discussion.[3] 7.6 sets the theme for chs. 7–8,[4] and 7.7 leads directly to a consideration of 7.7-25. Apart from the introductory remark of 7.7, vv. 7-13 are in the past tense, and vv. 14-23 are in the present tense. Both parts are introduced by comments in the first-person plural (vv. 7, 14), but then shift to the first-person singular.

The Identity of Paul's 'I' in Romans 7

Until W. Kümmel's definitive study of 1929, it was usually thought that the 'I' of Romans 7 referred straightforwardly to the experience of Paul, either as a Christian or in description of his pre-Christian struggle with the law. Kümmel strongly contested this approach, and many commentators since (especially German) have followed his view that the 'I' of 7.7-25 is a rhetorical means of illustrating a general train of thought, and *cannot* include Paul's experience.[5] Kümmel builds his case on three observations. First, he argues that the statement of 7.9 cannot be reconciled with Paul's pre-Christian life, since nowhere else does he speak of a life 'without law'.[6] Secondly, since Phil. 3.4-6 is clearly autobiographical, and since Romans 7 stands in contradiction to it (see below, p. 223), Paul's 'I' in Romans 7 cannot be autobiographical. Thirdly, Kümmel lists examples of the 'fictive I' in Paul,[7] Demosthenes, Xenophon, Horace and Philo.[8] On this third point, G. Theissen faults Kümmel for misappropriating parallels and offers a detailed critique.[9] But,

---

3. N. Elliott, *The Rhetoric of Romans: Argumentative Constraint and Strategy and Paul's Dialogue with Judaism* (JSNTSup, 45; Sheffield: JSOT Press, 1990), pp. 245-46 n. 3.

4. Theissen, *Psychological Aspects*, p. 187.

5. On the literature before 1963, see O. Kuss, 'Zur Geschichte der Auslegung von Röm 7.7-25', in *idem*, *Der Römerbrief* (2 vols.; Regensburg: Friederich Pustet, 1963), II, pp. 462-68. For a review of recent scholarship, see J. Lambrecht, *The Wretched 'I' and its Liberation: Paul in Romans 7 and 8* (LTPM, 14; Louvain: Peeters; Grand Rapids: Eerdmans, 1992), pp. 59-91; and M.A. Seifrid, 'The Subject of Romans 7.14-25', *NovT* 34 (1992), pp. 313-33.

6. Kümmel, *Römer 7*, pp. 67-90, 118-32. Cf. S. Yagi, 'Das Ich bei Paulus und Jesu—Zum Neutestamentlichen Denken', *Annual of the Japanese Biblical Institute* 5 (1979), pp. 133-53.

7. Rom. 3.5, 7; 1 Cor. 6.12, 15; 10.29b, 30; 11.31-32; 13.1-3, 11-12; 14.11, 14-15; Gal. 2.18, 19, 20; Rom. 7.7a, 9 (Kümmel, *Römer 7*, p. 121).

8. Kümmel, *Römer 7*, pp. 126-31.

9. Theissen, *Psychological Aspects*, pp. 191-201; see also U. Wilckens, *Der*

as we have seen in the previous chapters, Paul's 'I' style is so varied that an argument from style could not be considered conclusive for or against Kümmel.

What of the contradiction Kümmel identifies between Philippians 3 and Romans 7? Philippians 3.6 remains the strongest objection to allowing any autobiographical element to Rom. 7.7-25. The 'blameless' (ἄμεμπτος) pre-Christian Paul of Phil. 3.6 seems irreconcilable with the 'wretched man' of Rom. 7.24 (ταλαίπωρος ἐγὼ ἄνθρωπος), who is unable to do what the law requires (7.18).[10] In particular, Paul's absolute statement in Phil 3.6 does not seem to allow for the tension and feeling of moral impotence found especially in Rom. 7.14-25. He boldly claims in Phil. 3.6 that he was 'as to righteousness under the law, blameless'. This is undeniably autobiographical, which seems to imply that Romans 7 cannot be. But this tension is overstated since it may be maintained that Phil. 3.6 though autobiographical is incomplete, reflecting how Paul saw things *before* he was a Christian, while Romans 7 shows how he sees them *now* from his Christian perspective, a case made very well by J.M. Espy.[11] Perhaps in Phil. 3.6 Paul could claim that he kept the law blamelessly in an outward manner, but now with his increased self-knowledge he has become aware that he was not blameless after all, particularly since emphasis is made in Romans 7 on the command against coveting, an issue of inner consciousness rather than of outward conformity.[12] In support of this view, F. Thielman adds that claims of blamelessness in ancient Judaism were common, and comparative rather than absolute. For one example, in 2 Chron. 15.17 Asa is described as blameless, but ch. 16 goes on to catalogue his sins. Similarly, Thielman plausibly asserts Paul claims blamelessness vis-à-vis other sinners in Phil 3.6 without implying that he never sinned (NB Phil. 2.15; 3.12-14).[13]

Brief an die Römer (Röm, 6–11) (EKKNT, 6.2; Zürich: Benziger Verlag; Neukirchen–Vluyn: Neukirchener Verlag, 1980), pp. 76-77.

10. Kümmel, *Römer 7*, pp. 111-17; so also Sanders, *Paul and Palestinian Judaism*, pp. 443, 479.

11. J.M. Espy, 'Paul's "Robust Conscience" Re-Examined', *NTS* 31 (1985), pp. 161-88.

12. J.A. Ziesler, *Paul's Letter to the Romans* (London: SCM Press, 1989), p. 183. Similarly, Theissen's 'psychological analysis' of Rom. 7 suggests that in Rom. 7 we see a previously repressed conflict brought into consciousness (*Psychological Aspects*, pp. 222-75).

13. F. Thielman, *From Plight to Solution: A Jewish Framework for Under-*

Kümmel's observation about Rom. 7.9 may remain in force, since the Paul we know never speaks of a time when he was without the law.[14] However, there are elements of Romans 7 that express the deep feeling of an individual, and one cannot help but think that Paul felt something of what he wrote when he says, 'Wretched man that I am! Who will deliver me...', and 'I do not understand my own actions...I do the very thing I hate'. These statements are too pointed and even agonized to be concerned only with other people and not for oneself.[15] As C.H. Dodd aptly says, 'A man is not moved like that by an ideal construction'.[16] Furthermore, the command of 7.7 addresses all people, a category to which Paul belongs. It is probably an overstatement, then, that the 'I' of Romans 7 *cannot* include Paul, but Kümmel has made the case that Romans 7 is not merely about Paul.

A second distinctive approach to the identity of 'I' in Romans 7 identifies 7.7-13 (and not 7.14-25) as an allusion to the Genesis story of Adam's disobedience in the Garden of Eden, as S. Lyonnet has demonstrated.[17] In this view 'I' represents Adam, who in turn represents the human race in the progress of salvation history.[18] As Wedderburn points out:

standing Paul's View of the Law in Galatians and Romans (NovTSup, 61; Leiden: E.J. Brill, 1989), p. 110.

14. J. Ziesler, 'The Role of the Tenth Commandment in Romans 7', *JSNT* 33 (1988), pp. 41-56 (43-45), considers arguments for the time before Paul's *bar mitzvah* (recognizing the anachronism), and concludes this is possible but unlikely. See also G. Bornkamm, 'Sin, Law and Death: An Exegetical Study of Romans 7', in *idem*, *Early Christian Experience* (trans. P.L. Hammer; London: SCM Press, 1969), pp. 87-104 (92-93); Lambrecht, *The Wretched 'I'*, pp. 81-82.

15. Ziesler, *Romans*, p. 181; contra Sanders, *Paul, the Law, and the Jewish People*, pp. 71-81, who sees the anguish here resulting from the acute theological problem of the law that Paul faces, but this hardly accounts for the personal struggle and sense of bondage that are conveyed, culminating in 7.24.

16. C.H. Dodd, *The Epistle of Paul to the Romans* (MNTC; London: Hodder & Stoughton, 1932), p. 125.

17. S. Lyonnet, 'L'histoire du salut selon le ch 7 de l'épître aux Romains', *Bib* 43 (1962), pp. 117-51; *idem*, '"Tu ne convoiteras pas" (Rom 7.7)', in *Neotestamentica et Patristica* (NovTSup, 6; Leiden: E.J. Brill, 1962), pp. 157-65; and Theissen, *Psychological Aspects*, pp. 202-208, who counters the objections of Kümmel, *Römer 7*, pp. 85-87.

18. See E. Stauffer, 'ἐγω', *TDNT*, II, pp. 356-62 (358-62) who holds to the salvation-history view exclusively for this passage. D.J. Moo, 'Israel and Paul in

7. A Case in Point: Romans 7.7-25

Paul would have been only too aware that Adam by his very name stands for all men; just how aware he is of the interchangeability of Adam and ἄνθρωπος is indicated in 1 Cor. 15.45b where, having referred to ὁ πρῶτος ἄνθρωπος ᾿Αδάμ (᾿Αδάμ as a proper name), he refers to Christ, not as ὁ ἔσχατος ἄνθρωπος, but as ὁ ἔσχατος ᾿Αδάμ.[19]

Genesis 3 follows the same pattern as Romans 7: innocence, command, transgression, death. Moreover, Adam is the only person of whom it could be said he once lived apart from any law (7.9), but 'law' here stands for Torah and would rightly apply to anyone before Moses. Also, the reference to sin's deception (7.11; ἡ γὰρ ἁμαρτία...ἐξηπάτησέν με) echoes Gen. 3.13 (LXX), using almost the same verb for the serpent's deception of Eve (Ὁ ὄφις ἠπάτησέν με). The command not to eat was often seen as a symbol for the whole law.[20] There is in both Romans 7 and Genesis 3 an emphasis on knowledge, and sin is personified in both passages, in Genesis as the serpent. It seems undeniable that the story of Adam is incorporated into this passage, and the explicit direction of this passage to readers who 'know the law' in 7.1 strengthens this reading, since they would surely know the background to which Paul alludes. Even so, Käsemann overstates the case when he claims that 'There is nothing in our verses which does not match up with Adam, and everything matches up only with Adam'.[21] For example, this claim does not explain the use of 'law' as it refers to Torah, which came after Adam,[22] nor does it account for the personal emotion of what follows in 7.14-24.[23] While motifs from the Genesis story about

---

Romans 7.7-12', *NTS* 32 (1986), pp. 122-35, is a recent proponent of the view that the giving of the law to Israel at Sinai is the main focus of this text.

19. A.J.M. Wedderburn, 'Adam in Paul's Letter to the Romans', *Studia Biblica* 3 (1978), pp. 413-30 (422-23).

20. *Šab.* 145b-146a; Ecclus 17; *Targ. Neof.* on Gen. 1–3; Philo, *De spec. Leg.* 4.84-85. So Lyonnet, '"Tu ne convoiteras pas" '; A. Feuillet, 'Loi de Dieu, loi du Christ et loi de l'Esprit d'après les épîtres pauliniennes: Les rapports de ces trois lois avec la loi Mosaïque', *NovT* 22 (1980), pp. 29-65 (32-35).

21. Käsemann, *Römer*, p. 186. See the critique of Wedderburn, 'Adam', pp. 420-22.

22. Moo, 'Israel and Paul', p. 125.

23. See D.H. Campbell, 'The Identity of ἐγώ in Romans 7.7-25', *Studia Biblica* 3 (1978), pp. 57-64 (60-61).

Adam have been employed here, he is not the subject. Rather, Adam is a model that Paul has woven into the fabric of his argument.[24]

While it is true that there is an element of 7.7-13 that does not seem to fit Paul (e.g. 7.9), and that there are several elements that suit Adam very well, there still remains a personal aspect to this passage, an 'I' in which Paul expresses either himself or feelings he believes are common to the human experience of keeping the law. Thus Paul creates a composite character whom he labels 'I'. While 'I' does not refer straightforwardly to Paul, it incorporates his experience, especially in vv. 14-25.[25] Thus the tendency of recent commentaries in English to assume there is an element of autobiography is justified, though no one supposes it is only autobiographical.[26] Appeals to other sources, such as Ovid's *Metamorphoses* 7.19-20 or 1QS 11.9-15, can help us see Paul in connection with the ancient reflection on the contradiction of willing and doing, but they do not provide literary sources for the content or form of his argument here.[27]

A Diatribal Origin of Paul's 'I' Style?

The 'I' stylistic piece of Rom. 7.7-25 is found in a letter noted for its diatribal characteristics. The coincidence of these two features is highly suggestive of a possible origin of this 'I' style. If we look earlier in Romans at 3.6-7 we find a revealing clue. There, the change to the stylistic use of a rhetorical 'I' is preceded by the well-known diatribal

---

24. Theissen, *Psychological Aspects*, p. 203; Lambrecht, *The Wretched 'I'*, pp. 83-84.

25. Lofthouse, '"I" and "We"', p. 244; J.D.G. Dunn, 'Romans 7.14-25 in the Theology of Paul', *TZ* 31 (1975), pp. 257-73.

26. C.K. Barrett, *A Commentary on the Epistle to the Romans* (HNTC; New York: Harper & Row, 1957), p. 152; C.E.B. Cranfield, *The Epistle to the Romans*, I (ICC; Edinburgh: T. & T. Clark, 1975), pp. 342-47; Dunn, *Romans 1-8*, p. 388; Lambrecht, *The Wretched 'I'*, pp. 89-91; Theissen, *Psychological Aspects*, pp. 190-201; Ziesler, *Romans*, pp. 179-84. Cf. P. Althaus, *Der Brief an die Römer* (Göttingen: Vandenhoeck & Ruprecht, 1966), pp. 73-75; Feuillet, 'Loi de Dieu', pp. 33-34.

27. See Theissen, *Psychological Aspects*, pp. 212-21; R.V. Huggins, 'Alleged Classical Parallels to Paul's "What I want to do I do not do, but what I hate, that I do" (Rom. 7.15)', *WTJ* 54 (1992), pp. 151-61. Cf. the citation of 1QS 11.9-15 in J.A. Fitzmyer, *Romans* (AB, 33; London: Geoffrey Chapman, 1993), pp. 465-66.

ejaculatory μὴ γένοιτο.[28] The same combination of μὴ γένοιτο and punchy 'I' statement occurs at Gal. 2.17-18. These two texts raise the possibility that Paul's 'I' style may well be derived from a similar origin.[29] 'Diatribal style' is used here as Stowers has clarified, a flexible style of presentation set off by distinctive features that can vary widely.[30] Generally, diatribe is a dialogical form of argument conducted in a lively debate and familiar conversation style with an interlocutor. It is peppered with apostrophes, proverbs and maxims, short statements and rhetorical questions, among other features. Both Gal. 2.18 and Rom. 3.7 respond to rhetorical questions, and this technique seems to be a direct development of the diatribal style from its context. Throughout Romans, where the diatribal style is used most extensively, Stowers has argued that it is an indicator of the instructional intention of the letter, and it is that more developed stylistic usage there that may provide the clearest view to the origin of Paul's 'I' style.[31]

In Rom. 3.7 Paul frames a rhetorical question in the first-person singular, reminiscent of the style of Gal. 2.17-18: 'But if through my falsehood God's truthfulness abounds to his glory, why am I still being condemned as a sinner?' (Rom. 3.7). This occurs in Rom. 3.1-8, which is found in the first argumentative unit of the letter (1.18–4.25) as a part of the discussion of Jewish involvement in universal sin (3.1-20). The first part of this section (3.1-8) is identified by W.S. Campbell as the structural centre of Romans (3.21-26 as the theological centre), providing useful guidelines for tracing the argumentation that follows—3.1-6 anticipate chs. 9–11, and 3.8 introduces 6.1–7.6 and may anticipate Paul's discussion of the law in 7.7-25.[32] The transitional nature of 3.1-8 may account for much of the difficulty it poses to the interpreter.

---

28. A.J. Malherbe, '*Mē Genoito* in the Diatribe and Paul', in *idem*, *Paul and the Popular Philosophers* (Minneapolis: Fortress Press, 1989 [1980]), pp. 25-33.

29. Bachmann, *Sünder oder Übertreter*, pp. 30-54.

30. Rather than in Bultmann's sense of a literary *Gattung*; see Stowers, *The Diatribe*.

31. See A. Bonhöffer, *Epiktet und das Neue Testament* (Giessen: Alfred Töpelmann, 1911), pp. 136-46, for an overview of the stylistic comparison of Paul with 'Epiktets Diatriben'.

32. W.S. Campbell, 'Romans 3 as a Key to the Structure and Thought of Romans', in Donfried (ed.), *The Romans Debate*, pp. 251-64 (259); similarly H. Räisänen, 'Zum Verständnis von Röm. 3.1-8', *SNTU* 10 (1985), pp. 93-108 (106); J.D.G. Dunn, 'Paul's Epistle to the Romans: An Analysis of Structure and

Romans 3.1-8 utilizes a diatribal style as Paul guides an interlocutor through a discussion of objections to God's impartial judgment,[33] and he indicts a Jewish assumption of advantage over the non-Jew (3.1 and 9).[34] Stowers demonstrates how the structure of this passage and the awkward changes between first-person singular and plural are accounted for if this passage is read as a continuous dialogue between two people: Paul and his dialogue partner, the Jew.[35] In the midst of this diatribal discussion, Paul, as a Jew, poses the problem in the first-person bringing forward the assertion of v. 5b:[36] 'But if through my falsehood God's truthfulness abounds to his glory, why am I still being condemned as a sinner?' (3.7).[37] Stowers rightly observes that as Paul shifts to the first-person in 3.7 he 'puts on a *persona*':

> The words of this 'I' are meant to show the absurdity of an unjust partiality toward Israel. The sense of these verses can be clarified by means of a paraphrase with the interrogatives and the parenthetic comments

Argument', *ANRW*, II.25.4, pp. 2842-90 (2852); see also C.D. Myers, 'Chiastic Inversion in the Argument of Romans 3–8', *NovT* 35 (1993), pp. 30-47 (45-47).

33. As S.K. Stowers demonstrates, 'Paul's Dialogue with a Fellow Jew in Romans 3.1-9', *CBQ* 46 (1984), pp. 707-22. Though Stowers is unaware of the article by D.R. Hall ('Romans 3.1-8 Reconsidered', *NTS* 29 [1983], pp. 183-97), he answers Hall's objections against identification of the diatribe style here.

34. Following the traditional interpretation in, for example, Beker, *Paul the Apostle*, pp. 59-93. Even though Paul's answers to the questions in 3.1 and 3.9 are in tension with one another, this is not incongruent with his ambivalence in the letter. Dunn, 'An Analysis of Structure and Argument', p. 2851; Hall, 'Romans 3.1-8 Reconsidered', p. 184; contra Stowers, 'Paul's Dialogue', pp. 715, 719-20. Elliott, *Rhetoric*, pp. 284-87, stands alone in thinking Paul uses the diatribal mode of rhetoric to create an artificial environment where the Jewish interlocutor eventually submits to God's righteous judgment (3.4-9), and 'thus becomes a paradigm of trustful assent to God's will', an example for Gentile auditors to appropriate in their sense of freedom from the law (pp. 131-32). This conforms to his reading that Romans is a corrective of Gentile understanding from the freedom from the law, but it requires that we turn around the sense of 3.7, that there is a Jewish or Jewish-Christian attack on Paul's gospel that he seeks to refute. Entirely differently, C.H. Cosgrove, 'What If Some Have Not Believed? The Occasion and Thrust of Romans 3.1-8', *ZNW* 78 (1987), pp. 90-105, posits that it is specifically the rejection of the Messiah by Torah-faithful Jews that is in view here.

35. Stowers, 'Paul's Dialogue', pp. 709-10, 720; so also Elliott, *Rhetoric*, pp. 132-41.

36. Cranfield, *Romans*, I, pp. 185-87.

37. So Ziesler rightly says, 'in the context "I" is almost certainly to be taken as "I, as a Jew"' (*Romans*, p. 98).

7. *A Case in Point: Romans 7.7-25* 229

omitted: 'I, a Jew, should not be condemned for my sin because it only serves to display God's glory when he forgives his people. Let us Jews do evil that good may come'.[38]

This clearly has led to the wrong conclusion, as Paul's readers would agree, and results in the rejection of any thought of Jewish advantage over the non-Jew (3.9), though 3.2 steered the auditors in a different direction. Although Jewish people are entrusted with 'the words of God' (3.2), they have no exemption from God's impartial judgment (3.9).[39] Thus, the rhetorical question of 3.7, framed as a self-expression, serves as part of Paul's diatribal refutation of false inferences to be drawn from the gospel of Christ as he conceives it. It is entirely inferential, but it appears likely that Paul's highly polished usage of 'I' derives from the same style of diatribal argumentation, whether he learned it in school or imbibed it in everyday debates in the agora.

The composite identification of 'I' in Rom. 7.7-25 and the shift in 7.14 are adequately explained as an adaptation of the diatribal style. While the change of person is a common feature in Graeco-Roman letters,[40] the diatribal style of 7.7 is a direct clue to the origin of Paul's 'I' style here (cf. vv. 13, 14, 24).[41] It is likely that the diatribal form of 7.7 explains the form of our passage, as the diatribal style of 3.1-6 probably accounts for the 'I' style of 3.7-8 (cf. Gal. 2.17-18). One element of the diatribal style is to-personify the abstract as part of the argument.[42] We see this personification of law and sin in 7.7-25 'as actors on the stage of human history',[43] but it should not be overlooked that the 'I' is a virtual third literary character, and together their 'interpersonal' struggle portrays the theological points Paul wants to express. They have become agents with a volition, and Paul's 'I' emerges in this context as a third character in the struggle. Yet, law, sin and 'I' are not merely literary or rhetorical devices since they have literal referents, too. The law

---

38. Stowers, 'Paul's Dialogue', p. 718.
39. Contra Stowers, 'Paul's Dialogue', pp. 719-20.
40. See, for example, the illustrations from Dionysius of Halicarnassus, Epicurus, Plutarch and 2 Maccabees in M.L. Stirewalt, 'The Form and Function of the Greek Letter-Essay', in Donfried (ed.), *The Romans Debate*, pp. 147-71 (159-61).
41. As suggested by Kümmel, *Römer 7*, p. 127; so also Lambrecht, *The Wretched 'I'*, pp. 31-35; Fitzmyer, *Romans*, pp. 91, 432, 467. See Kümmel's examples on pp. 126-31 of *Römer 7*, and others in Stowers, *The Diatribe*, pp. 86-92.
42. T.C. Burgess, 'Epideictic Literature', *Studies in Classical Philology* 3 (Chicago: University of Chicago Press, 1902), pp. 89-261 (234-40).
43. Fitzmyer, *Romans*, p. 465.

explicitly refers to the tenth command, probably an implicit representation for the entire law.[44] Sin presumably refers to the experience of Jewish believers like Paul and perhaps Christian believers as well. The view adopted here is that 'I' is a composite of various elements which defy a single identification.[45] The 'I' of Romans 7 incorporates elements of Adam's story, elements of Paul's experience, and is somehow intended to relate to the experience of Jewish, and perhaps Christian, believers.[46] The diatribal introduction of 7.7 and the developed argument that flows from it seem to suggest that Paul's 'rhetorical' use of 'I' is really an adaptation of the common diatribal style, to clarify the argument in a striking, persuasive and memorable way.[47] The diatribal springboard of 7.7 makes it unlikely that Paul switches styles in what follows to a 'confessional' usage more akin to the Psalms, as Käsemann suggests.[48] Rather 7.7-25 is more likely an adaptation of the well-known Graeco-Roman diatribal style of didactic communication.

The Two Functions of 'I' in Romans 7
This creative use of 'I' in Romans 7 functions in two ways, which relate to the two distinct divisions of Romans 7, vv. 7-13 and vv. 14-25. These sections are set apart by the tense of the verbs they employ (vv. 7-13, past tense; vv. 14-23, present tense), and by the transitional 'for we know' at v. 14. In 7.7-13 Paul's 'I' participates as a 'defence' of the law, or more precisely a defence of the law in light of the claims of his

---

44. On the command against coveting as the essence of the whole Law, see *4 Macc.* 2.6; *Apoc. Mos.* 19.3; Philo, *De Decal.* 142, 150, 173; *Targ. Neof.* on Exod. 20.17; and cf. Num. 11.34; 1 Cor. 10.6; Bornkamm, 'Sin, Law and Death', pp. 90, 102 n. 7; Ziesler, 'Tenth Commandment', p. 47; Moo, 'Israel and Paul', p. 123.

45. Following Beker, Cranfield, Dunn, Lambrecht, Moo, Theissen, Ziesler. For a list of others see Moo, 'Israel and Paul', p. 135 n. 59.

46. Earlier proponents of Paul speaking as a Christian are J.I. Packer, 'The "Wretched Man" in Romans 7', in F. Cross (ed.), *Studia Evangelica*, II (Berlin: Academie, 1964), pp. 621-27; Dunn, 'Romans 7.14-25', pp. 257-73; Campbell, 'The Identity of ἐγώ', pp. 57-64.

47. So K. Stendahl, 'Paul and the Introspective Conscience of the West', in *idem, Paul among Jews and Gentiles and Other Essays* (Philadelphia: Fortress Press, 1976 [1963]), pp. 78-96 (92); Porter, *Idioms*, p. 76.

48. Käsemann, *Römer*, p. 183; Dunn, *Romans 1–8*, p. 378; and argued by Seifrid, 'Romans 7.14-25', pp. 313-33.

gospel. In 7.14-25, Paul's 'I' provides a showcase for the liberating power of Christ.[49]

It is generally held that 7.7 introduces the content of what follows as a defence of Paul's exclusion of the law from God's saving purpose (7.5-6).[50] Except for 3.31, mention of the law to this point in the letter has been largely negative. In the previous section (7.1-6) Paul seems to place the law in the same category as sin, and now he must deal with a potential objection to his argument: does he mean that the law 'is' sin (7.7)? His answer is 'no' (7.7, 12), but he goes beyond this to maintain that sin has 'exploited' the law (vv. 8-11) and this has led to death and not life (vv. 9, 10). Thus, it is fairly clear that Paul uses this 'I' statement initially as part of a clarification or defence of his earlier statements about the law. As we have already seen, it is a favourite argumentative move on Paul's part to make his case with either a literal (e.g. 1 Cor. 9) or hypothetical (e.g. 1 Cor. 13) 'I' statement.

At 7.14 there is a stylistic indicator of a transition ('For we know that...'), and in what follows all the verbs are present tense. This suggests that, although the characterization of the 'I' carries on, there is a new usage intended (cf. the change from Gal. 2.18 to 2.19-20). This is reinforced by the fact that the image is no longer built on the model of Adam in the Garden of Eden, but now turns to an analysis of the struggle of the divided self. In vv. 14-24, this 'I' is in a sorry state of affairs until v. 25, when Paul announces the release from bondage that comes through Jesus Christ, a theme developed further in 8.1-4.[51] A. Lincoln has identified the flow of the argument in Romans 1–4 as following the pattern of solution—plight—solution,[52] a pattern that is found also in chs. 5–8: chs. 5–6, solution; ch. 7, plight; ch. 8, solution (or, solution amid the plight).[53]

49. N.A. Dahl, *Studies in Paul: Theology for the Early Christian Mission* (Minneapolis: Augsburg, 1977), p. 85.
50. Kümmel, *Römer 7*, pp. 9-13; R. Bultmann, 'Romans 7 and the Anthropology of Paul', in *idem, Existence and Faith* (trans. S. Ogden; London: Hodder & Stoughton, 1960), pp. 147-57 (153-55); Bornkamm, 'Sin, Law and Death', p. 88; Beker, *Paul the Apostle*, p. 105; Wedderburn, 'Adam', p. 419; Dunn, 'An Analysis of Structure and Argument', p. 2862; Seifrid, 'Romans 7.14-25', p. 324; Lambrecht, *The Wretched 'I'*, p. 48. Contra Käsemann, *Römer*, pp. 182-83.
51. Fitzmyer, *Romans*, p. 476.
52. Lincoln, 'From Wrath to Justification', pp. 194-226.
53. Cf. Sanders, *Paul, the Law, and the Jewish People*, pp. 70-81; Thielman, *From Plight to Solution*, especially pp. 87-116.

We may easily identify Paul's second usage of 'I' here with the epistolary situation of Romans. The most obvious feature is that 7.25 forms an *inclusio* with 7.6. The reference of slavery to God in both of these verses is reminiscent of Paul's opening self-characterization as a 'slave of Christ' (1.1). In Rom. 1.16-17 he announced his confidence in the gospel's power to yield salvation. This theme was developed theologically in chs. 5–6, and when we come to 7.14-25, Paul illustrates the power of God's gospel by showing how it saves one-person ('I') who is unable to save himself.[54] Verses 14-24, whether or not they are based on personal experience, are a literary device that portrays the divided self's utter need for redemption. 'The cry of the enslaved'[55] in vv. 14-24 become the cry of the emancipated in v. 25. We find in Romans 7 what Lambrecht rightly calls 'the language of dramatic intensification and exaggeration' which Paul employs to highlight the liberating power of the gospel.[56] At v. 25 he expresses the gospel's solution to the human plight in the form of a crisp and concise thanksgiving, underlining the confidence Paul has in the gospel: 'Thanks be to God [who gives us the victory] through our Lord Jesus Christ'.[57] The occurrence of the first-person plural tips hints that Paul has had the readers in view, wanting them to visualize in a concrete way the joyful emancipation the gospel brings.[58]

Paul's usage of 'I' in Rom. 7.14-25 has similarities in form and content to Gal. 2.15-21, as Theissen and Betz have demonstrated.[59] But it

54. Bornkamm, 'Sin, Law and Death', p. 88; Seifrid, 'Romans 7.14-25', pp. 331-32.
55. Käsemann, *Römer*, p. 188.
56. Lambrecht, *The Wretched 'I'*, p. 136.
57. E.W. Smith, 'The Form and Religious Background of Romans 7.24-25a', *NovT* 13 (1971), pp. 127-35, believes he has identified the liturgical setting from which 7.24-25a was derived, but this does not change how these verses currently serve as an effective rhetorical climax to the plight Paul has described. Cf. R. Banks, 'Romans 7.25a: An Eschatological Thanksgiving?', *AusBR* 26 (1978), pp. 34-42, who sees the time frame of the deliverance as in the future.
58. E. Trocmé, 'From "I" to "We": Christian Life According to Romans, Chapters 7 and 8', *AusBR* 35 (1987), pp. 73-76. Cf. Dietzfelbinger, *Der Berufung des Paulus*, pp. 83-89, who understands Paul's self-presentation here as an autobiographical statement of his inner struggle before Damascus viewed from his post-Damascus perspective. Yet, Kümmel, *Römer 7*, pp. 139-60, has 'produced ample evidence to refute' this view (Munck, *Paul and the Salvation of Mankind*, pp. 11-12 n. 2).
59. Theissen, *Psychological Aspects*, pp. 197-99; Betz, *Galatians*, pp. 123-24.

must be noted that the characterization of the 'I' in these two passages affirm contradictory things. In Galatians 2 'I' is crucified with Christ, dethroned as Christ lives through him. In Romans 7 the 'I' struggles with the dilemma of a dual nature. Unless we are to conclude that Paul contradicts himself, it seems reasonable to take the 'I' of Rom. 7.14-25 as a characterization of the self under the law rather than the self in Christ (cf. Rom. 8.1-11).[60]

There are theological similarities of Rom. 7.7-24 with 1 Cor. 15.56 and Rom. 7.25 with 1 Cor. 15.57.[61] In fact, 1 Cor. 15.56 could function as a partial summary for Romans 7: 'The sting of death is sin, and the power of sin is the law'. 1 Cor. 15.57 sounds like a similar punchline to Rom. 7.25: 'But thanks be to God, who gives us the victory through our Lord Jesus Christ'. By content, 1 Cor. 15.56-57 is the closest Pauline parallel to Romans 7.[62]

By literary function, however, the 'I' statement in Romans 7, particularly vv. 14-25, has the most affinity with Paul's use of self-characterization in 1 Corinthians 1–4. If we adopt the straightforward view that Rom. 1.16-17 is programmatic for understanding Romans, Romans 7 shows the power of God's gospel for salvation using Paul's 'I' as the illustration. This use of 'I' is most similar to his use of self-presentation in 1 Corinthians 1–4, though there are significant differences. As I argued above in Chapter 2, Paul uses self-depreciation as a device to focus the Corinthians' attention on their unity in Christ, and the soteriological benefits they received from him (cf. 1 Cor. 3.21-23). The Corinthians were apparently overvaluing human leaders and dividing along party lines. In Romans, Paul illustrates the liberating power of the

---

60. Bornkamm, 'Sin, Law and Death'; Ziesler, *Romans*, pp. 191-94; K. Kertelge, 'Exegetische Überlegungen zum Verständnis der paulinischen Anthropologie nach Römer 7', *ZNW* 62 (1971), pp. 105-14; similarly, C.L. Mitton, 'Romans 7 Reconsidered', *ExpTim* 65 (1953–54), pp. 78-81, 99-103, 132-35. Differently see Packer, 'The "Wretched Man" in Romans 7', pp. 621-27, whose argument rightly nuances Paul's eschatological reserve displayed elsewhere, a view also maintained in Dunn, 'Romans 7.14-25'. In favour of the 'I' of vv. 14-25 representing Christians *simul iustus et peccator* are the commentaries of Bruce, Cranfield, Barrett and Dunn.

61. G. Bornkamm, 'The Letter to the Romans as Paul's Last Will and Testament', in Donfried (ed.), *The Romans Debate*, pp. 16-28 (24).

62. So Banks, 'An Eschatological Thanksgiving?', pp. 38-39, and see his treatment of the other formal parallels to the thanksgiving in 7.25 (Rom. 6.17; 1 Cor. 15.57; 2 Cor. 2.14; 8.16; 9.15).

gospel, demonstrating Christ's liberating power by portraying its effects on a person enslaved to the law. Though the *content* of his 'I' statements differs according to the distinct situations and usages in 1 Corinthians 1–4 and Romans, the *function* of his 'I' in both places, *mutatis mutandis*, is to highlight christological and soteriological concerns by a contrasting self-depreciation.

Summary

The Romans 7 'I' is used as part of a stylized theological portrayal in which Paul draws together diatribal and biblical elements (i.e. Adamic imagery), and probably combines them with personal experience or reflection (esp. 7.14-25). He imaginatively combines them to deflect antinomian charges against his gospel. The identity of the 'I' is not easily discerned because of this creative combination of elements—Paul is not excluded from 'I', but neither is he writing straightforwardly about himself. If the identity of 'I' is unresolved, the argumentative use of 'I' is clear. In this device, Paul brings forward the earlier contrast of life 'in Adam' with 'life in Christ' (5.12–6.23), and develops a new contrast between the effects of the law (death) and the effects of the Spirit (life; chs. 7–8). The end result for the 'I' culminates in a liberating reception of the gospel of Christ. Again, as we have observed in the other letters we have examined, Paul's literary self-portrayal serves as a vivid example for his readers to picture the main point of his argument. In this case, the stylistic 'I' of Romans 7 underlines Paul's central thrust that his gospel is able to result in salvation for all those who believe (Rom. 1.16-17). His 'I' models the main contention of his argument.

Chapter 8

CONCLUSION

A survey of Paul's use of personal example and paradigmatic and hypothetical 'I' statements leads to several literary, historical and theological conclusions pertinent to the study of Paul's letters. Generally we can approve what G. Lyons affirms, that Paul

> highlights his 'autobiography' in the interests of this gospel and his readers. He is concerned that, by imitating him, they too should incarnate the gospel. Their faithfulness or unfaithfulness to the gospel, as Paul understands it, determines which aspects of his life he brings to the fore. His autobiographical remarks rarely supplement the major concern of a letter, but rather support it by means of a flesh-and-blood illustration.[1]

I have argued that Paul presents his literary example as a model for Christian living and Christian response to the respective epistolary situations he addresses (e.g. 1 Corinthians, 1 Thessalonians; Philemon), often as an alternative in the face of competing claims on his auditors' loyalties (e.g. Gal. 1–2; Phil. 3). An attendant literary feature is the use of comparison where contrasting models are portrayed and ridiculed to accent rhetorically the appeal of Paul's model (e.g. Gal. 2.4-5, 11-14).

We may extend the literary implications even further. On the one hand, Paul uses larger blocks of material containing self-portrayal to ground or add weight to his argument (e.g. 1 Cor. 9; Gal. 1–2; Phil. 3). In 1 Corinthians 1–4, for example, he focuses on church unity in Christ by an accompanying and extended self-depreciation, setting a pattern of self-renunciation that he models later in the letter and calls his converts to emulate (1 Cor. 6.12; 7.7-8; chs. 8–9 and 13–14). It was suggested that Paul draws attention to the literary function of his use of personal example in 1 Corinthians 1–4 in the marker at 1 Cor. 4.6 (Chapter 2).

---

1. Lyons, *Pauline Autobiography*, pp. 226-27.

Likewise, it was suggested that the call to imitation in 1 Cor. 4.16 is presented in such a way as to draw attention to the detailed and thoroughgoing use of personal example in each of the main arguments that follow in 1 Corinthians (detailed in Chapter 3).

On the other hand, pithy, paradigmatic expressions are employed in 1 Corinthians 5–15 that indicate a precise and stylistic usage of personal example as a literary technique in introductions, transitions and perorations, providing exegetical markers for the main line of the prominent arguments and hortatory features of a letter. In Chapter 3, 1 Cor. 6.12 was identified as one such introductory, paradigmatic 'I' statement, a feature that was demonstrated in Chapter 4 for Gal. 1.10, and is universally recognized for Rom. 1.16-17. Philippians 1.21 is less striking, but may also function as one such introductory 'I' statement. Likewise, in conclusions and summary/transitions paradigmatic 'I' statements are common as punchline perorations, vivid, concrete and memorable (e.g. 1 Cor. 4.1-13; 5.12; 8.13; 9.24-27; 10.23–11.1; 15.30-32; Gal. 2.18-21). Also, in the midst of arguments Paul uses hypothetical 'I' statements that create a vivid picture for the reader, even though this 'I' is a persona rather than reflective of Paul himself (e.g. 1 Cor. 13–14; elements of Rom. 7?). Thus Paul uses both extended exemplification and short exemplary and hypothetical statements to ground his argument, to carry forward the argument into its next phase, and for transition to a fresh topic.

Occasionally Paul's self-portrayal verges on self-praise, creating a social need to employ accepted literary techniques to mitigate the odium and offence of his self-discussion. It was argued that this demand of etiquette explains several of the features that are found in 1 Corinthians 9 and 15. While this study has highlighted that Paul often portrays himself as a technique of argumentation, it is striking that he nowhere transgresses the stigma against self-praise except where he also offsets its offence.

In all of these literary features this study has supported Lyons's claim cited above. However, Lyons makes another claim that this study undermines:

> Succinctly and simply put, Paul's autobiographical remarks function not to distinguish him from his converts nor to defend his person or authority, but to establish his ethos as an 'incarnation' of the gospel of Jesus Christ.[2]

2. Lyons, *Pauline Autobiography*, p. 226.

This is a false and unnecessary dichotomy, and is undermined by elements of Galatians 1–2 that he overlooks (see Chapter 4 above), Philippians 3 which he does not treat, and is contradicted outright by Paul's extended self-defence in 2 Corinthians.[3] There is no justification for identifying a particular literary feature, as he has done in Galatians and 1 Thessalonians, and imposing it everywhere. This reductionistic tendency must be avoided as Paul's letters are treated on a case-by-case basis. If Lyons has correctly drawn attention to the hypothetical nature of many reconstructions that employ mirror-reading, he has not—as he has thought—changed the fact that hypotheses are needed in scientific exegesis. To be sure, hypotheses and theories about opponents and opposition must be tested, but to dismiss completely the use of hypotheses does not further the development of critical exegesis. In any case, Paul's letters display a diverse rather than uniform usage of self-portrayal, and one usage is in the face of antagonists who threaten his authority (e.g. 2 Corinthians).

It has been suggested that Paul's nascent usage of personal example in 1 Thessalonians already reflects a style that will be characteristic of his letters. By the time of Philemon, Paul's rhetorical use of self-portrayal has been developed and honed as a persuasive technique, along with other aspects of his nuanced epistolary persuasion. The seedling style of 1 Thessalonians comes to mature expression in the explicit literary strategy of 1 Corinthians, and is used to a somewhat lesser extent in Galatians and Philippians, and elements of this technique are not lacking in Rom. 7.7-25. An identifiable 'I' style and use of personal example are evident across Paul's undisputed letters.

As we have seen, Paul's literary self-portrayal is not to be separated sharply from the example that he set when he was present among his auditors, and it is noteworthy that he only uses this technique with churches that he founded himself. In 1 Thessalonians recollection of their past experience of his teaching and practice forms a foundation for his relatively minor use of personal example in the letter. In 1 Corinthians his argument at places is nonsensical if his epistolary claims did not reflect his actual condition (e.g. 1 Cor. 7.7-8; 9.1-27), and this is true of other arguments as well (e.g. Phil. 3; 4.9; 1 Thess. 2). Thus, Paul's literary style reflects his leadership style of modelling and embodying the teaching he propagated, and this is further underlined by

3. As has been pointed out by R.B. Hays in his review of Lyons in *JBL* 106 (1987), pp. 723-25.

epistolary theory of the time which urged the creation of a letter as an alter ego, a surrogate for one's personal presence with one's readers.

There has often been a facile equation of Paul's example with Christ's, and this has been called into question. The only place where this is possibly suggested in his letters, 1 Cor 11.1, is better explained as an indication of Paul's example for those who are 'of Christ', or in other Pauline terms, 'in Christ'. Paul's pattern is not exemplary because it reflects his portrayal of Christ's authoritative model, but his exemplification is meaningful because he *and his auditors* are 'in Christ', and thus able to achieve the same lifestyle because they live in the same redeemed sphere 'of Christ'. Paul bears the message of the risen Christ, both in proclamation and embodiment, but the collapsed distinction between Paul's pattern and Christ's saving work is a confusion found in contemporary scholarship rather than the letters of Paul (see Chapter 5).

It is not difficult to speculate on the question of why Paul chose to use this leadership and literary technique. Imitation was already suggested in his surrounding culture(s), and he utilizes a leadership style not unique to himself. Furthermore, we can suppose that—then, as now—this strategy was sound pedagogy and effective psychagogy. One wonders if there is not also a wise pastoral dimension to this technique, demonstrating for those 'in Christ' that the behaviour he demands is possible to achieve. As Epictetus says, 'God has sent you the man who will show in practice that it is possible. "Look at me", he says' (*Diss.* 3.22.46). Finally, persuasion trades on credibility. The coinage of the persuader is his or her believability. Credibility, then and now, may require the very practice that Paul employs, where his argument draws upon and requires a life-pattern that is consistent with spoken values. The contemporary 'Don't follow me, follow Christ', which *prima facie* sounds appropriately humble, may be completely ineffectual as a leadership style. It is against the nature of credibility to grant to a speaker the premise 'Do as I say, not as I do'. Rather, credence is given most naturally to leaders of integrity, where appearance and reality more closely approximate one another. Personal example, intrinsic to Paul's leadership and literary style, may be foundational to the leadership—and certainly the missionary—enterprise where all who follow expect those who lead to embody the values they represent and proclaim.

BIBLIOGRAPHY

Ahern, Barnabas Mary, 'The Fellowship of his Sufferings (Phil. 3.10): A Study of St. Paul's Doctrine on Christian Suffering', *CBQ* 22 (1960), pp. 1-32.
Alexander, Loveday C., 'Hellenistic Letter-Forms and the Structure of Philippians', *JSNT* 37 (1989), pp. 87-101.
Allo, E.-B., *Saint Paul: Première épître aux Corinthiens* (EBib; Paris: J. Gabalda, 1934).
Althaus, Paul, *Der Brief an die Römer* (Göttingen: Vandenhoeck & Ruprecht, 1966).
Aune, David E., *The New Testament in its Literary Environment* (LEC, 8; Philadelphia: Westminster Press, 1987).
Baarda, T., 'TI ETI ΔΙΩΚΟΜΑΙ in Gal. 5.11: Apodosis or Parenthesis?', *NovT* 34 (1992), pp. 250-56.
Baasland, Ernst, 'Persecution: A Neglected Feature in the Letter to the Galatians', *ST* 38 (1984), pp. 135-50.
Bachmann, Michael, *Sünder oder Übertreter: Studien zur Argumentation in Gal. ii. 15ff.* (WUNT, 2.59; Tübingen: J.C.B. Mohr [Paul Siebeck], 1992).
Bailey, Kenneth E., 'The Structure of 1 Corinthians and Paul's Theological Method with Special Reference to 4.17', *NovT* 25 (1983), pp. 152-81.
Baird, William, ' "One Against the Other": Intra-Church Conflict in 1 Corinthians', in R. Fortna and B. Gaventa (eds.), *The Conversation Continues: Studies in Paul and John in Honor of J. Louis Martyn* (Nashville: Abingdon Press, 1990), pp. 116-36.
—'Visions, Revelation, and Ministry: Reflections on 2 Corinthians 12.1-5 and Galatians 1.11-17', *JBL* 104 (1985), pp. 651-62.
Banks, Robert, 'Romans 7.25a: An Eschatological Thanksgiving?', *AusBR* 26 (1978), pp. 34-42.
Barclay, John M.G., 'Mirror-reading a Polemical Letter: Galatians as a Test Case', *JSNT* 31 (1987), pp. 73-93.
—'Paul, Philemon and the Dilemma of Christian Slave-Ownership', *NTS* 37 (1991), pp. 161-86.
Barr, James, *The Semantics of Biblical Language* (London: Oxford University Press, 1961).
Barrett, C.K., *A Commentary on the Epistle to the Romans* (HNTC; New York: Harper & Row, 1957).
—*A Commentary on the First Epistle to the Corinthians* (New York: Harper & Row, 1968).
—'Boasting (καυχᾶσθαι, κτλ.) in the Pauline Epistles', in A. Vanhoye (ed.), *L'Apôtre Paul: Personnalité, style et conception du ministère* (BETL, 73; ed. A. Vanhoye; Leuven: Leuven University Press, 1986), pp. 363-68.
—'Cephas and Corinth', in *idem*, *Essays on Paul* (London: SPCK, 1982 [1963]), pp. 28-39.
—*Freedom and Obligation: A Study of the Epistle to the Galatians* (London: SPCK, 1985).

Bartchy, S. Scott, *First-Century Slavery and the Interpretation of 1 Corinthians 7.21* (SBLDS, 11; Atlanta: Scholars Press, 1973).
—'Philemon, Epistle to', *ABD*, V, pp. 305-10.
—'Slavery (Greco-Roman)', *ABD*, VI, pp. 65-73.
Barth, Karl, *The Resurrection of the Dead* (trans. H.J. Stenning; London: Hodder & Stoughton, 1933).
Bassler, Jouette M., '1 Corinthians 4.1-5', *Int* 44 (1990), pp. 179-83.
Bauder, W., 'μιμέομαι', *NIDNTT*, I, pp. 490-92.
Beare, Francis Wright, *A Commentary on the Epistle to the Philippians* (BNTC; London: A. & C. Black, 1959).
Beker, J. Christiaan, *Paul the Apostle: The Triumph of God in Life and Thought* (Edinburgh: T. & T. Clark, 1980).
—'The Faithfulness of God and the Priority of Israel in Paul's Letter to the Romans', in K.P. Donfried (ed.), *The Romans Debate: Revised and Expanded Edition* (Edinburgh: T. & T. Clark, 1991), pp. 327-32.
Berchman, Robert M., 'Galatians (1.1-5): Paul and Greco-Roman Rhetoric', in J. Neusner and E. Frerichs (eds.), *Judaic and Christian Interpretation of Texts* (London: University Press of America, 1987), pp. 1-15.
Berényi, Gabriella, 'Gal. 2.20: A Pre-Pauline or a Pauline Text?', in A. Vanhoye (ed.), *L'Apôtre Paul: Personnalité, style et conception du ministère* (BETL, 73; Leuven: Leuven University Press, 1986), pp. 340-44.
Berger, Klaus, 'Apostelbrief und apostolische Rede / Zum Formular frühchristlicher Briefe', *ZNW* 65 (1974), pp. 190-231.
—'Hellenistische Gattungen im Neuen Testament', *ANRW*, II.25.2, pp. 1031-432.
—'Zur Geschichte der Einleitungsformel Amen, ich sage euch', *ZNW* 63 (1972), pp. 45-75.
Best, Ernest, *One Body in Christ: A Study in the Relationship of the Church to Christ in the Epistles of the Apostle Paul* (London: SPCK, 1955).
—*Paul and his Converts* (Edinburgh: T. & T. Clark, 1988).
—*The First and Second Epistles to the Thessalonians* (BNTC; London: A. & C. Black, 1972).
Betz, Hans Dieter, 'De laude ipsius (Moralia 539A-547F)', in *idem* (ed.), *Plutarch's Ethical Writings and Early Christian Literature* (Leiden: E.J. Brill, 1978), pp. 367-93.
—*Der Apostel Paulus und die sokratische Tradition* (BHT, 45; Tübingen: J.C.B. Mohr [Paul Siebeck], 1972).
—*Galatians* (Hermeneia; Philadelphia: Fortress Press, 1979).
—'In Defense of the Spirit: Paul's Letter to the Galatians as a Document of Early Christian Apologetics', in E. Schüssler Fiorenza (ed.), *Aspects of Religious Propaganda in Judaism and Early Christianity* (Notre Dame: University of Notre Dame Press, 1976), pp. 99-114.
—*Nachfolge und Nachahmung Jesu Christi im Neuen Testament* (Tübingen: J.C.B. Mohr [Paul Siebeck], 1967).
—'The Literary Composition and Function of Paul's Letter to the Galatians', *NTS* 21 (1974–75), pp. 353-79.
—'The Problem of Rhetoric and Theology According to the Apostle Paul', in A. Vanhoye (ed.), *L'Apôtre Paul: Personnalité, style et conception du ministère* (BETL, 73; Leuven: Leuven University Press, 1986), pp. 16-48.

Birdsall, J.N., 'ΠΡΕΣΒΥΤΗΣ in Philemon 9: A Study in Conjectural Emendation', *NTS* 39 (1993), pp. 625-30.
Bjerkelund, Carl J., *Parakalô: Form, Funktion und Sinn der parakalô-Sätze in den paulinischen Briefen* (Oslo: Universitetsforlaget, 1967).
Black, David Alan, 'A Note on "the Weak" in 1 Corinthians 9.22', *Bib* 64 (1983), pp. 240-42.
—*Paul, Apostle of Weakness: Astheneia and its Cognates in the Pauline Literature* (AUS, 3; New York: Peter Lang, 1984).
Black, Matthew, *Romans* (NCB; London: Marshall, Morgan & Scott, 2nd edn, 1989).
Blendinger, C., D. Müller and W. Bauder, 'Disciple, Follow, Imitate, After', *NIDNTT*, I, pp. 480-94.
Bligh, John, *Galatians: A Discussion of St Paul's Epistle* (London: St Paul Publications, 1970).
Bloomquist, L. Gregory, *The Function of Suffering in Philippians* (JSNTSup, 78; Sheffield: JSOT Press, 1993).
Boer, Willis Peter de, *The Imitation of Paul: An Exegetical Study* (Kampen: J.H. Kok, 1962).
Boers, Hendrikus, 'The Form Critical Study of Paul's Letters: 1 Thessalonians as a Case Study', *NTS* 22 (1976), pp. 140-58.
—'We Who Are by Inheritance Jews; Not from the Gentile Sinners', *JBL* 111 (1992), pp. 273-81.
Bonhöffer, Adolf, *Epiktet und das Neue Testament* (Giessen: Alfred Töpelmann, 1911).
Booth, Wayne C., *The Rhetoric of Fiction* (Chicago: University of Chicago Press, 1983).
Borgen, Peder, 'Paul Preaches Circumcision and Pleases Men', in M.D. Hooker and S.G. Wilson (eds.), *Paul and Paulinism* (London: SPCK, 1982), pp. 37-46.
Bornkamm, Günther, 'The Letter to the Romans as Paul's Last Will and Testament', in K.P. Donfried (ed.), *The Romans Debate: Revised and Expanded Edition* (Edinburgh: T. & T. Clark, 1991), pp. 16-28.
—'Sin, Law and Death: An Exegetical Study of Romans 7', in *idem*, *Early Christian Experience* (trans. P.L. Hammer; London: SCM Press, 1969), pp. 87-104.
Brewer, D. Instone, '1 Corinthians 9.9-11: A Literal Interpretation of "Do not muzzle the ox"', *NTS* 38 (1992), pp. 554-65.
Brinsmead, Bernard H., *Galatians: Dialogical Response to Opponents* (SBLDS, 65; Chico, CA: Scholars Press, 1982).
Brown, R.E., K.P. Donfried and J. Reuman (eds.), *Peter in the New Testament* (Minneapolis: Augsburg; New York: Paulist Press, 1973).
Bruce, F.F., *1 and 2 Corinthians* (NCB; Grand Rapids: Eerdmans, 1971).
—*1 and 2 Thessalonians* (WBC, 45; Waco, TX: Word Books, 1982).
—'Further Thoughts on Paul's Autobiography: Galatians 1.11–2.14', in E.E. Ellis and E. Grässer (eds.), *Jesus und Paulus* (Tübingen: J.C.B. Mohr [Paul Siebeck], 1975), pp. 21-29.
—*New Testament History* (Garden City, NY: Doubleday, 1971).
—'The Conference in Jerusalem: Galatians 2.1-10', in P.O'Brien and D. Peterson (eds.), *God Who Is Rich in Mercy* (Homebush, Australia: Lancer Books, 1986), pp. 195-212.
—*The Epistle of Paul to the Galatians: A Commentary on the Greek Text* (NIGTC; Exeter: Paternoster Press, 1982).
—*The Epistle of Paul to the Romans* (TNTC; Grand Rapids: Eerdmans, 1963).

—*The Epistles to the Colossians, Philemon, and to the Ephesians* (Grand Rapids: Eerdmans, 1984).
Buchanan, Colin O., 'Epaphroditus' Sickness and the Letter to the Philippians', *EvQ* 36 (1964), pp. 157-66.
Bultmann, Rudolf, 'Romans 7 and the Anthropology of Paul', in *idem, Existence and Faith* (trans. S. Ogden; London: Hodder & Stoughton, 1960), pp. 147-57.
—*Theology of the New Testament* (trans. K. Grobel; 2 vols.; New York: Charles Scribner's Sons, 1951–55).
Bünker, Michael, *Briefformular und rhetorische Disposition im 1. Korintherbrief* (GTA, 28; Göttingen: Vandenhoeck & Ruprecht, 1983).
Burgess, Theodore C., 'Epideictic Literature', *Studies in Classical Philology* 3 (Chicago: University of Chicago Press, 1902), pp. 89-261.
Burton, Ernest De Witt, *A Critical and Exegetical Commentary on the Epistle to the Galatians* (ICC; Edinburgh: T. & T. Clark, 1921).
Campbell, David H., 'The Identity of ἐγώ in Romans 7.7-25', *Studia Biblica* 3 (1978), pp. 57-64.
Campbell, William S., 'Romans 3 as a Key to the Structure and Thought of Romans', in K.P. Donfried (ed.), *The Romans Debate: Revised and Expanded Edition* (Edinburgh: T. & T. Clark, 1991), pp. 251-64.
Campenhausen, Hans F. von, *Ecclesiastical Authority and Spiritual Power in the Church of the First Three Centuries* (trans. J.A. Baker; London: A. & C. Black, 1969 [1953]).
Cancik, Hildegard, *Untersuchungen zu Senecas Epistulae morales* (Hildesheim: Georg Olms, 1967).
Caragounis, C.C., ' "Fornication" and "Concession"? Interpreting 1 Cor. 7,1-7', in R. Bieringer (ed.), *The Corinthian Correspondence* (BETL, 125; Leuven: Peeters, 1996), pp. 543-60.
Carrez, Maurice, 'Le "nous" en 2 Corinthiens: Contribution à l'étude de l'apostolicité dans 2 Corinthiens', *NTS* 26 (1979–80), pp. 474-86.
Carson, Donald A., 'Pauline Inconsistency: Reflections on 1 Corinthians 9.19-23 and Galatians 2.11-14', *Churchman: Journal of Anglican Theology* 110 (1986), pp. 6-45.
Castelli, Elizabeth A., *Imitating Paul: A Discourse of Power* (Louisville, KY: Westminster/John Knox Press, 1991).
Chadwick, Henry, ' "All Things to All Men" (1 Cor. 9.22)', *NTS* 1 (1954-55), pp. 261-75.
Chance, J.B., 'Paul's Apology to the Corinthians', *Philosophy of Religion Series* 9 (1982), pp. 145-55.
Chow, John K., *Patronage and Power: A Study of Social Networks in Corinth* (JSNTSup, 75; Sheffield: JSOT Press, 1992).
Church, F. Forrester, 'Rhetorical Structure and Design in Paul's Letter to Philemon', *HTR* 71 (1978), pp. 17-33.
Clarke, Andrew D., *Secular and Christian Leadership in Corinth: A Socio-Historical and Exegetical Study of 1 Corinthians 1–6* (Leiden: E.J. Brill, 1993).
Coenen, L., 'Bishop, Presbyter, Elder', *NIDNTT*, I, pp. 188-201.
Cole, G.A., '1 Cor. 5.4 "...with my spirit" ', *ExpTim* 98 (1987), p. 205.
Collange, Jean-François, *The Epistle of Saint Paul to the Philippians* (trans. A. Heathcote; London: Epworth Press, 1979).
Collins, Adela Yarbro, 'The Function of "Excommunication" in Paul', *HTR* 73 (1980), pp. 251-63.

Collins, Raymond F., 'Recent Scholarship on the First Letter to the Thessalonians', in *idem, Studies on the First Letter to the Thessalonians*, pp. 3-75.
—*Studies on the First Letter to the Thessalonians* (BETL, 66; Leuven: Leuven University Press, 1984).
—' "The Gospel of Our Lord Jesus" (2 Thess. 1.8): A Symbolic Shift of Paradigm', in *idem* (ed.), *The Thessalonian Correspondence* (BETL, 87; Leuven: Leuven University Press, 1990), pp. 426-40.
Colson, F.H., 'μετεσχημάτισα 1 Cor. 4.6', *JTS* 17 (1916), pp. 379-84.
Conzelmann, Hans, *1 Corinthians* (trans. J. Leitch; Hermeneia; Philadelphia: Fortress Press, 1975 [1969]).
Cosgrove, Charles H., *The Cross and the Spirit: A Study in the Argument and Theology of Galatians* (Macon, GA: Mercer University Press, 1988).
—'What If Some Have Not Believed? The Occasion and Thrust of Romans 3.1-8', *ZNW* 78 (1987), pp. 90-105.
Cousar, Charles B., '1 Corinthians 2.1-13', *Int* 44 (1990), pp. 169-73.
—'The Theological Task of 1 Corinthians: A Conversation with Gordon D. Fee and Victor Paul Furnish', in D. Hay (ed.), *Pauline Theology. II. 1 and 2 Corinthians* (Minneapolis: Fortress Press, 1993), pp. 90-102.
Craffert, Pieter F., 'Paul's Damascus Experience as Reflected in Galatians 1: Call or Conversion?', *Scriptura* 29 (1989), pp. 36-47.
Cranfield, C.E.B., 'Changes in Person and Number in Paul's Epistles', in M.D. Hooker and S.G. Wilson (eds.), *Paul and Paulinism* (London: SPCK, 1982), pp. 280-89.
—*The Epistle to the Romans*, I (ICC; Edinburgh: T. & T. Clark, 1975).
Culpepper, R. Alan, 'Co-Workers in Suffering: Philippians 2.19-30', *RevExp* 72 (1980), pp. 349-58.
Dahl, Nils A., 'Paul and the Church at Corinth According to 1 Corinthians 1.10–4.21', in W.R. Farmer, C.F.D. Moule and R.D. Niebuhr (eds.), *Christian History and Interpretation: Studies Presented to John Knox* (Cambridge: Cambridge University Press, 1967), pp. 313-35.
—'Paul and the Church at Corinth According to 1 Corinthians 1.10–4.21', in *idem, Studies in Paul*, pp. 40-61.
—*Studies in Paul: Theology for the Early Christian Mission* (Minneapolis: Augsburg, 1977).
Dalton, William J., 'The Integrity of Philippians', *Bib* 60 (1979), pp. 97-102.
—'The Meaning of "We" in Galatians', *AusBR* 38 (1990), pp. 33-44.
Daube, David, 'Onesimus', *HTR* 79 (1986), pp. 40-43.
Dautzenberg, G., 'Der Verzicht auf das apostolische Unterhaltsrecht: Eine exegetische Untersuchung zu 1 Kor 9', *Bib* 50 (1969), pp. 212-32.
Davis, J.A., *Wisdom and Spirit: An Investigation of 1 Cor. 1.18–3.20 against the Background of Jewish Sapiential Traditions in the Greco-Roman Period* (Lanham, MD: University Press of America, 1984).
Dawes, Gregory W., '"But if you can gain your freedom" (1 Corinthians 7.17-24)', *CBQ* 52 (1990), pp. 681-97.
Deidun, T.J., *New Covenant Morality in Paul* (AnBib, 89; Rome: Biblical Institute Press, 1981).
Derrett, J. Duncan M., 'Judgement and 1 Corinthians 6', *NTS* 37 (1991), pp. 22-36.
—'The Functions of the Epistle to Philemon', *ZNW* 79 (1988), pp. 63-91.

Dietzfelbinger, Christian, *Der Berufung des Paulus als Ursprung seiner Theologie* (WMANT, 58; Neukirchen–Vluyn: Neukirchener Verlag, 1985).
Dodd, B.J., 'Romans 1.17—A *Crux Interpretum* for the Πίστις Χριστοῦ Debate?', *JBL* 114 (1995), pp. 470-73.
Dodd, C.H., *The Epistle of Paul to the Romans* (MNTC; London: Hodder & Stoughton, 1932).
Dodds, E.R., *The Greeks and the Irrational* (Berkeley: University of California Press, 1951).
Donfried, Karl P., 'The Kingdom of God in Paul', in W. Willis (ed.), *The Kingdom of God in 20th-Century Interpretation* (Peabody, MA: Hendrickson, 1987), pp. 175-90.
Doohan, Helen, *Leadership in Paul* (GNS, 11; Wilmington, DE: Michael Glazier, 1984).
Dungan, David L., *The Sayings of Jesus in the Churches of Paul: The Use of the Synoptic Tradition in the Regulation of Early Church Life* (Oxford: Basil Blackwell, 1971).
Dunn, James D.G., 'Echoes of Intra-Jewish Polemic in Paul's Letter to the Galatians', *JBL* 112 (1993), pp. 459-77.
—*Jesus and the Spirit* (Philadelphia: Westminster Press, 1975).
—*Jesus, Paul and the Law: Studies in Mark and Galatians* (Louisville, KY: Westminster/John Knox Press, 1990).
—'Paul's Epistle to the Romans: An Analysis of Structure and Argument', *ANRW*, II.25.4, pp. 2842-90.
—'Prophetic I-Sayings and the Jesus Tradition: The Importance of Testing Prophetic Utterances within Early Christianity', *NTS* 24 (1977–78), pp. 175-98.
—'Romans 7.14-25 in the Theology of Paul', *TZ* 31 (1975), pp. 257-73.
—*The Epistle to the Galatians* (BNTC; London: A. & C. Black, 1993).
—'The Formal and Theological Coherence of Romans', in K.P. Donfried (ed.), *The Romans Debate: Revised and Expanded Edition* (Edinburgh: T. & T. Clark, 1991), pp. 245-50.
—'The Incident at Antioch (Gal. 2.11-18)', in *idem*, *Jesus, Paul and the Law: Studies in Mark and Galatians* (Louisville, KY: Westminster/John Knox Press, 1990), pp. 129-82.
—*The Partings of the Ways between Christianity and Judaism* (London: SCM Press, 1991).
—'The Relationship between Paul and Jerusalem According to Galatians 1 and 2', in *idem*, *Jesus, Paul and the Law: Studies in Mark and Galatians* (Louisville, KY: Westminster/John Knox Press, 1990), pp. 108-28.
—'The Responsible Congregation (1 Cor. 14.26-40)', in L. De Lorenzi (ed.), *Charisma und Agape (1 Kor 12–14)* (Rome: Abtei von St Paul vor den Mauern, 1983), pp. 201-36.
Ebeling, Gerhard, *The Truth of the Gospel: An Exposition of Galatians* (trans. D. Green; Philadelphia: Fortress Press, 1985 [1981]).
Ebner, Martin, *Leidenlisten und Apostelbrief: Untersuchungen zu Form, Motiv und Funktion der Peristasenkataloge bei Paulus* (FzB, 66; Würzburg: Echter Verlag, 1991).
Eidem, E., 'Imitatio Pauli', in *idem*, *Teologiska Studier Tillägnade Erik Stave* (Uppsala: Almqvist & Wiksell, 1922), pp. 67-85.
Elliott, John H., 'Patronage and Clientism in Early Christian Society', *Forum* 31.4 (1987), pp. 39-48.
—'Philemon and House Churches', *The Bible Today* 22 (1984), pp. 145-50.

Elliott, Neill, *The Rhetoric of Romans: Argumentative Constraint and Strategy and Paul's Dialogue with Judaism* (JSNTSup, 45; Sheffield: JSOT Press, 1990).
Ellis, E. Earle, 'Paul and his Co-workers', *NTS* 17 (1971), pp. 437-52.
—*Paul's Use of the Old Testament* (Grand Rapids: Baker Book House, 1981 [1957]).
—'*Soma* in First Corinthians', *Int* 44 (1990), pp. 137-49.
—'Traditions in 1 Corinthians', *NTS* 32 (1986), pp. 481-502.
—' "Wisdom" and "Knowledge" in 1 Corinthians', *TynBul* 25 (1974), pp. 82-98.
Ellison, H.L., 'Paul and the Law—"All Things to All Men"', in W.W. Gasque and R.P. Martin (eds.), *Apostolic History and the Gospel: Biblical and Historical Essays Presented to F.F. Bruce on his 60th Birthday* (Grand Rapids: Eerdmans, 1970), pp. 195-202.
Engels, Donald, *Roman Corinth: An Alternative Model for the Classical City* (Chicago: University of Chicago Press, 1990).
Espy, John M., 'Paul's "Robust Conscience" Re-Examined', *NTS* 31 (1985), pp. 161-88.
Everts, Janet Meyer, *Testing a Literary-Critical Hermeneutic: An Exegesis of the Autobiographical Passages in Paul's Epistles* (Ann Arbor, MI: University Microfilms, 1985).
Farahian, Edmond, *Le 'Je' Paulinien: Etude pour mieux comprende Gal. 2, 19-21* (Analecta Gregoriana, 253; Rome: Editrice Pontificia Universita Gregoriana, 1988).
Fee, Gordon D., *God's Empowering Presence: The Holy Spirit in the Letters of Paul* (Peabody, MA: Hendrickson, 1994).
—*The First Epistle to the Corinthians* (NICNT; Grand Rapids: Eerdmans, 1987).
—'Toward a Theology of 1 Corinthians', in D. Hay (ed.), *Pauline Theology. II. 1 and 2 Corinthians* (Minneapolis: Fortress Press, 1993), pp. 37-58.
Feuillet, A., '"Chercher à persuader Dieu" (Ga 1 10a)', *NovT* 12 (1970), pp. 350-60.
—'Loi de Dieu, loi du Christ et loi de l'Esprit d'après les épîtres pauliniennes: Les rapports de ces trois lois avec la loi Mosaïque', *NovT* 22 (1980), pp. 29-65.
Fiore, Benjamin, *The Function of Personal Example in the Socratic and Pastoral Epistles* (AnBib, 105; Rome: Biblical Institute Press, 1986).
Fitzgerald, John T., *Cracks in an Earthen Vessel: An Examination of the Catalogues of Hardships in the Corinthian Correspondence* (SBLDS, 99; Atlanta: Scholars Press, 1988).
—'Philippians, Epistle to the', *ABD*, V, pp. 318-26.
Fitzmyer, Joseph A., *Romans* (AB, 33; London: Geoffrey Chapman, 1993).
—'The Aramaic Background of Phil. 2.6-11', *CBQ* 50 (1988), pp. 470-83.
Forbes, Christopher, 'Comparison, Self-Praise and Irony: Paul's Boasting and the Conventions of Hellenistic Rhetoric', *NTS* 32 (1986), pp. 1-30.
Fortna, Robert T., 'Philippians: Paul's Most Egocentric Letter', in R. Fortna and B. Gaventa (eds.), *The Conversation Continues: Studies in Paul and John in Honor of J. Louis Martyn* (Nashville: Abingdon Press, 1990), pp. 220-34.
Fowl, Stephen E., *The Story of Christ in the Ethics of Paul: An Analysis of the Function of the Hymnic Material in the Pauline Corpus* (JSNTSup, 36; Sheffield: JSOT Press, 1990).
Fox, Michael V., 'The Identification of Quotations in Biblical Literature', *ZAW* 92 (1980), pp. 416-31.
Frame, James E., *A Critical and Exegetical Commentary on the Epistles of St. Paul to the Thessalonians* (ICC; Edinburgh: T. & T. Clark, 1912).

Fung, Ronald Y.K., *The Epistle to the Galatians* (NICNT; Grand Rapids: Eerdmans, 1988).
Funk, Robert W., 'The Apostolic *Parousia*: Form and Significance', in W. Farmer, C. Moule and R. Niebuhr (eds.), *Christian History and Interpretation: Studies Presented to John Knox* (Cambridge: Cambridge University Press, 1967), pp. 249-68.
Furnish, Victor Paul, 'Fellow Workers in God's Service', *JBL* 80 (1961), pp. 364-70.
—'The Jesus–Paul Debate: From Baur to Bultmann', *BJRL* 47 (1964–65), pp. 342-81.
—*Theology and Ethics in Paul* (Nashville: Abingdon Press, 1968).
—'Theology in 1 Corinthians', in D. Hay (ed.), *Pauline Theology. II. 1 and 2 Corinthians* (Minneapolis: Fortress Press, 1993), pp. 59-89.
—'The Place and Purpose of Philippians 3', *NTS* 10 (1963–64), pp. 80-88.
Garland, David E., 'The Composition and Unity of Philippians: Some Neglected Literary Factors', *NovT* 27 (1985), pp. 141-73.
Gaventa, Beverly R., 'Apostles as Babes and Nurses in 1 Thessalonians 2.7', in J. Carroll, C. Cosgrove and E. Johnson (eds.), *Faith and History: Essays in Honor of Paul W. Meyer* (Atlanta: Scholars Press, 1990), pp. 193-207.
—'Galatians 1 and 2: Autobiography as Paradigm', *NovT* 28 (1986), pp. 309-26.
—'The Maternity of Paul: An Exegetical Study of Galatians 4.19', in R. Fortna and B. Gaventa (eds.), *The Conversation Continues: Studies in Paul and John in Honor of J. Louis Martyn* (Nashville: Abingdon Press, 1990), pp. 189-201.
—'The Singularity of the Gospel: A Reading of Galatians', in J.M. Bassler (ed.), *Pauline Theology* (2 vols.; Minneapolis: Fortress Press, 1991), I, pp. 147-59.
Geoffrion, Timothy C., *The Rhetorical Purpose and Political and Military Character of Philippians* (Lewiston, NY: Edwin Mellen Press, 1993).
Getty, Mary Ann, 'The Imitation of Paul in the Letters to the Thessalonians', in R.F. Collins (ed.), *The Thessalonian Correspondence* (BETL, 87; Leuven: Leuven University Press, 1990), pp. 277-83.
—'The Theology of Philemon', in *SBL Seminar Papers 26* (Atlanta: Scholars Press, 1987), pp. 503-508.
Gillespie, Thomas W., 'Interpreting the Kerygma: Early Christian Prophecy According to 1 Corinthians 2.6-16', in J. Goehring, C. Hedrick, J. Sanders and H. Betz (eds.), *Gospel Origins and Christian Beginnings* (Sonoma, CA: Polebridge Press, 1990), pp. 151-66.
Gillman, John, 'Paul's ΕΙΣΟΔΟΣ: The Proclaimed and the Proclaimer (1 Thess 2:8)', in R. Collins (ed.), *The Thessalonian Correspondence* (BETL, 87; Leuven: Leuven University Press, 1990), pp. 62-70.
Gnilka, Joachim, *Der Philipperbrief* (HTK; Freiburg: Herder, 1968).
Goddard, A.J., and S.A. Cummins, 'Ill or Ill-Treated? Conflict and Persecution as the Context of Paul's Original Ministry in Galatia', *JSNT* 52 (1993), pp. 93-126.
Godet, F., *Commentary on St Paul's First Epistle to the Corinthians* (trans. A. Cusin; 2 vols.; Edinburgh: T. & T. Clark, 1886–87).
Gooch, Peter D. *Dangerous Food: 1 Corinthians 8–10 in its Context* (SCJ, 5; Waterloo, ON: Wilfred Laurier University Press, 1993).
Grayston, Kenneth, 'The Opponents in Philippians 3', *ExpTim* 97 (1986), pp. 170-72.
Gundry-Volf, Judith M., 'Controlling the Bodies: A Theological Profile of the Corinthian Sexual Ascetics (1 Cor. 7)', in R. Bieringer (ed.), *The Corinthian Correspondence* (BETL, 125; Leuven: Peeters, 1996), pp. 519-41.
—*Paul and Perseverance* (WUNT, 2.37; Tübingen: J.C.B. Mohr [Paul Siebeck], 1990).

Gunther, John J., *St. Paul's Opponents and their Background: A Study of Apocalyptic and Jewish Sectarian Teachings* (NovTSup, 35; Leiden: E.J. Brill, 1973).
Gutierrez, Pedro, *La paternité spirituelle selon Saint Paul* (Ebib; Paris: J. Gabalda, 1968).
Güttgemanns, Erhardt, *Der leidende Apostel und sein Herr: Studien zur paulinischen Christologie* (FRLANT, 90; Göttingen: Vandenhoeck & Ruprecht, 1966).
Habel, N., 'The Form and Significance of the Call Narratives', *ZAW* 77 (1965), pp. 297-323.
Hafemann, S.J., 'Corinthians, Letters to the', *DPL*, pp. 164-79.
Hall, Barbara, 'All Things to All People: A Study of 1 Corinthians 9.19-23', in R. Fortna and B. Gaventa (eds.), *The Conversation Continues: Studies in Paul and John in Honor of J. Louis Martyn* (Nashville: Abingdon Press, 1990), pp. 137-57.
Hall, David R., 'Romans 3.1-8 Reconsidered', *NTS* 29 (1983), pp. 183-97.
Hall, Robert G., 'Historical Inference and Rhetorical Effect: Another Look at Galatians 1 and 2', in D. Watson (ed.), *Persuasive Artistry: Studies in New Testament Rhetoric in Honor of George A. Kennedy* (JSNTSup, 50; Sheffield: JSOT Press, 1991), pp. 308-20.
—'The Rhetorical Outline for Galatians: A Reconsideration', *JBL* 106 (1987), pp. 277-87.
Harrington, Daniel J., *Interpreting the New Testament* (Dublin: Veritas, 1985).
Harris, Gerald, 'The Beginnings of Church Discipline: 1 Corinthians 5', *NTS* 37 (1991), pp. 1-21.
Harris, Murray J., *Colossians and Philemon* (EGGNT; Grand Rapids: Eerdmans, 1991).
Hartman, Lars, '1 Co 14,1-25: Argument and Some Problems', in L. De Lorenzi (ed.), *Charisma und Agape (1 Kor 12–14)* (Rome: Abtei von St Paul vor den Mauern, 1983), pp. 149-69.
Hawthorne, Gerald F., *Philippians* (WBC, 43; Waco, TX: Word Books, 1983).
Hays, Richard B., 'Christology and Ethics in Galatians: The Law of Christ', *CBQ* 49 (1987), pp. 268-90.
—*Echoes of Scripture in the Letters of Paul* (New Haven: Yale University Press, 1989).
—'Jesus' Faith and Ours: A Rereading of Galatians 3', in M. Lau Branson and C. Padilla (eds.), *Conflict and Context: Hermeneutics in the Americas* (Grand Rapids: Eerdmans, 1986), pp. 257-80.
—*The Faith of Jesus Christ: An Investigation of the Narrative Substructure of Galatians 3.1–4.11* (SBLDS, 56; Chico, CA: Scholars Press, 1983).
Héring, Jean, *The First Epistle of Saint Paul to the Corinthians* (trans. A. Heathcote and P. Allcock; London: Epworth Press, 1962).
Hester, James D., 'Placing the Blame: The Presence of Epideictic in Galatians 1 and 2', in D. Watson (ed.), *Persuasive Artistry: Studies in New Testament Rhetoric in Honor of George A. Kennedy* (JSNTSup, 50; Sheffield: JSOT Press, 1991), pp. 281-307.
—'The Rhetorical Structure of Galatians 1.11–2.14', *JBL* 103 (1984), pp. 223-33.
—'The Use and Influence of Rhetoric in Galatians 2.1-14', *TZ* 42 (1986), pp. 386-408.
Hill, David, *New Testament Prophecy* (London: Marshall, Morgan & Scott, 1979).
Hirsch, E., 'Zwei Fragen zu Gal 6', *ZNW* 29 (1930), pp. 196-97.
Hock, Roland F., *The Social Context of Paul's Ministry: Tentmaking and Apostleship* (Philadelphia: Fortress Press, 1980).
—'The Workshop as a Social Setting for Paul's Missionary Preaching', *CBQ* 41 (1979), pp. 438-50.
Hofius, Otfried, 'Gal. 1, 18: ἱστορῆσαι Κηφᾶν', in *idem*, *Paulusstudien* (WUNT, 51; Tübingen: J.C.B. Mohr [Paul Siebeck], 1989), pp. 255-67.

—'Herrenmahl und Herrenmahlsparadosis: Erwägungen zu 1 Kor 11.23b-25', *ZTK* 85 (1988), pp. 371-408.
Holladay, Carl R., '1 Corinthians 13: Paul as Apostolic Paradigm', in D. Balch, E. Ferguson and W. Meeks (eds.), *Greeks, Romans, and Christians: Essays in Honor of Abraham J. Malherbe* (Minneapolis: Fortress Press, 1990), pp. 80-98.
Holmberg, Bengt, *Paul and Power: The Structure of Authority in the Primitive Church as Reflected in the Pauline Epistles* (Philadelphia: Fortress Press, 1980 [1978]).
Holmes, M. (ed.), *The Apostolic Fathers* (trans. J.B. Lightfoot and J.R. Harmer; Grand Rapids: Baker Book House, 2nd edn, 1989).
Holtz, Traugott, 'Der antiochenische Zwischenfall (Galater 2.11-14)', *NTS* 32 (1986), pp. 344-61.
—*Der erste Brief an die Thessalonicher* (EKKNT, 13; Neukirchen–Vluyn: Neukirchener Verlag, 1986).
—'Zum Selbstverständnis des Apostels Paulus', *TLZ* 91 (1966), cols. 321-30.
Holtzmann, O., 'Zu E. Hirsch, Zwei Fragen zu Gal 6', *ZNW* 30 (1931), pp. 82-83.
Hooker, Morna D., ' "Beyond the things which are written": An Examination of 1 Cor. 4.6', *NTS* 10 (1963–64), pp. 127-32.
—'Interchange in Christ', *JTS* NS 22 (1971), pp. 349-61.
—'Philippians 2.6-11', in E. Grässer and E. Ellis (eds.), *Jesus und Paulus* (Göttingen: Vandenhoeck & Ruprecht, 1975), pp. 151-64.
—'ΠΙΣΤΙΣ ΧΡΙΣΤΟΥ', *NTS* 35 (1989), pp. 321-42.
Houlden, J.L., *Paul's Letters from Prison: Philippians, Colossians, Philemon, and Ephesians* (Philadelphia: Westminster Press, 1970).
Howard, George, *Paul: Crisis in Galatia. A Study in Early Christian Theology* (SNTSMS, 35; Cambridge: Cambridge University Press, rev. edn, 1990 [1979]).
Huggins, Ronald V., 'Alleged Classical Parallels to Paul's "What I want to do I do not do, but what I hate, that I do" (Rom. 7.15)', *WTJ* 54 (1992), pp. 151-61.
Hurd, John C., Jr, *The Origin of 1 Corinthians* (London: SPCK, 1965).
Hurtado, Larry W., 'Jesus as Lordly Example in Philippians 2.5-11', in P. Richardson and J. Hurd (eds.), *From Jesus to Paul: Studies in Honour of Francis Wright Beare* (Waterloo, ON: Wilfred Laurier University Press, 1984), pp. 113-26.
Jeremias, J., 'Chiasmus in den Paulusbriefen', *ZNW* 49 (1958), pp. 145-56.
—'Paulus als Hillelit', in E. Ellis and M. Wilcox (eds.), *Neotestamentica et Semitica: Studies in Honour of Matthew Black* (Edinburgh: T. & T. Clark, 1969), pp. 88-94.
Jervis, L. Anne, *The Purpose of Romans: A Comparative Letter Structure Investigation* (JSNTSup, 55; Sheffield: JSOT Press, 1991).
Jewett, Robert, 'Conflicting Movements in the Early Church as Reflected in Philippians', *NovT* 12 (1970), pp. 362-90.
—'Following the Argument of Romans', in K.P. Donfried (ed.), *The Romans Debate: Revised and Expanded Edition* (Edinburgh: T. & T. Clark, 1991), pp. 265-77.
—'The Agitators and the Galatian Congregation', *NTS* 17 (1970–71), pp. 198-212.
—'The Epistolary Thanksgiving and the Integrity of Philippians', *NovT* 12 (1970), pp. 40-53.
—*The Thessalonian Correspondence: Pauline Rhetoric and Millenarian Piety* (Philadelphia: Fortress Press, 1986).
Johanson, Bruce C., *To All the Brethren: A Text-Linguistic and Rhetorical Approach to 1 Thessalonians* (Stockholm: Almqvist & Wiksell, 1987).

Johnson, Luke T., *The Writings of the New Testament: An Interpretation* (Philadelphia: Fortress Press, 1986).
Jones, Peter R., '1 Corinthians 15.8: Paul the Last Apostle', *TynBul* 36 (1985), pp. 3-34.
Judge, E.A., 'Paul's Boasting in Relation to Contemporary Professional Practice', *AusBR* 16 (1968), pp. 37-50.
—'The Teacher as Moral Exemplar in Paul and in the Inscriptions of Ephesus', in D. Peterson and J. Pryor (eds.), *In the Fullness of Time* (Homebush, Australia: Lancer, 1992), pp. 185-201.
Karris, Robert J., 'Romans 14.1–15.13 and the Occasion of Romans', in K.P. Donfried (ed.), *The Romans Debate: Revised and Expanded Edition* (Edinburgh: T. & T. Clark, 1991), pp. 65-84.
Käsemann, Ernst, *An Die Römer* (HNT, 8a; Tübingen: J.C.B. Mohr [Paul Siebeck], 1973).
—'A Pauline Version of the *Amor Fati*', in *idem*, *New Testament Questions of Today* (trans. W. Montague; London: SCM Press, 1969 [1959]), pp. 217-35.
—'Die Legitimität des Apostels: Eine Untersuchung zu II Korinther 10–13', *ZNW* 41 (1942), pp. 33-71.
—'Kritische Analyse von Phil. 2.5-11', *ZTK* 47 (1950), pp. 313-60.
—'The Spirit and the Letter', in *idem*, *Perspectives on Paul* (trans. M. Kohl; London: SCM Press, 1971), pp. 138-66.
Kennedy, George A., *The Art of Persuasion in Greece* (London: Routledge & Kegan Paul, 1963).
—*New Testament Interpretation through Rhetorical Criticism* (Chapel Hill: University of North Carolina Press, 1984).
Kertelge, Karl, 'Exegetische Überlegungen zum Verständnis der paulinischen Anthropologie nach Römer 7', *ZNW* 62 (1971), pp. 105-14.
Kilpatrick, George D., 'Galatians 1.18: ΙΣΤΟΡΗΣΑΙ ΚΗΦΑΝ', in A.J.B. Higgins (ed.), *New Testament Essays. Studies in Memory of T.W. Manson* (Manchester: University of Manchester Press, 1959), pp. 144-49.
—'Peter, Jerusalem and Galatians 1.13–2.14', *NovT* 25 (1983), pp. 318-26.
Kim, Seyoon, *The Origin of Paul's Gospel* (Grand Rapids: Eerdmans, 1982).
Klauck, Hans-Josef, *1. Korintherbrief* (Würzburg: Echter Verlag, 1984).
Klein, G., *Die zwölf Apostel: Ursprung und Gehalt einer Idee* (FRLANT, 77; Göttingen: Vandenhoeck & Ruprecht, 1961).
Klijn, A.F.J., 'Paul's Opponents in Philippians 3', *NovT* 7 (1964), pp. 278-84.
Knox, John, *Philemon among the Letters of Paul* (London: Collins, 1960).
Koester, Helmut, '1 Thessalonians—Experiment in Christian Writing', in F. Forrester Church and T. George (eds.), *Continuity and Discontinuity in Church History* (Studies in the History of Christian Thought, 19; Leiden: E.J. Brill, 1979), pp. 33-44.
—Review of U. Wilcken's *Weisheit und Torheit*, in *Gnomon* 33 (1961), pp. 590-95.
—'The Purpose of the Polemic of a Pauline Fragment (Philippians 3)', *NTS* 8 (1961–62), pp. 317-32.
Kok, Ezra Hon-Seng, ' "The Truth of the Gospel": A Study of Galatians 2.15-21' (PhD Dissertation, Durham University, 1993).
Koptak, Paul E., 'Rhetorical Identification in Paul's Autobiographical Narrative: Galatians 1.13–2.14', *JSNT* 40 (1990), pp. 97-115.
Kosmala, Hans, 'Nachfolge und Nachahmung Gottes: Im griechischen Denken', *ASTI* 2 (1963), pp. 38-85.
—'Nachfolge und Nachahmung Gottes: Im jüdischen Denken', *ASTI* 3 (1964), pp. 65-110.

Kreuzer, Siegfried, 'Der Zwang des Boten—Beobachtungen zu Lk 14.23 und 1 Kor 9.16', *ZNW* 76 (1985), pp. 123-28.
Kümmel, Werner Georg, ' "Individualgeschichte" und "Weltgeschichte" in Galater 2, 15-21', in B. Lindars and S. Smalley (eds.), *Christ and Spirit in the New Testament* (Cambridge: Cambridge University Press, 1973), pp. 157-73.
—*Römer 7 und das Bild des Menschen im Neuen Testament* (TBü, 53; Munich: Chr. Kaiser Verlag, 1974 [1929]).
Kurz, William S., 'Kenotic Imitation of Paul and of Christ in Philippians 2 and 3', in F. Segovia (ed.), *Discipleship in the New Testament* (Philadelphia: Fortress Press, 1985), pp. 103-26.
Kuss, Otto, *Der Römerbrief* (2 vols.; Regensburg: Friederich Pustet, 1963).
Kyrtatas, Dimitris J., *The Social Structure of the Early Christian Communities* (London: Verso, 1987).
Ladd, George Eldon, 'Revelation and Tradition in Paul', in W.W. Gasque and R.P. Martin (eds.), *Apostolic History and the Gospel: Biblical and Historical Essays Presented to F.F. Bruce on his 60th Birthday* (Grand Rapids: Eerdmans, 1970), pp. 223-30.
Lambrecht, Jan, 'The Line of Thought in Gal. 2.14b-21', *NTS* 24 (1977–78), pp. 484-95.
—*The Wretched 'I' and its Liberation: Paul in Romans 7 and 8* (LTPM, 14; Louvain: Peeters; Grand Rapids: Eerdmans, 1992).
Lampe, G.W.H., 'Church Discipline and the Interpretation of the Epistles to the Corinthians', in W.R. Farmer, C.F.D. Moule and R.R. Niebuhr (eds.), *Christian History and Interpretation: Studies Presented to John Knox* (Cambridge: Cambridge University Press, 1967), pp. 337-61.
Lampe, Peter, 'Keine "Sklavenflucht" des Onesimus', *ZNW* 76 (1985), pp. 135-37.
—'Theological Wisdom and the "Word about the Cross": The Rhetorical Scheme in 1 Corinthians 1–4', *Int* 44 (1990), pp. 117-31.
Lang, F., *Die Briefe an die Korinther* (NTD, 7; Göttingen: Vandenhoeck & Ruprecht, 1986).
Lapide, Pinchas and Peter Stuhlmacher, *Paul: Rabbi and Apostle* (trans. L. Denef; Minneapolis: Augsburg, 1984).
Lassen, Eva M., 'The Use of the Father Image in Imperial Propaganda and 1 Corinthians 4.14-21', *TynBul* 42 (1991), pp. 127-36.
Lategan, Bernard C., 'Is Paul Defending his Apostleship in Galatians?', *NTS* 34 (1988), pp. 411-30.
—'Levels of Reader Instructions in the Text of Galatians', *Semeia* 48 (1989), pp. 171-84.
Lee, E. Kenneth, 'Words Denoting "Pattern" in the New Testament', *NTS* 8 (1961–62), pp. 166-73.
Lietzmann, H., *An die Korinther*, I–II (HNT, 9; Tübingen: J.C.B. Mohr [Paul Siebeck], 4th edn, 1949).
Lim, Timothy H., 'Not in Persuasive Words of Wisdom, but in the Demonstration of the Spirit and Power', *NovT* 29 (1987), pp. 137-49.
Lincoln, Andrew T., 'From Wrath to Justification: Tradition, Gospel and Audience in the Theology of Romans 1.18–4.25', in *SBL Seminar Papers 1993* (Atlanta: Scholars Press, 1993), pp. 194-226.
—*Paradise Now and Not Yet: Studies in the Role of the Heavenly Dimension in Paul's Thought with Special Reference to his Eschatology* (Cambridge: Cambridge University Press, 1981).

Litfin, A. Duane, 'St. Paul's Theology of Proclamation: An Investigation of 1 Cor. 1–4 in Light of Greco-Roman Rhetoric' (DPhil. Thesis, Oxford University, 1983).
—*St. Paul's Theology of Proclamation: 1 Corinthians 1–4 and Greco-Roman Rhetoric* (SNTSMS, 79; Cambridge: Cambridge University Press, 1993).
Lofthouse, W.F., ' "I" and "We" in the Pauline Letters', *ExpTim* 64 (1952–53), pp. 241-45.
Lohmeyer, Ernst, *Die Briefe an die Philipper, an die Kolosser und an Philemon* (Göttingen: Vandenhoeck & Ruprecht, 1964 [1930]).
Lohse, Eduard, *Colossians and Philemon* (Hermeneia; trans. W. Poehlmann and R. Karris; Philadelphia: Fortress Press, 1971 [1968]).
Longenecker, Richard N., *Galatians* (WBC, 41; Dallas: Word Books, 1990).
Lüdemann, Gerd, *Paul, Apostle to the Gentiles: Studies in Chronology* (trans. F. Jones; London: SCM Press, 1984).
Lyonnet, S., 'L'histoire du salut selon le ch 7 de l'épître aux Romains', *Bib* 43 (1962), pp. 117-51.
—' "Tu ne convoiteras pas" (Rom 7.7)', in *Neotestamentica et Patristica* (NovTSup, 6; Leiden: E.J. Brill, 1962), pp. 157-65.
Lyons, George, *Pauline Autobiography: Toward a New Understanding* (SBLDS, 73; Atlanta: Scholars Press, 1985).
MacArthur, S.D., ' "Spirit" in Pauline Usage: 1 Corinthians 5.5', in E.A. Livingstone (ed.), *Studia Biblica 1978*, III (JSNTSup, 3; Sheffield: JSOT Press, 1978), pp. 249-56.
Magee, Bruce R., *A Rhetorical Analysis of First Corinthians 8.1–11.1 and Romans 14.1– 15.13* (Ann Arbor: University Microfilms, 1989).
Malherbe, Abraham J., *Ancient Epistolary Theorists* (Atlanta: Scholars Press, 1988).
—'Exhortation in 1 Thessalonians', *NovT* 25 (1983), pp. 238-56.
—' "Gentle as a nurse": The Cynic Background to 1 Thessalonians 2', *NovT* 12 (1970), pp. 203-17.
—'Hellenistic Moralists and the New Testament', *ANRW*, II.26.1, pp. 267-333.
—'*Mē Genoito* in the Diatribe and Paul', in *idem*, *Paul and the Popular Philosophers* (Minneapolis: Fortress Press, 1989 [1980]), pp. 25-33.
—*Moral Exhortation: A Greco-Roman Sourcebook* (LEC; ed. W. Meeks; Philadelphia: Westminster Press, 1986).
—' "Pastoral Care" in the Thessalonian Church', *NTS* 36 (1990), pp. 375-91.
—*Paul and the Thessalonians: The Philosophic Tradition of Pastoral Care* (Philadelphia: Fortress Press, 1987).
—'The Beasts at Ephesus', *JBL* 87 (1968), pp. 71-80.
Malina, Bruce J., *The New Testament World: Insights from Cultural Anthropology* (Atlanta: John Knox Press, 1981).
Manson, T.W., 'The Corinthian Correspondence (1)', in M. Black (ed.), *Studies in the Gospels and Epistles* (Manchester: Manchester University Press, 1962), pp. 190-209.
Marrou, H.-I., *A History of Education in Antiquity* (trans. G. Lamb; London: Sheed & Ward, 1956).
—'Education and Rhetoric', in M.I. Finley (ed.), *The Legacy of Greece: A New Appraisal* (Oxford: Clarendon Press, 1981), pp. 185-201.
Marshall, I. Howard, *1 and 2 Thessalonians* (NCB; London: Marshall, Morgan & Scott, 1983).
Marshall, Peter, *Enmity in Corinth: Social Conventions in Paul's Relations with the Corinthians* (WUNT, 2.23; Tübingen: J.C.B. Mohr [Paul Siebeck], 1987).

—'Invective: Paul and his Enemies in Corinth', in E.W. Conrad and E.G. Newing (eds.), *Perspectives on Language and Text* (Winona Lake, IN: Eisenbrauns, 1987), pp. 359-73.

Martin, Brice L., 'Some Reflections on the Identity of the ἐγώ in Rom. 7.14-25', *SJT* 34 (1981), pp. 39-47.

Martin, Clarice J., 'The Rhetorical Function of Commercial Language in Paul's Letter to Philemon (Verse 18)', in D. Watson (ed.), *Persuasive Artistry: Studies in New Testament Rhetoric in Honor of George A. Kennedy* (JSNTSup, 50; Sheffield: JSOT Press, 1991), pp. 321-37.

Martin, Dale B., *Slavery as Salvation: The Metaphor of Slavery in Pauline Christianity* (New Haven: Yale University Press, 1990).

Martin, Ralph P., *Carmen Christi: Philippians 2.5-11 in Recent Interpretation and in the Setting of Early Christian Worship* (Grand Rapids: Eerdmans, rev. edn, 1983 [1967]).

—*Colossians and Philemon* (NCB; London: Marshall, Morgan & Scott, 1973).

—*Ephesians, Colossians, and Philemon* (Interpretation; Atlanta: John Knox Press, 1991).

—'Hymns, Hymn Fragments, Songs, Spiritual Songs', *DPL*, pp. 419-23.

—*New Testament Foundations: Acts–Revelation* (2 vols.; Exeter: Paternoster Press, 1978).

—*Philippians* (NCB; Grand Rapids: Eerdmans, 1980 [1976]).

—*The Spirit and the Congregation: Studies in 1 Corinthians 12–15* (Grand Rapids: Eerdmans, 1984).

Martyn, J. Louis, 'Events in Galatia, Modified Covenantal Nomism versus God's Invasion of the Cosmos in the Singular Gospel: A Response to J.D.G. Dunn and B.R. Gaventa', in J.M. Bassler (ed.), *Pauline Theology* (2 vols.; Minneapolis: Fortress Press, 1991), pp. 160-79.

Marxsen, Willi, *Der erste Brief an die Thessalonicher* (Zürich: Theologischer Verlag, 1979).

—*Introduction to the New Testament* (trans. G. Buswell; Oxford: Basil Blackwell, 1968 [1964]).

McLean, Bradley L., 'Galatians 2.7-9 and the Recognition of Paul's Apostolic Status at the Jerusalem Conference: A Critique of G. Luedemann's Solution', *NTS* 37 (1991), pp. 67-76.

McMichael, W.F., ' "Be ye followers together of Me": Συμμιμηταί μου γίνεσθε—Phil. 3.17', *ExpTim* 5 (1893–94), p. 287.

Mearns, Christopher, 'The Identity of Paul's Opponents at Philippi', *NTS* 33 (1987), pp. 194-204.

Meeks, Wayne A., *The First Urban Christians: The Social World of the Apostle Paul* (New Haven: Yale University Press, 1983).

—*The Moral World of the First Christians* (London: SPCK, 1987).

Merklein, Helmut, 'Die Einheitlichkeit des ersten Korintherbriefes', *ZNW* 75 (1984), pp. 153-83.

Metzger, Bruce M., *A Textual Commentary on the Greek New Testament* (New York: United Bible Societies, 1975 [1971]).

Michaelis, Wilhelm, 'μιμέομαι, κτλ.', *TWNT*, IV, pp. 661-78.

—'μιμέομαι, κτλ.', *TDNT*, IV, pp. 659-74.

Michel, Otto, *Der Brief an die Römer* (KEK; Göttingen: Vandenhoeck & Ruprecht, 4th edn, 1966).

Minear, Paul S., 'Singing and Suffering in Philippi', in R. Fortna and B. Gaventa (eds.), *The Conversation Continues: Studies in Paul and John in Honor of J. Louis Martyn* (Nashville: Abingdon Press, 1990), pp. 202-19.
—*The Obedience of Faith: The Purposes of Paul in the Epistle to the Romans* (London: SCM Press, 1971).
Misch, Georg, *A History of Autobiography in Antiquity* (trans. E.W. Dickes; 2 vols.; London: Routledge & Kegan Paul, 3rd edn, 1949–50).
Mitchell, Margaret M., 'Concerning περὶ δέ in 1 Corinthians', *NovT* 31 (1989), pp. 229-56.
—'New Testament Envoys in the Context of Greco-Roman Diplomatic and Epistolary Conventions: The Example of Timothy and Titus', *JBL* 111 (1992), pp. 641-62.
—*Paul and the Rhetoric of Reconciliation: An Exegetical Investigation of the Language and Composition of 1 Corinthians* (Louisville, KY: Westminster/John Knox Press, 1992).
Mitton, C. Leslie, 'Romans 7 Reconsidered', *ExpTim* 65 (1953–54), pp. 78-81, 99-103, 132-35.
Moffatt, James, *The First Epistle of Paul to the Corinthians* (London: Hodder & Stoughton, 1938).
Mohrlang, Roger, *Matthew and Paul: A Comparison of Ethical Perspectives* (SNTSMS, 48; Cambridge: Cambridge University Press, 1984).
Moo, Douglas J., 'Israel and Paul in Romans 7.7-12', *NTS* 32 (1986), pp. 122-35.
Morris, Leon, *1 Corinthians* (TNTC; Grand Rapids: Eerdmans, 1983 [1958]).
Moule, C.F.D., *An Idiom Book of New Testament Greek* (Cambridge: Cambridge University Press, 1959 [1953]).
—*The Epistles to the Colossians and to Philemon* (CGTC; Cambridge: Cambridge University Press, 1962).
Müller, H., 'Type, Pattern', *NIDNTT*, III, pp. 903-907.
Müller, P.-G., 'οὐ', *EDNT*, II, p. 539.
Mullins, Terrence Y., 'Visit Talk in New Testament Letters', *CBQ* 35 (1973), pp. 350-58.
Munck, Johannes, *Paul and the Salvation of Mankind* (trans. F. Clarke; London: SCM Press, 1959).
—'Paulus Tanquam Abortivus (1 Cor. 15.8)', in A. Higgins (ed.), *New Testament Essays: Studies in Memory of T.W. Manson 1893–1958* (Manchester: Manchester University Press, 1959), pp. 180-93.
Murphy-O'Connor, Jerome, 'Corinthian Slogans in 1 Cor. 6.12-20', *CBQ* 40 (1978), pp. 391-96.
—*St. Paul's Corinth: Texts and Archaeology* (Collegeville, MN: Michael Glazier, 1983).
Myers, Charles D., 'Chiastic Inversion in the Argument of Romans 3–8', *NovT* 35 (1993), pp. 30-47.
Myers, Jacob M. and Edwin D. Freed, 'Is Paul Also among the Prophets?', *Int* 20 (1966), pp. 40-53.
Nasuti, Harry P., 'The Woes of the Prophets and the Rights of the Apostle: The Internal Dynamics of 1 Corinthians 9', *CBQ* 50 (1988), pp. 246-64.
Neugebauer, Fritz, 'Das Paulinische "in Christo"', *NTS* 4 (1957–58), pp. 124-38.
Nickelsburg, George W.E., 'An ἐκτρώμα, Though Appointed from the Womb: Paul's Apostolic Self-Description in 1 Corinthians 15 and Galatians 1', *HTR* 79 (1986), pp. 198-205.

Niebuhr, Karl-Wilhelm, *Heidenapostel aus Israel: Die jüdische Identität des Paulus nach ihrer Darstellung in seinen Briefen* (WUNT, 62; Tübingen: J.C.B. Mohr [Paul Siebeck], 1992).
Nordling, John G., '*Onesimus Fugitivus:* A Defense of the Runaway Slave Hypothesis in Philemon', *JSNT* 41 (1991), pp. 97-119.
O'Brien, Peter T., *Colossians, Philemon* (WBC, 44; Waco, TX: Word Books, 1982).
—*Introductory Thanksgivings in the Letters of Paul* (SNT, 49; Leiden: E.J. Brill, 1977).
—*The Epistle to the Philippians: A Commentary on the Greek Text* (NIGTC; Grand Rapids: Eerdmans, 1991).
—'The Gospel and Godly Models in Philippians', in M.J. Wilkins and T. Paige (eds.), *Worship, Theology and Ministry in the Early Church: Essays in Honor of Ralph P. Martin* (JSNTSup, 87; Sheffield: JSOT Press, 1992), pp. 273-84.
Ollrog, Wolf-Henning, *Paulus und seine Mitarbeiter: Untersuchungen zu Theorie und Praxis der paulinischen Mission* (Neukirchen–Vluyn: Neukirchener Verlag, 1979).
Olson, Stanley N., 'Epistolary Uses of Expressions of Self-Confidence', *JBL* 103 (1984), pp. 585-97.
Omanson, Roger L., 'Acknowledging Paul's Quotations', *The Bible Translator* 43 (1992), pp. 201-12.
—'Some Comments about Style and Meaning: 1 Corinthians 9.15 and 7.10', *The Bible Translator* 34 (1983), pp. 135-39.
O'Neill, J.C., *The Recovery of Paul's Letter to the Galatians* (London: SPCK, 1972).
Packer, J.I., 'The "Wretched Man" in Romans 7', in F. Cross (ed.), *Studia Evangelica*, II (Berlin: Academie, 1964), pp. 621-27.
Paige, Terence, 'Stoicism, Ἐλευθερία and Community at Corinth', in M. Wilkins and T. Paige (eds.), *Worship, Theology and Ministry in the Early Church: Essays in Honor of Ralph P. Martin* (JSNTSup, 87; Sheffield: JSOT Press, 1992), pp. 180-93.
Panikulam, George, *KOINONIA in the New Testament: A Dynamic Expression of Christian Life* (AnBib, 85; Rome: Biblical Institute Press, 1979).
Patte, Daniel, *Paul's Faith and the Power of the Gospel: A Structural Introduction to the Pauline Letters* (Philadelphia: Fortress Press, 1983).
Patzia, Arthur G., 'Philemon, Letter to', in *DPL*, pp. 703-707.
Pearson, Birger A., *The Pneumatikos-Psychikos Terminology in 1 Corinthians: A Study in the Theology of the Corinthian Opponents of Paul and its Relation to Gnosticism* (SBLDS, 12; Missoula, MT: Scholars Press, 1973).
Perriman, Andrew, 'The Pattern of Christ's Sufferings: Colossians 1.24 and Philippians 3.10-11', *TynBul* 42 (1991), pp. 62-79.
Peterman, Gerald W., '"Thankless Thanks": The Epistolary Social Convention in Philippians 4.10-20', *TynBul* 42 (1991), pp. 261-70.
Petersen, Norman R., *Rediscovering Paul: Philemon and the Sociology of Paul's Narrative World* (Philadelphia: Fortress Press, 1985).
Petzer, J.H., 'Contextual Evidence in Favour of καυχήσωμαι in 1 Corinthians 13.3', *NTS* 35 (1989), pp. 229-53.
Pfitzner, Victor C., *Paul and the Agon Motif* (SNT, 16; Leiden: E.J. Brill, 1967).
Phipps, William E., 'Is Paul's Attitude toward Sexual Relations Contained in 1 Cor. 7.1?', *NTS* 28 (1982), pp. 125-31.
Plank, Karl A., *Paul and the Irony of Affliction* (Atlanta: Scholars Press, 1987).
Plevnik, Joseph, 'Pauline Presuppositions', in R. Collins (ed.), *The Thessalonian Correspondence* (BETL, 87; Leuven: Leuven University Press, 1990), pp. 50-61.

—'Paul's Appeals to his Damascus Experience and 1 Cor. 15.5-7: Are They Legitimations?', *Toronto Journal of Theology* 4 (1988), pp. 101-11.
Plunkett, Mark A., 'Sexual Ethics and the Christian Life: A Study of 1 Corinthians 6.12–7.7' (PhD Dissertation, Princeton University, 1988).
Pobee, John S., *Persecution and Martyrdom in the Theology of Paul* (JSNTSup, 6; Sheffield: JSOT Press, 1985).
Pogoloff, Stephen M., *Logos and Sophia: The Rhetorical Situation of 1 Corinthians* (SBLDS, 134; Atlanta: Scholars Press, 1992).
Pollard, T.E., 'The Integrity of Philippians', *NTS* 13 (1966–67), pp. 57-66.
Porter, Stanley E., *Idioms of the Greek New Testament* (Biblical Languages: Greek, 2; Sheffield: JSOT Press, 1992).
Preiss, Théo, *Life in Christ* (SBT, 13; trans. H. Knight; Chicago: Allenson, 1954).
Probst, Hermann, *Paulus und der Brief: Die Rhetorik des antiken Briefes als Form der paulinischen Korintherkorrespondenz (1 Kor. 8–10)* (WUNT, 2.45; Tübingen: J.C.B. Mohr [Paul Siebeck], 1991).
Proudfoot, C. Merrill, 'Imitation or Realistic Participation? A Study of Paul's Concept of "Suffering with Christ"', *Int* 17 (1963), pp. 140-60.
Rahtjen, Bruce D., 'The Three Letters of Paul to the Philippians', *NTS* (1960), pp. 167-73.
Räisänen, Heikki, 'Galatians 2.16 and Paul's Break with Judaism', *NTS* 31 (1985), pp. 543-53.
—*Paul and the Law* (Tübingen: J.C.B. Mohr [Paul Siebeck], 1983).
—'Zum Verständnis von Röm 3.1-8', *SNTU* 10 (1985), pp. 93-108.
Rapske, Brian M., 'The Prisoner Paul in the Eyes of Onesimus', *NTS* 37 (1991), pp. 187-203.
Reinhartz, Adele, 'On the Meaning of the Pauline Exhortation: "*mimētai mou ginesthe—*become imitators of me"', *SR* 16 (1987), pp. 393-403.
Richard, Earl, 'Contemporary Research on 1 (& 2) Thessalonians', *Biblical Theological Bulletin* 20 (1990), pp. 107-15.
Richards, E. Randolph, *The Secretary in the Letters of Paul* (Tübingen: J.C.B. Mohr [Paul Siebeck], 1991).
Richardson, Peter, '"I say, not the Lord": Personal Opinion, Apostolic Authority and the Development of Early Christian Halakah', *TynBul* 31 (1980), pp. 65-86.
—'Pauline Inconsistency: 1 Corinthians 9.19-23 and Galatians 2.11-14', *NTS* 26 (1979–80), pp. 347-62.
Riesenfeld, Harald, 'Faith and Love Promoting Hope: An Interpretation of Philemon v. 6', in M. Hooker and S. Wilson (eds.), *Paul and Paulinism: Essays in Honour of C.K. Barrett* (London: SPCK, 1982), pp. 251-57.
Robertson, A., and A. Plummer, *A Critical and Exegetical Commentary on the First Epistle of St Paul to the Corinthians* (ICC; Edinburgh: T. & T. Clark, 1953 [1914]).
Roetzel, Calvin J., 'The Judgment Form in Paul's Letters', *JBL* 88 (1969), pp. 305-12.
Roloff, Jürgen, *Apostolat–Verkündigung–Kirche: Ursprung, Inhalt und Funktion des kirchlichen Apostelamtes nach Paulus, Lukas und den Pastoralbriefen* (Gütersloh: Gerd Mohn, 1965).
Rosner, Brian S., 'Temple and Holiness in 1 Corinthians 5', *TynBul* 42 (1991), pp. 137-45.
Rousselle, Aline, *Porneia: On Desire and the Body in Antiquity* (trans. F. Pheasant; Oxford: Basil Blackwell, 1988).
Sampley, J. Paul, *Pauline Partnership in Christ: Christian Community and Commitment in Light of Roman Law* (Philadelphia: Fortress Press, 1980).

Sanders, Boykin, 'Imitating Paul: 1 Cor. 4.16', *HTR* 74 (1981), pp. 353-63.
Sanders, E.P., 'Jewish Association with Gentiles and Galatians 2.11-14', in R. Fortna and B. Gaventa (eds.), *The Conversation Continues: Studies in Paul and John in Honor of J. Louis Martyn* (Nashville: Abingdon Press, 1990), pp. 170-88.
—*Paul and Palestinian Judaism: A Comparison of Patterns of Religion* (Minneapolis: Fortress Press, 1977).
—'Paul on the Law, his Opponents, and the Jewish People in Philippians 3 and 2 Corinthians 11', in P. Richardson and D. Granskou (eds.), *Anti-Judaism in Early Christianity*. I. *Paul and the Gospels* (Waterloo, ON: Wilfred Laurier University Press, 1986), pp. 75-90.
—*Paul, the Law, and the Jewish People* (Philadelphia: Fortress Press, 1983).
Sanders, Jack T., 'First Corinthians 13: Its Interpretation Since the First World War', *Int* 20 (1966), pp. 159-87.
Sandnes, Karl O., *Paul—One of the Prophets? A Contribution to the Apostle's Self-Understanding* (WUNT, 2.43; Tübingen: J.C.B. Mohr [Paul Siebeck], 1991).
Sänger, Dieter, 'Die δυνατοί in 1 Kor. 1.26', *ZNW* (1985), pp. 285-91.
Sass, Gerhard, 'Zur Bedeutung von δοῦλος bei Paulus', *ZNW* 40 (1941), pp. 24-32.
Schenk, Wolfgang, 'Der Brief des Paulus an Philemon in der neueren Forschung (1945–1987)', *ANRW*, II.25.4, pp. 3439-95.
—*Die Philipperbriefe des Paulus: Kommentar* (Stuttgart: W. Kohlhammer, 1984).
Schlier, Heinrich, *Der Brief an die Galater* (KEK, 7; Göttingen: Vandenhoeck & Ruprecht, 1971 [1949]).
—'ὑπόδειγμα', *TDNT*, II, pp. 32-33.
Schmithals, Walter, *Gnosticism in Corinth* (trans. J. Steely; Nashville: Abingdon Press, 1971).
—*Paul and the Gnostics* (trans. J. Seeley; Nashville: Abingdon Press, 1972),
—'The False Teachers of the Epistle to the Philippians', in *idem*, *Paul and the Gnostics* (trans. J. Seeley; Nashville: Abingdon Press, 1972), pp. 65-122.
—*The Office of the Apostle in the Early Church* (trans. J. Steely; Nashville: Abingdon Press, 1969).
Schrage, Wolfgang, 'Das apostolische Amt des Paulus nach 1 Kor 4,14-17', in A. Vanhoye (ed.), *L'Apôtre Paul: Personnalité, style et conception du ministère* (BETL, 73; Leuven: Leuven University Press, 1986), pp. 103-19.
—*Der erste Brief an die Korinther (1 Kor 1,1–6,11)* (EKKNT, 7.1; Zürich: Benziger Verlag; Neukirchen–Vluyn: Neukirchener Verlag, 1991).
Schreckenberg, Heinz, *ANANKE, Untersuchungen zur Geschichte des Wortgebrauchs* (Zetemata, 36; Munich: C.H. Beck'sche, 1964).
Schulz, Anselm, *Nachfolgen und Nachahmen: Studien über das Verhältnis der neutestamentlichen Jüngerschaft zur urchristlichen Vorbildethik* (SANT, 6; Munich: Kösel, 1962).
Schüssler Fiorenza, E., 'Rhetorical Situation and Historical Reconstruction in 1 Corinthians', *NTS* 33 (1987), pp. 386-403.
Schütz, John H., *Paul and the Anatomy of Apostolic Authority* (SNTSMS, 26; Cambridge: Cambridge University Press, 1975).
Schweizer, Eduard, 'Dying and Rising with Christ', *NTS* 14 (1967–68), pp. 1-14.
—*The Letter to the Colossians: A Commentary* (trans. A. Chester; Minneapolis: Augsburg, 1982).
Seifrid, Mark A., 'The Subject of Romans 7.14-25', *NovT* 34 (1992), pp. 313-33.

Sellin, Gerhard, *Der Streit um der Auferstehunge der Toten* (FRLANT, 138; Göttingen: Vandenhoeck & Ruprecht, 1986).
Shanor, Jay, 'Paul as Master Builder: Construction Terms in First Corinthians', *NTS* 34 (1988), pp. 461-71.
Simon, W.G.H., *The First Epistle to the Corinthians* (London: SCM Press, 1959).
Smit, Joop, 'Argument and Genre of 1 Corinthians 12–14', in T. Olbricht and S. Porter (eds.), *Rhetoric and the New Testament: Essays from the 1992 Heidelberg Conference* (JSNTSup, 90; Sheffield: JSOT Press, 1993), pp. 215-34.
—'The Genre of 1 Corinthians 13 in the Light of Classical Rhetoric', *NovT* 33 (1991), pp. 193-216.
—'The Letter of Paul to the Galatians: A Deliberative Speech', *NTS* 35 (1989), pp. 1-26.
—'Two Puzzles: 1 Corinthians 12.31 and 13.3: A Rhetorical Solution', *NTS* 39 (1993), pp. 246-64.
Smith, Edgar W. 'The Form and Religious Background of Romans 7.24-25a', *NovT* 13 (1971), pp. 127-35.
Snyman, A. H., 'A Semantic Discourse Analysis of the Letter to Philemon', in P.J Hartin and J. Peter (eds.), *Text and Interpretation: New Approaches in the Criticism of the New Testament* (Leiden: E.J. Brill, 1991), pp. 83-99.
Soards, Marion L., 'Some Neglected Theological Dimensions of Paul's Letter to Philemon', *Perspectives in Religious Studies* 17 (1990), pp. 209-19.
Soden, Hans Freiherr von, 'Sacrament and Ethics in Paul', in W.A. Meeks (ed. and trans.), *The Writings of St. Paul* (New York: W.W. Norton, 1972 [1931]), pp. 257-68.
Spicq, Ceslaus, *Théologie morale du Nouveau Testament* (2 vols.; Ebib; Paris: J. Gabalda, 1965).
Stanley, Christopher D., *Paul and the Language of Scripture: Citation Technique in the Pauline Epistles and Contemporary Literature* (SNTSMS, 74; Cambridge: Cambridge University Press, 1992).
Stanley, David M., '"Become imitators of me": The Pauline Conception of Apostolic Tradition', *Bib* 40 (1959), pp. 859-77.
—'Imitation in Paul's Letters: Its Significance for his Relationship to Jesus and his Own Christian Foundations', in P. Richardson and J. Hurd (eds.), *From Jesus to Paul: Studies in Honour of Francis Wright Beare* (Waterloo, ON: Wilfred Laurier University Press, 1984), pp. 127-41.
Staudinger, Ferdinand, 'δεσμος, κτλ.', *EDNT*, I, pp. 288-90.
Stauffer, E., 'ἐγώ', *TDNT*, II, pp. 356-62.
Stendahl, Krister, 'Paul and the Introspective Conscience of the West', in *idem*, *Paul among Jews and Gentiles and Other Essays* (Philadelphia: Fortress Press, 1976 [1963]), pp. 78-96.
Stirewalt, Martin Luther, Jr, 'The Form and Function of the Greek Letter-Essay', in K.P. Donfried (ed.), *The Romans Debate: Revised and Expanded Edition* (Edinburgh: T. & T. Clark, 1991), pp. 147-71.
Stowers, Stanley K., 'Friends and Enemies in the Politics of Heaven', in J.M. Bassler (ed.), *Pauline Theology* (2 vols.; Minneapolis: Fortress Press, 1991), I, pp. 105-21.
—*Letter Writing in Greco-Roman Antiquity* (Philadelphia: Westminster Press, 1986).
—'Paul's Dialogue with a Fellow Jew in Romans 3.1-9', *CBQ* 46 (1984), pp. 707-22.
—*The Diatribe and Paul's Letter to the Romans* (SBLDS, 57; Chico, CA: Scholars Press, 1981).

Stuhlmacher, Peter, 'The Hermeneutical Significance of 1 Cor. 2.6-16', in G. Hawthorne and O. Betz (eds.), *Tradition and Interpretation in the New Testament: Essays in Honor of E. Earle Ellis for his 60th Birthday* (trans. C. Brown; Tübingen: J.C.B. Mohr [Paul Siebeck], 1987), pp. 328-47.
—'The Purpose of Romans', in K.P. Donfried (ed.), *The Romans Debate: Revised and Expanded Edition* (Edinburgh: T. & T. Clark, 1991), pp. 231-44.
—'The Theme of Romans', in K.P. Donfried (ed.), *The Romans Debate: Revised and Expanded Edition* (ed. K.P. Donfried; Edinburgh: T. & T. Clark, 1991), pp. 333-46.
Sumney, Jerry L., *Identifying Paul's Opponents: The Question of Method in 2 Corinthians* (JSNTSup, 40; Sheffield: JSOT Press, 1990).
Taylor, Nicholas, *Paul, Antioch and Jerusalem: A Study in Relationships and Authority in Earliest Christianity* (JSNTSup, 66; Sheffield: JSOT Press, 1992).
Theissen, Gerd, *Psychological Aspects of Pauline Theology* (trans. J. Galvin; Philadelphia: Fortress Press, 1987).
—*The Social Setting of Pauline Christianity: Essays on Corinth* (ed. and trans. J.H. Schütz; Philadelphia: Fortress Press, 1982).
Thielman, Frank, *From Plight to Solution: A Jewish Framework for Understanding Paul's View of the Law in Galatians and Romans* (NovTSup, 61; Leiden: E.J. Brill, 1989).
Thiselton, Anthony C., 'Realized Eschatology at Corinth', *NTS* 24 (1977–78), pp. 510-26.
Thrall, Margaret E., *1 and 2 Corinthians* (CBC; Cambridge: Cambridge University Press, 1965).
—'Christ Crucified or Second Adam? A Christological Debate between Paul and the Corinthians', in B. Lindars and S. Smalley (eds.), *Christ and Spirit in the New Testament* (Cambridge: Cambridge University Press, 1973), pp. 143-56.
Toit, A.B. du, 'Persuasion in Romans 1.1-17', *BZ* 33 (1989), pp. 192-209.
Trilling, Wolfgang, *Der zweite Brief an die Thessalonicher* (EKKNT; Zürich: Benziger Verlag; Neukirchen–Vluyn: Neukirchener Verlag, 1980).
Trocmé, Etienne, 'From "I" to "We": Christian Life According to Romans, Chapters 7 and 8', *AusBR* 35 (1987), pp. 73-76.
Tuckett, Christopher, 'The Corinthians Who Say, "There is no resurrection of the dead?" (1 Cor. 15.12)', in R. Bieringer (ed.), *The Corinthian Correspondence* (BETL, 125; Leuven: Peeters, 1996), pp. 247-75.
Tyson, Joseph B., 'Paul's Opponents at Philippi', *Perspectives in Religious Studies* 3 (1976), pp. 82-95.
Vos, Johan S., 'Die Argumentation des Paulus in Galater 1,1–2,10', in J. Lambrecht (ed.), *The Truth of the Gospel (Galatians 1.1–4.11)* (Rome: Benedictina, 1993), pp. 11-43.
Wallis, P., 'Ein neuer Auslegungsversuch des Stelle 1 Kor 4,6', *TLZ* 75 (1950), pp. 506-508.
Walter, Nikolaus, 'Paulus und die urchristliche Jesustradition', *NTS* 31 (1985), pp. 498-522.
Wanamaker, Charles A., *The Epistles to the Thessalonians: A Commentary on the Greek Text* (NIGTC; Grand Rapids: Eerdmans, 1990).
Watson, Duane F., '1 Corinthians 10.23–11.1 in the Light of Greco-Roman Rhetoric: The Role of Rhetorical Questions', *JBL* 108 (1989), pp. 301-18.
—'A Rhetorical Analysis of Philippians and its Implications for the Unity Question', *NovT* 30 (1988), pp. 57-88.

—'Paul's Rhetorical Strategy in 1 Corinthians 15', in T. Olbricht and S. Porter (eds.), *Rhetoric and the New Testament: Essays from the 1992 Heidelberg Conference* (JSNTSup, 90; Sheffield: JSOT Press, 1993), pp. 231-49.
Watson, Francis, *Paul, Judaism and the Gentiles: A Sociological Approach* (SNTSMS; Cambridge: Cambridge University Press, 1986).
—'The Two Roman Congregations: Romans 14.1–15.13', in K.P. Donfried (ed.), *The Romans Debate: Revised and Expanded Edition* (Edinburgh: T. & T. Clark, 1991), pp. 203-15.
Weaver, P.R.C., *FAMILIA CAESARIS: A Social Study of the Emperor's Freedmen and Slaves* (Cambridge: Cambridge University Press, 1972).
Webster, John B., 'The Imitation of Christ', *TynBul* 37 (1986), pp. 95-120.
Wechsler, Andreas, *Geschichtsbild und exegetische Studie über den antiochenischen Zwischenfall (Gal 2,11-14)* (BZNW, 62; Berlin: W. de Gruyter, 1991).
Wedderburn, A.J.M., 'Adam in Paul's Letter to the Romans', *Studia Biblica* 3 (1978), pp. 413-30.
—*Baptism and Resurrection* (WUNT, 44; Tübingen: J.C.B. Mohr [Paul Siebeck], 1987).
—'Paul and the Story of Jesus', in *idem* (ed.), *Paul and Jesus: Collected Essays* (JSNTSup, 37; Sheffield: JSOT Press, 1989), pp. 161-89.
—'Some Observations on Paul's Use of the Phrases "in Christ" and "with Christ"', *JSNT* 25 (1985), pp. 83-97.
—'The Problem of the Denial of the Resurrection in 1 Corinthians 15', *NovT* 23 (1981), pp. 229-41.
—*The Reasons for Romans* (Edinburgh: T. & T. Clark, 1988).
Wegenast, Klaus, *Das Verständnis der Tradition bei Paulus und in den Deuteropaulinen* (WMANT, 8; ed. G. Bornkamm and G. von Rad; Neukirchen–Vluyn: Neukirchener Verlag, 1962).
Weiss, Johannes, 'Beiträge zur Paulinischen Rhetorik', in *idem*, *Theologische Studien* (Göttingen: Vandenhoeck & Ruprecht, 1897), pp. 165-247.
— *Der erste Korintherbrief* (Göttingen: Vandenhoeck & Ruprecht, 1970 [1910]).
Welborn, L.L., 'A Conciliatory Principle in 1 Cor. 4.6', *NovT* 29 (1987), pp. 320-46.
—'On the Discord in Corinth: 1 Corinthians 1–4 and Ancient Politics', *JBL* 106 (1987), pp. 85-111.
—'Clement, First Epistle of', *ABD*, I, pp. 1055-60.
West, A., 'Sex and Salvation: A Christian Feminist Bible Study on 1 Corinthians 6.12–7.39', in A. Loades (ed.), *Feminist Theology: A Reader* (London: SPCK, 1990), pp. 72-80.
White, John L., *Light from Ancient Letters* (Philadelphia: Fortress Press, 1986).
—'The Structural Analysis of Philemon: A Point of Departure in the Formal Analysis of the Pauline Letter', in *SBL Seminar Papers 1971* (Atlanta: Scholars Press, 1971), pp. 1-47.
White, L. Michael, 'Morality between Two Worlds: A Paradigm of Friendship in Philippians', in D. Balch, E. Ferguson and W. Meeks (eds.), *Greeks, Romans, and Christians: Essays in Honor of Abraham J. Malherbe* (Minneapolis: Fortress Press, 1990), pp. 201-15.
Wickert, Ulrich, 'Einheit und Eintracht der Kirche im Präskript des ersten Korintherbriefes', *ZNW* 50 (1959), pp. 73-82.
Widmann, Martin, '1 Kor 2.6-16: Ein Einspruch gegen Paulus', *ZNW* 70 (1979), pp. 44-53.

Wilckens, Ulrich, *Der Brief an Die Römer (Röm 1–5)* (EKKNT, 6.1; Zürich: Benziger Verlag; Neukirchen–Vluyn: Neukirchener Verlag, 1978).
—*Der Brief an die Römer (Röm, 6–11)* (EKKNT, 6.2; Zürich: Benziger Verlag; Neukirchen–Vluyn: Neukirchener Verlag, 1980).
—'Der Ursprung der Überlieferung der Erscheinungen des Auferstandenen: Zur traditionsgeschichtlichen Analyse von 1 Kor 15.1-11', in W. Joest and W. Pannenburg (eds.), *Dogma und Denkstrukturen* (Göttingen: Vandenhoeck & Ruprecht, 1963), pp. 56-95.
—*Weisheit und Torheit* (Tübingen: J.C.B. Mohr [Paul Siebeck], 1959).
—'ὑποκρίνομαι, κτλ.', *TDNT*, VIII, pp. 559-71.
Williams, Donald M., 'The Imitation of Christ in Paul with Special Reference to Paul as Teacher' (PhD Dissertation, Columbia University, 1967).
Willis, Wendell L., 'An Apostolic Apologia? The Form and Function of 1 Corinthians 9', *JSNT* 24 (1985), pp. 33-48.
—*Idol Meat in Corinth: The Pauline Argument in 1 Corinthians 8 and 10* (SBLDS, 68; Chico, CA: Scholars Press, 1985).
—'The "Mind of Christ" in 1 Corinthians 2.16', *Bib* 70 (1989), pp. 110-22.
Wilson, Jack H., 'The Corinthians Who Say There Is No Resurrection of the Dead', *ZNW* 59 (1968), pp. 90-107.
Wilson, R. McL., 'Gnosis at Corinth', in M. Hooker and S. Wilson (eds.), *Paul and Paulinism* (London: SPCK, 1982), pp. 102-14.
Wimbush, Vincent L., *Paul the Worldly Ascetic: Response to the World and Self-Understanding According to 1 Corinthians 7* (Macon, GA: Mercer University Press, 1987).
Winter, Sara C., 'Paul's Letter to Philemon', *NTS* 33 (1987), pp. 1-15.
Wire, Antoinette Clark, *The Corinthian Women Prophets: A Reconstruction through Paul's Rhetoric* (Minneapolis: Fortress Press, 1990).
Wischmeyer, Oda, *Der höchste Weg: Das 13. Kapitel des 1 Korintherbriefes* (SNT, 13; Gütersloh: Gerd Mohn, 1981).
Wolff, Christian, *Der erste Brief des Paulus an die Korinther* (THKNT, 7.2; Berlin: Evangelische Verlagsanstalt, 1982).
—'Niedrigkeit und Verzicht in Wort und Weg Jesu und in der apostolischen Existenz des Paulus', *NTS* 34 (1988), pp. 183-96.
Wright, N.T., 'ἁρπαγμός and the Meaning of Philippians 2.5-11', *JTS* NS 37 (1986), pp. 321-52.
—*The Climax of the Covenant: Christ and the Law in Pauline Theology* (Edinburgh: T. & T. Clark, 1991).
— *The Epistles of Paul to the Colossians and to Philemon* (TNTC; Leicester: Inter-Varsity Press, 1986).
Wuellner, Wilhelm, 'Greek Rhetoric and Pauline Argumentation', in W. Schoedel and R. Wilken (eds.), *Early Christian Literature and the Classical Intellectual Tradition* (Paris: Beauchesne, 1979), pp. 177-88.
—'Paul as Pastor: The Function of Rhetorical Questions in First Corinthians', in A. Vanhoye (ed.), *L'Apôtre Paul: Personnalité, style et conception du ministère* (BETL, 73; Leuven: Leuven University Press, 1986), pp. 49-77.
—'Paul's Rhetoric of Argumentation in Romans: An Alternative to the Donfried–Karris Debate over Romans', in K.P. Donfried (ed.), *The Romans Debate: Revised and Expanded Edition* (Edinburgh: T. & T. Clark, 1991), pp. 128-46.
Yagi, Seiichi, 'Das Ich bei Paulus und Jesu—Zum Neutestamentlichen Denken', *Annual of the Japanese Biblical Institute* 5 (1979), pp. 133-53.

Yamauchi, Edwin, 'Pre-Christian Gnosticism, The New Testament and Nag Hammadi in Recent Debate', *Themelios* 10 (1984), pp. 22-27.
Yarbrough, O. Larry, *Not Like the Gentiles: Marriage Rules in the Letters of Paul* (SBLDS, 80; Atlanta: Scholars Press, 1985).
Zaas, Peter S., ' "Cast the evil man from your midst" (1 Cor. 5.13b)', *JBL* 103 (1984), pp. 259-61.
Ziesler, John A., *Paul's Letter to the Romans* (London: SCM Press, 1989).
—'The Role of the Tenth Commandment in Romans 7', *JSNT* 33 (1988), pp. 41-56.

INDEXES

INDEX OF REFERENCES

OLD TESTAMENT

Genesis		1.15	148	*1 Chronicles*	
2.24	93	8.31	148	4.1-13	131
3	178, 225	8.33	148	4.6	133
3.13	225	11.12	148	4.16	133
20.6	92	12.6	148	5.12	131
		13.8	148	7.8	133
Exodus		14.7	148	8.13	131
6.7	106	18.7	148	9.24-27	131
21.20	74	22.2	148	10.23–11.1	131
		22.4	148	11.1	133
Leviticus		22.5	148	12.31	133
1.45	17	24.29	148	15.30-32	131
11.44	17				
19.2	17	*Judges*		*2 Chronicles*	
20.26	17	2.8	148	1.3	148
		2.17	17	24.6	148
Numbers				32.31	207
11.34	230	*1 Samuel*			
		8.3	17	*Esther*	
Deuteronomy		12.23	117	4.2	86
15.32	82	17.43	74		
17.7	75, 82			*Psalms*	
19.9	75	*2 Samuel*		18.1	148
19.19	82	7.14	74	22.4	74
21.23	178			22.16	175
22.21	75, 82	*1 Kings*		22.20	175
22.24	75, 82	3.14	17	30.7	17
24.7	75, 82	9.4	17	31.8	117
25.4	97	11.33	17	32	178
34.5	148	11.38	17	32.8	117
				36.1	148
Joshua		*2 Kings*			
1.1	148	18.12	148	*Proverbs*	
1.13	148			6.29	92

10.13	74	3.22	149	33.5	149
13.24	74	5.19	150	34.6	149
		5.19	149	41.9	149
Isaiah		6.24	165	41.13	149
6	137	7.25	149	42.15	149
10.24	74	8.2	149	43.31	149
13.6	165	9.22-23	106	44.2	149
13.8	165	10.24	149	44.18	149
22.13	82	11.10	149, 150	51.4	149
40.13	82, 83	13.10	149, 150		
42.19	148	14.14-15	137	*Lamentations*	
48.17	117	15.14	149	3.1	74
49.1	149	16.11	149, 150		
52–53	178	16.13	149	*Ezekiel*	
56.10-11	175	20.9	106	13.6-9	137
		22.9	149, 150		
Jeremiah		23.32	137	*Amos*	
1.5	149	25.4	149	7.14-16	137
1.8-9	137	25.6	149		
2.14	149	25.11	149	*Micah*	
2.20	149	26.27-28	149, 150	4.10	165

APOCRYPHA

2 Esdras		*Ecclesiasticus*		14.22	207
4.14	86	17	225	14.44	86
		37.28	82		
Judith				*2 Maccabees*	
9–10	117	*1 Maccabees*		4.45	143
		10.42	199	11.34	207
Wisdom of Solomon		13.21	207		
9.8	17	14.21	207		

NEW TESTAMENT

Matthew		*Luke*		15	154
5.43-48	122	6.27-38	122	16.3	142
10.10	97	10.25-37	122	16.13	186
16.18	56			16.16	186
18.8	91	*John*		16.25	186
18.9	91	13.34-35	122	18.24-28	38
19.5	93	15.9-17	122	20.35	21
22.24-40	122				
28.14	143	*Acts*		*Romans*	
		5.1-11	75	1–4	231
		7.58	207	1.1	136, 148,
Mark		9.8-19	168		150, 232
12.28-34	122	12.20	143	1.12	81
14.21	91				

Romans (ctd)		7.1-6	231	11.8	47
1.16-17	32, 85, 146, 155, 221, 232-34, 236	7.5-6	231	11.12	59
		7.6	222, 232	11.26	47
		7.7-25	32, 220-22, 226, 227, 229, 230, 237	11.33-34	54
				11.33	59
				12	121
				12.2	165
1.17	47		233	12.11	148
1.18–4.25	221, 227	7.7-24		12.19	47
2–6	15	7.7-13	224, 226, 230	13.5	106
2.1-3	102			14.1–15.7	72
2.4	59	7.7	222, 224, 229-31	14.4	102, 148
2.24	47			14.11	47
3.1-20	227	7.8-11	231	14.18	148, 150
3.1-8	227, 228	7.9	222, 224-26, 231	15	15
3.1-6	227, 229			15.1-3	21
3.1	228			15.3	47
3.2	229	7.10	231	15.5	55
3.4-9	228	7.11	225	15.7	211
3.4	47	7.12	231	15.9	47
3.5	222, 228	7.13	117, 222, 229	15.14-32	15
3.6-7	226			15.14	118, 167
3.7	222, 227-29	7.14-25	224, 226, 230-34	15.21	47
				16.17-18	42, 177
3.8	227	7.14-24	225, 231, 232		
3.9	228, 229			*1 Corinthians*	
3.10	47	7.14-23	230	1–6	41
3.21-26	227	7.14	222, 229-31	1–4	21, 24, 33, 40, 41, 42, 44, 51, 61-63, 65, 66, 71, 131, 233-35
3.31	231				
4.17	47	7.24-25	232		
4.24–5.1	157	7.24	229		
5–8	221, 231	7.25	231-33		
5–6	89, 231, 232	8	165, 231		
		8.1-11	233		
5.1-11	122	8.1-4	231	1–3	50, 56, 70
5.12–6.23	234	8.15-17	106		
6	147	8.16-17	164		
6.1–7.6	227	8.17	179	1.1–4.13	33, 63
6.3-6	158	8.22-23	165	1.1	29, 40, 136
6.4-6	158	8.29	179		
6.6	160	8.35-39	122	1.2	72
6.12-23	88	8.36	47	1.4-9	48
6.13-15	160	9–11	147, 227	1.4	48
6.17	233	9.2	176	1.5	48, 50, 59, 60, 115, 118, 123
7–8	222, 234	9.13	47		
7	222, 224, 225, 230-34, 236	9.20	102		
		9.23	59		
		9.33	47		
		10.15	47	1.7-8	48

Index of References

1.7	48	1.31	47, 62,	3.6-10	55		
1.8	116, 123		69, 82,	3.6-8	56		
1.9-11	48		106, 115	3.6	42, 55		
1.10–4.21	41, 42, 65	2	51	3.8-13	122		
		2.1-16	53, 55	3.8	55, 56		
1.10–4.13	43, 51, 66, 67, 70	2.1-5	51-54, 57, 58, 66	3.9-17	56		
				3.9	55, 56, 69		
1.10–4.5	48	2.1-4	72	3.10-11	56		
1.10-31	51	2.1	52, 58, 119	3.10	56		
1.10-17	52			3.11-23	56		
1.10-12	42	2.2-16	120	3.11	22, 56		
1.10	36, 45, 48, 49, 57, 65-67	2.2	55	3.12	56		
		2.4	52	3.16-17	73		
		2.6–4.21	51	3.16	62		
		2.6–3.3	54	3.17	62		
1.11	36, 37	2.6-16	42, 53, 54	3.18-22	50		
1.12-16	36			3.18-20	50		
1.12	29, 34, 37-40, 48, 56, 82, 187	2.6	54, 123	3.18-19	36		
		2.7	54	3.19	47, 62, 82		
		2.9	47, 69, 82, 115	3.20	47, 82		
1.13-16	38	2.10	53	3.21-23	39, 56-58, 233		
1.13	48, 49, 56	2.11	53				
		2.12	53	3.21	36, 57, 60, 62, 106, 115		
1.14-17	49	2.13	52, 53, 140				
1.14	37						
1.15	56	2.14	54	3.22–4.1	42		
1.16	56	2.15	53, 54	3.22	36, 57, 59		
1.17-20	52	2.16	40, 54-56, 82, 83, 187				
1.17-18	22			3.23	29, 40, 56-58, 187		
1.17	50, 52						
1.18–3.4	45	3	55				
1.18–2.16	51, 52	3.1-17	52	4	62		
1.18–2.5	54	3.1-5	66	4.1-13	54, 56, 57, 86, 236		
1.18-31	49	3.1-4	25, 68, 165				
1.18	57						
1.19	47, 69, 82	3.1-3	46	4.1-7	59		
		3.1	52, 56	4.1	29, 40, 58, 116		
1.21	106	3.3-4	55				
1.23-24	22	3.3	115	4.3-5	25, 66, 141		
1.25	123	3.4	56, 82				
1.26	61	3.5–4.5	45	4.3-4	42		
1.27	123	3.5-9	51	4.3	54		
1.29	62, 106, 115	3.5	33, 45, 55-57, 148	4.6-13	58, 64, 68		

1 Corinthians (ctd)		4.15	28, 42, 62, 70, 71	5.7	56
4.6	15, 33, 45-47, 49, 58, 62, 63, 66, 67, 69, 70, 82, 85, 196, 235			5.9-11	87
				5.9	69
		4.16-17	17, 62, 130	5.11-12	77
				5.11	69
		4.16	15, 19, 28, 62, 64-67, 71, 72, 81, 85, 100, 113, 116, 122, 125, 130, 150, 186, 187, 196, 212, 236	5.12	77, 78, 84-86, 99, 111, 123, 130, 147, 236
4.7-13	68				
4.7-8	58				
4.7	32, 59, 62, 106, 115			5.13	47, 75, 82, 83
				6–10	85, 89
4.8-13	25			6	86
4.8	35, 59			6.1-11	86
4.9-13	60-63, 66, 72, 114, 121, 130			6.1	86
		4.17–5.13	126, 131	6.3	35, 86
		4.17-19	76	6.7–10.33	98
		4.17	28, 65, 70, 72, 115, 122	6.7-8	115
4.9-10	60			6.8-10	87
4.9	35, 60, 62, 115			6.9-12	86
		4.18-19	73, 75, 76	6.9-11	87
				6.9-10	87
4.10	50, 58, 60-62, 123	4.18	40, 62, 64, 76	6.11	87, 88
				6.12	61, 63, 77-90, 95, 99-101, 111, 130, 222, 235, 236
		4.19	62, 123		
4.13	61, 67	4.20	76		
4.14–15.58	67, 130	4.21	28, 65, 70, 72-74, 115		
4.14–5.13	72, 73, 76, 78				
4.14-21	22, 26, 28, 63, 65-67, 70, 71, 204	5–15	61, 236		
		5–10	36	6.13	79, 83, 87, 176
		5–6	83, 84, 90	6.15-20	87
		5	25, 43, 65, 67, 69, 72, 73, 115	6.15	40, 56, 88, 187, 222
4.14-17	64				
4.14-16	65, 164, 218			6.16	47, 82
				6.18	79
4.14-15	73, 165	5.1–8.13	38	6.19	62
4.14	28, 33, 43, 59, 61, 66-71, 74, 115, 164	5.1-13	65, 72	6.20	88
		5.1	74	7–11	83, 125
		5.2	62, 73-75, 84	7–10	107
				7	63, 87, 91, 92, 94, 95, 98, 149, 201
4.15-17	131	5.3-5	72, 74		
4.15-16	70	5.3	76		
		5.6	36, 75, 84, 106, 115		

7.1-24	91	7.40	93-95,	9		15, 25,
7.1-6	94		120, 130			43, 44,
7.1	69, 82,	8–11	90			96-105,
	83, 90-	8–10	84, 96,			107, 109,
	95		98, 110,			110, 115,
7.2-5	93-95		113			121, 127,
7.2	93	8–9	63, 235			128, 146,
7.3-5	95	8	89, 98,			155, 217,
7.3	93		99, 101,			231, 236
7.5	93, 94		105, 115,	9.1-27		237
7.6-7	28		123	9.1-15		105, 131
7.6	42, 81,	8.1–11.1	176	9.1-5		101
	93-95	8.1-13	42	9.1-2		97
7.7-8	90, 92,	8.1-11	36	9.1		96-99,
	93, 95,	8.1-8	99			102, 107,
	235, 237	8.1-6	89			110
7.7	15, 93-	8.1	62, 82,	9.2		96
	95, 98		86, 99,	9.3		42, 54,
7.8	66, 90-		110, 111,			96, 102,
	95, 116,		113, 115,			105
	125, 130,		123	9.4-15		100
	196	8.3	115	9.4		97, 98,
7.9	94, 95	8.4	82			100
7.10-16	94, 95	8.7-13	98, 100	9.5-12		100
7.10	93	8.7-12	111	9.5		38, 42,
7.12	94	8.7	115, 123			97, 98
7.17-24	36, 94	8.8-9	98, 100	9.6		97, 101
7.21-22	203	8.8	83, 99	9.7		101
7.21	98	8.9-12	99	9.8-10		101
7.22	22, 29,	8.9	85, 87,	9.9		47, 82,
	40, 56,		99, 100			85
	106, 148,	8.10-11	99, 102	9.11-12		101
	150, 187	8.10	38, 102,	9.12-15		25
7.25	94, 130		111, 115,	9.12		87, 97,
7.26-27	94		123			98, 101
7.26	91, 94,	8.11-12	56	9.13		62, 102
	106	8.11	115, 123	9.14		102
7.27	93, 95	8.12-13	99	9.15-23		109
7.28	94	8.12	99	9.15-18		102, 105,
7.29	81, 94,	8.13–9.27	130			131
	95	8.13	77, 78,	9.15		44, 91,
7.31	94		86, 99,			92, 98,
7.32-35	93-95		101, 107,			101,
7.32	94		111, 112,			105-107,
7.35	81		114, 116,			115
7.36	93-95		123, 130,	9.16-18		106
7.37	106		146, 155,	9.16		105, 106,
			169, 236			115

268   Paul's Paradigmatic 'I'

1 Corinthians (ctd)			89, 98, 111	11.2-34	33
9.17-23	106			11.2-16	15
9.17-18	107	10.24	89, 98, 112, 115	11.2	42, 113, 114, 130
9.18	97, 98, 101	10.25-26	110	11.3	114
9.19-23	25, 101, 107, 108, 111, 112, 142, 149	10.25	111	11.10	35
		10.26	47, 82	11.13-16	42
		10.27	111	11.16-18	36
		10.28–11.2	77	11.16	72
9.19-22	102, 107	10.28–11.1	77, 78, 111, 123	11.17-34	37, 67
9.19	85, 106, 107, 110			11.17	81
		10.28-33	142	11.23-26	22
9.20-21	115	10.28-29	112	11.23-25	114
9.21	56, 164	10.28	82, 89, 111	11.24	82
9.22	21, 98			11.25	82
9.23-27	102, 130	10.29–11.2	110	11.27	70
9.23	98, 105, 107	10.29–11.1	130	11.31-32	222
		10.29-30	111-13	12–14	35, 36, 53, 116
9.24-27	86, 101, 108, 109, 114, 236	10.29	110, 111, 147, 222	12	84, 88, 114-16, 121, 201
		10.30	222		
9.24	109	10.31–11.1	107, 112, 113	12.1	53
9.25	109				
9.26	109	10.31-33	110	12.3	48, 54, 82
10–13	96	10.31-32	111, 113		
10	85, 98, 105, 110, 115	10.31	88, 113	12.4	53
		10.32-33	21, 25	12.7	53
		10.32	39, 113	12.8	53, 54, 115, 123
10.1-33	38	10.33–11.2	111		
10.1-11	110	10.33–11.1	113	12.9	53
10.6	230	10.33	21, 89, 98, 111, 115	12.10	140
10.7	47, 82			12.11	53
10.8	84			12.12-31	55
10.9	84	11–14	37	12.12-13	56
10.11	35, 123	11.1-2	111, 114	12.13	59
10.12	84	11.1	15, 19-22, 28, 29, 40, 56, 63, 66, 67, 72, 81, 85, 100, 110, 113, 116, 122, 125, 130, 131, 150, 187, 196, 212, 238	12.15	82
10.15	110			12.16	82
10.16-18	110			12.18	57
10.16	56, 110			12.21	82
10.22	123			12.22	106
10.23–11.2	110, 111			12.27	56, 187
10.23–11.1	86, 100, 101, 110, 111, 114, 236			12.28	120
				12.29-30	116
				12.31–13.13	116
				12.31–13.3	78
10.23-24	111			12.31	66, 116, 117, 125,
10.23	79, 81, 85-87,				

Index of References

	130, 146, 169, 196	14.6	78, 119, 120, 123-25, 156	15.12-58	127
13–14	63, 114, 235, 236			15.14-15	125
				15.23	29, 40, 187
13	56, 84, 114-19, 121, 122, 124, 125, 131, 146, 231	14.7	123	15.24	123
		14.9	123	15.27	47, 82
		14.11	78, 124, 125, 156, 222	15.29-34	129, 130
				15.30-32	86, 125, 129, 130, 236
		14.12	124		
13.1-13	117	14.14-15	222	15.31	115
13.1-3	77, 117-19, 123, 124, 130, 156, 222	14.14	78, 124, 125, 156	15.32	47, 83
				15.33	82
		14.15	77, 125	15.35	82
		14.17	124	15.45	47, 82, 225
13.1-2	118, 121	14.18-19	125		
13.1	35, 114	14.18	78, 119, 124	15.50	81
13.2-3	118			15.54-55	47, 82
13.2	114, 115, 118, 119, 121-23	14.19	77, 125	15.56-57	233
		14.20	54, 123	15.56	233
		14.21	47, 82	15.57	233
13.3	115, 121	14.25	82	16.3-11	76
13.4-7	118, 120-23	14.26	124	16.10-11	76
		14.29	140	16.12-18	70
13.4	62, 115	14.30	53	16.12	56
13.7	122	14.33	160	16.14	115
13.8-13	118	14.36-37	127	16.15-18	38
13.8-10	123	14.37-38	76	16.21	129
13.8	123	14.37	42, 53, 120	16.24	115
13.10	123				
13.11-12	78, 123, 124, 222	15	33, 35, 36, 42, 43, 56, 66, 126, 129, 236	*2 Corinthians*	
				1.5	168
13.11	123			1.6-7	62, 179
13.12-14	118			1.8	117
13.12	123			1.12	30, 141
13.13	122	15.1-11	127	1.17	30
14–16	64	15.3-12	22	2.1	136
14	61, 84, 86, 114-16, 124, 125, 130	15.5-8	131	2.5-11	43
		15.5-7	38, 126, 128	2.5	30
				2.9-10	30
		15.5	38	2.14	148, 233
14.1-25	125	15.7	97	2.17	30, 141
14.1	115, 116	15.8-11	125, 126	3.1-3	70
14.2	116	15.8-10	126, 129, 131	3.1	131
14.3-5	124			3.3	40
14.3	121	15.8-9	128	3.4	141
14.5	94	15.8	165	3.6	148
		15.11	127	3.8	165

2 Corinthians (ctd)		10.10	30, 52, 76	1.6-9	134, 137, 143-45
4.2	30, 131				
4.5	30, 106, 131, 148, 149	10.12	131	1.6	166
		10.18	131	1.7	137, 155, 166
		11.1	60		
4.7-15	146	11.4	44	1.8-9	138, 143, 151, 153, 154
4.8-11	122	11.5-7	30		
4.10-11	62, 179	11.7-11	217		
4.10	158, 168	11.7	107	1.8	137, 152
4.11	179	11.11-13	44	1.9	138, 144
4.12	62	11.13	176	1.10-24	142
4.14-21	43	11.21-33	129	1.10-13	144
4.16	168	11.23–12.10	146	1.10	32, 85, 86, 106, 133, 141, 143-53, 155, 159, 162, 166-69, 236
4.17	117	11.23	39, 40		
5.11	143	11.30	30		
5.12	131	12.10	106		
5.14	122	12.11-13	30		
5.16-17	168	12.11	30		
5.20	163, 207, 208	12.14-18	217		
		12.14-15	204		
6.3-10	129	12.14	70, 165	1.11–2.21	151
6.4	106, 131	12.17	30	1.11–2.14	163
6.10	59	13.3-4	30, 168	1.11–2.10	153, 155
6.13	204	13.3	135	1.11-12	138, 139, 144
7.2	30	13.10	70		
7.4	167	13.11	166	1.11	141, 144, 145
7.8	131				
7.16	167	*Galatians*		1.12-16	144
8	201	1–2	15, 42, 134, 137, 138, 141, 149, 150, 152, 155, 161, 162, 195, 235, 237	1.12	139, 158, 168
8.7	118				
8.9	21, 59			1.13–2.14	141
8.15	47			1.13-24	162
8.16	233			1.13	117, 144, 145, 167
8.23	210				
9.1-2	167			1.15-16	120, 135, 137, 149
9.5	106				
9.6	81	1	149, 162	1.15	163
9.7	106	1.1-26	149	1.16-17	139
9.9	47	1.1-10	134	1.16	139, 158, 168
9.15	233	1.1-9	138, 141		
10–13	39, 42, 97, 135	1.1-5	136	1.17	155
		1.1	138, 139, 149, 155, 159, 168	1.18-20	139
10	29			1.18	152
10.1	30			1.20	139
10.2	30	1.2	160	1.21-24	139
10.7	29, 39, 40	1.4	136, 159	1.21	155
		1.6-11	143	1.23	145, 167
		1.6-10	134, 144	1.24	145

Index of References

2	154, 156, 162, 233		166-68, 231	4.8-10 4.8	161 149, 150
2.1-10	152	2.19	156, 157, 222	4.9-10 4.9	162 149, 162
2.1-3	139				
2.2	139	2.20	135, 158, 163, 166, 222	4.10-11 4.11-20 4.11	133 134, 161 161, 166
2.3-5	150				
2.3-4	141				
2.4-6	155	2.21	152, 153, 155, 156, 159, 160 161, 170	4.12-20	133, 161, 162
2.4-5	133, 149, 151, 155, 162, 235			4.12-14 4.12	163 15, 25, 133, 134, 162, 163, 169, 196, 212
2.4	149, 151	3–4			
2.5	151	3	133		
2.6-10	139, 140	3.1–5.25	134		
2.6	139, 140	3.1-14	134		
2.7	140	3.1-7	147		
2.9	139, 140	3.1-6	170	4.13-15	32
2.10	140	3.1	134, 137, 143, 156, 166	4.13-14 4.13	162 150, 162, 163
2.11-21	133, 141, 155	3.2-5	161	4.14	135, 150, 163, 168
2.11-14	141, 151-53, 162, 235	3.4 3.6-14 3.9	146 161 145	4.15 4.16	168 166
2.11	152	3.10	47, 153	4.17	134, 137, 143
2.12-14	152	3.13	47, 146, 149, 153, 178	4.19	70, 134, 164-66, 204, 218
2.12-13	153				
2.12	153, 159				
2.13	153	3.15–4.7	161		
2.14	106, 152, 153	3.17 3.22-23	81 149	4.20 4.21–5.1	164 149
2.15-21	120, 133, 146, 152, 155, 159, 160, 169, 232	3.22 3.23–5.15 3.23 3.26-29 3.26	157 88 149 158 150	4.21-31 4.21 4.22-23 4.22 4.24	161 162 149 47 149
2.15	155	3.27-28	163, 203	4.25	149
2.16	150, 156	3.27	150	4.26	150
2.17-18	227, 229	3.28	149	4.27-31	164
2.17	150, 156	3.29–4.9	149	4.27	47
2.18-21	85, 86, 159-61, 164, 236	3.29	29, 148, 150	4.29 4.30-31 5	145 150 42, 166
2.18	156, 159, 160, 222, 227, 231	4 4.1-3 4.1 4.3	15, 133 27 149 149, 162	5.1-2 5.1 5.2-6	161, 162 149, 150 168
2.19-21	146, 159	4.5	149	5.2-5	156, 160
2.19-20	157, 158, 160, 163,	4.7 4.8-11	149, 150 162	5.2-4 5.6	153 150, 161

Galatians (ctd)		1.8	59	2.1-5	189
5.7	166	2.7	59	2.1	181, 188,
5.8	166	2.8-10	59		194
5.9	166	3.8	59	2.2	166, 175
5.10-11	133, 134	3.16	59	2.3	188, 189,
5.10	134, 137,	4.1	206, 209		191
	143, 150,	5.4	199	2.4-5	72
	166	5.31	93	2.5-11	21, 191
5.11-12	135	6.5-9	203	2.5	20, 166,
5.11	62, 142,	6.5	150		175, 181,
	145, 167	6.20	207, 208		188, 194
5.12	134, 137,			2.6	188
	138, 143	*Philippians*		2.6-11	173, 188,
5.13-15	122	1	42, 206		190-92
5.13	89, 149,	1.1	148, 150,	2.6-8	190
	150, 162,		181, 183,	2.7-8	188
	163		187, 189	2.7	189
5.14–6.1	89	1.3-11	173, 186	2.8-11	178, 180,
5.14-26	137	1.6-7	180		184
5.14-15	163	1.6	178, 184	2.8	177, 178,
5.24-25	146	1.7	177, 206		188-91
5.24	29, 148,	1.8	187	2.9-11	191, 192,
	150, 168	1.10-12	180		194
5.25	162	1.10-11	178, 184	2.11	189
6–7	106	1.10	113	2.12	191
6.1-5	72	1.12-18	177	2.15	164
6.2-5	162	1.12-14	190	2.16	178, 184
6.2	122	1.12-13	189	2.17	172, 177,
6.11-18	167	1.12	178		189, 190
6.11	168	1.13	181, 187	2.19-24	190
6.12-13	134, 137,	1.15-18	175	2.19-22	183
	142, 143,	1.16	206	2.19	178, 184
	160	1.19-21	178, 184	2.22	70, 189,
6.12	106, 145,	1.20-23	191		204
	167	1.20-21	187	2.23-24	178, 184
6.13	167	1.20	189	2.25-30	177, 190
6.14-15	146	1.21-26	177	2.25	106, 172,
6.14	133, 134,	1.21	184, 236		211
	167-69	1.23	181, 189	2.26-28	174
6.15	161, 168	1.24-26	185	2.27	190
6.16-17	166	1.24	106	2.30	172, 190
6.16	168	1.25-30	174	3	15, 42,
6.17	135, 146,	1.26	181		172, 180,
	158, 168	1.27-30	27		181, 194,
		1.27-29	190		217, 235,
Ephesians		1.28	191		237
1.1	136	1.29-30	177, 189	3.15	175
1.7	59	2	190		

3.1-2	175, 176, 180	3.14	181, 184-86, 191	4.13	186
3.1	181			4.14	189
3.2	175, 176, 181	3.15-17	181, 195	4.15	187
		3.15	166, 181, 186, 190	4.19-20	178, 184
3.3-14	182			4.19	59, 181, 187
3.3-5	181	3.16-21	27	4.21	172, 181
3.3-4	177, 181	3.16	20, 22, 186		
3.3	175, 181-84			*Colossians*	
		3.17-21	179	1.1	136
3.4-11	184	3.17-18	177, 186	1.27	59
3.4-9	186	3.17	15, 17, 19, 22, 26, 29, 150, 170, 177, 182, 183, 187, 190, 194, 196, 212	2.2	59
3.4-8	188			2.5	32
3.4-6	31, 175, 182, 183			3.18	199
				3.22	142
3.4	181-83			4.1	203
3.5-6	181			4.12	150
3.6	181, 182			4.16	32
3.7-14	25				
3.7-11	181	3.18-19	175, 177, 180, 181	*1 Thessalonians*	
3.7-10	187			1.3	213
3.7-9	175	3.18	176-81	1.5-6	15, 190, 212
3.7-8	188	3.19-21	177		
3.7	181, 184	3.19	166, 175-77, 181	1.5	16, 213
3.8	181, 184, 188			1.6	16, 19-21, 24, 29, 62, 179, 190, 212
3.9-10	184	3.20-21	177, 184, 185, 191		
3.9	181, 184, 188				
		3.20	179, 181	2	30, 237
3.10-21	178-80, 184	3.21	188, 189, 191	2.1-12	214-19
3.10-17	108	4.1-2	186	2.1	213
3.10-11	179, 191	4.2	166, 175	2.2	212, 213
3.10	62, 158, 165, 168, 177, 179, 181, 182, 184, 189	4.5	178, 184	2.3	218
		4.6-7	186	2.4-5	217
		4.7	181, 186	2.4	141
		4.8	16	2.5-12	107
		4.9	15, 32, 183, 186, 190, 195, 196, 237	2.5	213, 218
3.11-14	185			2.7	165, 204, 217
3.11	184				
3.12-16	177, 180			2.8	214
3.12-14	185	4.10	172, 175	2.9	213, 217-19
3.12	181, 185, 187	4.11-20	180		
		4.11-14	177	2.11	165, 204, 213, 218
3.13	185, 186	4.11-13	186, 187		
		4.11	101, 186	2.14-16	190, 212
		4.12	188, 189	2.14-15	179
		4.13-14	189		

1 Thessalonians (ctd)		2 Timothy		13	107, 198, 200, 206
2.14	16, 19, 20, 24, 29, 190, 212	1.13	21	14	106, 198, 199, 202, 203, 206, 208, 209
		2.1	136		
		2.12	136		
		3.10	21		
3.3-5	212				
3.3	213	Titus		15-16	198, 200, 202
3.4	213	1.10-16	42		
3.7	106	2.7	182	15	197, 198
4.1	214			16	199, 201, 204, 211
4.2	213	Philemon			
4.6	218	1-2	205	17-20	198
4.7	218	1	106, 199, 204, 206, 210, 211	17	198, 201, 203-206, 210
4.10-12	218, 219				
4.11	218				
4.12	218	2-3	200	18-19	204
5	165	2	211	18	198, 204
5.2	213	3	200	19	197, 198, 201, 206
5.11-15	72	5	199, 204		
5.13	216	6	200, 201, 205, 210	20	199, 201, 203, 210, 211
5.14	217-19				
5.19-22	140	7	199, 204, 211	21-22	203
				21	167, 200-202, 205, 209, 212
2 Thessalonians		8-21	49		
3.4	167	8-11	198		
3.6-13	218-20	8-9	203		
3.6-11	217	8	198, 199, 201, 202, 208, 209	22-25	200
3.6-9	17			22	197, 204, 206, 209
3.6	219				
3.7	19, 29, 219	9-10	201, 202, 209	23-24	205
3.8	219	9	107, 199, 204, 206-10	23	201, 206, 211
3.9	19, 29, 182, 219			24	210
3.10	219	10-12	198	25	200
3.11	219	10-11	198		
3.12	219	10	165, 200, 206, 211	James	
				1.1	148
1 Timothy		11	200, 204, 208, 211		
1.1	136			Revelation	
1.16	21	12	197, 204, 200, 211	5.12	60
4.12	182				
		13-14	200		

Index of References

OTHER ANCIENT REFERENCES

Pseudepigrapha
1 En.
89.41-50   175

4 Ezra
4.3   117

3 Macc.
1.11   87

4 Macc.
2.6   230
5.18   87
9.23   17

T. Ash.
4.3   17

T. Benj.
4.1   17

Early Christian
Apoc. Mos.
19.3   230

1 Clem.
47   39

Ignatius Smyr.
11   207

Polycarp Phil.
3.2   32

Talmuds
b. Šab.
145b-146a   225

b. Sanh.
19b   71

Targums
Targ. Isa.
48.16-17   117

Targ. Neof. Exod.
20.17   230

Targ. Neof. Gen.
1–3   225

Qumran
1QS
11.9-15   226

Philo
Decal.
142   230
150   230
173   230

Op. Mund.
16   17
25   17

Quod Lib.
156–59   106
21–25   106

Spec. Leg.
4.84-85   225

Josephus
Ant.
13.66   199
20.268   87

Classical
Aeschylus
Prom.
648   86

Aristotle
Rhet.
1.9.38-39   153
2.6.2-3   69
2.6.11-12   103
2.6.12   68
2.23   147

Democritus
Frag.
39   16

Demosthenes
De Cor.
4   104
101   104
128   104
321   104

Dio Chrysostom
Dis.
55.4-5   17
32.11-12   216

Diogenes Laertius
2.24   101

Epictectus
Diss.
2.123   106
4.1   106
3.2.95   27
3.22.45-50   18
3.22.46   238
3.22.48   101

Herodotus
1.183   86

Ovid
Metamorphoses
7.19-20   226

Plato
Tim.
38   17
48   17

Pliny
Ep.
9.21   202

Plutarch		100.12	24	Xenothon	
Mor.		29.4	24	*An.*	
7.539-47	103	52.2	24	7.1.21	86
7.543-544	128	52.7	24		
8.544	104	52.8	24	*Mem.*	
				1.2.3	16
Seneca		*Test. Epict.*			
Ep.		4.28	208		
6.3-5	24	6.29	208		

INDEX OF AUTHORS

Ahern, B.M. 179, 182
Alexander, L.C. 7, 172, 173
Allo, E.-B. 82, 85
Althaus, P. 226
Aune, D.E. 147

Baarda, T. 167
Baasland, E. 145, 146
Bachmann, M. 146, 159, 160, 227
Bailey, K.E. 65, 73
Baird, W. 36, 37, 149
Balch, D. 115, 173
Balz, H. 81, 86
Banks, R. 232, 233
Barclay, J.M.G. 134, 135, 202, 203
Barr, J. 165
Barrett, C.K. 35, 39, 54, 59, 77, 80, 92, 94, 106, 158, 226, 233
Bartchy, S.S. 197-99, 201-204
Barth, K. 35, 127, 194
Bassler, J.M. 58, 135, 138, 173
Bauder, W. 13
Bauer, J. 199
Baur, F.C. 34, 126
Beare, F.W. 172, 175
Beker, J.C. 134, 228, 230, 231
Bentley, R. 207-209
Berchman, R.M. 136
Berényi, G. 160
Berger, K. 134, 135
Best, E. 7, 19, 23, 24, 30, 45, 62, 201, 215, 216
Betz, H.D. 16, 18, 23, 52-54, 57, 105, 128, 134, 136, 137, 139, 141, 143-46, 148, 160, 164, 167, 168, 191, 232
Betz, O. 51

Bieringer, R. 35, 90, 92
Birdsall, J.N. 207
Bjerkelund, C.J. 49, 65, 66, 201, 202
Black, D.A. 102
Black, M. 38
Bligh, J. 149, 153-55, 168
Bloomquist, L.G. 173, 177-79, 181, 191, 193, 194
Boer, W.P. de 18, 20-22, 24-26, 31, 162-64, 183, 186, 188
Boers, H. 153
Bonhöffer, A. 227
Booth, W.C. 14, 138
Borgen, P. 142
Bornkamm, G. 38, 224, 230-33
Branson, M.L. 157
Brewer, D.I. 101
Brinsmead, B.H. 135, 160
Brown, R.E. 152
Bruce, F.F. 80, 141, 146, 149, 152, 153, 160, 162, 168, 208-10, 215, 217, 233
Buchanan, C.O. 172
Bultmann, R. 127, 227, 231
Bünker, M. 42, 51, 129
Burgess, T.C. 229
Burton, E.D.W. 139, 143, 146, 160, 162, 163, 168

Campbell, D.H. 225, 230
Campbell, W.S. 227
Campenhausen, H.F. von 76
Cancik, H. 24
Caragounis, C.C. 92
Carrez, M. 30
Carroll, J. 216
Carson, D.A. 107

Castelli, E.A. 19, 26-28, 31, 32, 65, 67, 113, 164, 165
Chadwick, H. 108
Chance, J.B. 41, 51, 53
Chow, J.K. 34, 44
Church, F.F. 199, 200, 202, 204, 214
Clarke, A.D. 34, 50, 51, 73
Cole, G.A. 76
Collange, J.-F. 172, 173, 176, 179, 180, 185
Collins, A.Y. 73
Collins, R.F. 18, 75, 213-15
Colson, F.H. 46
Conrad, E.W. 40
Conzelmann, H. 35, 54, 59, 78, 80, 81, 85, 88, 89, 91, 92, 96, 97, 109, 110, 124
Cosgrove, C.H. 134, 135, 216, 228
Cousar, C.B. 34, 52, 53
Cranfield, C.E.B. 228, 230, 233
Cross, F. 230
Culpepper, R.A. 173
Cummins, S.A. 146, 162, 163

Dahl, N.A. 40-41, 43, 47, 74, 231
Dalton, W.J. 156, 173
Daube, D. 203
Dautzenberg, G. 101
Davies, M. 7
Davis, J.A. 50
Dawes, G.W. 94
Deidun, T.J. 88
Derrett, J.D.M. 78, 200, 202
Dietzfelbinger, C. 96, 232
Dodd, C.H. 224
Dodds, E.R. 68, 105
Donfried, K.P. 58, 152, 221, 227, 229, 233
Doohan, H. 14, 72, 164
Dungan, D.L. 96
Dunn, J.D.G. 120, 135, 136, 138-42, 144-46, 152-54, 157-62, 226-28, 230, 231, 233

Ebeling, G. 145, 159
Ebner, M. 59, 61
Eidem, E. 18
Elliott, J.H. 203

Elliott, N. 222, 228
Ellis, E.E. 34, 36, 42, 47, 54, 75, 77, 97, 114, 149, 173
Ellison, H.L. 107
Engels, D. 80
Espy, J.M. 223
Everts, J.M. 152, 159, 160

Farahian, E. 30
Farmer, W.R. 39, 75
Fee, G.D. 35, 59, 60, 62, 73, 75, 81, 90, 92, 93
Ferguson, E. 115, 173
Feuillet, A. 141, 225, 226
Finley, M.I. 105
Fiore, B. 16-19, 23-29, 31, 33, 46, 65, 66, 68-71, 107, 119, 154, 186
Fitzgerald, J.T. 41, 42, 45-47, 59-62, 65, 68, 179
Fitzmyer, J.A. 178, 226, 229, 231
Forbes, C. 154
Fortna, R. 36, 108, 157, 164, 171, 173
Fowl, S.E. 7, 173, 192
Fox, M.V. 83
Frame, J.E. 215
Freed, E.D. 120
Frerichs, E. 136
Fung, R.Y.K. 136
Funk, R.W. 75, 76
Furnish, V.P. 31, 35, 55, 57, 70, 181, 193

Garland, D.E. 172, 184
Gasque, W.W. 107, 114
Gaventa, B.R. 30, 36, 108, 134, 135, 138, 140, 142, 144, 147, 157, 163-66, 172, 173, 216
Geoffrion, T.C. 188, 190
George, T. 214
Getty, M.A. 18, 205, 214, 218
Gillespie, T.W. 54, 61
Gillman, J. 214
Gnilka, J. 172, 175, 181
Goddard, A.J. 146, 162, 163
Godet, F. 60, 79, 85
Goehring, J. 54
Gooch, P.D. 100
Granskou, D. 176

Index of Authors

Grässer, E. 149, 173
Grayston, K. 175
Green, J. 7
Grob, R. 93
Grotius, H. 220
Gundry-Volf, J.M. 73, 75, 90, 93
Gunther, J.J. 174, 176, 177, 185
Gutierrez, P. 18, 22-25, 27, 69-71, 165, 166, 204
Güttgemanns, E. 146

Habel, N. 137, 149, 150
Hafemann, S.J. 126
Hall, B. 107
Hall, D.R. 228
Hall, R.G. 136, 154
Harrington, D.J. 81
Harris, G. 75
Harris, M.J. 209
Hartin, P.J. 198
Hartman, L. 125
Hawthorne, G. 51, 171, 174, 175, 183-85, 188
Hay, D. 34, 35, 62
Hays, R.B. 82, 157, 163, 164, 237
Hedrick, C. 54
Héring, J. 80
Hester, J.D. 134-36, 159
Higgins, A.J.B. 128, 139
Hill, D. 118
Hirsch, E. 168
Hock, R.F. 96, 218
Hofius, O. 114, 139
Holladay, C.R. 115, 117-21
Holmberg, B. 14, 23, 28, 29, 154, 164, 165, 201, 209
Holmes, M. 39
Holtz, T. 149, 152, 215, 218
Holtzmann, O. 168
Hooker, M.D. 46, 47, 80, 142, 157, 164, 173, 178, 187, 189, 191, 210
Houlden, J.L. 174, 198
Howard, G. 135, 138, 153, 155
Hübner, H. 219
Huggins, R.V. 226
Hurd, J.C., Jr 20, 40, 83, 91, 94, 100, 101, 110, 112, 192
Hurtado, L.W. 192

Jeremias, J. 97, 99, 115, 155
Jewett, R. 146, 173, 174, 176, 179, 185, 215, 216, 219-21
Joest, W. 126
Johanson, B. 217
Johnson, E. 216
Johnson, L.T. 100
Jones, P.R. 127
Judge, E.A. 31, 52

Käsemann, E. 29, 105, 191, 225, 230-32
Kennedy, G.A. 52, 136
Kertelge, K. 233
Kilpatrick, G.D. 139, 141, 181
Kim, S. 54
Klauck, H.-J. 81
Klein, G. 127
Klijn, A.F.J. 175
Knox, J. 200, 202, 211
Koester, H. 49, 174, 176, 178, 179, 184, 214
Kok, E.H.-S. 156
Kok, J.H. 20, 157-59
Koptak, P.E. 147, 151, 156
Kosmala, H. 16, 18
Kreuzer, S. 106
Kuhn, H.-W. 138
Kümmel, W.G. 30, 159, 222-24, 229, 231, 232
Kurz, W.S. 176, 182, 187
Kuss, O. 222
Kyrtatas, D.J. 148

Ladd, G.E. 114
Lambrecht, J. 136, 156, 222, 224, 226, 229-32
Lampe, G.W.H. 75
Lampe, P. 50, 52, 54, 197
Lang, F. 37
Lapide, P. 107
Lassen, E.M. 65, 68, 74
Lategan, B.C. 134, 136, 140, 142, 148
Lee, E.K. 182
Lietzmann, H. 87
Lim, T.H. 52
Limbeck, M. 94
Lincoln, A.T. 7, 147, 179, 185, 231
Lindars, B. 88, 159

Litfin, A.D. 35, 50, 51, 53, 56, 68
Livingstone, E.A. 75
Loades, A. 88
Lofthouse, W.F. 30, 85, 86, 226
Lohmeyer, E. 174, 178, 200, 207
Lohse, E. 199, 207, 209
Longenecker, R.N. 142-46, 155, 157, 159-61, 168
Lorenzi, L. De 120, 125
Lüdemann, G. 135, 141
Lyonnet, S. 224, 225
Lyons, G. 15, 16, 30, 134, 147, 159, 162, 167, 215-18, 235-37

MacArthur, S.D. 75
Magee, B.R. 99
Malherbe, A.J. 31, 35, 100, 104, 129, 183, 186, 214-17, 227
Malina, B.J. 68
Manson, T.W. 39, 42, 56
Marrou, H.-I. 104, 105
Marshall, I.H. 215
Marshall, P. 34, 40, 44, 47, 74, 96, 108, 137, 218
Martin, C.J. 198
Martin, D.B. 100
Martin, R.P. 7, 100, 106-108, 114, 116, 127, 129, 149, 154, 174-76, 179-81, 185, 186, 188, 192, 198-201, 208, 209, 211
Martyn, J.L. 134, 135
Marxsen, W. 215, 220
McLean, B.L. 135
McMichael, W.F. 187
Mearns, C. 174, 176, 179, 180
Meeks, W.A. 35, 38, 84, 100, 115, 173
Merklein, H. 34
Metzger, B.M. 207
Michaelis, W. 17, 19-21, 23-27, 29, 162, 190, 212
Minear, P.S. 173, 187, 188, 191, 221
Misch, G. 133, 147
Mitchell, M.M. 34, 37, 61, 65, 67, 72, 75-77, 81, 83, 86, 91, 94, 99, 100, 118, 121, 124, 125, 128, 131, 146
Mitton, C.L. 233
Moffatt, J. 79, 80
Mohrlang, R. 88, 122

Moo, D.J. 224, 230
Morris, L. 80, 81
Moule, C.F.D. 39, 75, 80, 137, 143, 150, 197, 200, 207
Müller, P.-G. 97
Mullins, T.Y. 75
Munck, J. 37, 128, 140, 141, 154, 232
Murphy-O'Connor, J. 79, 80, 83
Myers, C.D. 228
Myers, J.M. 120

Nasuti, H.P. 100
Neugebauer, F. 201
Neusner, J. 136
Newing, E.G. 40
Nickelsburg, G.W.E. 128
Niebuhr, R.D. 39, 75, 142, 175
Nordling, J.G. 197, 202

O'Brien, P.T. 48, 137, 140, 174, 176, 181, 185, 186, 189, 190, 199, 207, 208, 210
O'Neill, J.C. 141
Olbricht, T. 116, 127
Ollrog, W.-H. 77
Olson, S.N. 85, 94, 167
Omanson, R.L. 79, 83, 106

Packer, J.I. 230, 233
Padilla, C. 157
Paige, T. 34, 38, 59, 189
Panikulam, G. 210, 211
Pannenburg, W. 126
Patte, D. 177, 181, 213
Patzia, A.G. 197, 199
Pearson, B.A. 54
Perriman, A. 185
Peter, J. 198
Peterman, G.W. 187
Petersen, N.R. 56, 197, 201-203, 208-11
Peterson, D. 31, 140
Petzer, J.H. 115
Pfitzner, V.C. 108, 109, 185
Phillips, J.B. 85
Phipps, W.E. 90, 95
Plank, K.A. 41, 59, 60
Plevnik, J. 126, 213
Plummer, A. 47, 79, 92, 109

Index of Authors

Plunkett, M.A. 82, 93
Pobee, J.S. 179
Pogoloff, S.M. 34, 38, 44, 50, 52, 53, 57-60
Pollard, T.E. 173
Porter, S.E. 116, 127, 144, 230
Preiss, T. 201
Probst, H. 100, 110
Proudfoot, C.M. 179
Pryor, J. 31

Rad, G. von 38
Rahtjen, B.D. 172
Räisänen, H. 157, 227
Rapske, B.M. 197
Reinhartz, A. 25, 43
Reuman, J. 152
Richard, E. 215
Richards, E.R. 105, 129
Richardson, P. 20, 76, 107, 108, 176, 192
Riesenfeld, H. 210
Robertson, A. 47, 79, 92, 109
Roetzel, C.J. 31, 73
Roloff, J. 22, 23
Rosner, B.S. 73
Rouselle, A. 95

Sampley, J.P. 210
Sanders, B. 18, 62, 68, 71, 85
Sanders, E.P. 157, 176, 177, 223, 224, 231
Sanders, J.T. 54, 114, 115
Sandnes, K.O. 53-55, 105, 117, 118, 120, 137, 149, 162
Sänger, D. 61
Sass, G. 141, 149
Schenk, W. 31, 172, 182, 185, 198
Schlier, H. 46, 143, 158, 163, 164
Schmithals, W. 34, 127, 174, 176, 179, 215, 216
Schneider, G. 92
Schoedel, W. 41
Schrage, W. 34, 41, 87
Schreckenberg, H. 106, 206
Schulz, A. 18, 22, 25
Schüssler Fiorenza, E. 41, 43, 44, 134

Schütz, J.H. 14, 29, 62, 72, 127, 128, 134, 138, 142, 153, 155, 218
Schweizer, E. 158, 199
Segovia, F. 176
Seifrid, M.A. 222, 230-32
Sellin, G. 35
Shanor, J. 56
Simon, W.G.H. 80
Smalley, S. 88, 159
Smit, J. 115-18, 136
Smith, E.W. 232
Snyman, A.H. 198
Soards, M.L. 201, 206, 209
Soden, H.F. von 35, 112
Spicq, C. 85, 86, 219
Stanley, C.D. 47
Stanley, D.M. 18, 20, 21, 24-26, 82, 148
Staudinger, F. 206
Stauffer, E. 224
Stendahl, K. 230
Stirewalt, M.L. 229
Stowers, S.K. 41, 59, 100, 102, 112, 173, 181, 187, 227-29
Stuhlmacher, P. 51, 54, 107
Sumney, J.L. 102

Taylor, N. 154
Theissen, G. 30, 34-37, 39, 96, 97, 101, 222, 224, 226, 230, 232
Thielman, F. 223, 231
Thiselton, A.C. 35, 36
Thrall, M.E. 80, 88
Trilling, W. 220
Trocmé, E. 232
Tuckett, C. 35
Tyson, J.B. 176, 179

Untergassmair, F. 57

Vanhoye, A. 42, 53, 59, 106, 160
Vos, J.S. 136, 143-45, 153, 162

Wallis, P. 46
Walter, N. 139
Wanamaker, C.A. 213, 215-17, 220
Watson, D.F. 110, 111, 127, 129, 130, 134, 154, 173, 185, 198

Watson, F. 56, 112-14
Weaver, P.R.C. 148
Webster, J.B. 194
Wechsler, A. 152, 156
Wedderburn, A.J.M. 35, 36, 191-93, 201, 224, 225, 231
Wegenast, K. 38, 114
Weiss, J. 79, 81, 82, 92, 138
Welborn, L.L. 34, 37, 39, 46, 47, 54
West, A. 88
White, J.L. 105, 174, 189, 200, 202, 205, 206
White, L.M. 173
Wickert, U. 72
Widmann, M. 54
Wilckens, U. 49, 50, 126, 153, 222
Wilcox, M. 97
Wilken, R. 41
Wilkins, M.J. 38, 189
Williams, D.M. 16, 23, 24, 218-20

Willis, W.L. 30, 54, 55, 58, 96, 98-100, 107, 110, 112
Wilson, J.H. 35
Wilson, R.M. 80
Wilson, S.G. 80, 142, 210
Wimbush, V.L. 91
Winter, S.C. 197, 198, 202, 210
Wire, A.C. 35, 43
Wischmeyer, O. 30, 114, 116, 118-24
Wolff, C. 100, 101, 187, 193
Wolter, M. 58
Wright, N.T. 188, 199, 205
Wuellner, W. 41, 59, 86, 100, 108, 113, 116, 125, 130

Yagi, S. 222
Yamauchi, E. 81
Yarbrough, O.L. 90, 92

Zaas, P.S. 75
Ziesler, J.A. 223, 224, 226, 228, 230

JOURNAL FOR THE STUDY OF THE NEW TESTAMENT
SUPPLEMENT SERIES

25 David E. Orton, *The Understanding Scribe: Matthew and the Apocalyptic Ideal*
26 Timothy J. Geddert, *Watchwords: Mark 13 in Markan Eschatology*
27 Clifton C. Black, *The Disciples According to Mark: Markan Redaction in Current Debate*
28 David Seeley, *The Noble Death: Graeco-Roman Martyrology and Paul's Concept of Salvation*
29 G. Walter Hansen, *Abraham in Galatians: Epistolary and Rhetorical Contexts*
30 Frank Witt Hughes, *Early Christian Rhetoric and 2 Thessalonians*
31 David R. Bauer, *The Structure of Matthew's Gospel: A Study in Literary Design*
32 Kevin Quast, *Peter and the Beloved Disciple: Figures for a Community in Crisis*
33 Mary Ann Beavis, *Mark's Audience: The Literary and Social Setting of Mark 4.11-12*
34 Philip H. Towner, *The Goal of our Instruction: The Structure of Theology and Ethics in the Pastoral Epistles*
35 Alan P. Winton, *The Proverbs of Jesus: Issues of History and Rhetoric*
36 Stephen E. Fowl, *The Story of Christ in the Ethics of Paul: An Analysis of the Function of the Hymnic Material in the Pauline Corpus*
37 A.J.M. Wedderburn (ed.), *Paul and Jesus: Collected Essays*
38 Dorothy Jean Weaver, *Matthew's Missionary Discourse: A Literary Critical Analysis*
39 Glenn N. Davies, *Faith and Obedience in Romans: A Study in Romans 1–4*
40 Jerry L. Sumney, *Identifying Paul's Opponents: The Question of Method in 2 Corinthians*
41 Mary E. Mills, *Human Agents of Cosmic Power in Hellenistic Judaism and the Synoptic Tradition*
42 David B. Howell, *Matthew's Inclusive Story: A Study in the Narrative Rhetoric of the First Gospel*
43 Heikki Räisänen, *Jesus, Paul and Torah: Collected Essays* (trans. D.E. Orton)
44 Susanne Lehne, *The New Covenant in Hebrews*
45 Neil Elliott, *The Rhetoric of Romans: Argumentative Constraint and Strategy and Paul's Dialogue with Judaism*
46 John O. York, *The Last Shall Be First: The Rhetoric of Reversal in Luke*
47 Patrick J. Hartin, *James and the Q Sayings of Jesus*
48 William Horbury (ed.), *Templum Amicitiae: Essays on the Second Temple Presented to Ernst Bammel*

49 John M. Scholer, *Proleptic Priests: Priesthood in the Epistle to the Hebrews*
50 Duane F. Watson (ed.), *Persuasive Artistry: Studies in New Testament Rhetoric in Honor of George A. Kennedy*
51 Jeffrey A. Crafton, *The Agency of the Apostle: A Dramatistic Analysis of Paul's Responses to Conflict in 2 Corinthians*
52 Linda L. Belleville, *Reflections of Glory: Paul's Polemical Use of the Moses–Doxa Tradition in 2 Corinthians 3.1-18*
53 Thomas J. Sappington, *Revelation and Redemption at Colossae*
54 Robert P. Menzies, *The Development of Early Christian Pneumatology, with Special Reference to Luke–Acts*
55 L. Ann Jervis, *The Purpose of Romans: A Comparative Letter Structure Investigation*
56 Delbert Burkett, *The Son of the Man in the Gospel of John*
57 Bruce W. Longenecker, *Eschatology and the Covenant: A Comparison of 4 Ezra and Romans 1–11*
58 David A. Neale, *None but the Sinners: Religious Categories in the Gospel of Luke*
59 Michael Thompson, *Clothed with Christ: The Example and Teaching of Jesus in Romans 12.1–15.13*
60 Stanley E. Porter (ed.), *The Language of the New Testament: Classic Essays*
61 John Christopher Thomas, *Footwashing in John 13 and the Johannine Community*
62 Robert L. Webb, *John the Baptizer and Prophet: A Socio-Historical Study*
63 James S. McLaren, *Power and Politics in Palestine: The Jews and the Governing of their Land, 100 BC–AD 70*
64 Henry Wansborough (ed.), *Jesus and the Oral Gospel Tradition*
65 Douglas A. Campbell, *The Rhetoric of Righteousness in Romans 3.21-26*
66 Nicholas Taylor, *Paul, Antioch and Jerusalem: A Study in Relationships and Authority in Earliest Christianity*
67 F. Scott Spencer, *The Portrait of Philip in Acts: A Study of Roles and Relations*
68 Michael Knowles, *Jeremiah in Matthew's Gospel: The Rejected-Prophet Motif in Matthaean Redaction*
69 Margaret Davies, *Rhetoric and Reference in the Fourth Gospel*
70 J. Webb Mealy, *After the Thousand Years: Resurrection and Judgment in Revelation 20*
71 Martin Scott, *Sophia and the Johannine Jesus*
72 Steven M. Sheeley, *Narrative Asides in Luke–Acts*
73 Marie E. Isaacs, *Sacred Space: An Approach to the Theology of the Epistle to the Hebrews*
74 Edwin K. Broadhead, *Teaching with Authority: Miracles and Christology in the Gospel of Mark*

75 John K. Chow, *Patronage and Power: A Study of Social Networks in Corinth*
76 Robert W. Wall & Eugene E. Lemcio, *The New Testament as Canon: A Reader in Canonical Criticism*
77 Roman Garrison, *Redemptive Almsgiving in Early Christianity*
78 L. Gregory Bloomquist, *The Function of Suffering in Philippians*
79 Blaine Charette, *The Theme of Recompense in Matthew's Gospel*
80 Stanley E. Porter & D.A. Carson (eds.), *Biblical Greek Language and Linguistics: Open Questions in Current Research*
81 In-Gyu Hong, *The Law in Galatians*
82 Barry W. Henaut, *Oral Tradition and the Gospels: The Problem of Mark 4*
83 Craig A. Evans & James A. Sanders (eds.), *Paul and the Scriptures of Israel*
84 Martinus C. de Boer (ed.), *From Jesus to John: Essays on Jesus and New Testament Christology in Honour of Marinus de Jonge*
85 William J. Webb, *Returning Home: New Covenant and Second Exodus as the Context for 2 Corinthians 6.14–7.1*
86 B.H. McLean (ed.), *Origins of Method: Towards a New Understanding of Judaism and Christianity—Essays in Honour of John C. Hurd*
87 Michael J. Wilkins & T. Paige (eds.), *Worship, Theology and Ministry in the Early Church: Essays in Honour of Ralph P. Martin*
88 Mark Coleridge, *The Birth of the Lukan Narrative: Narrative as Christology in Luke 1–2*
89 Craig A. Evans, *Word and Glory: On the Exegetical and Theological Background of John's Prologue*
90 Stanley E. Porter & Thomas H. Olbricht (eds.), *Rhetoric and the New Testament: Essays from the 1992 Heidelberg Conference*
91 Janice Capel Anderson, *Matthew's Narrative Web: Over, and Over, and Over Again*
92 Eric Franklin, *Luke: Interpreter of Paul, Critic of Matthew*
93 Jan Fekkes III, *Isaiah and Prophetic Traditions in the Book of Revelation: Visionary Antecedents and their Development*
94 Charles A. Kimball, *Jesus' Exposition of the Old Testament in Luke's Gospel*
95 Dorothy A. Lee, *The Symbolic Narratives of the Fourth Gospel: The Interplay of Form and Meaning*
96 Richard E. DeMaris, *The Colossian Controversy: Wisdom in Dispute at Colossae*
97 Edwin K. Broadhead, *Prophet, Son, Messiah: Narrative Form and Function in Mark 14–16*
98 Carol J. Schlueter, *Filling up the Measure: Polemical Hyperbole in 1 Thessalonians 2.14-16*
99 Neil Richardson, *Paul's Language about God*
100 Thomas E. Schmidt & M. Silva (eds.), *To Tell the Mystery: Essays on New Testament Eschatology in Honor of Robert H. Gundry*

101 Jeffrey A.D. Weima, *Neglected Endings: The Significance of the Pauline Letter Closings*
102 Joel F. Williams, *Other Followers of Jesus: Minor Characters as Major Figures in Mark's Gospel*
103 Warren Carter, *Households and Discipleship: A Study of Matthew 19–20*
104 Craig A. Evans & W. Richard Stegner (eds.), *The Gospels and the Scriptures of Israel*
105 W.P. Stephens (ed.), *The Bible, the Reformation and the Church: Essays in Honour of James Atkinson*
106 Jon A. Weatherly, *Jewish Responsibility for the Death of Jesus in Luke–Acts*
107 Elizabeth Harris, *Prologue and Gospel: The Theology of the Fourth Evangelist*
108 L. Ann Jervis & Peter Richardson (eds.), *Gospel in Paul: Studies on Corinthians, Galatians and Romans for R.N. Longenecker*
109 Elizabeth Struthers Malbon & Edgar V. McKnight (eds.), *The New Literary Criticism and the New Testament*
110 Mark L. Strauss, *The Davidic Messiah in Luke–Acts: The Promise and its Fulfillment in Lukan Christology*
111 Ian H. Thomson, *Chiasmus in the Pauline Letters*
112 Jeffrey B. Gibson, *The Temptations of Jesus in Early Christianity*
113 Stanley E. Porter & D.A. Carson (eds.), *Discourse Analysis and Other Topics in Biblical Greek*
114 Lauri Thurén, *Argument and Theology in 1 Peter: The Origins of Christian Paraenesis*
115 Steve Moyise, *The Old Testament in the Book of Revelation*
116 Christopher M. Tuckett (ed.), *Luke's Literary Achievement: Collected Essays*
117 Kenneth G.C. Newport, *The Sources and Sitz im Leben of Matthew 23*
118 Troy W. Martin, *By Philosophy and Empty Deceit: Colossians as Response to a Cynic Critique*
119 David Ravens, *Luke and the Restoration of Israel*
120 Stanley E. Porter & David Tombs (eds.), *Approaches to New Testament Study*
121 Todd C. Penner, *The Epistle of James and Eschatology: Re-reading an Ancient Christian Letter*
122 A.D.A. Moses, *Matthew's Transfiguration Story in Jewish-Christian Controversy*
123 David Lertis Matson, *Household Conversion Narratives in Acts: Pattern and Interpretation*
124 David Mark Ball, *'I Am' in John's Gospel: Literary Function, Background and Theological Implications*
125 Robert Gordon Maccini, *Her Testimony is True: Women as Witnesses According to John*

126	B. Hudson Mclean, *The Cursed Christ: Mediterranean Expulsion Rituals and Pauline Soteriology*
127	R. Barry Matlock, *Unveiling the Apocalyptic Paul: Paul's Interpreters and the Rhetoric of Criticism*
128	Timothy Dwyer, *The Motif of Wonder in the Gospel of Mark*
129	Carl Judson Davis, *The Names and Way of the Lord: Old Testament Themes, New Testament Christology*
130	Craig S. Wansink, *Chained in Christ: The Experience and Rhetoric of Paul's Imprisonments*
131	Stanley E. Porter & Thomas H. Olbricht (eds.), *Rhetoric, Scripture and Theology: Essays from the 1994 Pretoria Conference*
132	J. Nelson Kraybill, *Imperial Cult and Commerce in John's Apocalypse*
133	Mark S. Goodacre, *Goulder and the Gospels: An Examination of a New Paradigm*
134	Larry J. Kreitzer, *Striking New Images: Roman Imperial Coinage and the New Testament World*
135	Charles Landon, *A Text-Critical Study of the Epistle of Jude*
136	Jeffrey T. Reed, *A Discourse Analysis of Philippians: Method and Rhetoric in the Debate over Lierary Integrity*
137	Roman Garrison, *The Graeco-Roman Contexts of Early Christian Literature*
138	Kent D. Clarke, *Textual Optimism: The United Bible Societies' Greek New Testament and its Evaluation of Evidence Letter-Ratings*
139	Yong-Eui Yang, *Jesus and the Sabbath in Matthew's Gospel*
140	Tom Yoder Neufeld, *Put on the Armour of God: The Divine Warrior from Isaiah to Ephesians*
141	Rebecca I. Denova, *The Things Accomplished Among Us: Prophetic Tradition in the Structural Pattern of Luke–Acts*
142	Scott Cunningham, *'Through Many Tribulations': The Theology of Persecution in Luke–Acts*
143	Raymond Pickett, *The Cross in Corinth: The Social Significance of the Death of Jesus*
144	S. John Roth, *The Blind, the Lame and the Poor: Character Types in Luke–Acts*
145	Larry Paul Jones, *The Symbol of Water in the Gospel of John*
146	Stanley E. Porter & T.H. Olbricht (eds.), *Rhetorical Analysis of Scripture: Essays from the 1995 London Conference*
147	Kim Paffenroth, *The Story of Jesus According to L*
148	Craig A. Evans and James A. Sanders (eds.), *Early Christian Interpretation of the Scriptures of Israel: Investigations and Proposals*
149	J. Dorcas Gordon, *Sister or Wife?: 1 Corinthians 7 and Cultural Anthropology*
150	J. Daryl Charles, *Virtue Amidst Vice: The Function of the Catalog of Virtues in 2 Peter 1.5-7*
151	Derek Tovey, *Narrative Art and Act in the Fourth Gospel*

152   Evert-Jan Vledder, *Conflict in the Miracle Stories*
153   Christopher Rowland & Crispin H.T. Fletcher-Louis (eds.), *Understanding, Studying and Reading: New Testament Essays in Honour of John Ashton*
154   Craig A. Evans and James A. Sanders (eds.), *The Function of Scripture in Early Jewish and Christian Tradition*
155   Kyoung-Jin Kim, *Stewardship and Almsgiving in Luke's Theology*
156   I.A.H. Combes, *The Metaphor of Slavery in the Writings of the Early Church: From the New Testament to the Begining of the Fifth Century*
158   Jey. J. Kanagaraj, *'Mysticism' in the Gospel of John: An Inquiry into its Background*
159   Brenda Deen Schildgen, *Crisis and Continuity: Time in the Gospel of Mark*
160   Johan Ferreira, *Johannine Ecclesiology*
161   Helen C. Orchard, *Courting Betrayal: Jesus as Victim in the Gospel of John*
162   Jeffrey T. Tucker, *Example Stories: Perspectives on Four Parables in the Gospel of Luke*
163   John A. Darr, *Herod the Fox: Audience Criticism and Lukan Characterization*
164   Bas M.F. Van Iersel, *Mark: A Reader-Response Commentary*
165   Alison Jasper, *The Shining Garment of the Text: Gendered Readings of John's Prologue*
166   G.K. Beale, *John's Use of the Old Testament in Revelation*
167   Gary Yamasaki, *John the Baptist in Life and Death: Audience-Oriented Criticism of Matthew's Narrative*
169   Derek Newton, *Deity and Diet: The Dilemma of Sacrificial Food at Corinth*
172   Casey Wayne Davis, *Oral Biblical Criticism: The Influence of the Principles of Orality on the Literary Structure of Paul's Epistle to the Philippians*
174   J.D.H. Amador, *Academic Constraints in Rhetorical Criticism of the New Testament*
177   Brian Dodd, *Paul's Paradigmatic 'I': Personal Example as Literary Strategy*

GENERAL THEOLOGICAL SEMINARY
NEW YORK